D1061831

THE LEE HARVEY OSWALD FILES

FLIP DE MEY

THE LEE HARVEY OSWALD FILES

WHY THE CIA KILLED KENNEDY

LANNOO

For all women and girls
and in particular
for my dear sisters, Veerle and Annelies,
and in memory of Hilde and Mieke – we came
to know the world in the agreements and differences
we had together on a swing – and my dear daughter Lotte,
for the indescribable things that she understands much better than I;
and for my wife Martine, who is in my heart every second.

"Too often we enjoy the comfort of opinion
without the discomfort of thought."

John Fitzgerald Kennedy

Let it not be overlooked that due process of law is not for the sole benefit of an accused. It is the best insurance for the Government itself against those blunders which have lasting stains on a system of justice but which are bound to occur on ex parte consideration.

Justice Robert Jackson

Shaugnessy v. United States ex rel Mezei, 345 U.S. 206,225 (1953)

CONTENTS

PREAMBLE

What really happened in Dallas on November 22, 1963? This simple question opens the door to a vast labyrinth. Conspiracy authors and supporters of the lone-crazy gunman theory unwind a storyline from this, like Ariadne's thread, which leads you through the labyrinth, and brings you to the only real exit. But a murder investigation is not mythology. Selective production of evidence is ultimately counterproductive, and leads to an answer in which the result cannot subsequently withstand the infiltration of the hard facts from the case.

In my book *Cold Case Kennedy*, my research remained close to the victim, both in space and time. Kennedy is the central figure. Now that the basic facts are known about the crime and the crime scene, it's time to shift the focus to the possible perpetrator(s). Lee Harvey Oswald is obviously the central figure here. But is he also the perpetrator? This is often assumed to be true for lack of a better explanation. On the other hand, dissatisfaction with the errors and gaps in the case often leads one to opt for a speculative conspiracy theory. Kennedy was murdered because the Mafia was seething with anger at his brother Bobby, the Cuban exiles were furious, nobody had the CIA under control, and Vice President Johnson was willing to do anything to become President. There is a great temptation to quickly connect these identifiable points, but the truth exists only by the grace of facts. Trying to pick the solution to a mystery from the air is dangerous. As far as possible, I will therefore refer to the original documents and will correctly quote the statements. I will always state the source, so that the reader can check the accuracy and the context. The original 'fragrance' and 'color' of a statement are often decisive for its credibility. The findings are sometimes so unbelievable that the direct quote will help to convince the reader that this is not some interpretation by the author, but a concrete historical fact. The best starting point for the original sources is and remains the website of the Mary Ferrell Foundation www.maryferrell.org. All the witness statements can be found in alphabetical order on jfkassassination.net/russ/wit.htm. The anonymous British website 22november1963.org/ is certainly a must, being thematically organized and having an excellent click-through function to the original sources.

This book follows the footsteps of Lee Harvey Oswald. He has become one of the most notorious figures in the history of the 20th century. This is, of course, the result of the significance and fame of the victim of the crime of which he stands accused. But Oswald was actually involved in no less than four murder cases. He was not only thought to have assassinated the president, but also Officer Tippit and is also suspected of a failed attack on the ultra-conservative General Walker. Finally, he was himself the victim of a murder. But Oswald is also a human being, a child of his time, a neglected boy lost in a strange world of shadows and mirrors. Oswald is the central link in the events of November 22. If we remain close to him, we will inevitably come closer to a solution of the many puzzles in the Kennedy case. This is what matters: the truth. The Kennedy file is sometimes referred to as a puzzle as big as a football field. Quite rightly so. That's why I'm trying to work as systematically as possible. The aim is to precisely outline a part of the terrain, and to then work as thoroughly as possible within that particular area. I referred to this as 'forensic archeology' in *Cold Case Kennedy*. But however logically I approach the case, the emotions always remain just below the surface. Searching for the truth is often a frustrating business. Anger at each manipulation of the investigation, at the illegal destruction of documents or false declarations, is still required. Keep this outrage alive. The adrenaline will help to fuel the arduous journey, because it is a fascinating but very unruly case.

My main goal is to first of all reduce the complexity. We will first investigate whether Oswald could have been Kennedy's murderer. We will not go through all the evidence again. This time we base the analysis solely on a very careful selection of *irrefutable* arguments and undeniable facts, which together should prove beyond reasonable doubt whether Oswald could have been the sniper on Dealey Plaza or not. One hundred pages in order to perhaps unravel one of the greatest mysteries of the 20th century cannot be a bad investment. I say 'perhaps' because the reader always has the last word. I am not infallible, and, with a puzzle the size of a football field, it's possible that there are elements or documents that I have mistakenly overlooked.

There are no doubt also elements or documents that I have mistakenly assumed to be true. It is the privilege of every investigator who enters an extensive area to evolve and to learn – this is one of the greatest qualities of Man. But you can count on my sincerity. I have tried, after much research, to summarize a limited set of objective data that in my opinion allows to reasonably decide on Oswald's guilt. Through hearing the facts the reader becomes part of a virtual jury. Once we have formed our opinion whether or not Lee Harvey Oswald killed John F. Kennedy, we can proceed to the other Oswald files. To start, two more murders and an attempted murder require our attention. Here also, the facts cannot be ignored. No murder case is simple, and every detail matters and can have its consequences for the overarching file. In the last months of his life, Oswald seemed entangled in a web of intrigues. Step by step, we will carefully, systematically and objectively reduce the number of possible scenarios until only one logical explanation for the totality of the events remains. Finally, after the questions how, when, and who the most important question remains: why was John Kennedy murdered?

Although I try to remain as unbiased as possible, I have to admit that, after this intensive search for the truth, I feel a mix of compassion and remote friendship for Lee Harvey Oswald. Not many historians, not even those who believe in his innocence, or partial innocence, have much symptathy for this mousy man. But he deserves some kindness. He was a sensible, but never loved, boy of only 24 years of age in a world that on the one hand did not understand him, and made opportunistic use of him on the other. Lee Harvey Oswald was condemned, even executed, without a trial, by partial judges ignoring the fundamental facts. He is entitled, at the start of this investigation, to our renewed complete neutrality, our careful attention for nothing but the objective facts, and ultimately our common sense and wisdom at the moment of our final judgment on what really happened on Friday, November 22, 1963.

Flip de Mey
Tuesday, June 2, 2015

INTRODUCTION

FRIDAY, NOVEMBER 22, 1963

President Kennedy is assassinated in the Dealey Plaza in Dallas on November 22, 1963, at 12.30 p.m. The assassin seems to have shot at the open limousine from a corner window on the sixth[1] floor of a book depository. The Governor of Texas, John Connally, who was sitting in front of Kennedy on a folding seat, is also seriously wounded, but survives the attack.

Shortly afterwards, a little further on, Police Officer Tippit is brutally shot down. The police arrest the 24-year-old Lee Harvey Oswald in a cinema, as a suspect in the murder of the police officer. He soon also becomes the prime suspect in the murder of the president. An old Italian army weapon of the Carcano brand was found in the book depository. Oswald had bought a similar weapon a few months earlier, and his hand print was also on the Carcano that was found in the depository. When it is seen that Oswald had also flirted with communism, everything seems to indicate that he is the culprit: a misfit who shot at the president out of frustration.

Vice President Lyndon Johnson is sworn in as Kennedy's successor in the sweltering and crowded presidential plane. Two days later, the seedy nightclub owner Jack Ruby shoots Oswald down in the basement of the police station. There is thereby no longer a suspect who can defend himself, and no contradictory process takes place. The homicide squad of the Dallas police had interrogated Oswald in the Texan tradition, without any tape recording, without any clear written record of the statements and without the presence of a lawyer, although Oswald repeatedly and explicitly requested one.

The further investigation is carried out in accordance with the guidelines of the new president, a power politician *par excellence*. Lyndon Johnson allows the Secret Service, which operates under his command, to immediately carry out measures that will not benefit the investigation for the truth.

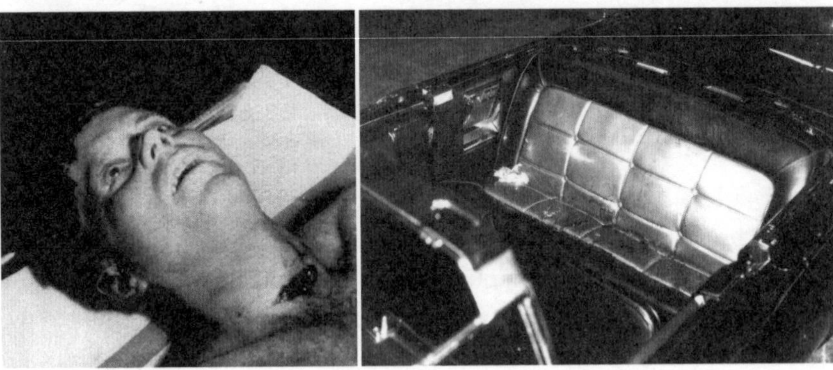

The limousine, which was in fact the crime scene, is dismantled down to the chassis within the shortest time. The doctors who attended to Kennedy's last moments in Dallas, and those who performed the autopsy in Washington, are placed under severe pressure. Just about everything that could go wrong with the official autopsy of the murdered president did go wrong, to the extent that the intention could only seem to have been to conceal the circumstances of the attack, rather than clarify them.

Johnson entrusts the case to his friend and neighbor Edgar Hoover, the corrupt FBI director. Hoover had held the federal police in an iron grip for more than 40 years, and could take the investigation in any direction he wanted. Hoover does not doubt for a second that he can give the new president what he wants. The Kennedy assassination, and the political castration of his brother Bobby, is not unwelcome for Hoover. In his eyes, the palace revolution after the elimination of John Kennedy restored the natural order. The findings of the FBI are fixed from the very beginning of the investigation. Oswald was the perpetrator, and he acted completely alone.

In order to increase the credibility of the conclusions, and to cut off any other possible investigations at the pass, Johnson arbitrarily installs a seven-member presidential commission of inquiry. Chief Justice Earl Warren was appointed Chairman of this Commission. Warren is the highest magistrate in the country. Furthermore, the President only appoints political dignitaries to the Commission who have no forensic or police experience. These include Allen Dulles and Gerald Ford, who are mainly in the Commission to act as watchdogs for the interests and secrets of the powerful CIA and FBI. It is the Deputy Director (and later Director) of the CIA, Richard Helms, who personally asks Johnson to include Dulles in the Commission. Even a child can see that Dulles is not there to help dig up the truth, but to help keep the cabinet of CIA skeletons closed. An example of how Ford acted as a telltale for the FBI is the FBI memorandum of December 12, 1963, from Cartha DeLoach.[2] The FBI Deputy Director proudly notes how the subservient Gerald Ford will 'confidentially' keep him up to date with the activities of the Commission, and rewards his dutiful acolyte with a signed copy of Hoover's book, *A Study of Communism:*

Ford indicated he would keep me thoroughly advised as to the activities of the Commission. He stated this would have to be on a confidential basis, however, he thought it should be done. He also asked if he could call me from time to time and straighten out questions in his mind concerning our investigation. I told him by all means he should do this. He reiterated that our relationship would, of course, remain confidential.

We have had excellent relations with Congressman Ford for many years. He has been given an autographed copy of the Director's book "A Study of Communism" and has been in touch with my office on numerous occasions in the past.

Even worse is the fact that the Commission itself does not employ its own team of investigators. They support the findings in the field completely and without criticism of what the FBI considers useful to find out or to communicate.

THE SUCCESSIVE INVESTIGATIONS

The major shortcomings of the first investigation lead to so much controversy that the call for a new and improved investigation never disappears completely. What really happened on that day in Dallas has been investigated[3] by the government eight times in the meantime, and hundreds of times by individual citizens. The riddles, nevertheless, remain remain and, in a sense, continue to increase. A summary of the investigations:

THE WARREN COMMISSION

The final conclusions of the Warren Commission look suspiciously like the marching orders that were given at the start:

— Oswald is the sole perpetrator, a *lone nut*, a lonely madman with leftist sympathies, but without a motive;
— Oswald shot at Kennedy with a pre-war carbine that was incorrectly adjusted;
— In order to limit the number of bullets to the desired number – three – the Commission attributed seven wounds to a single bullet;
— Jack Ruby, who murdered Oswald, is also a lone nut;

— No government agency bore any blame. The president was assassinated, but that was nobody's fault. Not a single bureaucrat or politician had to worry that his sinister secrets would be dragged into the light of day.

The truth about the attack is clearly subordinated to reasons of state.

The 27 volumes of the Warren Commission are beautifully bound and impressive to the eye, but, as a murder investigation, are a shameful piece of political theater. The committee members, and above all their boss Warren, know they are being lied to and duped by the FBI and the CIA, but remain silent. Walt Brown summarizes it well: 'Hoover passed along what he saw fit, usually worthless, sanitized, or misworded voluminous garbage, to Earl Warren, whose understaffed fact-finding body could neither wade through the mass nor understand it.'[4] Brown did not actually say it, but the work also had to be completed before the elections of 1964. Time constraints also impeded the search for truth, and played into the hands of those who wanted to sabotage the investigation.

ON TRIAL

As a result of the death of Oswald, a proper trial has never been carried out against him. In 1967, District Attorney Jim Garrison investigates the New Orleans link to the assassination of Kennedy. Oswald had lived in New Orleans for a while, and the wheelings and dealings of a number of shady figures from the *Big Easy* in 1963 seemed suspicious. In particular, Garrison wanted to cross-examine the crazy pilot David Ferrie, but the latter died under mysterious circumstances shortly before his arrest. Garrison then pursued businessman Clay Shaw, but was hardly able to present any evidence against him. The jury ultimately needed less than an hour to acquit Shaw.

The 16-hour long BBC television documentary On Trial, broadcast in 1986, was intended to be an alternative to a real trial of Oswald. A major plus is that the real witnesses are to be heard. But, apart from its sober, brown wood court appearance, it is never convincing at any time. Oswald's lawyer, Gerry Spence, does not know the case well enough.[5]

The person who comes closest to presenting an Oswald trial is Walt Brown, with his strongly written book *The People vs. Lee Harvey Oswald*.[6]

THE HSCA INVESTIGATION

Bobby Kennedy and Martin Luther King Jr., the leader of the civil rights movement, are also murdered. The similarities between the three murders are striking. A parliamentary investigation commission, the *House Select Committee on Assassinations* (HSCA), is formed in 1976 to delve deeper into the three murder cases. Because it's an election year, the members of the House of Representatives agree. 'But', adds Bob Tanenbaum, first deputy counselor for the JFK case, 'there was no commitment to really do it. [...] They pulled our budget, they pulled our long-distance phone privileges, our franking privileges, we couldn't even send out mail. And all of this was happening at a time when we were making some significant headway.'[7] The HSCA does expose many of the errors of the first investigation, and comes to the surprising conclusion that Kennedy was indeed assassinated by means of a conspiracy. But this investigation was also subject to severe constraints in both time and available resources[8]. As a former investigator of the parliamentary committee, Gaeton Fonzi relates a shocking tale of the HSCA investigation in *The Last Investigation*. Nevertheless, the HSCA does draw attention to a number of major issues in the Warren investigation. The controversy about the Kennedy case thereby hardly subsides.

THE ARRB

In 1991, Oliver Stone stirs up even more controversy with his acclaimed film JFK. Thanks to this film, the call for the release of documents became so great that it was finally heard in 1992, which was an election year. The Congress approved the *JFK Records Act*. This law stipulates that: 'each assassination record be publicly disclosed in full, and be available in the collection [of the national archive] no later than the date that is 25 years after the date of enactment of the Act.'

Every document that is eligible for release will, of course, be reviewed first. In order to do this, Congress set up a separate civil service department, the *Assassinations Record Review Board* (ARRB). In order to decide whether a document is eligible for release, the ARRB must, of course, examine the content and know its context. As a result, the ARRB eventually becomes a sort of official investigation into the murder. A number of AARB investigators, such as Douglas Horne, later become strongly convinced of the conspiracy theory.

It is a recurring phenomenon that the more you consider the file in detail, the greater becomes the belief that Kennedy was the victim of a conspiracy.

FURTHER RELEASE OF DOCUMENTS

Americans do not easily give away their freedom. The *Freedom of Information Act* (FOIA) guarantees citizens that they can request all government documents to the extent that there are no obstacles in terms of privacy or national security. The JFK Act goes one step further, and requires the government to release all the relevant documents on its own initiative on the fiftieth anniversary of the FOIA law, i.e. in 2017. The government is determined to exploit this delay to the maximum. Even President Obama refused to release 1,171 top-secret CIA documents in 2013 that related to a murder that was committed when he was still wearing diapers.[9]

The real heroes in the Kennedy case are unknown to the general public. They are the motivated citizens who doggedly fought against the juggernaut of bureaucracy at the cost of their career and their health. Jim Lesar, chairman of the AARC *(Assassination Archives and Research Center)*, has pleaded for the release of documents as a public defender in case after case. According to him, the FBI hates the FOIA.[10] When the FBI eventually has to release a document, they seem to wait until the ink in the copying machine has run out so that they can make copies that are virtually illegible. According to Lesar, the FBI, CIA, NSA and military intelligence also do not shy away from manifest lies. Robert Blakey, the former Chief Counsel of the HSCA, confirms that the National Archives (NARA) deliberately make use of bureaucratic jargon 'to obfuscate its failure to vindicate the public interest in transparency'. According to Lesar, this is due above all to a 'bureaucratic mind-set'. As a last resort, the bureaucrats have been given an ultimate loophole in the JFK law to deny the release of documents: it is sufficient to confer the status of "NBR" (*Not Believed Relevant* or irrelevant) to a document, and then, if a document has nothing to do with the murder, it is no longer subject to the law. Legal experts such as Jim Lesar can then dispute the administration's position before a court of law, but this takes many years of expensive procedures. In many cases, the importance of the documents subsequently turns out to be disproportionate to the enormous effort that was needed to obtain its release. But there are also startling results. For example, a set of documents emerged in

2007 that has been described as the "family jewels" of the CIA. Now we at least know that the CIA was very busy with regard to Oswald[11] from 1959 to 1963.

The released information usually involves details that are important for the specialists, small mosaic tiles that can be incorporated into the growing overall picture. Very occasionally, another astonishing document pops up. Very occasionally, a now-elderly witness says something new in an interview. Barry Ernest interviewed Dorothy Garner in 2011. It turns out that, despite her age of 83, she was a very strong and important witness. One minute after the assassination, Ms. Garner was at a place where she had to see Oswald if he had been the perpetrator. But she did not see him. She was officially interviewed about this at the time, but there was no trace of this interrogation afterwards. The name of this essential witness is not even included in the 880-page Warren Report. A late, spectacular breakthrough in the case can never be excluded. But time is pressing, because Henry Hurt's gloomy prediction is gradually becoming reality: 'Finally [...]the whole exercise will become as academic as today's parlor debate over who poisoned Napoleon.' Then, from the government's standpoint, the truth can quietly and safely emerge. In the end, it seems sure, victory will belong to those agencies that hold the keys to the many mansions of U.S. Intelligence.'[12]

INVESTIGATION BY THE RESEARCH COMMUNITY

A large majority of Americans do not believe the findings of the Warren investigation. They are convinced that there was indeed a conspiracy. They are also served by a wide range of conspiracy authors of various levels of volatility. Although much of the data that initially seemed very suspicious has long been refuted dozens of times in the meantime, that doesn't prevent 'weekend authors' from continuing to recycle outdated stories. The situation has not been improved by the Internet. The total absence of the media in the investigation is striking. Investigative journalism has hardly contributed at all. The hard core of the *conspiracists*, those who believe that Kennedy was the victim of a conspiracy, are stubborn researchers who are fascinated by the case, and the basis of their criticism largely remains intact. The number of unexplained riddles and – to put it mildly – bizarre coincidences is astounding. Robert Blakey has even coined an alternative name for the *believers* who are convinced that Oswald was a lone nut who killed Kennedy. He calls them *coincidence-nuts*.[13] The believers need so many improbable coincidences to prop up their version of the facts that, in the end, their story doesn't need to play second fiddle to even the wackiest theories of the conspiracists. The gaps in the case force the conspiracy authors into questionable speculation. They are often faulted for this. But, all things being considered, the official bodies are to blame for the many gaps that remain in the case.

The politically correct minority still stubbornly defends the stronghold of the Warren Commission. They stand firm: it has been proven beyond any doubt that Oswald was the only perpetrator. This certainty of conviction is generally inversely proportional to the case knowledge of the person stating this view. Believers can therefore often be recognized by their patronizing tone and the worn-out arguments that actually have nothing to do with the case, such as:

— conspiracy theory authors earn money from their books;
— if there really was a conspiracy, someone would have revealed it long ago;
— the conspiracy theories are ridiculous, and are entirely made up;
— the investigation was the most thorough murder investigation ever carried out;
— the belief in a dark conspiracy can be explained psychologically. People want a conspiracy. Kennedy should not be the victim of a layabout, he must have died in a confrontation worthy of him.

The new gods of 'science", "television' and 'computer' are often invoked as evidence that Oswald acted alone. Then somebody wrote the following, totally unhindered by any knowledge of the case: 'The conclusion that Oswald acted alone is supported by scientific evidence, and is only disputed by those who have not made an effort to gather all the facts. The A&E Network, CBS News have all analyzed the data with modern computer technology and all come to the same conclusion – that Oswald acted alone.'[14] And 50 years of tireless digging by the Conspiracists is thereby simply swept off the table by a believer. The believers like to see themselves as the right-thinking elite. They thereby do not spare the superlatives. For example, the eminent lawyer Louis Nizer said the following in the preface to a popular reprint of the Warren Report: "The reader who assesses the report in dispassionate approach and objective quest for truth will be overwhelmed by the exhaustive scientific and documentary evidence which support the main theses of the report. [...] This is the incalculable service rendered by the Commission.'[15] A minimum knowledge of the case is sufficient to reject this prose full of gasping admiration as poetic exaggeration. Anyone who goes into the case a little more deeply encounters a whole range of questions that the believers haughtily refuse to answer. Vincente Bugliosi seemed willing to take on the task.[16] He wrote an impressive work in 2007, enclosing a CD-ROM with an even more impressive set of endnotes. Bugliosi was an authoritative author, with an aura of impartiality and thoroughness.[17] He knew the Kennedy case, and played the role of the prosecutor in *On Trial*, the British film adaptation of the fictitious trial of Oswald. Expectations were high at the time of the publication of his long-awaited book on the assassination. His *Reclaiming History* was intended to be the objective and comprehensive record of the assassination case. At last, the many pressing questions would be patiently and quietly answered, and the fabrications of the conspiracy authors would be unmasked. It was a letdown. Bugliosi's book is full of haughty contempt for anyone who does not agree with his position. Almost all conspiracists are 'caught up in their fertile delusions' and indulge in 'crazy, incredibly childlike reasoning and mentality.'[18] The few exceptions who are not maliciously trying to fool everyone are dumb-bells who let themselves be led by the nose. Up to the last day of his life, on June 6, 2015, Bugliosi remained firmly convinced that he was right. If Bugliosi's arguments are correct, the haughtiness should not be important. But *Reclaiming History* is not the final book about the assassination that it pretends to be. Even after struggling through the whole thing, dozens of riddles remain.

For me, the most plausible believer book is still *Case Closed* by Gerald Posner. An advantage of this book is that the story is structured chronologically. It is also less pushy, less condescending and better written. The book is most convincing if you see it as the only piece of Kennedy literature – but only 'if.' The margins of my paperback version are much too narrow for the persistent series of objections that could be made against Posner's advocacy of Oswald's guilt.

The believers have the advantage that they defend an identical story. The conspiracists have to compete in disarray. Impressive early books, like Sylvia Meagher's *Accessories After the Fact* in 1967, are now somewhat dated. Fortunately, we now know more than was known in 1967. Many writers specialize in one aspect of the case. Vince Palamara, for example, knows almost everything about the role of the Secret Service, which was responsible for

Kennedy's security. In his book *The Girl on the Stairs*, Barry Ernest has followed up everything about one person, Vicki Adams. The Irish author Anthony Summers carried out a lot of fieldwork and interviewed many witnesses directly. His *Not in Your Lifetime* is still a classic. *The Last Investigation* by Gaeton Fonzi is very important for the same reason. As a researcher for the HSCA, Fonzi can report irreplaceable information first-hand. For more insight into the political background of the murder, Douglas's' 'JFK and the Unspeakable' is a must-read. And so there are many very interesting books that deserve a recommendation. The range of conspiracy books is very diverse, and is growing daily.

But we mustn't get carried away in the controversy between the two irreconcilable camps. Only the truth counts. From that perspective, we must once again look carefully at the real data.

PART I

THE FILES

There is really only one way to run an investigation, and that is with thoroughness. Take every scrap of evidence, add to each of those scraps by dauntless investigation until the saturation point is reached, then begin to see where all the evidence points, and only then narrow the focus.

Walt Brown, *Treachery in Dallas*, p. 125

FILE 1

THE MURDER OF J.F. KENNEDY

Chapter 1 – The shot from the sniper's nest

In solving a problem of this sort, the grand thing is to be able to reason backwards. That is a very useful accomplishment, and a very easy one, but people do not practise it much. In the every-day affairs of life it is more useful to reason forwards, and so the other comes to be neglected. There are fifty who can reason synthetically for one who can reason analytically.

Sherlock Holmes in Arthur Conan Doyle's *A Study in Scarlet*

A cursory glance at the official evidence is sufficient to confirm that Oswald *seems* to be the perpetrator of the Kennedy assassination. In every interview, Vincent Bugliosi, the godfather of the believers, emphasized that, according to him, there were 53 indications of Oswald's guilt. 'Only in a fantasy world can you have 53 pieces of evidence against you and still be innocent',[19] he concludes. Bugliosi thereby simply refutes all contradictions – they must be based on a mistake, given that Oswald's guilt is established. The validity of this reasoning depends, of course, on the number and weight of the contradictions. What if there were also 53 indications showing that the official story of the *lone nut* or lone madman cannot be correct? Then the shoe starts to pinch in the Kennedy case. According to a large part of the evidence, Oswald is clearly a lone nut who assassinated Kennedy, but according to other evidence he cannot be the perpetrator, or at least not the only culprit. The analytical method of the fictional British detective Sherlock Holmes can help us here. The fact that he's a fictional character does not make his unsurpassed method less valuable. Synthetic reasoning proves its usefulness in everyday life, but is a dangerous step in a murder investigation. It absorbs the conflicting data into a general resolution. Holmes's analytical approach works the other way, upstream, as it were. On closer examination, is something really what it seems to be? One fact, however lonely among the mass of indications of guilt, may suffice as proof that it is impossible for the accused to be the culprit. But this approach is not self-evident in a gigantic case such as the assassination of Kennedy. With an eye to procedural economy, we must try to find one crucial question whose answer is decisive for Oswald's guilt. We must then unravel the evidence relating to that one question, down to the smallest detail. The truth will remain inexorably present in the details, and if we carefully examine the smallest detail, it will be difficult for Bugliosi to claim that we are moving in a world of fantasy.

The ultimate question in this case seems to be quite obvious: Did *Oswald* shoot at Kennedy? If the answer is negative, someone else shot Kennedy, and the president is then the victim of a conspiracy. But as the debate about the question has dragged on for more than fifty years, and still has no conclusive answer, we may assume it's not the right question. The question of whether Oswald shot Kennedy can never be answered directly. The answer always requires an explanatory component, such as: 'Yes, because his gun was found in the book depository.' An answer of this kind immediately raises a new question: Does finding a weapon prove that the owner shot with it? So we basically have to split the ultimate question into more specific sub-questions, for which it is perhaps possible to find an answer. It's a case of finding the right set of sub-questions that can be answered in a way that's not susceptible to dispute, and that, together, lead to a needed conclusion about the main question.

The three statements below meet those two conditions. In its most reduced form, the hypothesis of the lone nut has three components: Oswald (1) fired (2) the Carcano (3). If Oswald killed Kennedy on his own, there must be evidence of the following three assumptions:

1. There were shots from the sniper's nest;
2. The shots were fired with the Carcano;
3. The shots were fired by Oswald.

It is sufficient to rebut one of these three points to prove that Oswald was unfairly blamed.

We can immediately answer the first question in the affirmative: there is no doubt that the limousine was fired at from the sniper's nest in the book depository. Robert Hill Jackson, a reporter for the *Dallas Times Herald*, was riding in one of the cars behind Kennedy in the parade. He saw a weapon being aimed at Kennedy's car from the sniper's nest.[20] Jackson drew this to the attention of his colleague, Malcolm O. Couch, a camera man from WFAA-TV in

Dallas. Couch stated: 'I remember [...] seeing about a foot of a rifle being – window'.[21] Fifteen-year-old Amos Euins stood right beneath the window of the sniper's nest. He saw a 'piece of pipe' projecting from the window.[22] Brennan,[23] the chief witness of the Commission, and James Worrell[24] also saw the weapon.

There is much controversy regarding the question of whether the shots came *exclusively* from the sniper's nest. There are two problems. According to the hypothesis of the lone nut, a single bullet caused seven different injuries to Kennedy and Governor Connally. The second problem is whether Kennedy was also shot at from the front. It is undeniable that, in the Zapruder film, Kennedy's head makes an abrupt backward movement after the head shot. There are also many 'ear-witnesses' of a front shot. The nursing team at the Parkland Hospital is unanimous. They all saw a large gaping wound on the back of Kennedy's head. The wound had miraculously disappeared at the autopsy in Bethesda. The one-bullet theory and the frontal shot are key points of contention. The question of whether a single bullet could cause the seven injuries ascribed to it is also crucial. If the answer is negative, there was more than one shooter, and the president is the victim of a conspiracy. *Cold Case Kennedy* objectively and verifiably demonstrated that the improbable single bullet is actually mathematically possible.[25] But the questions about the single bullet and the frontal shot are only relevant if it is established that *Oswald* did indeed shoot from the sniper's nest. Then we have to actually verify that Oswald was the *only* perpetrator. If it turns out that it was *not* him who shot, the existence of a conspiracy has been proved, regardless of the debate about the *single bullet* and the frontal shot. We want evidence that is made up of indisputable facts that everybody acknowledges. It is therefore a plus point that we can remove controversies about the single bullet and the frontal shot from the evidence here.

In the following chapters, we examine the two other questions that indicate whether Oswald acted alone.

Chapter 2 – The weapon in the sniper's nest

It is a capital mistake to theorize before one has data. Insensibly one begins to twist facts to suit theories, instead of theories to suit facts.

Sherlock Holmes in Arthur Conan Doyle's *A Study in Scarlet*

The second crucial question that we ask here is whether shots were fired with the Carcano. The believers consider this to be proven: the weapon was at the crime scene, and the grooves on the bullet that was found show that it came from the barrel of the Carcano, to the exclusion of all other weapons. Furthermore, Oswald's palmprint was on it. More evidence is unnecessary for them, but the conspiracists claim that Oswald was a *patsy*, a scapegoat, and that the evidence produced against him was fabricated. In this hypothesis, the weapon is a false trail to incriminate Oswald. But is the Carcano a real or a false trail to the perpetrator? If Oswald was a scapegoat, the evidence of his guilt must be false. The answer to this question is decisive. We can follow the outcome of the further analysis step-by-step on the mind map below, and thereby arrive at a final decision.

From an analytical point of view, the question of whether the weapon is a false trail again consists of three components. The Carcano that was found in the book depository is a false trail if one of the three following assumptions is true:

1. The Carcano that was found is not Oswald's Carcano;
2. The shots were not fired with the Carcano that was found;
3. The shots were fired with the Carcano that was found, but not by Oswald.

We will examine each of these questions.

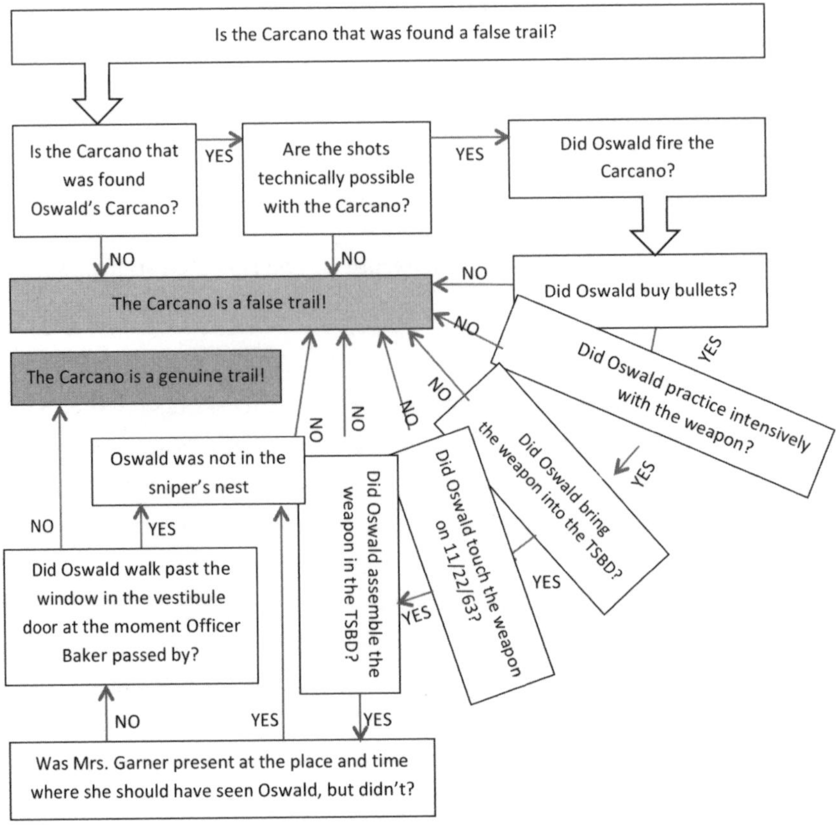

IS THE CARCANO THAT WAS FOUND THE WEAPON THAT WAS OWNED BY OSWALD?

We know that Oswald owned a Carcano. Let's call this 'Carcano 1'. We'll call the Carcano that was found at the crime scene, the sixth floor of the school book depository, 'Carcano 2'. For the believers, it's obvious that Carcano 1 and 2 are the same weapon. But if we have learned anything during the Kennedy investigation, it's that nothing can be taken for granted.

The Carcanos were originally intended for the Italian army. So they were produced in series of many hundreds of thousands. The weapons should be virtually identical, but their production took place in five different plants spread over decades, and the weapons were sometimes produced for very different destinations. The members of the extended Carcano family seem very much alike, but there are also striking differences. The length of the barrel may be different, as can the 'shark fin' at the front, and, of course, the sight, which was mounted after production. The attachment points for the strap were sometimes placed differently. Each weapon also has a serial number, but that number only consisted of four digits and one letter. So there could perhaps be several Carcanos in circulation bearing the same serial number. Time also played a part. A weapon that is more than 25 years old will, of course, have acquired many unique characteristics. Each of these differences provides an opportunity to determine whether Oswald's Carcano was also the weapon that was found in the book depository.

Ownership and serial number of the weapon

There is no doubt that Oswald purchased a Carcano: the microfilm with the coupon was found at Klein's Sporting Goods on November 23. Oswald had filled it in using the pseudonym Hidell. The FBI did not let any grass grow over this. One day after the assassination, the Federal Bureau of Investigation already reported: 'We have definitively identified the hand printing on the gun order and the handwriting on the envelope in which it was originally enclosed with the writing of Lee H. Oswald.'[26] Oswald placed the order under a pseudonym, and had the weapon delivered to a mailbox. That is not illogical. If the police ever connected the weapon to Hidell, they would then also have to link the pseudonym to a real individual. But why did Oswald let himself be arrested with a fake identity card in the name of Hidell?[27] It's even more striking that when the police asked him his name after his arrest, he answered with Hidell.[28] He might just as well have had his name engraved on the weapon. According to the official version, Oswald had the intention of carrying out an attack with the weapon. But he apparently also intended to stubbornly deny any involvement in the attack after an arrest. Yet when he left that morning, he took with him the clear evidence that he was the owner of the weapon. This is one of the many details in the proof of Oswald's guilt that doesn't really tie up.

It is also certain that Oswald bought a Carcano with the serial number C2766. Carcano 2, the weapon at the crime scene, had the same serial number. The identical serial number is a strong argument, but is not decisive, because it may not be a unique number. But, so far, no other Carcano 91/38 has surfaced with the serial number C2766.[29] The serial number is thereby still a slightly stronger argument than first assumed.

The backyard photos

On March 31, 1963, the spring sun is shining in the backyard of the house rented by Lee Oswald and his Russian wife, Marina, on Neely Street in Dallas. Marina makes use of the good weather to hang out the laundry. As she's doing this, Oswald comes down the steep stairs to the backyard. He's wearing black pants, a black polo shirt and has a pistol fastened to his belt. In addition, he has a carbine in his hand, two communist newspapers and a primitive camera. Marina has to take some photos of her husband. Oswald looks into the lens with a tough expression, and the shadow of the midday sun gives him a Hitler-like mustache. The photos with the weapon in the backyard also prove to be the only pictures on the roll of film. They look as though they had been intended to deliver the perfect proof that Oswald was the assassin of Kennedy eight months later. Oswald was confronted with this evidence after his arrest, and was the first to claim that the pictures are fakes. For decades some investigators continued to say the same. The HSCA set up a panel of forensic photographic experts in 1978. The *Photographic Evidence Panel* examined the photos closely and wrote an extensive report.[30] It was scientifically explained why the length of an object or a person may vary from photo to photo. The panel concluded that the backyard photos were not forgeries. In order to do this, they used a stereoscope, which exposes any striking manipulations in a photograph. The panel analyzed the defects caused by the lens of the cheap camera and the typical scratches that the mechanism of the unit made on the film, and was confident that the backyard photos are authentic. That is very incriminating evidence for Oswald. In the *On Trial* television trial, Oswald's lawyer, the experienced criminal lawyer Gerry Spence, undertakes a hopeless attempt to raise doubts about the pictures. Sergeant Cecil Kirk, head of the *Mobile Crime Laboratory* of the Metropolitan Police in Washington DC and a leading member of the photographic panel of the HSCA, sits in the witness chair. The lawyer asks how Kirk could see that the CIA or KGB had perfectly faked a picture. 'Have you ever examined a photo that the CIA had phonied up?' 'As far as I know, no', replies Kirk. 'Have you ever seen one that was messed with by the KGB?' Kirk has to admit that he doesn't know. Spence responds: 'You really don't know, mister, how sophisticated the methods of the KGB and the CIA are in making fake photographs.'[31] He actually wants to demonstrate that the fact that no CIA and KGB forgeries have been unmasked proves that these fakes are very good, but not that they do not exist. But that does not prove that the backyard photos were KGB forgeries. The witness sighs and calmly maintains his point of view: according to the HSCA panel there was no tampering with the backyard pictures. If Spence had known his dossier a little better, or if *On Trial* had been more like a genuine trial for Oswald, he would probably not have discussed the backyard photos in front of the jury. The police had searched Oswald's belongings on November 22 without a search warrant.[32] The Commission asked Agent Gus Rose, who had led the house search: 'Did you have a search warrant?' 'No, we didn't.'[33] answered the agent, as if it was the most normal thing in the world in Dallas to search through the belongings of a suspect in a murder case without an order from a magistrate.[34] They found no photos in the first search. The police came back the next day, this time with a search warrant, and suddenly found the backyard photos. There are judges who would exclude a piece of evidence for much less. But even if the validity of the photos as evidence is accepted, the further defense is weak. No single jury believed the CIA/KGB story. Why would the CIA or the KGB make three false photos if one was sufficient? Why three photos, and then make three different copies of Photo A and two copies of Photo C? There are now six copies on which you could detect a fraud, while one forgery would achieve the same result as six. Furthermore, another copy of the photo emerges later with Oswald's aristocratic acquaintance, Georges de Morenschildt. On the back, Oswald has dedicated the photograph to his close friend, and Marina had written a note in Russian full of contempt for her husband: 'Ha ha ha! The hunter of fascists.' So it really is Oswald standing there with the Carcano.

Now that we are sure that the Carcano in the backyard photos is Carcano 1, we can look for the similarities and differences with Carcano 2, the copy held in the evidence. There is one striking difference: Carcano 1 seems to have a metal tab at the bottom for the attachment of the carrying strap, but Carcano 2 is of the type with the attachment for the belt on the side.

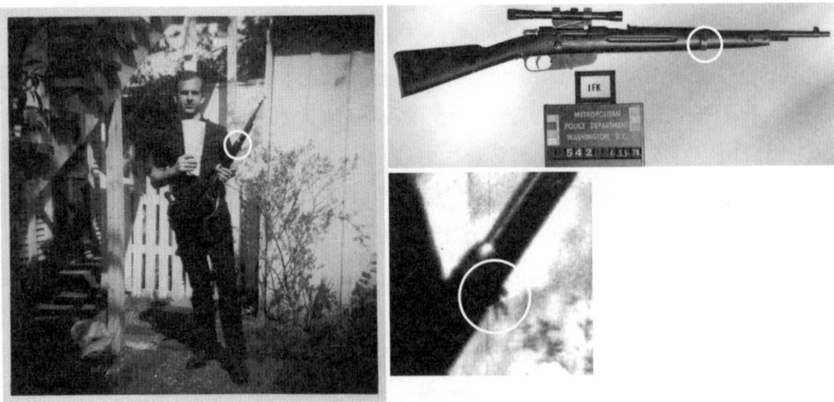

Figure 12. The tab under Carcano 1 is missing in Carcano 2.

But you should always be careful with photographs. Is the tab underneath the Carcano a chimera or a reality?

My investigations into the existing reports yielded little. Even the Warren Commission never confirmed anywhere that Carcano 1 and Carcano 2 are one and the same weapon. The photographic panel that the HSCA set up consisted of twenty experts. They, and Cecil Kirk above all, were convinced that the weapon in the backyard photographs was identical to the weapon in the evidence.[35] The panel based its conviction on a scratch, 'Mark S'. This scratch is definitely on Carcano 2, but is apparently also recognizable on backyard photo 133-A-dem.[36] The HSCA report only illustrates the existence of scratch S with a picture the size of a postage stamp:

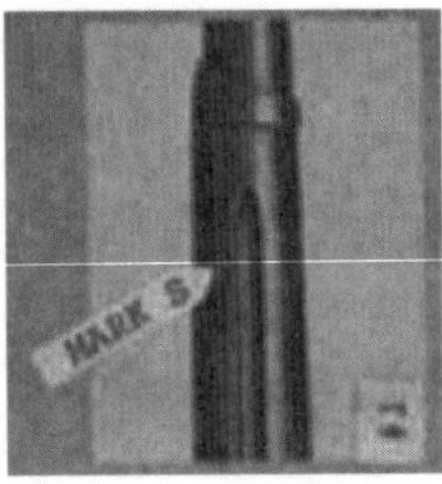

Figure 13.
Mark S as printed in the report of the photographic panel of the HSCA Vol.VI p. 88

But if the photo is printed in this way, the scratch can, of course, hardly be seen. Sergeant Cecil Kirk testified three times before the HSCA about his investigation in connection with this and other photos of the weapon. He was a man with an opinion, and made condescending remarks in his testimony about the kind of investigation that is based on 'a lot of second and third generation prints'. They see what they want to see in a picture. Very satisfied with his own work, Kirk added to this: 'This panel only looked at the original prints, and we all came to one seeing and one telling, in effect.' But that is, of course, not fair. He examined the original photographs, and we only have the print the size of a postage stamp.

The original HSCA photos

Cecil Kirk died in 2011, and a number of bundles with photos were found in his legacy. In 1978, it was still not possible to display a picture with more or less contrast, or more or less exposure, at the click of a mouse. Kirk had apparently made a series of copies of every photo that could be used as evidence. Some of these reserve copies, but also the 21 original 13x11 cm negatives of photographs of the Carcano, were offered as lot 1318 on the J. Levine auction site in 2014 (www.jlevines.com). This offered me a unique opportunity to solve the riddle, and I therefore didn't hesitate to buy the lot. The original photo on which Cecil Kirk based his position in 1978 is indeed a good deal clearer. It's finally visible what was meant by 'scratch S'.

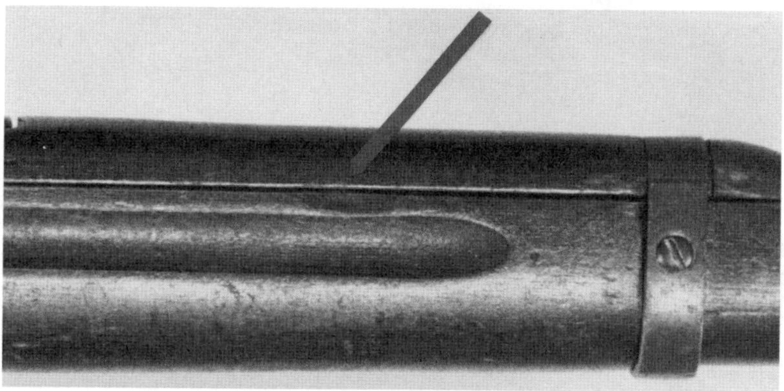

Figure 14. Photo of scratch S, as found in the estate of Cecil Kirk.[37]

The panel of photographic experts from the HSCA had the following to say about scratch S: 'Significantly, the largest and most prominent mark, mark S, a gouge mark that appears on the backyard picture, also appears in [...] post-assassination photographs of the rifle as well.'[38]

But the backyard photos are and remain what they are. Even in their highest resolution, they give no more details than when they were recorded on the original celluloid. Luckily, the bundle from Kirk also includes photos from the backyard photo series. Given the high resolution of Kirk's photos, we can assume that this is the best he could make from them. The photos from the panel are also considerably larger than the originals. There is indeed some noticeable discoloration at the place where scratch S should be. This is not strong enough to make this clear with a print here, but there is certainly a slight color difference on Carcano 1 at the site of scratch S on Carcano 2. Other details reinforce the belief that the weapon in Oswald's hands is the same weapon that was found at the crime scene. For example, the metal support plate for the telescopic sight exhibits a striking X-pattern that you can also see in the backyard picture.

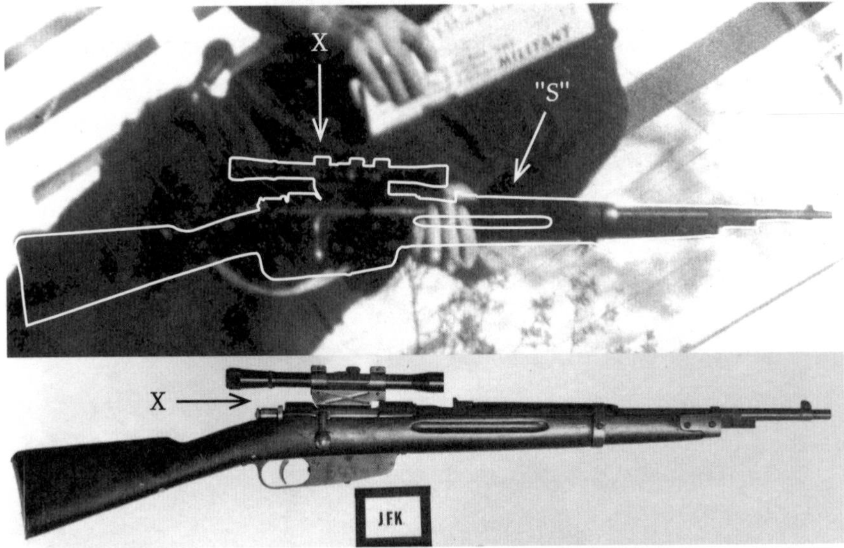

Figure 15. Backyard photo 133-A DEM and photo of the weapon. A vague, but unmistakable scratch S is visible. Other characteristics, such as the X-pattern in the support plate of the sight, can also be seen in the backyard photo.

The sharper version of backyard photo 133-B also confirms the belief that it is the same weapon. On the magnification, it's more clearly visible that the strap is *not* attached at the bottom of the Carcano, but extends to the side of the weapon. Oswald is holding the weapon here with the underside facing the camera. There is clearly no metal lip to be seen on the underside.

Figure 16.
Backyard photo – enlargement of the improvised strap.

For me, the investigation of the photographic material from the estate of Cecil Kirk is persuasive. The *Photographic Evidence Panel* of the HSCA rightly states that the Carcano that was found in the schoolbook depository is the Carcano with which Oswald proudly poses in the backyard photos. There is therefore no Carcano 1 and 2. It is Oswald's Carcano that was found at the crime scene. We also know that the bullet and fragments that were found after the assassination carry unique traces from the barrel of the Carcano.

The first opportunity to exclude a falsification of evidence is thereby concluded. Now there only remains the questions as to whether the shots were fired with *this Carcano* and whether they were fired by *Oswald*.

WAS OSWALD'S CARCANO FIRED ON NOVEMBER 22?

Investigation of the weapon

The bullet and the fragments that were found carry unique traces from the barrel of the Carcano. It is therefore logical to assume that the Carcano was fired on Friday, November 22. But that's not quite certain, because it's technically possible to produce a Carcano bullet in advance by firing the weapon into a bucket of wadding. You could then fit a *sabot* or 'shoe' around the 6.5 mm bullet and[39] then use the bullet in a weapon with a higher caliber. The shoe would be lost when the bullet is fired. The bullet would then retain the unique characteristics of the previous shot into the bucket of wadding.

If the Carcano was *not* fired on November 22, and the bullet fragments in the limousine *do* carry the traces of the Carcano, it would become immediately clear that the evidence was manipulated to incriminate Oswald. But, unfortunately, no one came up with the simple idea of determining whether the weapon had actually been used on the day of the assassination. Weapon expert Frazier himself even denied the possibility of such an investigation. Other experts confirm his point of view in certain terms.[40] You can only consider whether the weapon has been used since the last time it was cleaned. Unless you know that the gun was cleaned the day before a murder, you achieve little with this test. Nevertheless, Warren Commissioner McCloy asked FBI weapons expert Frazier the following: 'Was there metal fouling in the barrel?' Frazier answered: 'I did not examine it for that.' And, a little later, he said: 'If a barrel is allowed to rust, one round will remove that rust.'[41] But checking the barrel for rust is not so difficult, is it? Three rounds would certainly be enough to remove the rust. So if corrosion was still found, the weapon was not fired that day. But the test was deemed unnecessary, as it could only fall in Oswald's favor. Test shots with the weapon quickly followed, with the result that any further investigation into rust formation in the barrel was impossible. From the weapon itself, we cannot therefore determine whether it had been fired on November 22.

We can try this out indirectly, however. A common claim is that the Carcano was technically inadequate for the attack. If the shots that were fired are technically impossible with the Carcano, then they were obviously shot with a different weapon. There are doubts about the Carcano, and they relate to the speed and accuracy of the weapon.

Were the shots possible with the Carcano within the time available?

The Carcano does not have the best reputation. Silvia Maegher unjustly launched the nickname *the humanitarian rifle*,[42] and she also suggested, with some exaggeration, that 'it could not hurt anyone on purpose'. This nickname has been echoed in many JFK books. It is also not really the weapon you would expect to be used in an attack on a president. The Carcano was a mass product from the war industry. The weapon often produced a misfire. The loading system with its stiff bolt is also impractical and time consuming, even to the extent that there have often been doubts as to whether it is possible to carry out the alleged performance of Oswald within the given time. But the timing is not really a problem, at least as far as there is a clip (cartridge holder) available for loading the bullets.[43] A whole series of doubts again arose about this.[44] The final report of the Commission states that the clip was present in the weapon when it was found.[45] The conspiracists find this suspicious, because the last of Oswald's four bullets was loaded and ready to shoot. The clip was therefore empty, and the weapon would normally automatically eject the magazine.[46] Investigator Lattimer, however, who owned four different Carcanos, testified that the clip sometimes remains stuck in the weapon after loading the last bullet.[47] In any event, the clip was not found on the floor in the sniper's nest. In fact, no one actually knows how the clip ended up in the evidence. The police from Dallas once again ignored the elementary rules of evidence. It is also strange that no fingerprints were found on this sleek, metallic object.[48] In any case, there was a clip in the Carcano at the time that it was carried from the book depository. The archives of Cecil Kirk contain an illuminating photo that shows that.

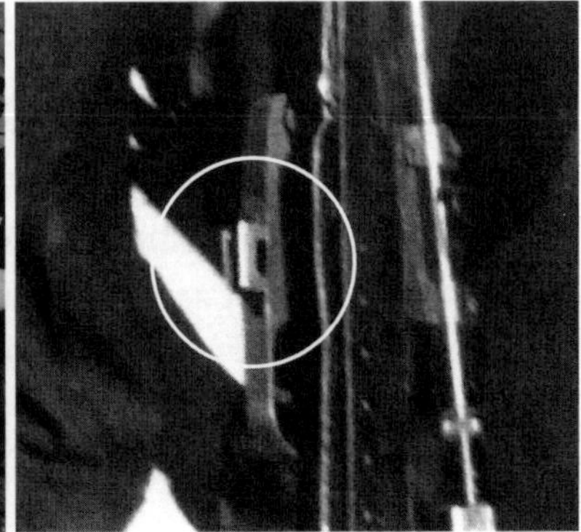

Figure 17. The clip in the Carcano is visible when the weapon is carried out of the TSBD.

So the shooter definitely possessed a clip. It was therefore technically possible to shoot three times in 5.5 seconds. That's the time between the *single bullet*, the single bullet with its infamous seven injuries, and the fatal head shot. The FBI assumed that the missed shot was fired between the two hits. In that sequence, you actually need only 5.5 seconds for the following seven actions: shot 1, reload, aim, shot 2, reload, aim, shot 3. This is just possible with a clip to push the bullets through. The CBS television network carried out a test with eleven sharpshooters in 1967.[49] Seven shooters were able to fire three times at a moving target within 5.5 seconds. The slowest of the ten shooters did it in 6.16 seconds. The weapon of the eleventh shooter jammed. This was the most striking problem with the Carcano. Of the 37 attempts, no fewer than 17 produced no result because one of the three shots jammed. But in 60 percent of cases in which the shooters were able to load three bullets in a row, firing 3 shots in 5.5 seconds was not an unsurmountable problem. Even if Oswald was much slower than the master marksman of the CBS, the timing is no problem. The shooter in the Dealey Plaza had, in fact, much longer than 5.5 seconds. The mysterious third shot that hit nothing or nobody did not occur *between* but *before* the other two shots. The action is then limited to just four steps: shot 2, reload, aim, shot 3. The available 5.5 seconds are thereby certainly more than adequate.

The HSCA investigation had another suggestion: shooting without the use of the telescopic sight. The firearms experts questioned by the commission felt that, in the circumstances at the Dealey Plaza, 'the open sights on Oswald's Mannlicher Carcano would have been preferred.'[50] That would save the time needed to regain the target in the 4x4 sight after reloading. If we look at the time aspect alone, the shooter would even have a bit more time if necessary.

Is the Carcano accurate enough to carry out an attack?

The Carcano in the book depository also shot with amazing accuracy. We know this because Oswald's Carcano was tested twice, once by the FBI and once by the military. Both agencies carried out their research independently from each other, and they were not informed of the results of the other investigation.

The FBI tested the deviation of the weapon over a distance of 15 yards (13.71 meters), 25 yards (22.86 meters) and 100 yards (91.44 meters). In the tests, three agents[51] each fired three rounds at each distance. That's a total of 27 bullets. As usual with the FBI, there's something strange going on, and, as always, the anomaly is detrimental to Oswald. From a distance of 15 yards, the bullets ended up between 2.5 and 4 inches (6.35 to 10.16 centimeters) above the target. From a distance of 25 yards, the bullets still ended up somewhat higher above the target, 4 to 5 inches (10.16 to 12.7 centimeters) too high. This appears consistent with the expectation that the deviation will only increase as the bullet flies straight ahead over a greater distance. If the bullet is 4 inches off course after 15 yards, it should therefore be 26 inches (66.04 centimeters) off course with a shot over 100 yards. But this is not the case with the FBI. The Carcano was suddenly much more accurate over 100 yards than it had been over 15 yards. The deviation was suddenly only 3 to 5 inches (7.62 to 12.7 centimeters) above the target, even less so than the deviation from 25 yards.

The graph in Fig. 18 shows how implausible the FBI measurement was from 100 yards. The dotted line shows the normally expected deviation for the shots from 15 and 25 yards. In fact, the deviation should, of course, be even greater than the linear extrapolation. The human error in this shot will, in fact, be higher due to aiming at a more remote target.

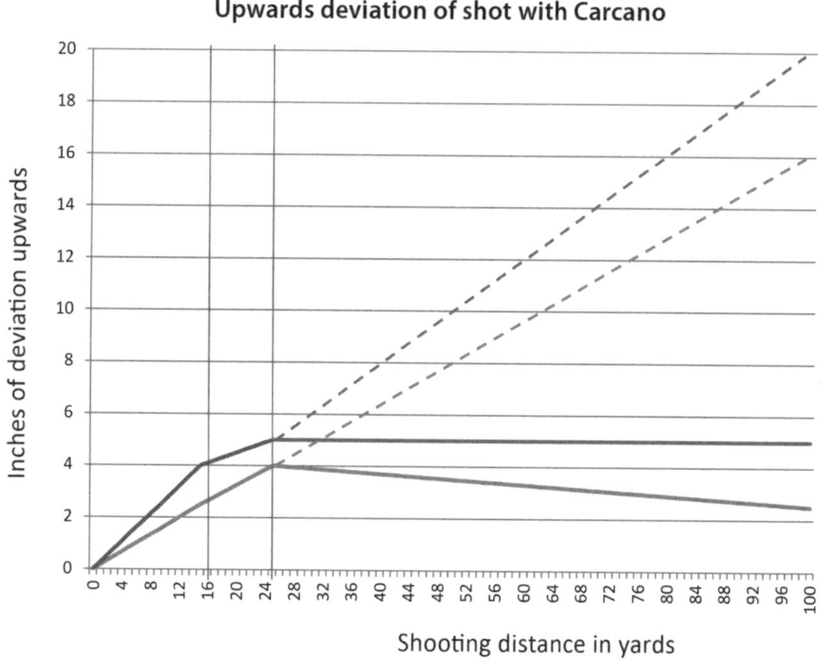

Figure 18. The deviation of the Carcano in the FBI tests

In the best case scenario, the FBI did not tamper with the results, and the anomaly is only the result of an inconsistency in the tests. That could, for example, be due to the shooters now taking account of the deviations they had established in the previous shots during the 100 yard shot. The most striking finding is: the deviation with regard to the target is consistently too high and too far to the right. Once you disregard this, the bullets appear to be incredibly strongly grouped.

FBI experts Frazier and Cunningham shot a total of six times, and each time the bullet landed within the same circle of ? inches (1.9 centimeters). Their colleague Killion took slightly longer to aim, and his three bullets ended up slightly lower, but all three were within the area of a coin.[52]

Test shots at 25 yards (13.7 meters)

Shooter	Sec. for 3 shots	Inches above target	Inches to the right of target	Spread of the hits
Frazier	6	4	1	3/4 inch circle
Killion	9	2.5	1	"size of a dime"
Cunningham	7	4	1	3/4 inch circle

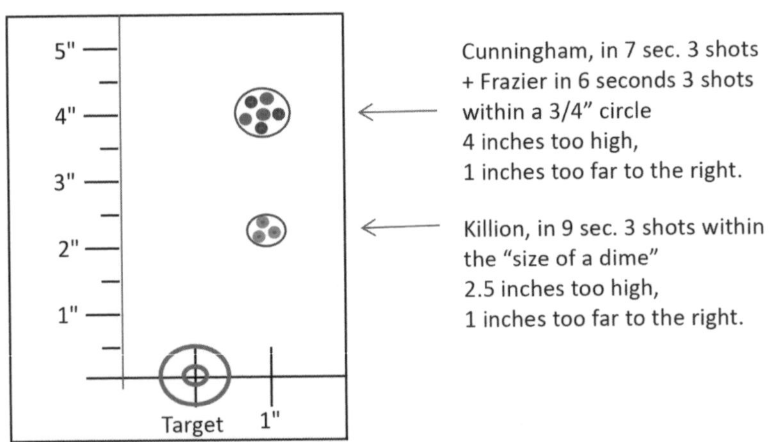

Figure 19. The deviation of the Carcano in the FBI tests

The problem is therefore not the accuracy of the weapon. Weapon expert Simmons also confirmed that the Carcano 'is as accurate as the current American military rifles.'[53] Apparently, the problem is above all the incorrect adjustment of the sight. The shots by the FBI weapons experts shown above were fired after the weapon had been adjusted as accurately as possible. 'We sighted the scope in relatively close, fired it, and decided rather than fire more ammunition through the weapon, we would use these targets which we had fired.' And yet the bullets all landed too high and too far to the right. In addition, the sight was very difficult to adjust. 'The spring mounting in the crosshair ring did not stabilize until we had fired five or six shots',[54] said Frazier.

But if, according to Frazier, you adjust the weapon as accurately as possible, fire six rounds to stabilize the sight, measure the deviation of the weapon and take account of this when aiming – and take more time because you are shooting at a moving target – then anyone who had practiced intensively could keep the three shots within a circle of 6 inches (15.2 centimeters) from a distance of 100 yards (91 meters).[55]

At the moment of the fatal shot, Kennedy's head was 89 yards (81 meters) from the sniper's nest. Because of the shorter distance flown by the bullet on November 22, Frazier's accuracy circle can therefore be somewhat smaller. A circle with a diameter of 14 centimeters is the size of a saucer under a coffee cup – and that's also the accuracy required to hit Kennedy in the head. According to the FBI, an excellent sharpshooter could hit Kennedy in the head with the Carcano from 81 meters if the preconditions stated above by Frazier are fulfilled.

In addition to the FBI, the Ballistics Research Laboratory, the ballistics laboratory of the military, also carried out an investigation. The army approached the matter more scientifically. Simmons, the head of the laboratory, explained to the commission how the weapon was adjusted. There were at least two, possibly three, *shims* or wedges to be adjusted. These are thin plates (two of 0.38 millimeter thickness and one of 0.2 millimeter thickness) that are placed under the sight because the original deviation was too large to compensate with the control mechanism.[56] The enigmatic third *shim*, about which weapons expert Simmons was very vague,[57] is used to orient the sight slightly to the left. This was necessary, because 'the gunsmith observed that the scope as we received it was installed as if for a left-handed man'[58] Oswald was right-handed. Authors who consider themselves more competent than the army armorer challenge whether a sight can be mounted for a right or left-hander. But, in any case, the sight was originally poorly adjusted, not only in height, but also in the left-right axis. After the gun has been adjusted as accurately as possible, the deviation from the target could be limited to 1.2 mil[59] over a distance of 91 meters. This corresponds to a deviation of 3.5 inches (8.9 centimeters) from the target. This is only the deviation of the weapon itself, fired from a tripod. But the deviation that has to be added due to the human error of the shooter is very small, according to experts, or at least in the case of the very experienced shooters deployed by Simmons (with the rank of 'master' in the National Rifle Association).[60] The deviation measured by the military is also constant in one direction, too high and too far to the right. A possible deviation of 3.5 inches (8.89 centimeters) in *all* directions would mean that a shot at a point 91 meters away would fall within a circle of 7 inches (17.78 centimeters). But if all the bullets deviate 3.5 inches in one direction, the circle would, of course, be much smaller. Simmons therefore did not contradict the investigation of the FBI weapon specialists. According to the FBI, a top shooter firing from 100 yards and with the weapon adjusted as well as possible would shoot about 2.5 to 5.0 inches too high. According to the military, this would be 3.5 inches. In any case, both studies confirm that the Carcano performs reasonably reliably. But is 'fairly reliable' also sufficient for the attack on the Dealey Plaza?

Simmons had a small target (4 inches or 10 inches in diameter) placed at 270 feet (82 meters). That is an approximation of the distance that the bullet traveled in the shot that hit Kennedy's head. He then used three top shooters. The chance of them hitting within the circle with a diameter of 4 inches turned out to be relatively small: 39 percent.[61] But the probability became 100 percent with a larger target with a diameter of 9 inches (22.86 centimeter). Kennedy's head was, of course, not 9 inches wide. Simmons also thought that the fact that the limousine was moving (from 16 to 24 kilometers per hour), had little impact on the calculations.[62]

The conclusion of the army was also that the Carcano fired accurately, in the sense that the bullets always ended up in approximately the same place, but that the weapon had a deviation above and to the right that could not be corrected. That made it relatively difficult to hit a target with a diameter of 10 centimeters, but it was easy to fire the bullet into a slightly larger circle.

Other tests

Oswald's Carcano was tested by the FBI and the army, but there were, of course, many tests that were also carried out using other Carcanos. Dr. John Lattimer tested the accuracy of four Carcanos together with his son. He noted the following: 'After two weeks of practice, it was relatively easy for each of us to place three bullets in the central area of the head (or the torso) of a military-type silhouette target if five seconds were used between shots.'[63]

In 1967, CBS also conducted a test for a television as mentioned above program. In the CBS test, eleven shooters were usually able to hit the target twice – provided the weapon did not jam. But it was of no consequence to CBS where Kennedy was hit (see photograph below on the left). The president had also been given a very broad head. In this test, the gunmen were instructed to aim for the center of this very large, bright orange surface. Simmons's statement already indicated that a Carcano is perfect for aiming at a target of more than 20 centimeters in diameter, but that it is much harder to hit a target of only 10 centimeters in diameter. In order to fatally hit Kennedy, the real sniper had to aim for the small circle representing the back of Kennedy's head. In the photograph below on the right, the huge orange surface of the CBS test has been replaced by the real target. It's not surprising that the shooters in the documentary hit the target with two out of three shots. It is 50 centimeters wide and 40 centimeters high. Furthermore, CBS seemed to assume that Kennedy had hydrocephalus (water on the brain). Kennedy's shoulder width is indeed 50 centimeters. But his head

Figure 20. CBS target: 50 centimeters wide, 40 centimeters high: 2 hits possible

Actual target, back of JFK's head: 14 centimeters wide

is turned with the narrowest side towards the book depository. This side has a width of 14 centimeters. If we take this into account (adjusted photo below on the right), it becomes clear just how misleading the successful CBS test is. The real assassin did not have to hit the orange surface, but the small circle in the adjusted photograph on the right.

In its final report, the Warren Commission was intellectually dishonest in the same way when it stated: 'The Commission agrees with the testimony of Marine marksmanship expert Zahm that is was an easy shot to hit some part of the President's body.'[64] Hitting a target of 50 by 40 centimeters is, of course, an easy shot, but there is a difference whether the president is hit in his arm or shoulder, or in the head. CBS therefore only proved that it was possible to make a documentary in which Oswald's performance with a Carcano was *seemingly* repeated. But, nevertheless, even with only a 40 percent chance of hitting the small circle, three attempts would probably be sufficient for a good marksman.

The crucial importance of the correct adjustment

According to the official version of the story, the Carcano was not properly adjusted at the time of the assassination. The importance of this fact was explained to the Commission by an independent and experienced expert. Floyd Davis was the manager of the Sports Drome Rifle Range, the shooting range where Oswald had been sighted several times in November. Davis had a lot of professional experience in setting up rifles. He claimed that he was able to correctly adjust a rifle with 8 to 10 shots, but that adjustment was an absolute must: 'If the gun was anywhere near accurate, it would have to be an accident, because the slightest jar can knock a scop 2 or 3 foot out of balance, and there is no way that you could ship a gun and carry a gun around a little bit and make sure it being accurate. That is why your deer hunters practice and shoot their guns in every year before they go deer hunting. And I have saw them waste almost five boxes of shells trying to get them accurate down there after having sighted them in the year before.'[65] Davis's view is convincing, as it indeed seems impossible that a dismantled rifle that is reassembled in the worst possible conditions would be able to shoot accurately.

We can therefore answer the question as to whether the head shot with the Carcano was possible with 'yes'. It is 'yes' in the sense that it cannot be completely ruled out that it is possible, on condition that the rifle is at least correctly adjusted. On the basis of the technical features of the weapon, we can therefore neither confirm nor exclude that the Carcano was fired on that fatal Friday.

Did Oswald fire the Carcano?

We know in the meantime that Oswald's Carcano was found at the crime scene. Oswald worked there, and it cannot be ruled out that the Carcano was actually fired on that day. Technically, the shots with the Carcano are not impossible, provided the right conditions were met. The bullets and the fragments that were found bear traces that indicate that the Carcano was fired. But the subsequent claim that it was not Oswald who shot Kennedy with this rifle cannot be made lightly. After all, he bought the Carcano, and he was carrying a suspicious package with him that day. The Carcano was found on the fifth floor, from where the shots were fired. Oswald's fingerprints and palmprints were found on the boxes in the sniper's nest. He had no direct alibi for the time of the assassination, and he behaved very suspiciously after the attack. That is too much to simply dismiss.

Let's therefore assume that Oswald indeed fired the Carcano on November 22, and verify whether this could be true. We again split up the question into necessary components. If Oswald fired the Carcano on November 22, then Oswald must have had the necessary marksman qualifications to carry out the assassination, and – in chronological order – he must have purchased the bullets, practiced intensely with the rifle, smuggled the weapon into the TSBD, and then touched, assembled and fired the Carcano. What evidence exists of these seven essential assumptions?

1. Was Oswald sufficiently prepared to fire the fatal shots?

The experts who tested the weapon during the investigation had a 40 percent chance of hitting a small disc with a shot from a distance of 81 meters. Was Lee Harvey Oswald also able to hit Kennedy's head from that distance? Courtesy of the army, we know reasonably well how good Oswald's performance was on the shooting range.

The army has three categories of snipers, measured on a scale of 190 to 250:

1) *expert* is the highest category, and requires a score above 220;
2) *sharpshooter* is the middle category, and requires a score of 210 or higher;
3) *marksman* is the lowest category, with a score between 190 and 209.

In December 1956, after three weeks of intensive training in the Marine Corps,[66] Oswald obtained a score of 212. Sherman Cooley was in Oswald's training squad. He testified twenty years later that 'Oswald was known as a s***bird, who couldn't qualify with his weapon. It was a disgrace not to qualify and we gave him holy hell.'[67] But Oswald eventually succeeded on January 20, 1957. He obtained a score two points above the lower limit of the middle category. That was 22 points above the absolute minimum, and 38 points below the absolute top.[68] Not brilliant, but still creditable for the clumsy Oswald. Believers refer to this one-off score of 212 as evidence that Oswald was a 'sharpshooter'. At the next test, however, in May 1959, Marine Oswald only managed to score 191, one point above the absolute minimum, i.e. barely the level of *marksman*. It is clear that Oswald rapidly deteriorated as a rifleman due to a lack of training. Lieutenant Colonel Folsom of the Marine Corps explained the score of 191 to the Commission as follows: 'A low marksman qualification indicates a rather poor "shot".'[69] The Commission failed to mention the opinion of this Lieutenant Colonel in its final report, but made sure to cite two other witnesses. Major Anderson declared: 'Oswald was a good shot, somewhat better or equal to better than the average let us say.' Sergeant Zahm stated: 'I would say in the Marine Corps he is a good shot, slightly above average.'[70] According to author Leo Sauvage, a score of 190 'was for all practical reasons a score of Zero.'[71] How can one point above the minimum be better than the average of the 175,571 marines who were enlisted at that moment? Did the others score zero? The 'somewhat better than the average' score relates to the one-off performance in January 1957, after three weeks of intensive training. But the proper benchmark is, of course, the more recent score of May 1959, and Oswald had not practiced intensely for three weeks before the assassination of Kennedy took place.

The Carcano is also a more difficult weapon than the M16 with which Oswald used to practice in the Marine Corps. The locking system of the Carcano must be operated with the right hand, so that the shooter has to find his target in his sight again after reloading the rifle. John Lattimer had his fourteen year old son, Gary, fire at a stationary target from a distance of 263 feet (87.7 yards or 80.16 meters) with a comparable Carcano that was optimally adjusted. Gary hit the target three times in twelve seconds.[72] Lattimer also owns Oswald's original score book. From a sitting position, Oswald scored 49/50 and 48/50 respectively for shots at 200 yards (182.88 meters), more than double the distance at Dealey Plaza.[73] 'His sitting position scores were excellent.'[74] This does not alter the fact that Oswald was definitely not as good a shot as the experts who were used later in the comparative tests. Commission Counsel Liebeler even wrote this down in the margin of the proof sheets: 'The fact is that most of the experts were much more proficient with a rifle than Oswald could ever be expected to be.'[75]

The believers, headed by Bugliosi, assess the probability of each question about the feasibility of the shot separately. They *consider* it possible to hit a target with a worn and poorly adjusted rifle. They *consider* it possible that a former marine could hit a moving target at 60 to 82 meters, even though he was a mediocre shooter. But a positive reply to the question as to whether *Oswald* could have fired two *master shots with a poorly adjusted Carcano*, is much less likely than a positive reply to the separate elements of this question. The improbability, in fact, increases with each subsequent question. The answer to the question as to whether Oswald could have fired two master shots is again not yes or no. The answer is: 'He needed some luck, but it was not entirely impossible.'

2. Did Oswald buy bullets?

The believers do not deny that Oswald had only four bullets. These are the three bullets he alledgedly used in the attack, and the fourth unused bullet that remained in the rifle. The investigators found not a single additional bullet in Oswald's belongings, or even packaging that could have contained bullets.[76] Four bullets or one hundred bullets make little difference for the believers. It seems quite logical to them that Oswald was aware that he could not target the president five times, and therefore only took four bullets with him. But not a single bullet could be found anywhere, either at Oswald's home or with his belongings in the garage of Ruth Paine. Marina stated that 'she had never seen any ammunition around the houses in which they had lived.'[77] Her statement to the FBI on December 17, 1963, is even clearer:

'Oswald did not have any ammunition for the rifle to her knowledge in either Dallas or New Orleans, and he did not speak about buying ammunition.'[78] But that's odd, because bullets are sold per dozen, or per hundred. One of the two stores that sold bullets purchased them for 45 dollars per thousand.[79] Even Oswald was not so stingy that he would save on a bullet that cost a few cents. The 6.5 mm caliber is relatively common as such, but only bullets that have been produced in Italy can be used for the Carcano.[80] The cartridge clip was not supplied with the gun,[81] and Oswald must therefore have purchased it somewhere. The Commission realized that this was, once more, a problem. They were well aware that the weapon was delivered without a cartridge clip, but still kept this possibility open, and wrote: 'The rifle was *probably* sold without cartridge clip.'[82] The word *probably* says it all. If the cartridge clip had indeed been sold together with the weapon, the Commission would, of course, have known this, and would also have had this on record. They questioned the salesmen who sold the weapon, and could simply have asked the question. The question of where Oswald had purchased the reasonably common cartridge clip was, in fact, the least of our concerns. But where had he purchased the four bullets – or actually five if he had indeed taken a shot at General Walker on April 10, 1963? This question proved difficult, or even impossible, to answer. Intensive investigation revealed that only two gun stores in the Dallas neighborhood sold Carcano bullets. Both stores had sole proprietors, and the proprietors were always present when the store was open. They were both convinced that they never sold a bullet to Oswald. No Carcano bullets were sold in the gun store in Irving where a certain 'Oswald' allegedly had the sight adjusted.[83]

It is possible that Oswald only had four bullets, but it does seem quite unlikely. And this improbability is added to the improbability of the replies to the other questions.

3. Did Oswald practice with the weapon?

The commission asked gun expert Simmons whether 'a marksman who is less than a highly skilled marksman' could be capable of a shot with the required accuracy under those conditions. The army expert replied: 'Obviously considerable experience would have to be in one's background to do so. And with this weapon, I think also considerable experience with this weapon, because of the amount of effort required to work the bolt.'[84] So you absolutely need 'considerable experience' to match the performance of the sniper with the Carcano at Dealey Plaza. About three years after his fairly decent results with an M16 in January 1957, Marine Oswald achieved a score just one point above the absolute minimum. He barely touched a weapon in the next four years. Although he was a member of a hunting club in Russia, and owned a rifle,[85] his wife, Marina, scornfully said that hunting in Russia usually means that you catch a bottle of vodka.[86] These hunts were therefore mainly a get-together for men, and hunting was ancillary. After his return to the United States, Oswald also never practiced to improve his poor marksmanship level of 1959. According to the official story, the weapon was stored in Ruth Paine's garage during the last two months before the attack. Ruth, who provided accommodation to Marina, never saw Oswald with this weapon.[87] She never even saw him practice with it. As a fervent opponent of firearms, Ruth Paine would certainly have noticed. According to an FBI statement of December 3, 1963, Marina also never saw her husband practice with the rifle: 'Marina said she had never seen Oswald practice with the rifle or any other firearm and he had never told her that he was going to practice with his rifle or any other firearm.'[88] In a later statement, on December 17, Marina repeated her point of view: 'She cannot recall that he ever practiced firing the rifle either in New Orleans or in Dallas.'[89] She also never saw Oswald take the weapon with him when he left the house in New Orleans. She never saw him handling the rifle, not even to clean it. The only device for which Oswald was trying to improve his skills at the time was a typewriter, and that did not seem to be going too smoothly either. Oswald and mechanical devices were not a good combination; he couldn't even drive a car. Despite the above two clear statements of December 3 and 17, Marina said the following in her questioning before the Commission on February 3, 1964: 'I think that he went once or twice. I didn't actually see him take the rifle, but I knew that he was practicing [...] He told me.'[90] Marina had a good reason to change her statement: 'I said before I had never seen it before. But I think you understand. I want to help you.' It is pathetic to see how the Commission Counsel rushed to her aid: 'She says she was not sworn in before. But now inasmuch as she is sworn in, she is going to tell the truth.' On February 22, 1964, Marina proved that even her sworn truth still left room for improvement. The FBI asked her the same question for the fourth time, and was finally satisfied to record: 'He had his rifle wrapped up in a raincoat and told Marina he was going to practice firing with the rifle.

She said the police would get him. He replied he was going anyway and it was none of her business. He did not say where he was going to practice firing the rifle, other than he was going to a vacant spot.'[91]

In its final report, the HSCA put the responsibility for the lies entirely in the hands of Marina: 'She gave incomplete and inconsistent statements at various times to the Secret Service, the FBI and the Commission.'[92] But that is not entirely fair: the FBI also bears a lot of the responsibility for this. Marina unilaterally changed her statements in the direction the FBI wanted. In February, Marina no longer feared that she would be extradited to the Soviet Union if she did not cooperate sufficiently with the investigation. She no longer adapted her statement in her own interest. It was the FBI that put her under pressure. Ultimately, it makes little difference. Even if Marina did speak the truth in her final statement, Oswald only practiced with the rifle in the house in Neely Street. The couple lived there for seven weeks, from March 2. The rifle was shipped to Oswald at the Hidell post office box on March 20. Oswald moved to New Orleans on April 24. Marina stated that the rifle would then have traveled in her luggage to Ruth Paine's garage in Irving.[93] It remains possible that the weapon was disassembled and traveled to New Orleans in one of Oswald's NAVY duffel bags, but there are no witnesses who ever saw Oswald practice with a gun in New Orleans. So, at best, Marina only confirmed that Oswald allegedly practiced very sporadically with the rifle for a period of four weeks, seven months before the attack. In any case, Oswald was only near the weapon in the weekends in the last ten weeks before the attack. Besides, where would he have practiced? Practicing with a weapon is prohibited in Dallas. A storekeeper stated that it occasionally happened that someone came to practice with a weapon in a particular deserted spot along the highway. In Ruth's community, Irving, there were 46 people who lived near places where someone could potentially practice with a gun. All of them were questioned, but no one had seen Oswald or noticed anything that could be an indication of shooting practice.[94] There was a flash of hope when someone had found two empty boxes of 6.5 mm bullets, but it turned out they were not Carcano bullets.[95] The *Report of investigation of possible target practice by Lee Harvey Oswald* section amounts to no more than eighteen pages in the entire FBI report containing 971 pages. This is how meager the findings on the possible practice sessions of Oswald were. Oswald therefore did not practice with the weapon in the months prior to the attack.[96]

It would appear that Oswald was spotted at a shooting range, but what he was doing there could hardly be regarded as practice. The 35-year-old heart patient Malcolm Price was often hanging around the Sports Drome Rifle Range shooting range, where he gave the owner, Floyd Davis, a hand. Price claims he saw Oswald three times at the range. But there are some problems with the dates.[97] According to the shooting range manager, the dates were finally established as November 9, 10 and 17. These dates don't fit into Oswald's agenda, however. The weapon is in Irving,[98] where Marina was living in Ruth Paine's house. During the weekend of November 9 and 10, Oswald was in Irving, but did not leave the house.[99] They had a Turkey Shoot at the shooting range on November 17, but it is highly unlikely that Oswald was there on that day because he did not visit his wife and daughter in Irving that weekend.[100] He could therefore not have drawn the attention of the other shooting range customers to his rifle on that day.

Drawing attention appears to be the only thing Oswald seemed to have done when he was at the shooting range. He allegedly took a shot at the target of the range next to him, much to the annoyance of the other amateur shooter, Mr. Slack. Oswald is said to have told those present ostentatiously that his sight had cost 18 dollars, and that it had been mounted by a gunsmith in Ceddar Hill.[101] Yet there was not a single gun store in Ceddar Hill, and the sight on Oswald's weapon had already been mounted when he purchased it. These are not the only remarkable contradictions that emerged. Mr. Greener, the manager of a gun store in Irving, found an undated ticket bearing the name 'Oswald'. Between November 4 and 8, someone who claimed to be 'Oswald' had had three holes drilled for fixing the sight. But closer investigation revealed that this customer was not Lee Harvey Oswald, and the weapon was not a Carcano.[102] Oswald allegedly used a ten-year-old Chevrolet to travel to the shooting range, but the real Oswald didn't have a car, or even a driver's license. Oswald is also said to have worn a hat, which is not so easy for someone who did not own a hat. Moreover, he seems to have temporarily assumed the habit of chewing tobacco especially for his visits to the shooting range.[103]

Davis, the manager of the range, confirmed Price's story in broad outline. He had heard talk about the incident at the shooting range, but, in the end, he was not able to either confirm or deny much about Oswald, his rifle, his company, his means of transport, and similar aspects.

Two strong witnesses, who had seen Oswald practice with an Italian weapon on November 16, remained, however. Dentist Homer Wood[104] and his thirteen-year-old[105] stated that Oswald was firing a Carcano on the range next to them. The father swore on the bible that the man they had seen was Oswald. This man allegedly shot several bull's-eyes from a distance of 100 yards (91.44 meters), but only used eight to ten bullets. They saw Oswald step into a passenger car when he left. Whether or not Oswald took place behind the wheel is not clear.[106] According to young Sterling, the car was a new Ford model.[107]

An old Chevrolet or a new Ford, Oswald as driver or as passenger... The Commission was not eager to go any deeper into these witness statements. If Oswald was a passenger in the car, he had an unknown accomplice. But he also could not have been the driver, because he had no driver's license nor a car. The FBI also examined the shells that had been left at the shooting range, but the shells and Oswald's Carcano did not match. The very attentive young Sterling, however, had noticed that, after each shot, the gunman had picked up the shell and put it in his pocket. It is also notable that Oswald only fired eight or ten shots at each of his alleged visits. There mainly seems to have been an intention to draw attention, and to clearly show the Italian weapon. Sterling Wood, who seemed to have an eye for weapons, also believed that the sight he had seen differed from the sight on the Carcano from the book depository.

After the publication of the Warren Report, Sterling proudly showed a girlfriend that it actually mentioned his name. He boasted a little, and also exaggerated his story. By chance, investigator Gus Russo heard this 'dressed up' version,[108] and this caused additional doubts to arise. Father and son Wood rather aggressively kept the press at bay after this. All this also did not contribute to the credibility of their story.

So what can we actually believe about Oswald's presence in the Sports Drome Rifle Range? We have a whole list of witnesses: Price the heart patient, Davis the manager, Slack the angry neighbor at the shooting range, and, finally, father and son Wood. But the number of contradictions in their observations is very high, and, all in all, the credibility of these incidents is not entirely convincing. The believers consider this as evidence that Oswald was planning an attack. The conspiracists assume that someone took conspicuous pains in passing himself off as Oswald in order to create evidence against him afterwards.

The Warren Commission would, of course, have liked the fact that Oswald had practiced with the rifle at the shooting range, but the fact that he would have needed an accomplice to take him there took things a step too far, even for them. The Commission therefore decided that all the witnesses had been mistaken.[109] There are arguments for and against, but even if we accept the fact that Oswald had indeed been present at the shooting range, the question remains as to whether he did a lot of practicing. At best, he would have fired eight to ten shots three times, and that is not enough to be regarded as practice. This would just about be enough to adjust the sight, and this could not have been the intention, because any use this adjustment would have had would have been lost by the disassembly for transportation to the book depository. If the encounters at the shooting range did indeed take place as related, and the person in question was indeed Oswald, the practice sessions in preparation of the attack still hardly meant anything.

Oswald therefore never practiced intensively with the Carcano, and that certainly plays a role in his chances of hitting the target twice in 5.5 seconds on November 22. Lattimer highlights that practicing was particularly important in terms of getting used to the stiff bolt: 'It must be emphasized that a leisure period of repeated manipulation and dry-firing was essential for acquiring the proficiency demonstrated by the assassin.'[110] But there is no evidence at all regarding any such practice.

4. Did Oswald smuggle the weapon into the TSBD?

The paper bag that allegedly contained the weapon when Oswald smuggled it into the school book depository causes a lot of problems.[111] The best known problem is that the bag that Oswald had with him that morning was not long enough (about 61 to 68 centimeters) to contain the disassembled weapon (88 centimeters).[112] From now on, we will call this Bag O. Two witnesses, Buell (Wesley) Frazier and his sister Linnie Mae Randle, kept to their original estimate of the length of the paper bag, despite the pressure that was put on them. Immediately after the assassination, Buell Frazier said under oath: 'It must have been about 24 inches long.'[113] He kept to this statement before the Commission.[114] In 1987, he stated to author Gus Russo: 'They had me in one room and my sister in another. They were asking us to hold our hands apart to show how long the package was. They made me do it over and over – at least ten times. Each time they measured the distance and it was always 25 inches, give or take an inch. They did the same with my sister and she gave the same measurement.'[115] Linnie described the bag as follows: 'He carried it in his right hand, had the top sort of folded down and had a grip like this [...] and it almost touched the ground as he carried it.'[116] Linnie also verified the measurement: 27 inches (69 centimeters). The Commission Counsel was anxious to make it 28.5 inches, but she did not give in.[117]

The bag that was found at the crime scene – we'll call this Bag C – also looks quite different from what witness Buell Frazier remembered about Bag O: 'It is right as you get out of the grocery store, just more or less out of a package, you have seen some of these brown paper sacks you can obtain from any, most of the stores, some varieties.' To be sure, Commission Counsel Ball asked once again: 'The paper, was the color of the paper, that you would get in a grocery store, is that it, a bag in a grocery store?' Frazier replied: 'Right. [...] you have seen these kinds of heavy duty bags you know like you obtain from the grocery store, something like that.' Bag C does not look like a typical bag from a grocery store at all. It is clearly a self-made one. Linnie believed that the paper corresponded to what she had seen, but she had, of course, only seen the bag briefly, and from some distance away. Marina had never seen the bag, and she hadn't seen Oswald doing something with paper on the eve of the murder.[118] Oswald claimed that Bag O contained curtain rods. He had already told Buell Wesley Frazier on Thursday that these curtain rods were the reason why he had been in Irving outside the weekend. Linnie confirmed that Oswald had said that to her brother, as Buell mentioned that detail on the same evening when she went shopping with him.[119] Oswald claimed he needed the curtain rods for his rented room. But that was, of course, a lie: someone as stingy as Oswald would not spend money on curtains for a rented room where he could be asked to leave any day. Logically, Oswald should also have taken his package of curtain rods with him when he returned home after the attack. He didn't do so, and no curtain rods were found in the Book Depository later. Curtain rods[120] were found in Ruth Paine's garage, however, together with brown wrapping paper and sellotape.[121] This was apparently not investigated further, however.

If we leave aside the problem with the length for a moment, the question arises whether Bag O and Bag C are actually the same bag. The investigation would normally have demonstrated this very quickly, but the chain of evidence with regard to Bag C is once again typical for the quality of a murder investigation in Texas. As encountered several times in this case, the last step relating to this evidence seems reasonably kosher. Lieutenant Day, the person who was ultimately responsible for the crime scene, neatly identified Bag C by putting his signature and place where it was found on it. But this identification is pretty worthless, because not a single witness has confirmed *when* Day put it there.[122] The experience we have of the case, however (the lies about the marking of the shells, the withheld discovery of a handprint on the gun etc.), demonstrates that Day was completely unreliable. It is therefore best to have a closer look at the chain of evidence from the beginning.

1. Deputy Sheriff Mooney found the sniper's nest, but did not see a paper bag lying in the corner.[123]
2. The people who next saw the sniper's nest, Deputy Sheriff Craig[124] and Sergeant Hill,[125] also don't remember seeing a paper bag.
3. The next person was Detective Sims. He was the first to confirm the presence of a bag in the sniper's nest. But he was so cautious in his statement that we can almost be sure that he is lying. 'We saw some wrappings – a brown wrapping there', he said, already using the first person plural in order to share the responsibility. Where was this bag then? To this, his reply contained no less than five attenuations in one sentence: 'As well as I remember (1) – of course, I didn't pay much attention at that time (2), but it was, I believe (3), the east side of where the boxes were piled up – that would be a guess (4) – I believe (5) that's where it was.'[126] There is yet another indication that he lied, and didn't know where the bag was supposed to be. The paper bag and the bullet shells (hulls) that were found were officially situated only one meter apart. Yet Sims stated: 'I was going back and forth, from the wrapper to the hulls.' Walking back and forth over a distance of one meter?
4. Captain Fritz then appeared on the scene. The head of the homicide squad was the first to enter the sniper's nest behind the wall of books. He picked up the shells to make it easier for reporter Tom Alyea to film them. That's correct, a television reporter was trailing along be-

hind the head of the homicide squad during the initial investigation of the crime scene. Large sections of Alyea's coverage disappeared without trace – read: were censored. But in the fragment that was preserved, Fritz is standing with his big feet on top of the evidence in the sniper's nest. He claimed, however, that the paper bag was only found 'a little later', and not while he was there.[127]

5. Lieutenant Day arrived on the scene, and obviously confirmed the presence of the bag.
6. Just like every poor liar, Day also mentioned that someone else could confirm his statement. Supervisor Truly was also supposed to have seen the bag lying in its original position.[128] But Truly denied this.[129]
7. The guarding of the sniper's nest was then left to agents Johnson and Montgomery. Marvin Johnson believed that his partner Montgomery picked up the bag: 'My partner picked it up and we unfolded it.'[130]
8. Montgomery denied that: 'I didn't pick it up. I believe Mr. Studebaker did it.'[131]
9. Studebaker was the klutz who had just been transferred from the Car Theft department to the Crime Scene Search Section. He was immediately entrusted with the task of taking the photos of the most important crime scene of the 20th century. His experience as a photographer[132] was not much better than his forensic expertise. Studebaker did indeed pick up the bag: 'I picked it up and dusted it and *they* took it down there and sent it to Washington ...'[133]
10. Studebaker thereby removed the bag and only then began to photograph the crime scene. The bag is not on the pictures of the sniper's nest. This did not, however, prevent the Commission from saying in its final report that the photos were taken 'before anything had been moved.'[134] We are no longer surprised by one lie more or less.[135]
11. 'They took it down there', said Studebaker regarding the subsequent procedure with the paper bag. But who are 'they'? Lieutenant Day was heard by the Commission exactly five months after the assassination. You might expect that, by then, he had already had enough time to determine who, under his responsibility, had finally added the bag to the evidence. But Day hid behind Hicks and Studebaker, by claiming that he had fully delegated the formalities to them in this matter.[136]

12. Unfortunately, Hicks once again knew nothing at all. 'Did you ever see a paper sack in the items that were taken from the Texas School Book Depository building?' the Commission asked him. Hicks acted surprised. 'Paper bag?' Commission Counsel Ball pressed on by asking once again whether Hicks had seen a 'bag made out of brown paper'. The answer was: 'No, sir; I don't believe I did.'[137]
13. Studebaker had also not added the bag to the evidence. He stated, in fact: "... they took it down there..." The opinion of Lieutenant Day is therefore again a waste of time.
14. In the end, we become a little wiser thanks to an external document. Photo Reporter William Allen took a picture of Detective Montgomery carrying a paper bag out of the book depository at 3.00 p.m. The bag in the photo corresponds to the bag subsequently numbered CE142[138] in the evidence. The stains and the pleats are recognizable.[139]

We now know at least something: bag C existed two hours after the assassination. It was therefore 'made' before that time, but when exactly? Another big problem arises here. The laboratory investigation indicates that the paper from which the bag is made is completely 'identical' in all respects to the paper that was found on the roll in the packing department of the TSBD on Friday afternoon.[140] But the FBI did not want the word 'identical' to remain in the report under any circumstances.[141] Hoover himself gave the instruction to falsify the finding of his own FBI expert. What was going on now?

It is quite a complex matter, but I will try to keep things simple. The expert investigated the bag using various methods, including microscopic examination of the paper. He found that the paper and the adhesive tape from two different rolls are not 'identical'. Another roll means different paper. The police took a sample of the paper from the roll on the packing counter on Friday. That paper is identical to the paper from which the bag was made. Presuming normal use, however, the roll of paper and the adhesive tape on the packing counter would have been replaced in the course of Friday morning. If Oswald had made the bag on Thursday, the paper from this bag should not be identical to the paper that was found on the roll on Friday afternoon. After careful investigation, however, the FBI expert insisted that the paper was identical. The unavoidable conclusion from this is that the bag was made on Friday.

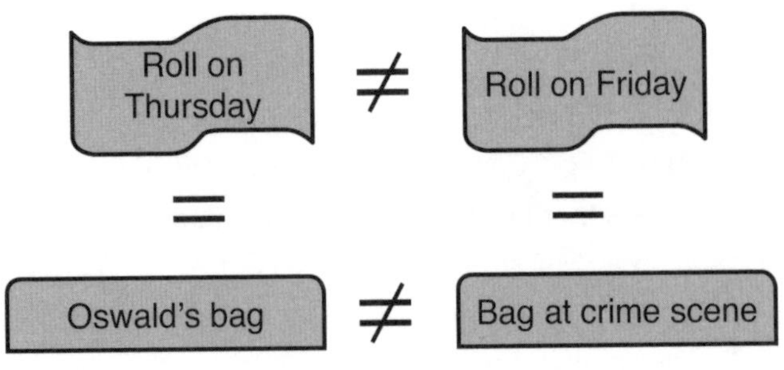

Figure 21. The bag included in the evidence would therefore have been made on Friday.

As soon as the FBI realized this, the agency applied the emergency brake. Despite the statement by expert Cadigan[142] that the paper and the adhesive tape were 'identical', the FBI changed this to 'similar'. But we can believe Cadigan, because he carried out his investigation very thoroughly. The bag was therefore made with material identical to the paper and the adhesive tape that were found on the roll at the packing counter on that Friday afternoon. We also know for sure that the bag in the evidence was made at this counter. The adhesive tape shows unique traces of the mechanism by which the gum is humidified. This is important, because it indicates that no paper and dry adhesive tape were taken in order to make the bag elsewhere. And that, in turn, is important, because Troy West, the worker responsible for the packaging department, never left his workplace. He ate, and even made his coffee there. West never saw Oswald in the packing department, and certainly did not see him making an elongated paper bag.[143] So when the bag was made is another mystery in the official story, and then we haven't even mentioned the problems with the bag itself as evidence yet.

A first problem with the bag itself as evidence is that it does not show the slightest sign that it once held the weapon.[144] Fibers were, however, found that could have come from the blanket in which the weapon was wrapped in Ruth Paine's garage. But the Dallas Police cleverly put all the evidence together first for a photograph.[145] We can see the blanket lying on top of the opening of the paper bag. This means that these fibers don't bring us any further either. There are no other traces. The Carcano was 'well oiled' and was disassembled into twelve pieces. There were also five screws, four bullets and the clip, so altogether 22 objects. But not even a tiny drop of oil was found on the bag. The structure of the bag also did not show any indication that it had ever contained 22 objects of different sizes and different structures.

A second problem is that there are no fingerprints on the bag, although Oswald must have touched it several times in the course of the morning. Lieutenant Day found no fingerprints.[146] His assistant Studebaker also found hardly anything: 'There wasn't but just smudges on it – is all it was. There was one little ole piece of a print and I'm sure I put a piece of tape on it to preserve it ... just a partial print.'[147] FBI specialist Latona found nothing either. Only when he treated the bag with silver nitrate in order to make any latent prints visible to the naked eye did a hitherto unseen handprint and a fingerprint[148] appear. But as a result of the aggressive chemical process, the bag, as evidence, was severely damaged. A replica was then made as a solution, which from now on served as evidence. From the two imprints, Latona determined nine points of agreement with those of Oswald. He waved away the objection that the court should have at least twelve points of agreement – and is even at least 16 points of agreements in Europe. He claimed that his conclusion was correct because of his experience and professional conviction, and that it was not only the number of agreements that counted. Latona was convinced that the prints on the paper bag were Oswald's. Two very vague, incomplete prints on a bag that had been so intensively handled by Oswald, and only nine points of agreement were, in his opinion, sufficient as evidence. It is not much, but this could possibly indicate that bag C could also be bag O.

The essential question is whether Oswald had the paper bag with him on Friday morning in order to smuggle the weapon into the book depository. Once again, we cannot rule that out, but in order to believe that the bag that was found is identical to the bag which Oswald had with him that morning, we must simultaneously acknowledge the following:

- The police officers who found the sniper's nest, but who did not see the bag on the floor, made a mistake;
- The fact that the paper bag is not in the photo of the crime scene does not mean anything, because replacing the evidence by a dotted line is an acceptable forensic method;

- The vague, incomplete fingerprint and palmprint are indeed from Oswald;
- Buell Frazier was mistaken about the length of the bag;
- His sister Linnie was mistaken about the length of the bag;
- The roll of paper on the packing desk of the TSBD was not changed on Friday morning;
- The roll of adhesive tape was also not replaced on Friday morning;
- The ever-present assistant at the packing desk was mistaken when he claimed that he never saw Oswald in the vicinity;
- It is possible to make a bag and to carry a heavy object in it without leaving hardly any fingerprints behind;
- It is possible to put the disassembled weapon in the bag without leaving any trace on the inside or on the structure of the bag;
- All the ambiguities in the chain of evidence for the bag are only the result of random errors and innocent mistakes by the police. The incredibly high number of contradictions does not indicate an underlying problem with the evidence, but only a problem with the intelligence of the Dallas Police.

The Carcano that was found is Oswald's property. It's not illogical to assume that he had the weapon with him that morning. You could accept this if the package had been long enough, or if there had been lots of fingerprints, or if there had been even a trace, however small, of the weapon, or if the evidence chain had been reliable, or if the findings of the FBI had proven trustworthy... But there is very little of all this. The very least that we can determine is that it is not proven that Oswald brought in the gun that morning.

5. Did Oswald touch the weapon?

The shells, the unused bullet and the clip inexplicably show not a single fingerprint from Oswald. But he must have touched the smooth copper objects if he was the gunman. No visible fingerprints were also found on the weapon itself. Only a palmprint was found under the wooden stock. Lieutenant Day – him again – is said to have found the imprint on Friday evening. Nobody was there to witness this, and he also informed nobody about it. He then transferred the imprint from the weapon to a file card using adhesive tape. But the file card only came into the hands of the FBI on November 29,[149] almost a full week after the facts. The police kept the press constantly informed of the evidence against Oswald, even fabricated evidence. For example, the Dallas Police repeatedly declared, through, among others, District Attorney Wade, that a map of Dallas was found in Oswald's rented room on which the parade route was marked in pencil. The Warren Commission had to admit afterwards in its final report that this was a pure invention of the police.[150] It is strange, however, that if you are making statements about fictional evidence, you would omit to make a statement about the ultimate proof that actually was found. A fingerprint on the weapon would provide very important evidence. Police Chief Curry stated the following about the available evidence in an interview with the WFAA television station on Saturday afternoon: 'I don't know whether it will be enough to convict him or not, but if we can put his prints on the rifle, it'll certainly connect him with the rifle...'[151] Curry was very well informed at that time: he knew exactly what was happening with the paraffin test, how much communist literature Oswald had in his room, that Officer Baker had met Oswald shortly after the assassination, that Buell Frazier had been arrested in connection with the assassination because he had once been identified at a meeting of a left-wing group, and so on. But, more than 24 hours afterwards, Curry did not know anything about a full-fledged palmprint of Oswald being found on the weapon by his direct subordinate Day. The only logical explanation for this is that the palmprint wasn't there at the time. There is, however, the explicit mention of the useless 'smudged fingerprints that have been found on the rifle', but not a word was said about the palmprint under the butt. Up to November 24, there is no reference at all to the palmprint on the weapon. Another interesting detail is that this print only emerged after Oswald's death. While the undertaker was preparing Oswald's body, he suddenly was made to leave the room with the corpse because post mortem fingerprints of Oswald had to be urgently taken, although this had already been done three times while he was still alive. It is also strange that Day – although being a self-proclaimed specialist in photographing latent fingerprints – did not take any photos when the spectacular palmprint was discovered. He still had three hours before he had to hand over the weapon to the FBI, however. Nevertheless, Day claimed that he refrained from taking a photo due to lack of time. He also lied when he said he had pointed out the presence of the palmprint to the FBI agent who collected the weapon from him. It is inconceivable that the FBI agent would not remember such conclusive evidence. The FBI in Washington found no trace of the palmprint and also no trace of the treatment to which the weapon had been subjected in order to find the palmprint. Lieutenant Day had, on the other hand, taken a photo of the so-called partial fingerprints near the trigger. But FBI specialist Latona also found nothing of these prints.[152] The prints that should be visible in the photo were labeled as useless by the FBI: 'Too fragmentary and indistinct to be of any value for identification purposes'. An attempt to create new, better photos was also unsuccessful: 'Failed to produce prints of sufficient legibility for comparison purposes.'[153] The FBI also found fibers on the weapon that could have come from the shirt that Oswald was wearing at his arrest, but they could just as well not have originated from this shirt,[154] as it turned out afterwards that Oswald had changed shirts in the meantime.

So there is nothing to suggest that Oswald actually touched the weapon. Moreover, the palmprint is irrelevant because we know that the weapon that was found was actually Oswald's Carcano. An old palmprint on his rifle does not prove that he actually touched the weapon on that *Friday*. No evidence was also found on the shells, the clip, or the remaining bullet that was still in the magazine that Oswald had held them in his hands. Oswald also did not have the time to perfectly clean off all the marks before, according to the official story, he rushed down the stairs to the lunchroom. He had to be on the first floor within ninety seconds after the first shot, because he met a police officer there.

6. Did Oswald assemble the weapon?

It's not easy to assemble a Carcano without a screwdriver. FBI agent Cunningham claimed that he could do this in six minutes,[155] but mentioned that this time had never really been measured. The retired British detective Ian Griggs took the acid test.[156] In June 1994, he thoroughly investigated a Carcano identical to the Oswald model, and dismantled the weapon twelve times in order to assemble it again. He was intrigued by the question as to why Oswald would have disassembled the Carcano to bring it into the book depository. The metal barrel protruded just 5.4 inches or 13.7 centimeters beyond the wooden butt. In other words, dismantling the weapon made it less than 14 centimeters shorter.[157] That only provided a small advantage in comparison with the gigantic disadvantages of the disassembly. The Warren

Commission claimed with evidence item 1304[158] (photo on the top) that the weapon was brought into the book depository in only two parts. That is hogwash. In reality, twelve wooden and metal parts and five screws of different sizes had to be put together (photo on the bottom).[159]

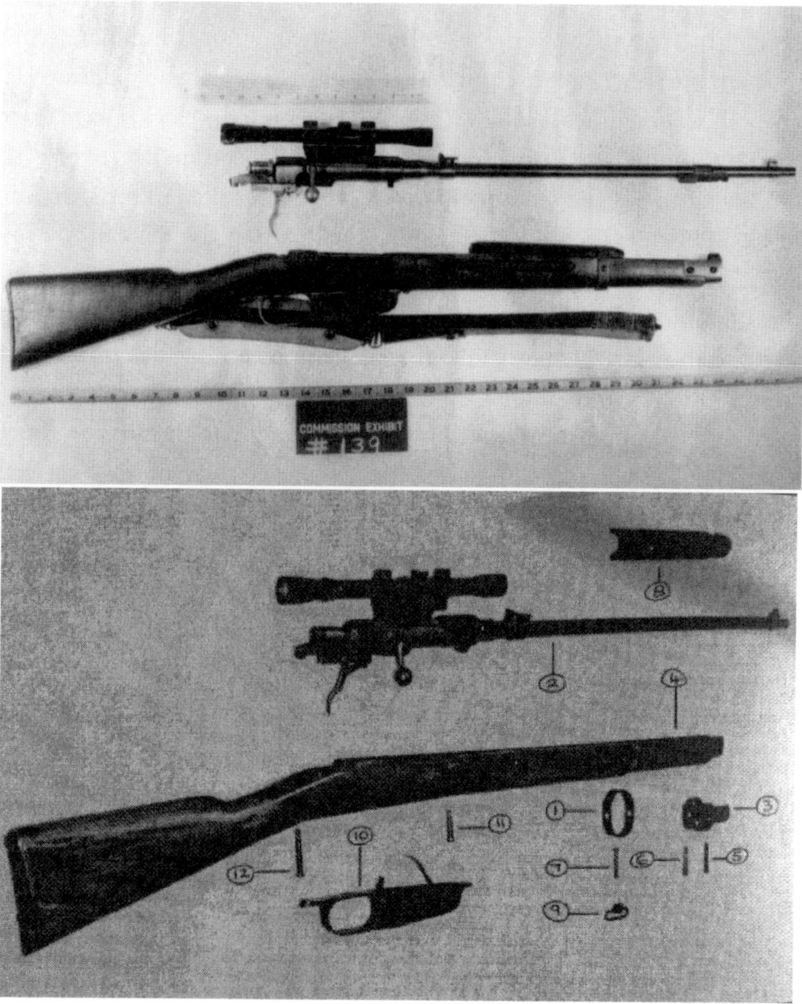

Figure 22. According to the Warren Commission, the dismantled weapon consisted of two parts, but, in reality, it consisted of twelve parts.

The paper bag in the official version therefore contained twelve weapon parts and five screws. Add to that four bullets and a brass cartridge-holder, and you end up with seventeen items. Although Griggs practiced many times, he never managed to assemble the weapon within a reasonable time. He sat in a comfortable chair in a well-lit room, with the parts nicely arranged before him in the order of assembly.[160] But putting all the parts of the Carcano together – like Oswald would have – using only a coin, a *dime*, as a tool, remained impossible. Griggs wrote: 'How long did it take me to reassemble the Mannlicher Carcano? Well my best time was two minutes and four seconds with a screwdriver. I have to confess that I admitted defeat using a dime. Having begun several times and fallen hopelessly behind the clock, I have to look upon SA Cunningham's time of six minutes with a certain degree of suspicion. Trying to put the gun together with a dime resulted in me sustaining two blood blisters on my fingers and a small cut on the joint of my right thumb.' Griggs emphasized that his attempt, unlike Oswald's, was carried out without any stress factors. The whole story also raises new questions about the absence of fingerprints. If we take into account a period of more than six minutes, then it also seems totally impossible that Oswald would have found the opportunity to imperceptibly assemble the weapon during his shift. Below, we also demonstrate that Oswald could not have been in the sniper's nest before 12.20 p.m. Kennedy drove past at 12.30 p.m., although the motorcade was expected to be at Dealey Plaza at 12.25 p.m. Oswald therefore also had very little time to assemble the weapon without a screwdriver during the lunch break. But sometimes the less striking details raise the most doubt. Why, for example, did Oswald, who must have practiced assembling the weapon at home, not simply put a screwdriver in the paper bag? Cunningham and Griggs agree that the job is quite feasible with a screwdriver. Without a screwdriver, it's certainly more difficult, takes a lot more time, or it is downright impossible. If Oswald had smuggled in the disassembled Carcano, he would certainly have done himself the small favor of taking a screwdriver with him. Simple arguments are sometimes the most convincing. No screwdriver was found in the TSBD, and that raises serious doubts as to whether Oswald assembled the weapon in the book depository on Friday afternoon.

Another example of a simple but intriguing argument is why Oswald did not have the obvious idea of removing the strap when he dismantled the weapon. A heavy, awkward, leather strap was attached to the weapon. Neither Marina nor Ruth Paine, in whose garage the weapon was stored, recognized the wide leather strap. The strap also interferes when shooting. Weapon expert Frazier explained this to the Commission: 'I find it very difficult to use the rifle with a sling at all. The sling is too short, actually, to do more than put your arm through it.'[161] What could have motivated Oswald to leave a useless and annoying strap attached to his weapon while preparing the attack?

Figure 23. The clumsy, heavy strap. Did Oswald take the weapon with him that day?[162]

7. Did Oswald shoot the Carcano on November 22?

After Oswald's arrest, the Dallas police used paraffin to determine whether there were traces of gunpowder on the cheek of the suspect, but did not find any.[163]

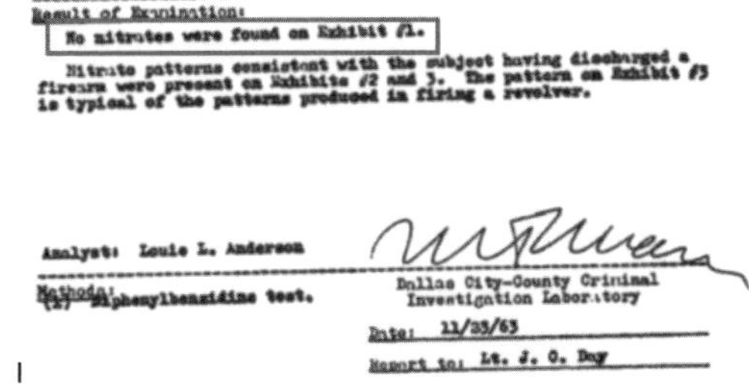

Result of Examination:

No nitrates were found on Exhibit #1.

Nitrate patterns consistent with the subject having discharged a firearm were present on Exhibits #2 and 3. The pattern on Exhibit #3 is typical of the patterns produced in firing a revolver.

Analyst: Louie L. Anderson

Methods:
(1) Diphenylbenzidine test.

Dallas City-County Criminal
Investigation Laboratory

Date: 11/23/63

Report to: Lt. J. C. Day

Figure 24. Exhibit 1 is the paraffin test that was performed on Oswald's cheek. No nitrates were found on the wax.

Harold Weisberg and his lawyer Jim Lesar obtained this document during one of their many FOIA actions. It was originally not part of the Warren Report nor of the annexes. It's clear why. The result was favorable for Oswald. It was, of course, known that a paraffin test had been carried out. A journalist even explicitly put the question to Police Chief Curry, who replied that the test was 'positive'. 'What does that mean?' asked the journalist. 'It only means that he fired a gun', answered the Chief of Police. The journalist also wanted to know whether the gunpowder traces were found on Oswald's cheek or shoulder. Curry said that he did not know. The journalist persisted: 'That he fired a gun, Chief, not the rifle?' Curry answered: 'That's right. We just say a gun.'[164] With this, he stated clearly and publicly that the result of the test on the cheek was negative. The police could therefore no longer sweep the problem under the carpet or keep silent about it. The FBI intervened, and FBI agent Gallagher came before the Commission to testify that the paraffin test was actually worthless. He formulated this as follows: 'The diphenylamine or the diphenylbenzidine tests are not specific. They react with many ingredients and, for this reason, the results obtained from such tests are difficult to interpret.'[165] A nitrate trace can also be obtained from urine, toothpaste or paint. A positive test therefore provides little evidence of any value. But if no nitrate is present, then that's another matter. The paraffin test penetrates deep into the pores. It's not enough to wash your face if you want to remove a nitrate trace. In other words, if no nitrate could be found on Oswald's cheek, this would seem to prove that he did *not* shoot a rifle that day. In order to remedy that 'shortcoming', FBI weapons expert Cunningham was brought in, the man who, according to his own statement, could assemble the Carcano so easily. He stated before the Commission that the locking mechanism of the Carcano, the *bolt action*, prevented any nitrate traces from depositing themselves on the cheek of the shooter.[166] A nitrate test on his colleague Killion, who had fired the weapon three times, also turned out to be negative.[167] We have to take Cunningham at his word here again, because there are no documents available to support his thesis. The Commission did not ask Killion anything about it. Or they did, but again in a suspiciously late and meaningless statement. On July 31, 1964, Killion was presented with a paper to confirm that he was entirely in agreement with the testimony of Cunningham.[168] We should perhaps read Killion's 'sworn affidavit' as follows: 'No, my immediate superior, who can determine my future career with one stroke of a pen, did not lie under oath in his testimony before the Commission.' Why did the Commission find it so important for Killion to explicitly declare that FBI agent Cunningham had not lied under oath in the most important criminal case in American history? The reason is obvious. Despite Killion's confirmation, the Commission remained concerned that the paraffin test had not been sufficiently neutralized. The negative nitrate test on the cheek remained potentially dangerous. This is evident from the fact that, after Gallagher, Cunningham and Killion, even FBI boss Edgar Hoover, as a model of an unimpeachable witness, quickly explained the following in a letter: 'The assassination rifle was then rapid-fired three times by the same man on which the control tests were made. Paraffin casts of the examiner's right cheek and both hands were then prepared. These paraffin casts were also treated with diphenylbenzidine and there were no reactions.'[169] Even this statement still did not provide complete reassurance. To be absolutely sure, FBI agent Gallagher made one more appearance as the final witness. He came – literally in the final seconds of the investigation – once again to explicitly state that the NAA test on the paraffin samples was totally unreliable.[170] Commission interrogator Redlich even put the words into his mouth: 'As I understand it, Mr. Gallagher, one of the reasons why this test is considered unreliable for purposes of determining whether or not someone has fired a weapon is...' No lawyer was present to represent Oswald, who could have objected on the grounds of leading the witness. The important distinction between the traces on the cheek and on the hands were carefully circumvented in the questions to and the answers from Gallagher. And the fact that an unreliable positive test says nothing about the reliability of a negative result was not mentioned at all.

According to the FBI, the locking system of the worn-out and poorly maintained Carcano still closed *perfectly* hermetically. Bugliosi accepted that assumption uncritically, but there are other opinions. G. Paul Chambers, a specialized physicist, wrote as follows: 'Even if the rifle's firing chamber were perfectly sealed, as Bugliosi argues, the hot gases would escape as soon as the firing bolt mechanism was operated to eject the spent cartridge and chamber the next round.'[171] In addition, the FBI may not have told the whole truth. In reality, in addition to Killion, seven other test persons had been subjected to the paraffin test on the cheek after they had fired a Carcano. Nitrate was apparently found on each of these test persons.[172] These tests were kept out of the investigation, and only came to light after a tedious FOIA procedure carried out by the persistent Weisberg and his tireless lawyer Jim Lesar.

In the hope of still being able to raise doubts about the negative nitrate test, the FBI thought up another plan in the course of the investigation: to carry out a more thorough examination to find traces using spectro-analysis. The finding of this research was again formulated in very ambiguous words: 'The deposits found on the paraffin casts from the hand and cheek of Oswald could not be specifically associated with the rifle cartridges.'[173] The FBI threw the residues of the hands and cheek into one heap, and then claimed that it was impossible to determine whether the traces that were only found on the hands, came from the shots at Officer Tippit with the revolver or from the rifle shots at President Kennedy. The formulation carefully avoids acknowledging that there was still not a single piece of evidence of a rifle shot after the spectro-analysis. So the FBI had to look for an even better story. The wax was therefore sent to the Oak Ridge Laboratory in Tennessee for an even more thorough check, the state of the forensic art *Neutron Activation Analysis* (NAA). Spectro-analysis shows which elements are present, but neutron activation analysis also indicates the *quantity* of the elements, and that in *parts per million (ppm)* or in thousandths of a gram.[174] The technique was quite revolutionary in 1963. The question about whether it would be useful to make use of the NAA technology as a flagship in the Kennedy case was raised as early as November 27. FBI agent Jevons felt that this investigation was not necessary 'in view of the massive evidence already available indicating Oswald's guilt'.[175] But he also warned that 'relatively highly placed individuals in the *Atomic Energy Commission* (AEC)' could see the potential publicity for their product. These men could – quite unjustly, of course – accuse the FBI of negligence if they were to forgo the use of their extremely meticulous test, so the FBI had better make use of it in one way or another, merely to avoid criticism. The paraffin specimens were the most suitable for this test, according to Jevons. 'They represent the best possibility of applying the neutron activation technique for the detection of powder residues'. The information about and dissemination of the results would, of course, remain completely secret. But even in the internal secret FBI report about the NAA, the result of the test was formulated in such an ambiguous way that it is not better than the description of the results from the spectrograph test. 'No characteristic elements were found by neutron activation which could be used to distinguish the rifle from the revolver cartridges.'[176] The FBI had jumped from the frying pan into the fire, and once again had to come up with a reason for the negative result of the NAA test. The bureau therefore had Gallagher explain before the Commission that the neutron activation test could really only provide negative results, because the paraffin casts had been 'cleansed' by the previous tests. The barium and the antimony, the specific elements for which the NAA test was looking, had actually been flushed away in the first investigation – which moreover also exonerated Oswald.

That the reason for this could also be that Oswald had actually not fired a rifle did not occur to the FBI. Another strange thing emerged from Gallagher's testimony. The traces that were found in the paraffin casts of Oswald's cheeks mainly came from the wrong cheek. There was more barium and antimony on the cheek that was not turned towards the rifle. The laboratory therefore suspected that the few traces that were found originated from the revolver fired at Tippit. Oswald must have transferred these to his face by touching his cheeks with his hands. Otherwise there could never have been more gunpowder on the cheek that was turned away from the weapon. For all these reasons, the conclusion of the test was undecided. The Warren Commission therefore firmly kept the lid on the NAA investigation. Evidence that exonerated Oswald did not count.

In 1978, the HSCA hoped that some progress had surely been made with the NAA technology that had still been experimental in 1964. It appointed Doctor Vincent P. Guinn as an expert, a real authority in the field of neutron activation analysis. Among other things, he was the manager and technical director of the *Activation Analysis Program*, a research assistant in chemistry at the University of California, and the author of books and numerous articles on the subject. The parliamentary investigation commission posed Guinn a series of questions.[177] But these questions were only about the composition of the bullets and bullet fragments, not about the paraffin casts. But Guinn would certainly have been able to provide interesting information on this. We know this because he later wrote an article in a magazine about nuclear science that specifically dealt with the casts of Oswald's cheek. In the article, the scientist stressed the importance of the tests on the cheeks. 'The important casts in rifle studies are those of the cheeks. Large amounts of Ba and Sb on the cheeks would indicate that a rifle had been fired, as these elements would not be expected to be deposited on the cheeks when a revolver or pistol was fired.'[178] In the investigation that he described in his article, Guinn had four persons shoot with a Carcano in a manner that was as close as possible to the shots in the Kennedy case. He then let a few hours pass by – just like Oswald – between the assassination and his arrest. He then first carried out the diphenylamine test, the rough nitrate test as in Dallas, on two of the persons, and only then the hypersensitive NAA test. He noted that the first rough test did make the NAA method unusable for the chemical element barium, but that the NAA test worked perfectly well for antimony, despite the initial nitrate test. Consequently, the NAA test found clear traces of antimony on the cheeks of the four test persons who had shot with the Carcano.[179] The argument of the hermetically sealed Carcano could consequently also be consigned to the realm of fables, at least for the tests at the atomic level. If the nitrate test in 1963 did not make the paraffin samples unusable for the NAA test for antimony, the fact that no antimony was found on Oswald's cheek indicates that it is highly probable that Oswald did not shoot with the Carcano on November 22.

Could Oswald have shot with the Carcano?

The circumstances of the assassination make it less likely that Oswald did not shoot with the Carcano. He worked in the building from which President Kennedy was shot, and a weapon was found in the sniper's nest that was the same type as the one he owned. We determined that if Oswald did not shoot, one of the three following assumptions must be true:

1. The Carcano that was found was not Oswald's;
2. The shots were not fired with the Carcano that was found;
3. The shots were fired with the Carcano that was found, but not by Oswald.

The first possibility is excluded because the weapon did turn out to be Oswald's Carcano. We have not been able to completely exclude the second assumption. At the time that it was still possible, there was no investigation into whether it was possible to exclude shots being fired with the Carcano on November 22. In any case, it is technically possible that the Carcano was used for the assassination: the weapon could have been fired twice without any problem within the available 5.5 seconds, and it is also sufficiently precise to hit the target, provided that it is correctly adjusted. The question of whether the Carcano was fired therefore still remains open. It also remains theoretically possible that the Carcano bullets were fired with a technically better weapon through the use of a *sabot* or shoe.

The third possibility was the question as to whether Oswald was actually the gunman. We assumed that, if he really was the gunman, eight important consequences would have to follow:

0. The assassination was technically possible with the Carcano;
1. The assassination had to be possible for Oswald as the gunman;
2. Oswald had bought bullets;
3. He had practiced intensively with the weapon;
4. He had smuggled the weapon into the TSBD;
5. He had touched the weapon;
6. He had assembled the weapon;
7. He fired with the Carcano.

On closer investigation, considerable doubts arose for each of items 1 to 7. The believers underestimate above all the accumulating effect of this uncertainty. The questions cannot be simply ticked off one by one. A poor shot can, of course, sometimes hit the target, even twice in a row. Hitting the target with an incorrectly adjusted rifle is also not impossible. Hitting the target without practicing is also possible. But the combination of two master shots being made with an incorrectly adjusted rifle by a moderate marksman who had not previously practiced... that's something else again.

To this we must add the other uncertainties. It is not proven that the paper bag Oswald carried with him contained the weapon. There is no evidence that Oswald handled the weapon on November 22. The older palmprint that was added to the evidence later is of no value whatsoever in that respect. The Carcano belonged to Oswald, so an old palmprint doesn't mean anything. Or perhaps it does: it proves that the metal in at least this place was smooth enough to leave a fingerprint. Did Oswald assemble the weapon without touching it? Oswald also had no screwdriver with him. This makes it very unlikely that he entered the TSBD that morning with a plan to assemble the Carcano. The fact that no gunpowder residue was found on Oswald's left cheek provides a strong indication that he did not shoot with the Carcano that day.

The believers consider it to be unrealistic that the Carcano could be falsified evidence, merely left to incriminate Oswald. Now that we have analyzed the concrete facts, we can determine on the mind map whether it is really as improbable as the believers claim. In addition, we can rearrange the information that we have gathered in an attempt to achieve a better hypothesis with the same elements.

There is a direct correlation between the above-mentioned precondition that the Carcano must be technically suitable for the assassination (Question 0) and whether the weapon in the book depository had been reassembled (Question 6). If Oswald had reassembled the weapon, it could not be properly adjusted and was consequently unsuitable for the assassination.[180] The answers to Question 0 and Question 6 are in any case the opposite of each other: if the answer to one of the questions is yes, the answer to the other question is no. The crucial question becomes then whether the weapon entered the building disassembled. We can rearrange the findings of the investigation with respect to this question:

— Oswald is supposed to have assembled the weapon under stress and time pressure. Do the expected fingerprints provide proof of this?
— Answer: No.
— The level of difficulty of the assembly process implies that Oswald must have practiced in advance. Is there any evidence of this?
— Answer: No.
— If Oswald had practiced enough to be able to put the weapon together again, he must have been aware of the crucial importance of a screwdriver. Did Oswald have a screwdriver with him in order to be able to assemble the weapon in the book depository?
— Answer: No.
— Oswald knew that the weapon would only be useful again after the assembly if the sight was correctly adjusted on the basis of six to ten shots. Was he able to do that?
— Answer: No.
— The benefit of the disassembly of the weapon was to make it shorter in order to smuggle it undetected into the book depository. With the Carcano, only a very short part of the barrel protrudes beyond the wooden butt. The result is that the dismantled weapon is only 14 centimeters shorter than the full length of the weapon. Does the advantage of a reduction of 14 centimeters in length make up for the disadvantages of disassembly?
— Answer: No.
— Buell Frazier and his sister saw the paper bag on Friday morning. Buell was certain that the package was only 61 centimeters long, while his sister thought it was up to 68 centimeters. The dismantled weapon is 88 centim-

eters long. Could Oswald have brought in a weapon with a dismantled length of 88 centimeters in a paper bag with a length of 61 to 68 centimeters without being seen?

— Answer: No.
— Oswald went to bed at 9.00 p.m. on Thursday evening, and got up at 6.30 a.m. on Friday. Did anyone see Oswald disassemble the weapon in Irving on Thursday evening or Friday morning?
— Answer: No.
— Not only when looking at it separately, but especially when considered as a whole, all these points very strongly suggest that the weapon was *not* brought into the book depository in a dismantled state.

We can now align the other information further based on that assumption:

— The Carcano was certainly in the book depository.
— The presumption that the weapon was dismantled is a result of the assumption that it was brought into the book depository in a paper bag on Friday morning. If the weapon was not brought in in this paper bag, there is no reason to bring it in disassembled.
— If the weapon was brought in in one piece, there is no reason whatsoever to assume that it was not perfectly adjusted.
— If the Carcano was perfectly adjusted, there is no technical problem in carrying out the attack with that weapon.

Assuming that the weapon was not dismantled, we now have a plausible answer to four of the above-mentioned eight questions, not based on speculation, but on sound evidence and logical deduction:

0) The assassination is technically possible with the Carcano;
5) Traces that show that Oswald had intensive contact with the weapon are not necessary because
6) He did not reassemble the weapon in the book depository. From this, it immediately follows that
4) Oswald did not necessarily bring the weapon into the book depository that morning.

Four questions now remain:

1) Was Oswald able to carry out the master shots?
2) Did he buy bullets?
3) Did he practice sufficiently with the weapon?
7) Did Oswald fire with the Carcano on Friday afternoon?

Here also, it is clear that a negative answer to the last question makes the answer to the three other questions superfluous. The absence of gunpowder residue on Oswald's cheek is a strong indication that he did not shoot with the Carcano, but is not 100 percent conclusive. The answer to the three other questions (1, 2 and 3) also point in the direction of Oswald's innocence. He was, at best, a mediocre marksman. He apparently didn't buy bullets anywhere, and he never practiced intensively with the weapon. But, on the basis of this, it can never be conclusively proven that Oswald was not the gunman. It is not entirely impossible that, as a former Marine and without any practice, he fired accurately twice with the only four bullets in his possession.

But the four remaining questions need no answer if Oswald was not in the sniper's nest at the time of the assassination. So let's have a closer look at this point.

Chapter 3 – The perpetrator in the sniper's nest

Once you eliminiat the impossible, whatever remains,
no matter how improbable, must be the truth.

Sir Arthur Conan Doyle's Sherlock Holmes, several works

The presence of the perpetrator at the crime scene is, of course, crucial. If Oswald was not in the sniper's nest at the time of the assassination, he was not the sniper.

Oswald must have touched some of the boxes in the sniper's nest at some point or other, because two palmprints and one fingerprint of Oswald were found on four of the boxes.[181] One of the palmprints was reasonably fresh, the others could only be detected through the use of silver nitrate. Oswald touched at least two of the four examined boxes. This is an important fact. Consciously or unconsciously, the believers confuse the question of whether Oswald was in the sniper's nest at some point in time with the question of whether he was there at the time of the attack. If you don't make a distinction between the two, the fingerprints on the boxes can be seen as proof of Oswald's guilt. But these fingerprints could have been caused because Oswald worked in the building or was an accomplice to the attack, without him being Kennedy's assassin himself. In this chapter, we will therefore focus our attention exclusively on the question of whether Oswald was present in the sniper's nest at the time of the assassination. Because, in the end, these fingerprints and palmprints don't say anything about this.

Once more, the believers consider Oswald's presence in the sniper's nest at the time of the attack as being obvious. They point to the indirect evidence: the weapon, the suspicious paper bag that Oswald brought in, his behavior after the attack, and so on. Oswald's guilt is a given, and, consequently, he had to be present at the crime scene at the time of the assassination. This extrapolation is the only thing the believers have to cling on to, because there is no concrete evidence of Oswald's presence in the sniper's nest at the moment of the assassination. The Chief of Police in Dallas was unusually formal regarding this in 1969: 'We don't have any proof that Oswald fired the rifle, and never did. Nobody's yet been able to put him in that building with a gun in his hand.'[182]

But the absence of evidence doesn't actually prove that he wasn't there either. Can we credibly defend the position that Oswald was not in the sniper's nest?

WITNESS FOR THE DEFENSE: BONNIE RAY WILLIAMS

Bonnie Ray Williams was a 20-year-old, tough black laborer. He wanted to watch the presidential motorcade from a window at the front of the school book depository with some friends. Bonnie was sure that they had agreed to meet on the sixth floor. Because of the parade, the lunch break started a little earlier on that day, at 11.50 a.m. The workers first went downstairs to wash their hands and to pick up their lunch boxes. This must have been around 12 'clock. Bonnie Williams subsequently took the elevator up to the sixth floor again, and picked a spot near a window. There was a wall made of book boxes immediately next to this window, and the sniper's nest was behind this makeshift wall. Bonnie didn't see anybody on that floor, and assumed his friends would arrive soon. He took out his lunch and started eating while waiting for his friends. But he gradually began to wonder whether their appointment really was on the sixth floor. He left the remains of his lunch behind and walked back to the staircase in the northwest corner. He then found his friends one floor lower. Meanwhile, it was now after 12.20 p.m.

Sargeant Hill testified about the abandoned lunch: 'On top of the larger stack of boxes that would have been used for concealment, there was a chicken leg bone and a paper sack which appeared to have been about the size normally used for a lunch sack.'[183] According to Officer Mooney, who found the sniper's nest, the chicken leftovers were 'on top of one of the boxes, about five feet away from the window in the southeast corner.'[184] Williams therefore placed the remainder of his food on one of the walls of the sniper's nest, a stack of boxes with a height of no more than five feet. The remains of the lunch were so close to the sniper's nest that it was, in fact, initially assumed that the assassin had calmly eaten a chicken leg in anticipation of the arrival of Kennedy.

The FBI was aware that Williams's timing was very problematic for the official version of the facts. That's why they moved his departure from the sixth floor to 12.05 p.m., more than fifteen minutes earlier. The claim that Bonnie

Williams could have already left the sixth floor at 12.05 p.m. is simply poppycock. He must have really been in a hurry if he arrived on the sixth floor just after 12 o'clock, walked thirty meters, found a spot near the window, unwrapped his lunch, ate and drank, and then went back to the staircase to descend to the fifth floor. But Williams didn't need to hurry, because the president was only scheduled to drive by at around 12.25 p.m., and, moreover, he was waiting for his friends. It must have been at least ten minutes before he started wondering where his friends could be.

Even the Commission did not believe the FBI timing, and admitted that Williams was on the sixth floor for almost twenty minutes: 'Williams went down to the fifth floor, where he joined Norman and Jarman at approximately 12:20 p.m.'[185] If the commission sticks to twenty minutes, we can be reasonably sure that it was certainly not less than that. Further investigation actually confirms this. In any case, Williams arrived at the fifth floor after his friends. Let's therefore have a look at their timings. Junior Jarman started his lunch break at 11.55 a.m. He went to the first floor (two minutes), washed his hands (two minutes), picked up his lunch from the Domino room (one and a half minutes), walked 30 meters back to the staircase and up to the second floor (one and a half minutes), took a soda from the vending machine (one minute) and then returned to the first floor (one minute), where he finished his sandwich in the hall and drank his soft drink (five minutes). He then went to the sidewalk of the book depository with Norman to wait for Kennedy. By then – roughly estimated – it must have been 12.10 p.m. According to his statement before the Warren Commission, he stood there until 'about 12.20 p.m., between 12.20 and 12.25 p.m.'[186] He then walked the whole way around the book depository with his friend Norman, entering the building through the back door (one and a half minutes) before taking the elevator to the fifth floor. There, they had to cover 30 meters to come to the front windows in the corner opposite to where the sniper's nest was situated one floor above (one and a half minutes). According to his own statement, Bonnie's friend therefore only arrived at the fifth floor between 12.23 and 12.28 p.m. at the earliest. Jarman also stated that Bonnie Ray Williams arrived there 'a few minutes later'[187]. Williams therefore joined his friends at 12.25 p.m. at the earliest.

It is interesting to see how the Commission once again omitted to ask Jarman the obvious question: how many minutes after the arrival of Bonnie

Williams did Kennedy drive by? We would then only have to estimate one step in the timing, which would, of course, be much more accurate. The unsolicited reply to this was given by Norman, Jarman's buddy, in 1993. In the PBS documentary *Who was Lee Harvey Oswald?* for the Frontline program, Norman stated: '[Bonnie Williams] came down to find us just before the motorcade passed by.'[188] Kennedy drove by the book depository five minutes behind schedule at 12.30 p.m. People who are waiting for something have a tendency to overestimate the elapsed time. 'Just before' therefore confirms that Bonnie Williams arrived on the fifth floor at 12.25 at the earliest. That wouldn't even give Oswald enough time to assemble the weapon with a coin. The smarter ones among the believers therefore ignore the implausible FBI timing of 12.05, and stick to the timing of the Warren Commission: 12.20 p.m. But this estimate is still debatable, even though it is fifteen minutes later than the FBI version. We should actually assume that Williams left the vicinity of the sniper's nest at 12.24 p.m. at the earliest.

When faced with the fact that Williams did not see Oswald, Gerald Posner, the author of *Case Closed*, a fixed reference point for believers, therefore wisely concentrates his response on something else. He writes that Oswald was actually in the sniper's nest, but that Williams didn't *see* him because of the wall of boxes.[189] But that really doesn't make any sense either. From the photographs of the location of the lunch bag, it appears that the stack of boxes on which the bag was found was less than five feet high. Williams would certainly have seen Oswald if he had been there, at the latest when he put the remains of his lunch on top of the stack of boxes. Moreover, Oswald could not possibly have remained so quiet that Williams also didn't *hear* him for fifteen minutes. The wall of boxes did not form an obstacle for sound. Posner omits the fact that Williams explicitly confirmed to Commissioner Dulles that he was completely on his own on the floor.[190]

Williams stated he saw nobody on the sixth floor, and no one explicitly asked him whether he might have heard anything, but Williams confirmed this himself:

> Mr. DULLES: You were all alone as far as you knew at that time on the sixth floor?
> Mr. WILLIAMS: Yes, sir.

Mr. DULLES: During that period from 12 o'clock about to – 10 or 15 minutes after?

Mr. WILLIAMS: Yes, sir. I felt like I was all alone. That is one of the reasons I left – because it was so quiet.

Bonnie Ray Williams therefore not only didn't see Oswald, he also didn't hear him.

Incidentally, according to the official story, Oswald was also supposed to have completely noiselessly assembled the weapon in this time frame. The time required by an FBI weapon expert to assemble the rifle without a screwdriver – which was actually never proven – is six minutes. The President was expected at Dealey Plaza at 12.25 p.m. At 12.15 therefore, Oswald could not have waited any longer to start assembling his weapon, and, at that time, even according to the Warren Commission, Bonnie Williams was still looking out of the window just a few meters away.

WITNESS FOR THE PROSECUTION: CHARLES GIVENS

The Commission assumed that Oswald was already on the sixth floor shortly after 12 o'clock, and that he stayed there. They based this on the statement of Charles Givens, a 38-year-old black worker. He claimed to have seen Oswald shortly after 12 o'clock in the sniper's nest, at least according to his last version of the facts. In his first – and therefore most reliable – testimony, he said that the last time he saw Oswald was at 11.50 a.m., but that this was on the first (ground) floor:[191]

about 7 A.M. On the morning of November 22, 1963, GIVENS observed LEE reading a newspaper in the domino room where the employees eat lunch about 11:50 A.M.

This statement of November 22 was recorded by two FBI agents, Griffen and Odum.

Givens also stated the following about his whereabouts immediately after the facts:[192]

I went downstairs and into the bathroom. At twelve o'clock I took my lunch period. I went to the parking lot at Record and Elm street. I have a friend who works at the parking lot. We walked up to Main and Record when the President passed by. We then walked back to the parking lot after the President had passed by. We had just got back to the lot when we heard the shooting. I think I heard three shots. I did not see anyone in the building that was not supposed to be there this morning.

Charles Douglas Givens

Givens was therefore on the ground floor at 11.50 a.m., where he saw Oswald; he ate his lunch at 12 o'clock, and subsequently went to the parking lot to wait for Kennedy to drive past.

How could Givens ever have been a key witness for Oswald's presence in the sniper's nest? The answer to this question is: by completely changing his first statement during his hearing on April 8, 1964. Counsel Belin asked the witness 'Did you ever tell anyone that you saw Lee Oswald reading a newspaper in the domino room around 11:50, 10 minutes to 12 on that morning on November 22? ' Givens replied without batting an eyelid: 'No, sir.'[193] He had indeed gone downstairs, had washed his hands, but had then returned to the sixth floor because he had forgotten his cigarettes. There, he claims he not only saw Oswald at around 11.55 a.m. but that he also spoke to him, 'Boy are you going downstairs?' It's near lunch time.'[194]

This modified statement is completely implausible. Posner props up Givens's shaky credibility with the testimony of Police Officer Revill.[195] He confirmed to the Warren Commission that Givens had already stated on the day of the assassination itself that he had seen *mister* Lee on the sixth floor.[196] But the cigarette story doesn't confirm this at all. There is no doubt that Givens saw Oswald on the sixth floor. The question is whether this was shortly before twelve o'clock. He didn't mention anything about this in his statement to Revill. There was also no mention of cigarettes yet. Immediately after his verbal statement to Revill, Givens stated in writing that he had gone to the parking lot at around 12 o'clock. Posner's argument (the confirmation by Police Officer Revill) therefore in no way refutes the fact that Givens drastically changed his previous statement. In any case, we know that it is quite unlikely that Oswald was still on the sixth floor shortly before 12.00. William Shelley was Oswald's direct superior, so he knew him well. Shelley saw Oswald on the ground floor near the phone ten or fifteen minutes before twelve.[197] Eddie Piper also stated on two occasions that he had seen Oswald on the ground floor at 12 noon.[198] We also know that Givens is a liar. In a report, the FBI itself confirmed that they considered Givens capable of changing his testimony for money.[199]

Another noteworthy detail is that the believers often point out that Oswald must have been guilty because he did not return to his workplace after the attack, and that it was this that put the police on the trail of his guilt. They always add that he was the only one who didn't return to work, but

Oswald was not the only one missing from the roll call. Givens was also missing.[200] But there was no recrimination of Givens in this context. The same tunnel vision applies for the defenders of the Warren Commission in their selective outrage about witnesses who deviate from their original statement. When it comes to Givens, however, they suddenly no longer have a problem with this.

It is indisputable that Givens lied about Oswald's presence on the sixth floor. Yet the believers hopelessly cling to this straw. In order to put Oswald on the sixth floor by whatever means necessary, Bugliosi brings up the name Givens three times in nineteen lines: 'Givens saw Oswald ostensibly dallying on the sixth floor. [...] That Oswald did go up to the upper floors [...] is supported, as we have seen, by four witnesses – Givens, Williams, Lovelady, and Arce. [...] Givens, who saw Oswald minutes later on the sixth floor with a clipboard.'[201] This demonstrates how indispensable the man is for this essential element of the evidence. We know for sure that Givens lied, because we have the incontestable and reliable testimony of Bonnie Williams. Bonnie was eating his lunch on the sixth floor, and didn't see Givens there. Givens also did not see Williams. This means that even if Givens had seen Oswald, this would have been before the arrival of Bonnie Williams, and Oswald would then have had to leave the floor again before Williams got there. In brief, the evidence in the file still demonstrates that Oswald was *not* on the sixth floor between 12 and about 12.20 p.m.

WITNESS FOR THE PROSECUTION: HOWARD BRENNAN

The Commission found another witness who was willing to link Oswald to the sniper's nest. Howard Brennan was a construction worker, a pipe fitter, and it is therefore easy to recognize him on the photographs of Dealey Plaza and in the Zapruder film by his silver gray helmet. He was also an avid bible reader. The relevance of this fact in the case is unclear, but the Commission asked him a question about it anyway. At the moment of the attack, Brennan was sitting on a low wall on the other side of Elm Street, opposite the book depository. He had a perfect view of the sniper's nest – a windfall for the Warren Commission. Brennan clearly and unmistakably saw Oswald. According to the believers, he also recognized Oswald during the line-up in the police station.

Brennan is therefore the Commission's key witness. But there are at least thirteen serious objections:

1. On page 62 of its final report, the Commission published a photograph of Brennan on the wall across from the school book depository. Commissioner Gerald Ford asked him: 'Is this the true location of where you were sitting November 22nd?' Brennan replied: 'Yes, sir.'[202] But he was mistaken. Brennan was sitting at least one meter more to the right. This distance is important. From where he was actually sitting, he did not have such a good view of the sniper's nest.[203] At best, the witness made a mistake about the place where he was sitting on one of the most memorable moments of his life.

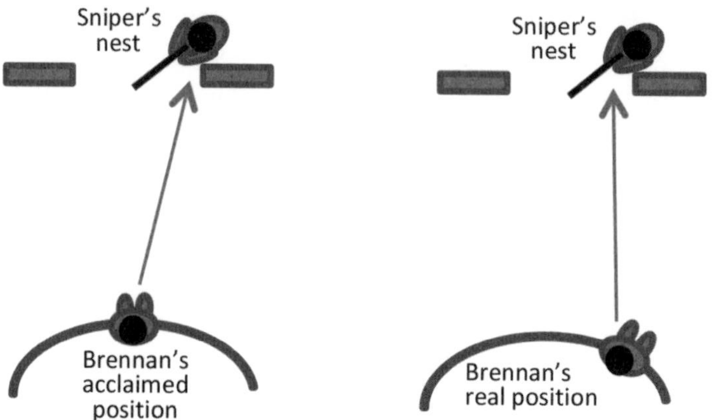

2. Brennan only heard two shots, probably the second and third shots. Although he was sitting in an ideal position to hear the shots from the book depository, he apparently missed the first shot. This is understandable, but it also says something about his quality as a witness.
3. Brennan saw the gunman standing upright: 'Well as it appeared to me he was standing up and resting against the left window sill.' He was even able to estimate that the man in the window was about 178 cm (5 feet 10 inches) tall. But Oswald could never have stood upright. The part of the window that was open in the sniper's nest was only half a meter in size. The glass was barely transparent enough to be able to look at the sunlit Plaza from the inside. Looking into the dark deposi-

tory from the outside, Brennan could certainly not have seen anything through the glass.

Figure 25.
Photo from the private collection of Cecil Kirk. Brennan could not possibly have seen the clothes and facial features of an upright man. The glass was simply not transparent enough.

4. Brennan saw a much larger portion of the weapon sticking out of the window than was possible: 'I could see all of the barrel of the gun.'[204] He estimated the portion of the weapon that was sticking out of the window as 70 to 85 percent. That is impossible if he saw Oswald, because, if Oswald was the shooter, he used the Carcano, and the section of the barrel of the Carcano that is not part of the wooden butt is 14 centimeters. Officially, the barrel of the weapon, which measures 41.12 inches in total, slightly over one meter, rested on a book box that was placed on the inside of the window. Then add the width of the window and the window sill on the outside to this. The weapon could therefore never have been outside of the window as far as Brennan claimed.
5. 'If you could put on Exhibit 482 the direction that you saw the rifle pointing, sir?' the Commission asked. Brennan placed the arrow on the photograph as follows:[205]

Figure 26.
Brennan's arrow indicates the wrong place and the wrong direction of the shot.

This angle is completely wrong: in actual fact, the third shot, the shot that Brennan claimed to have seen,[206] only needed an angle of less than 20 degrees downwards. Gerald Ford asked once again: 'That is the angle that you believe the rifle was pointed?' Brennan confirmed again.

6. Brennan also put the arrow way too high, which indicates that he believed that the shots came from the upper half of the window, and not from the bottom quarter, where the window was open. Was this really what he meant: Did the arrow also indicate the spot where he had seen the rifle, or only the direction in which the weapon was pointing? This time, Commissioner Allen Dulles asked, puzzled: 'And that is from the area in the window from which the rifle was pointing?' It was indeed what Brennan meant, because he replied: 'That's right, yes.' But his arrow is completely in the wrong place. That part of the window was closed during the attack – it is not even possible to open it – and the shots could therefore not have come from there.

   The photo also more or less reflects the view that Brennan could have had. Notice how dark it is in the sniper's nest, and how opaque the glass is.

7. In his first written statement under oath, immediately after the facts, Brennan described the clothing of the man he had seen as follows: 'He had on light colored clothing but definitely [sic] not a suit.'[207] During his first verbal hearing on November 22, he stated the following about the color of the clothing: 'No, other than light, and a khaki color – maybe in khaki. I mean other than light color – not a real white shirt, in other words. If it was a white shirt, it was on the dingy side.'[208] The other witnesses who noticed the man in the window of the sniper's nest also mentioned light-colored clothing. Don Thomas, in his excellent essay *Rewriting History: Bugliosi Parses the Testimony*,[209] brought the five other testimonies together: (1) Carolyn Arnold: 'The man was wearing a white shirt and had blond or light brown hair';[210] (2) Arnold Rowland: 'He had on a light shirt, a very light-colored shirt, white or a light blue or a color such as that';[211] (3) Ronald Fisher: 'A sport shirt or a T-shirt. It was light in color; probably white';[212] (4) Robert Edwards: 'A light colored shirt',[213] and, finally (5) James Crawford: 'It was a profile, somewhat from the waist up, but it was a very quick movement and rather indis-

tinct and it was very light colored'.[214] The sixth witness in this list is Brennan. During his hearing before the Commission, Brennan also described the color of the clothing of the man he had seen: 'Light colored clothes, more of a khaki color.'[215]

Figure 27. Oswald's shirt– Commission evidence CE150 [216]

But when the Commission showed Brennan the shirt Oswald was wearing on that day, he could only stammer: 'I would have expected it to be a little lighter – a shade or so lighter.'[217] The witness clearly wanted to be helpful to the Commission. A shade lighter than this shirt is not light-colored or khaki. The question of the Commission was whether Brennan could positively identify this shirt as the shirt of the man in the window. Brennan did not answer this question, but the reply seems clear: this was not the garment that Brennan thought he had seen on November 22. Officer Baker had pressed his revolver against Oswalds shirt, so he had seen it close up. When he was shown the photograph of the shirt, he replied: 'Yes, sir; I believe that is the shirt that he had on when he came.'[218] The taxi driver who took Oswald to his rented room also said that he was wearing a brown shirt,[219] with a T-shirt underneath and a gray jacket over it. Linnie Mae Randle, Buell Frazier's sister, also recalled Oswald's brown-yellow shirt.[220] Based on the six testimonies, a problem therefore emerged. The man in the sniper's nest was wearing light-colored clothing, but Oswald was not. In the few seconds that he had to reach the second floor, it's virtually impossible that he also managed to button up his open shirt. But, apart from this, the problem that arises with regard to Brennan is that the witness was immediately willing to describe dark brown as 'a shade lighter'.

8. Brennan also remembered the pants the gunman was wearing: 'I remembered them at that time as being similar to the same color of the shirt or a little lighter.'[221] But the gunman had to lie down or crouch in order to be able to shoot through the open window, so Brennan could never have seen the color of his pants. When Oswald was arrested, he was wearing black pants,[222] but he had already changed his pants in his rented room by then.[223] Taxi driver Whaley, who took Oswald there, recalled the color of Oswald's pants, before he had changed, as 'blue faded' and 'like a blue uniform'. In any case, not the same color as his brown shirt, whether or not that was a shade or so lighter.
9. The description Brennan gave of the man is, of course, also essential. In his very first statement, he said: 'He was a white man in his early 30s, slender, good looking, slender and would weigh about 165 to 175 pounds.' In his testimony before the Commission, he estimated the man 'between 160 and 170 pounds'. According to his autopsy report, Oswald weighed 150 pounds[224] (68 kilograms), a difference from the initial estimate of 7 to 11 kilograms. Oswald was also not in his early thirties, he was 24. Brennan explicitly confirmed that the man he had seen in the window looked older than Oswald: 'I had saw (*sic*) the man in the window and I had saw him on television. He looked much younger on television than he did from my picture of him in the window – not much younger, but a few years younger – say 5 years younger.'[225] Also note here that, according to the Commission, Brennan's description prompted Officer Tippit to stop Oswald. The Commission clearly had no problem with the fact that a police officer stopped a 150-pound, 24-year-old dressed in a dark brown shirt and black pants on the basis of the description 'slightly over thirty, white, 165 to 175 pounds and light clothing'.
10. Brennan was later asked to identify Oswald in a line-up, but only after the police had let him go home first. By then, Brennan had seen photographs of Oswald on television at his home.[226] That was, of course, not

Brennan's fault, but it makes the line-up obviously worthless, and reduces his quality as a witness.

11. Mark Lane threw himself on the case in his capacity of lawyer for Oswald's mother. According to him, Oswald was placed between five teenagers in the line-up. Oswald protested vehemently and shouted: 'This is not a fair line-up.'[227] Brennan still did not pick Oswald out of the line, however. He explained later that he had certainly recognized Oswald, but that he feared for his life and that of his family. He had assumed that his testimony was not so important, because there were enough other witnesses against Oswald, and his identification would therefore not have been decisive.
12. On May 7, 1964, Brennan again had to correct his statement, because it obviously made no sense that he could be murdered as a witness while there were still plenty of other witnesses around. So, basically, Brennan had meant exactly the opposite: he believed that he was the only witness, and that, consequently, his life and that of his family could be at risk if he picked Oswald out of the line-up.[228] Not a very steadfast witness, it would appear.
13. Before the Commission, Brennan stated that he was looking at the sniper's nest when the third shot was fired. When he then looked in the direction of the president again, something obstructed his view: 'I looked towards where President Kennedy's car should be, and there was something obstructing my view. I could not see the President or his car at that time.'[229] On September 27, 1964, CBS news broadcast an interview with Brennan, in which Brennan spoke about how he saw with his own eyes that 'the President's head just exploded'.[230] This witness certainly enjoyed dramatizing and exaggerating his statements.

Yet this Brennan was the Commission's key witness linking Oswald to the sniper's nest. This was the man who Gerald Ford called 'the most important witness to appear before the Warren Commission.'[231] It is clear that Brennan saw *someone* in the sniper's nest, because the shots came from there. The question is, however, whether this person was Lee Harvey Oswald. From this perspective, Brennan's testimony is very weak, and even completely impossible in many points. The evidence supplied by this key witness was, in fact, so weak that the HSCA did not even use Brennan's testimony in the new investigations.[232]

In any case, we know that Oswald was already back on the second floor at 12.31 p.m. Strictly speaking, Oswald could therefore have taken his position between 12.20 and 12.25 p.m. and could have quickly assembled his rifle without a screwdriver. Making grateful use of Kennedy's five-minute delay on the schedule, Oswald could have assembled the rifle with a coin. Kennedy drove by within seconds of him finishing this job. Oswald fired three times, cleaned the rifle, hid it, buttoned up his shirt and then ran head over heels downstairs for the meeting with Police Officer Baker. All this is just about possible with a lot of imagination. But there is another witness.

WITNESS FOR THE DEFENSE: DOROTHY GARNER

Police motorcyclist Marrion Baker was driving somewhere halfway down the motorcade. He had only just turned onto the square when the first shot fell. Thanks to his experience as a hunter, Baker was one of the few who recognized the sound he heard at Dealey Plaza as a gunshot. He hurried to the book depository, ran inside and asked how he could get to the roof, the place he suspected the shots had come from, because he had seen a flock of pigeons fly up. The building superintendent, Roy Truly, pointed the way out to him. They tried to take the elevator on the first floor, but, when this failed, they ran up the stairs together. Through a glass window in the door of a small vestibule, the officer saw someone move on the second floor. This vestibule led to a lunchroom. The officer drew his gun and stormed into the lunchroom. There, he faced a surprised, but icily calm Oswald. This seemed to rule out that this man had just carried out a fatal attack on the most powerful man in the world, seconds before and several floors higher. The officer and the superintendent then continued their trip to the roof.

Two young ladies, Victoria 'Vicki' Adams and her friend Sandra Styles,[233] watched the parade from the window of their office on the fourth floor.[234] After the attack, the girls ran immediately to this same staircase at the back of the building. They descended to the first floor and left the book depository through the back door. There was therefore quite a lot of movement on the staircase in the seconds after the attack, In the official story, Oswald has to get from the sixth to the second floor. The girls are on their way from the fourth floor to the first floor, and the motorcycle officer and superintendent are running from the first floor up to the second floor. Yet the girls neither saw nor heard Oswald on the staircase, and they did not bump into officer Baker and superintendent Truly. According to the Commission, this was impossible, and therefore Vicki Adams had made a mistake! She had come minutes later, the Commission[235] decided, and that ended the discussion – debate closed. Decades later, Kennedy researcher Barry Ernest tracked Vicki Adams down. She maintained that she had descended the staircase immediately after the attack, and not minutes later. She told him how her story met with strong opposition from the FBI. Her testimony was ignored and publicly labeled as false. That was embarrassing, but she was young and managed to give her life a new direction after this terrible event, in the hope of being able to leave the bad experience behind her.

In Chapter 40 of *Cold Case Kennedy*, we reconstructed the timeline of the five people on the staircase. Vicki and Sandra could indeed start going down the staircase *immediately without* meeting Oswald on his rush downstairs, and also *without* meeting Baker and Truly, who were running up the stairs.[236] According to the timeline, the girls had already left through the back door of the building 41 seconds after the third shot. At that moment, Baker and Truly were situated on the first floor, and not even near the stairs. Oswald could indeed descend the stairs after the girls, starting two floors higher. He would just be able to reach the lunchroom ahead of the officer and the superintendent. On his website, Barry Ernest correctly drew attention to an additional witness who was not mentioned in my timeline: 'Flip has written a very interesting book and I would recommend reading it. A couple of things regarding his timeline, however, require further consideration. Flip's timeline has Vicki and Sandra descending the stairs in advance of Lee Oswald. This would conflict with what office superintendent Dorothy Garner told me in an exclusive interview in 2011. Mrs. Garner, who followed Vicki and Sandra to the fourth-floor landing and remained there long enough to see Officer Marrion Baker and Roy Truly come up and emerge onto that floor (which would have been after the lunchroom encounter between Baker, Truly, and Oswald), said she did not see Oswald come down the stairs after Vicki and Sandra had left. That might explain why the document containing her statement corroborating the timing of Vicki's action was suppressed for 35 years, and why Mrs. Garner was never officially questioned as part of the Warren Commission's investigation.'[237]

With the help of one of the readers of his excellent book *The Girl on the Stairs*, Barry Ernest managed to track down Dorothy Garner in 2011. This now 83-year-old lady was on the fourth floor near the stairs just after the attack. The Warren Commission completely ignored her, just like Vicki, perhaps even more so. Her name is not mentioned in the report, and she was not even questioned officially. That certainly says a lot already. Here is a solid witness for the crucial minute immediately after the attack, and she was in the book depository in a place where Oswald had to pass through if he was the perpetrator. It is unthinkable that the Commission would not have heard her. The only logical conclusion is that her statement was undesirable, and consequently disappeared without a trace. As not even a statement by Mrs. Garner can be found,[238] the believers have no difficulties in completely ignoring her. Bugliosi's 1,600 pages don't mention Mrs. Garner even once. Her name does not appear in the 590-page index of Posner's book *Case Closed* either. But Mrs. Garner was, of course, questioned. When Barry Ernest visited her 48 years later, Dorothy Ann Garner had not yet realized herself just how decisive her statement could be.

Mrs. Garner is a punctual witness of top quality. Barry Ernest introduced her as follows during the introduction of the interview: 'Mrs. Garner was an office superintendent for the Scott, Foresman Co., publishers of textbooks, with headquarters in Chicago. The company's Dallas regional office was located on that floor. She had been employed there for more than 10 years. Her employees would describe her as a very dedicated, professional woman. According to one she was "detail-oriented" and "never missed a thing". "She demanded the best, watched the clock like a hawk and tolerated no nonsense or talking while she ruled her kingdom", Victoria Adams would say. "If you can picture an old fashioned prim librarian telling everyone to 'shush,' you have an idea of the power and demeanor of Dorothy Garner."'[239]

In 2011, this Mrs. Garner repeated the statement that she believed everyone had already known for all those years. She had seen Vicki Adams go down the stairs, and then saw Officer Baker and superintendent Truly run upstairs, although she was a little less certain of the latter after so many years. Of course she had seen police officers on the staircase soon after the assassination – the place was soon buzzing with activity – but she was no longer completely sure about superintendent Truly. Can you still consider the testimony of an 83-year-old after 48 years? Indeed you can, because there is an indisputable confirmation of her story that even comes straight from the time of the investigation. Thirty-five years after the assassination, Barry Ernest was able to put his hands on a letter from Assistant U.S. Attorney Martha Stroud, dated June 2, 1964. This letter, often called the 'Stroud-document', is actually on the subject of rectifications and corrections which 'the girl on the stairs', the very conscientious Vicki Adams, wanted to have made to the report of her statement. The Assistant U.S. Attorney informed the Commission of the small corrections Vicki wanted to apply, and used the opportunity to also casually report something about the statement of a certain Dorothy Garner in the last paragraph of her letter: 'Mr. Bellin [sic] was questioning Miss Adams about whether or not she saw anyone as she was running down the stairs. Miss Garner, Miss Adams' superintendent, stated this morning that she (Miss Garner) saw Mr. Truly and the policeman come up after Miss Adams went downstairs.'[240]

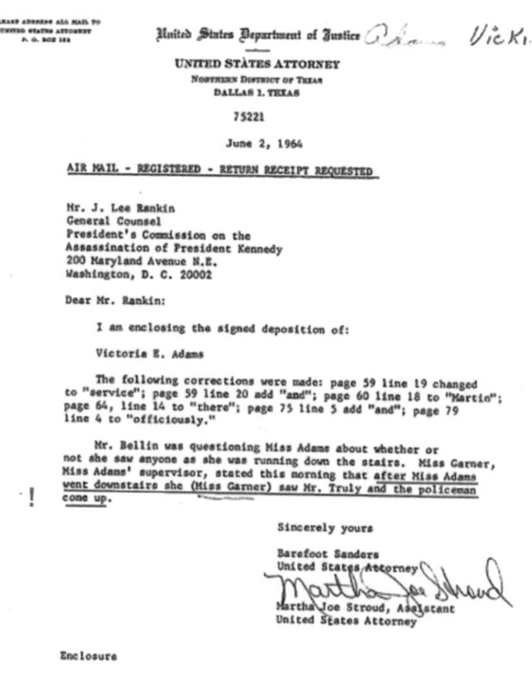

PLEASE ADDRESS ALL MAIL TO
UNITED STATES ATTORNEY
P. O. BOX 188

United States Department of Justice Adams Vicki.

UNITED STATES ATTORNEY
NORTHERN DISTRICT OF TEXAS
DALLAS 1, TEXAS

75221

June 2, 1964

AIR MAIL - REGISTERED - RETURN RECEIPT REQUESTED

Mr. J. Lee Rankin
General Counsel
President's Commission on the
Assassination of President Kennedy
200 Maryland Avenue N.E.
Washington, D. C. 20002

Dear Mr. Rankin:

I am enclosing the signed deposition of:

Victoria E. Adams

The following corrections were made: page 59 line 19 changed to "service"; page 59 line 20 add "and"; page 60 line 18 to "Martin"; page 64, line 14 to "there"; page 75 line 5 add "and"; page 79 line 4 to "officiously."

Mr. Bellin was questioning Miss Adams about whether or not she saw anyone as she was running down the stairs. Miss Garner, Miss Adams' supervisor, stated this morning that after Miss Adams went downstairs she (Miss Garner) saw Mr. Truly and the policeman come up.

Sincerely yours

Barefoot Sanders
United States Attorney

Martha Joe Stroud

Martha Joe Stroud, Assistant
United States Attorney

Enclosure

Figure 28. The letter from Assistant U.S. Attorney Stroud.

So it was actually all there in black and white in 1964, and that perhaps explains why also this letter 'went missing' within the Commission. It was deliberately lost somewhere in the many tons of unimportant Commission documents, and Ernest found it purely by coincidence. The Commission was certainly aware of the Stroud document, because the corrections requested by Vicky that it mentioned were indeed made to her unpublished statement. The reason why the letter had to disappear is also clear. The Assistant U.S. Attorney explicitly referred to Mrs. Garner's testimony, and, officially, this testimony did not exist. The letter also reflects the content of what Mrs. Garner testified, from a non-suspect perspective. It is to her credit that she was so cautious with her reply in 2011, when she was asked whether she had seen Truly and Baker on the stairs together: 'I could have, but there was so much confusion. It was, after all, a few years ago!' But the letter of Assistant U.S. Attorney Stroud leaves no doubt that Dorothy Garner saw the police officer and Mr. Truly come up the staircase. The recipient of the letter was J. Lee Rankin, the big boss of the Commission's staff. Mr. 'Bellin', who apparently had questioned Mrs. Garner, is David Belin, the deputy counsel to the Warren Commission. The fact that no trace of that interview can be found in the meanwhile well-known Commission Documents strongly suggests the bad faith of the Commission in the whole affair. The significant statement of the very correct and punctual Mrs. Garner did not fit into the hypothesis of the lone nut, and therefore disappeared into the trash bin. A letter from an attorney of the United States to the head of staff of the Commission goes missing because it happens to contain a reference to a witness testimony that disappeared. It is rather a cowardly and hypocritical act, unworthy of this Commission, which was made up of distinguished and learned gentlemen – the bearers of moral authority – who accept payment and bask in the public glory as conscientious and independent fighters for the truth – and I'm carefully considering my words here. But what surprises me perhaps most is that there are still distinguished and learned gentlemen even now who deny and explain all this away, and who still claim, without batting an eyelid, that the Warren Commission alone has a monopoly on truth, while mustering nothing but contempt for the brave private researchers who fight this official lie machine with their bare hands.

So Mrs. Garner confirmed in 2011 that Vicki Adams and Sandra Styles rushed down the stairs immediately after the assassination. The girls were not mistaken about the time of their departure; it was the Warren Commission that violated the truth.[241] But Mrs. Garner's statement also contained another important aspect. She herself was also in the vicinity of the stairway a few seconds after the attack: 'I remember hearing them [the girls], after they started down.' Mrs. Garner confirmed in 2011 that the girls made quite a bit of noise on the stairs. This implies that also Oswald, if he had rushed down the stairs, would also have been audible. Mrs. Garner was already in the vicinity of the stairway at the moment the girls were only one floor lower. This means she arrived at the stairs about 26 seconds after the last shot. In order to arrive at the third floor in time, Oswald should have been audible 11 seconds after the arrival of Mrs. Garner at the stairs, and after 20 seconds, he should also have been visible, according to the timeline.

The diagram of the movements on the stairs can be summarized as follows:

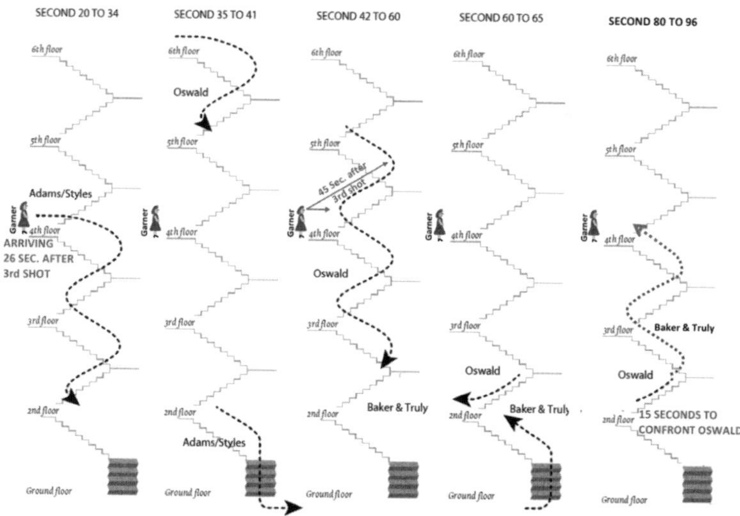

Figure 29. Movements on the stairs with the presence of Mrs. Garner

Mrs. Garner stayed long enough at the staircase to see Truly and officer Baker come up after their meeting with Oswald in the lunchroom. During this time, she neither heard nor saw Oswald pass by. In 2011, during her interview with Barry Ernest, the witness was formal: she had in any case *not* seen Oswald that day, except on television that evening. If Mrs. Garner had not seen or heard Oswald on the stairs, then the only possible explanation is that Oswald was not on the sixth floor at the moment of the attack.

David von Pein, a pure-blood believer, does not let himself be fooled by Dorothy Garner. She must be mistaken, because he is convinced that Oswald is the only culprit. He wrote: 'It's a thousand times easier to explain away Garner's 6/2/64 statement provided to Barry Ernest than it is for conspiracists to explain away all of that incredibly incriminating evidence against Lee H. Oswald that was discovered on the sixth floor.'[242] But Mrs. Garner is by all means a reliable witness. The fact that the Warren Commission and the FBI did not want to hear from her in 1963, is not her fault. There were five other persons on the fourth floor at the moment of the assassination from whom no statement was taken, or, at least, from whom no statement was found in the file.[243] It looks very much as though any possible confirmation of the presence of Dorothy Garner was carefully avoided. But the testimony of Dorothy Garner becomes indisputable by the letter written by Assistant U.S. Attorney Stroud in 1964, which was found in 2011. She is not the type of witness who, after many decades, shows up with a gripping story on the eve of the publication of a sensational bestseller, nor is she a person who yearns for five minutes of fame, but simply a stern, straightforward woman without airs and graces.

WHERE WAS OSWALD THEN?

Carolyn Arnold

If Oswald was not on the sixth floor, he must, of course, have been somewhere else. The major witness who the conspiracists quote for this is Carolyn Arnold, the then 20-year-old secretary of the vice president of the TSBD. She left her office on the second floor between 12 noon and 12.15, together with five colleagues.[244] They waited near the TSBD entrance for the moment the president would drive by. On November 26, Carolyn testified to the FBI that '... she caught a fleeting glimpse of Lee Harvey Oswald standing in the hallway between the front door and the double doors leading to the warehouse, located on the first floor. She could not be sure that this was Oswald, but said she felt it was and believed the time to be a few minutes before 12:15 p.m.'[245]

Although Arnold had not signed this testimony, it was included as part of an FBI report. This report was a 'Commission Document', yet it never made it into the nonetheless 26 volumes thick annex to the Warren Report. It was only a 'glimpse', of course, and Mrs. Arnold 'could not be sure'. To weaken her testimony as much as possible, the FBI also had her state that she barely knew Oswald. The fact that this 'dilution' was initiated by the FBI only became apparent in 1978. The Commission was, however, content with this poor FBI interview. They preferred not to be faced with a witness who had seen Oswald on the first floor, even if she could not be sure.

In the course of the investigation, Counsel Rankin asked FBI boss Hoover, on behalf of the Commission, to provide six specific details about every TSBD employee. The fourth item in this list was whether the employee had seen Lee Harvey Oswald at the exact time the shots were fired. As if Hoover enjoyed winding up the Commission, he carried out this duty quite literally, by instructing that only those six specific questions be asked in the interviews. Afterwards, he said: 'Every effort was made to comply with your request that six specific items be incorporated in each statement.'[246] The FBI therefore literally asked each of the 73 employees of the book depository[247] whether he/she had seen Oswald exactly at 12.30 p.m. Carolyn Arnold was asked this question on March 18, 1964. In this statement, the time when she had left the building is ten minutes later than in her original timeline: 'about 12:25'. But her colleagues Betty Dragoo,[248] Judy Johnson,[249] and Bonnie Richey,[250] who had accompanied her, insisted that it was 12.15, therefore the time of 12.25 had to be a mistake. Many conspiracists turn this into the holy grail by linking the 'glimpse' Carolyn Arnold had possibly seen of Oswald to the incorrect time of 12.25. If Oswald was still on the first floor at 12.25 p.m., he could, of course, hardly be the assassin. But when asked whether she had seen Oswald at the time of the shots, Carolyn Arnold's response was naturally negative. She was not asked the key question as to whether she had seen him before the attack, because this question was not literally on Rankin's list.

Fifteen years later, author Anthony Summers appeared on the scene with a strong story in his thoroughly documented book *Not in Your Lifetime.* This title refers to a remark by Earl Warren: when asked whether the Commission would disclose its documents, the Chief Justice replied: 'Yes, there will come a time. But it might not be in your lifetime.'[251] Summers contacted Carolyn Arnold in 1978 to hear her story first hand. In order to find out whether or not she had seen Oswald on the first floor at 12.15, he presented her with the FBI report on her statement in 1963. Carolyn, who thereby saw the minutes of her testimony for the first time, claimed that this did not at all reflect what she had told the FBI agent. Although it was fifteen years ago, her memory of what happened was crystal clear. Contrary to what the FBI took down, she did know Oswald quite well. He came to see her regularly to get change for the vending machine. Fifteen minutes before the assassination, she went to get a glass of water from the lunchroom on the second floor. She remembered this because she was pregnant for the first time at the time, and didn't feel too well. Oswald sat in the lunchroom, in other words, on the second floor, not on the first floor. She clearly recognized him, and did not just catch a glimpse of him. The time was 'about 12.15. It may have been slightly later.'[252] What Carolyn Arnold told Summers confirms Oswald's statement to the police that he was in the lunchroom on the second floor in the minutes before the attack.[253] The lunchroom on the second floor is also the place where Officer Baker met Oswald immediately after the attack.

The conspiracists welcomed Summers's story about Carolyn Arnold with cheers, but Bugliosi did not believe it. If Carolyn Arnold had seen Oswald shortly before the murder, she would have immediately stated this, and not have waited fifteen years to do so. Bugliosi also laughed off any insinuations that the FBI would knowingly have recorded her statement falsely. According to him, the statements of all the witnesses who had not seen Oswald had been correctly recorded, so why would the statement of Carolyn Arnold that she had seen Oswald then be taken down incorrectly? Why indeed? The conspiracists know the answer to this question. But Bugliosi had an argument that was somewhat stronger. Accounting clerk Pauline Sanders stated in March 1964[254] that she had taken her lunch break in the lunchroom in question on the second floor. She had only left her desk at 12.20 p.m. and had not seen Oswald at any time that day. There is no reason to doubt that statement: either Oswald only arrived in the lunchroom on the first floor after 12.20, when Sanders had already left again, or Carolyn Arnold made a mistake in her statement that she saw Oswald in the lunchroom on the first floor. The latter is likely to have happened. Oswald would undoubtedly have mentioned to his interrogators that he met her so shortly before the assassination. Not affected, however, is Arnold's original statement, that when she left the building around 12.15 she caught a glimpse of Oswald near the entrance on the first floor. We'll come back to this later.

Eddie Piper and William Shelley

Charles Givens, our cigarette man, undoubtedly lied when he claimed in his amended version that he had seen Oswald on the sixth floor shortly before 12 noon. Because doorman Eddie Piper had seen Oswald on the first floor at 12 noon.[255] This corresponds to Givens's first statement of November 22nd: then he had seen Oswald reading a newspaper in the domino room on the first floor at 11.50 a.m.[256] The domino room is the lunch area for workers where Oswald usually ate his lunch. The small lunchroom in the northeast corner at the back of the first floor was mainly used by black workers, a Mexican, a disabled man and crypto-communist Oswald.[257] The canteen owed his nickname to the fact that the workers often played dominoes there during their lunch break. The lunchroom for staff with a better status was on the second floor, on the other side of the building. There were vending machines for snacks and soft drinks in this lunchroom. Oswald is said to have been on the first floor at 12 o'clock. That makes sense, because he was not on the sixth floor, and obviously had to be somewhere in the building.

Witness William Shelley also saw Oswald on the first floor near the phone ten or fifteen minutes before twelve.[258]

Oswald's statement

Where was Oswald according to his own statement? To find that out, the Commission relied solely on the memory of Captain Fritz. Fritz was literally old school. He was 68 at the time of the most important challenge in his career. He dated back to the time that it was still possible to make it to chief of the homicide squad without any noteworthy forensic training.[259] He had conducted Oswald's questioning for two days without making any sound recordings or having notes taken by a stenographer, or at least making a decent official transcript of the interrogation. FBI agent James Bookhout mentioned that seven interrogators were surrounding Oswald in the small office of the homicide squad.[260] Even Police Chief Curry was aware of it: 'We were violating every principle of interrogation... It was just against all principles of good interrogation practice.'[261] Fritz therefore only had his own scribbled notes when he appeared before the Commission on April 22, 1964. During the interrogation, he had quickly jotted down that Oswald ate his lunch, and that two 'negroes' came in, one of them 'Jr,' and the other one a short man:

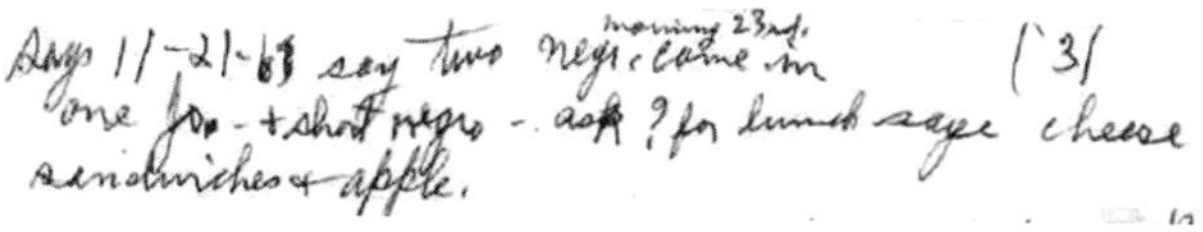

Says 11-21-63 say two negr. came in (morning 23rd.) (3/
one Jr. - + short negro - ask ? for lunch says cheese
sandwiches + apple.

Figure 30. Fritz's scribbled notes. The police couldn't afford a tape recorder.

This prompted Fritz to state the following before the Commission, five months later: 'He told me he was eating lunch with some of the employees.'[262] But that is wrong: the scribbles only mention the following: 'two negr. came in'. There is no mention that Oswald claimed that he had had lunch together with those two black boys. The fact that Oswald merely stated that he had seen the two black guys is confirmed by the FBI report of the interrogation, prepared by FBI agent Bookhout. He wrote down more correctly: 'Oswald stated that he had had lunch in the lunchroom of the Texas School Book Depository on his own on 22 November, but recalled that two black employees might have walked through the room during this period. He stated that one of these employees was possibly called "Junior", and that the other one was a short man whose name he could not remember, but whom he would certainly recognize.'[263] Other documents also refer to Oswald's correct statement.[264] He was in the 'domino room' on the first floor at 12 o'clock: the two black employees passed by there, and Oswald noticed them.

Junior Jarman and Harold Norman

'Junior' was James Jr. Jarman, and his short companion was Harold Norman. They were the friends with whom Bonnie Ray Williams had arranged to meet on the fifth floor. Jarman stated that he stopped work around 11.55 a.m. and then went to wash his hands. He indeed picked up his sandwich from the domino room – and therefore walked through the room, as Oswald had said – and then went to the other lunchroom on the second floor for a soda. Jarman then returned to the first floor, where he ate his sandwich in the hall.[265]

Commission Counsel Ball then asked him: 'After his arrest, he [Oswald] stated to a police officer that he has lunch with you. Did you have lunch with him?" The answer from Junior was, of course, negative. Instead of recognizing that old Fritz had got it wrong, Bugliosi was quick to accuse Oswald of a blatant lie: 'The real question is whether Oswald had lunch *with*[266] Jarman and Norman, as he told Captain Fritz he did [...]. The big problem with Oswald's story is that when Warren Commission Counsel asked Jarman [...]: "Did you have lunch with him?" Jarman answered: "No Sir, I didn't."'[267] But the real, big question seems to me to be whether Oswald had seen Jarman and Norman. Because that is what he had actually told Fritz. All this makes it poignantly clear what the consequences are for a suspect who is liquidated before he has a chance to defend himself, and, moreover, who is tried by a blatantly partisan court who doesn't even award him a lawyer posthumously.

The short black man Fritz mentioned in his scribbles was Harold Norman. He stated that he had lunch in the domino room. He thought there was someone else in the room, but he did not remember who. He afterwards joined James Jarman, and they went to the first floor together.[268] On Friday at lunch time, Oswald was still 'nobody.' It is therefore quite possible that Norman didn't pay any attention to who the other person in the domino room was. I am convinced that Oswald was sitting in the domino room. Givens – at least according to his first statement – saw him there, as did Eddie Piper, and William Shelley saw him there in the vicinity. But the decisive point is that none of the other TSBD employees has stated that he or she was in the domino room at 12 o'clock. One of the six standard questions on Rankin's list was what the employee had done during the lunch break.[269] Apart from Jarman and Norman, nobody else mentioned the domino room. If Norman therefore remembered someone, we can only conclude that this person was indeed Oswald, the only person who stated that he was there.

Oswald saw Junior Jarman and Harold Norman on the first floor. This can only be the case if he was actually there himself at that time. The statements made by Piper, Shelley and possibly also the 'glimpse' Carolyn Arnold caught, confirm that Oswald was still on the first floor after 12 o'clock. We don't know how long he was there afterwards. But before a point in time between 12.20 and 12.25 p.m., he could not have been on the sixth floor, because Bonnie Ray Williams did not meet him there.

There is another element that places Oswald in the domino room. A month after the assassination, someone found Oswald's jacket in the lunchroom on the first floor. Marina recognized the jacket, and the hair that was found on it corresponded to Oswald's hair.[270]

Cigarette-man Givens, the only witness who saw Oswald elsewhere around 12 o'clock, lied. We can therefore add his very first statement to the list of reliable testimonies again. On the basis of all this, we can conclude that Oswald was in the domino lunchroom after 12 o'clock. After that, we lose track of him, until Baker meets him in the lunchroom on the second floor after the assassination.

Prayer Man

It would be very strange if, with his interest in politics, Oswald would have been the only employee of the TSBD who would not have gone to watch the parade. The question as to whether he saw the parade, for example from the front steps of the book depository, has never been asked directly. The seven members of the homicide squad fired their questions about the backyard photographs, the purchase of the weapon, the taxi drive after the assassination, etc. ... But they apparently never worked systematically. At some point in time, Oswald had enough of it, and he simply replied that the detectives should sort it out. If and where Oswald had seen the parade drive by was irrelevant for the interrogators, who had already decided that he must have seen the parade through the sight of the Carcano. From the replies to Rankin's questionnaire, it appears that nobody from the TSBD employees had seen Oswald at the exact moment of the assassination. That is not a big surprise, because, naturally, all eyes were on the president. Oswald was a loner, with a mousy appearance who always kept in the background, and who spoke sparingly and only when he was spoken to. Immediately after the assassination, he was still a 'nobody', certainly in the general chaos and hectic of crowds of people running around and talking. Could he just have stood somewhere unnoticed? Carolyn Arnold believes to have caught a glimpse of him near the entrance door around 12.15. That's coming close to what Oswald stated himself. Oswald claimed that he was close to William Shelley when Kennedy drove by, and Shelley was indeed standing on the front steps of the book depositary at that time. But was Oswald standing there too? In the famous Alt-

Figure 31. Prayer Man on the front steps of the book depository.

gens photograph, about ten people are visible in the hall of the book depository. Only three of them, namely Lovelady, Shelley and Frazier, were questioned about this. The man in the photograph, who many conspiracy authors still identify as Oswald, is certainly Billy Lovelady. He looks a little like Oswald, but that's as far as it goes. But in two news films from Dave Wiegman and Jimmy Darnell (photograph on the left), a white man who was never identified can be seen standing in the corner at the back of the steps. Sean Murphy nicknamed this stranger *Prayer Man*, because he holds his hands in a kind of prayer position.

In the recording of Darnell, Officer Baker rushes past this man a little later. The man also seemed to have already been there at the moment the motorcade drove past (photo on the right). The position of this person on the front steps seems to imply that he was employed at the book depository. A casual passerby would probably not have stood so far into the doorway. All other people on the steps were identified[271] as employees of the book depository, so we may assume that Prayer Man was also a TSBD employee.

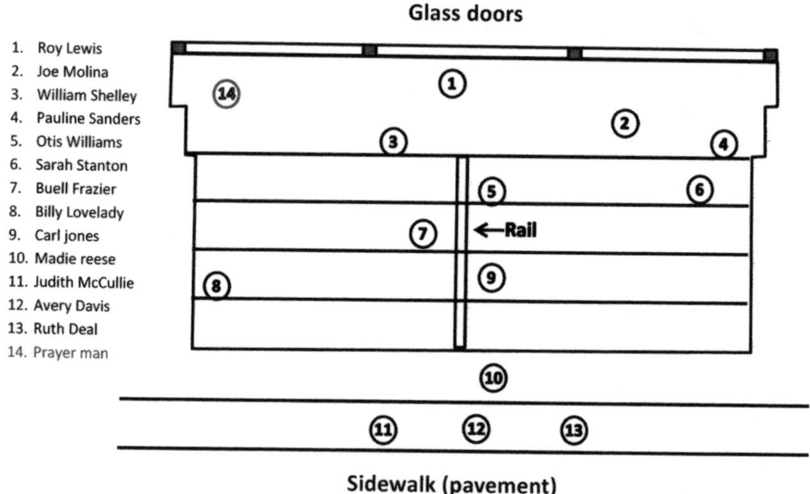

Figure 32. The position of the spectators in the doorway of the TSBD.

According to the anonymous, but excellent British website 22november1963.org.uk, there are fourteen people on the front steps. The seven women and two black men can certainly not be Oswald. Employees Joe Molina, Bill Shelley and Otis Williams can also be excluded, because they were wearing a suit and tie, unlike the Prayer Man. We can rule out Billy Lovelady because he is the man who is more in the front, as the endless debate on this has clearly demonstrated. Buell Frazier, Oswald's friend, is standing on the left of the steps. The position of all other male employees of the TSBD at the time of the assassination can be established on the basis of Rankin's list: they are not situated on the steps. Oswald is the only person whose location we do not know at the time of the attack. And one of the fourteen people on the front steps has not been identified. Could it be that this person was murdered two days later, so that he would later become the only staff member the FBI was unable to question on this? If we exclude the other possibilities, the man at the back of the steps has to be Oswald. The physical characteristics and the clothing of Prayer Man are, in any case, not inconsistent with what we know about Oswald.

Yet there is a major contradiction for Oswald's presence in the doorway. If Oswald really stood in the doorway, then there was another gunman, which means we have a conspiracy. In this plot, Oswald was to play the role of the patsy, and that meant that the real culprits had to prevent Oswald from having an alibi for the time of the assassination. Based on this hypothesis, it is unthinkable that they would have let him stand around in the doorway. It would have been sufficient for Buell Frazier to notice his presence to wreck the whole plan. We will presumably never find out whether Oswald was indeed Prayer Man.

WALKING EAST

The first witness who saw Oswald after the assassination was Officer Baker. He saw Oswald passing by through a window in a door on the second floor. Oswald was therefore moving at the moment Baker noticed him. The direction in which he moved determines where he was before, and this, in turn, could be decisive for the gap in Oswald's schedule at the time of the assassination. From which direction did Oswald come when Baker noticed him?

There are two possibilities. Firstly, there is the official hypothesis: Oswald left the sniper's nest head-over-heels in the direction of the lunchroom. The alternative is Oswald's statement that he was on the first floor. As soon as

Kennedy had driven past, Oswald went to the second floor to pick up a soda from the vending machine. He very calmly bumped into Officer Baker there. Let us look at the meeting between Baker and Oswald once again to determine which hypothesis is the most likely.

Superintendent Roy Truly was a brave man. Well aware that he was running towards a sniper who had targeted the president, he was nevertheless the first to run up the stairs, unarmed. On the second floor, he took a turn towards the staircase leading to the upper floors. Officer Baker followed him. When Baker also arrived on the second floor, he caught a glimpse of a man walking past the window of a door. That was the door of a small vestibule, leading to the lunchroom (figure 33).

Figure 33. The door of the vestibule to the lunchroom as Baker saw it.

The door opened counterclockwise in the direction of the camera. An important detail is that the door closed automatically with a pump system. It took three seconds for the door to close completely. This is important, because when Truly arrived on the second floor, this door was already completely closed. Officer Baker ran up several meters behind him. He stated the following about this: 'As I came out to the second floor there, Mr. Truly was ahead of me, and as I come out I was kind of scanning, you know, the rooms, and I caught a glimpse of this man walking away from this – I happened to see him through this window in this door.' When asked in which direction the man walked, Baker replied: 'He was walking east.' As most American cities have a linear street plan, everyone knows the cardinal points. On the photograph, walking east means passing the window from right to left. Both Bugliosi[272] and Posner[273] carefully omit the explicit mention of this direction in their quote from Baker.

The annex to the Warren Report includes a floor plan of the entire second floor.[274] On the basis of this, and with Baker's statement, we are able to make the following sketch of the official version of the story:

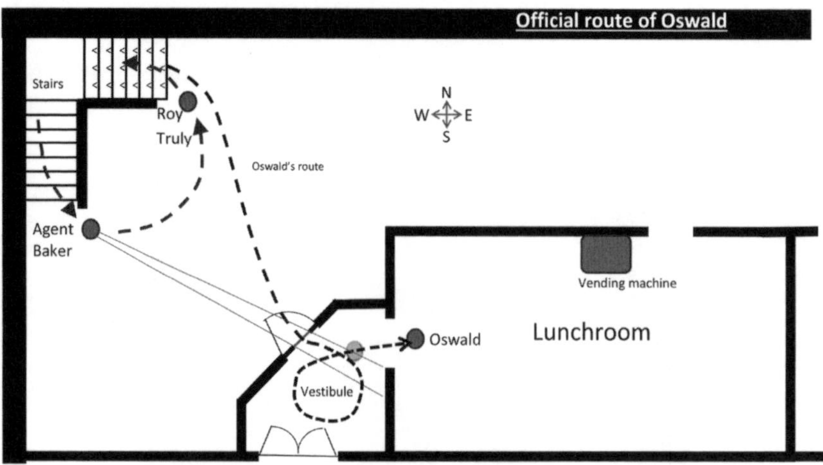

Figure 34. Plan of Oswald's movement according to the official version.

When superintendent Roy Truly passed by, the automatic door was already completely closed. Oswald had therefore already passed through this door at least three seconds earlier. Officer Baker followed Truly, who bravely showed him the way. Note the distance that Truly covered in the time Baker needed to also arrive on the second floor. Oswald had still not made it past the 1-foot (30 centimeter) window. Five seconds – three for the door to close and two for the delay Baker had on Truly – after Oswald would have opened the door to enter the vestibule, he could not have walked past the window from right to left. By then, he should already have been near the vending machine, which – incidentally – was the reason he gave for his presence in the lunchroom on the second floor. Moreover, if he had come down the stairs, he would never have walked east past that window. According to Baker, he remained on the left side of that window, and moved away in a straight line towards the lunchroom. If Oswald had walked past the window eastwards, the only possible explanation is that he very calmly walked a circle in the vestibule (taking more than five seconds). That seems difficult to reconcile with an assassin on the run.

The alternative route seems more realistic. Baker's statement that he saw Oswald walk past the window from right to left can only mean that Oswald entered the vestibule through the double swinging doors, at the bottom of the map. That is fully compatible with the other data in the file.

One of the many peculiarities of the school book depository is that there is another staircase, leading only to the second floor, next to the entrance in the front. On the map of the entire second floor, the Warren Commission outlined how Oswald left the building afterwards:[275] he walked from the vending machine to the door in the lunchroom, through the vestibule and the double swinging doors, and then to the other staircase at the front of the building. But the reverse route, through the corridor or the office, is, of course, equally possible.

If Oswald could go from the lunchroom to the hall, then the reverse was also possible:

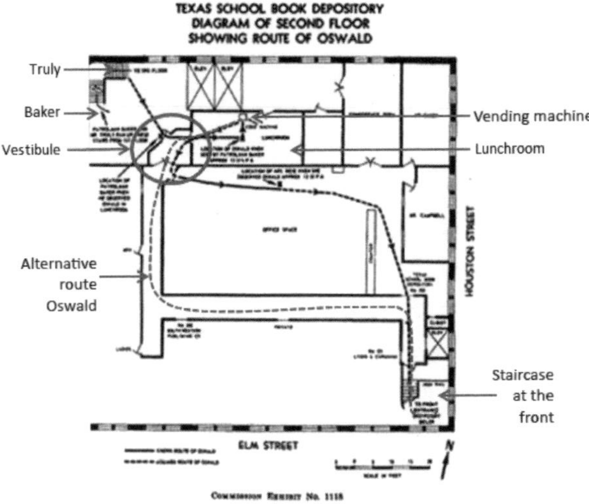

Figure 36. Floor plan of the second floor and possible route Oswald took from the first floor to the lunchroom on the second floor.

Around 12.15, after he had left the domino room, Oswald was near the telephone in the hall on the first floor. Maybe it was there that Carolyn Arnold caught a glimpse of him. Did Oswald see the president drive past the front door of the book depository from the hall, perhaps because he had been asked to stay near the phone, for example? Or was he indeed Prayer Man, and stood watching in the second or third row of spectators on the steps in front of the building? In any case, Oswald never left the building. Meanwhile, Vicki Adams and Sandra Styles were already walking down. When Baker finally went through the third entrance door in a row on the first floor, and obtained a view of the central hall, the girls had already left the building through the back door. After Baker and Truly had run past Oswald, he went to the second floor using the stairs at the front to get a soda, as he himself stated afterwards. That is not illogical, because Junior Jarman had done exactly the same thing less than half an hour before. But does it make sense that a witness to an attack on the president then calmly finds himself a vending machine immediately afterwards? We must not forget, however, that Oswald was in any case involved in the assassination. There is also no need to figure out logical explanations for his behavior. The only thing we need to find out is whether or not he was the gunman.

WHICH HYPOTHESIS IS THE MORE REALISTIC ONE?

In hypothesis A, Oswald stood at the back of the doorway, or elsewhere in a less conspicuous place near the steps at the front of the building. Baker and Truly hurriedly stormed into the building in order to search for the assassin on the top floor. Oswald calmly took the stairs to the second floor at the front of the building. Meanwhile, Baker and Truly attempted to get the elevator on the ground floor. Oswald walked towards the lunchroom on the second floor. Baker and Truly realized that they could not use the elevator to go up, and rushed to the stairs. Truly hurried past the vestibule door on the second floor. That door was closed, and nobody could be seen behind the window. Officer Baker followed him. At that moment, he saw how Oswald leisurely wandered past the window from right to left. Oswald was not out of breath, and responded calmly to the policeman, who had drawn his gun.

In hypothesis B, Oswald wiped clean his weapon in a flash and sprinted thirty meters to the other side of the sixth floor. Baker and Truly stormed into the building at that same moment. Oswald hid the rifle under several boxes. Baker and Truly reached the elevator. Oswald soundlessly – and apparently also invisibly – rushed down the stairs and past Dorothy Garner. He opened the door to the vestibule on the second floor. Baker and Truly decided not to wait for the elevator any longer, and ran to the staircase. The door of the vestibule closed after three seconds. Oswald started walking in circles. Roy Truly arrived on the second floor and continued to the next flight of stairs. Officer Baker also arrived on the second floor at the exact moment that Oswald, still walking in circles, passed by the door into the vestibule he had come through five seconds earlier, from right to left. Oswald was not out of breath, and responded calmly to the policeman, who had drawn his gun.

In the official version, Oswald also walked in the wrong direction for someone who would be on the run. This is a detail the believers never mention. They claim that his behavior after the assassination is an indication of his guilt. But if Oswald had fled into the vestibule, he would then have ran to the right, through the hallway and to the stairs in the front, where he could leave the building. Why would he have gone to the left, where his escape route came to a dead-end in the lunchroom? What seems to be the most logical choice for a man on the run?

WAS OSWALD IN THE SNIPER'S NEST?

We will briefly go through our findings to try and determine whether or not Oswald was in the sniper's nest at the time of the assassination:

- Brennan and Givens, the two witnesses for the prosecution and the key witnesses of the Warren Commission, appear to be very weak and unreliable upon closer inspection. Givens changed his statement to meet the wish of the Commission to link Oswald to the sniper's nest by means of a testimony. Brennan clearly did see someone in the sniper's nest, and he also saw the weapon and he claims to have seen the last shot. But on the basis of his testimony, there is no reason to believe that Oswald was that person. On the contrary, his statement contains clear indications that the person he saw was not Oswald at all. Brennan was too keen on pleasing the Commission.
- The two witnesses for the defense, on the other hand, are very reliable. The statement from Bonnie Williams makes it as good as certain that Oswald could only have been present in the sniper's nest at the earliest five to ten minutes before the assassination. The testimony of Mrs. Garner irrefutably confirms that Oswald was not on the upper floors immediately after the assassination. Assistant U.S. Attorney Stroud wrote on June 2,

1964: 'Miss Garner, Miss Adams's superintendent, stated this morning that after Miss Adams went downstairs she (Miss Garner) saw Mr. Truly and the policeman come up.' In the time in between, Oswald had not passed by, and therefore he could not have been on the sixth floor.

- Some witnesses saw Oswald on the first floor before the attack, and Oswald made a statement that contains information that he could only have known if he indeed had been present on the first floor. There was only one person that was never identified in the doorway of the book depository. All thirteen other spectators in the doorway are staff of the TSBD. We can therefore assume that the fourteenth person, standing at the very back, was also working at the TSBD. The whereabouts of all 73 other staff members at the moment Kennedy drove by is known. Except for the thirteen known persons in the doorway, none of the other employees were situated there. The logical conclusion is that Oswald is the only remaining employee who qualifies to be this person. Perhaps Oswald was indeed Prayer Man, the non-identified man who physically looked like him and wore the same type of clothing.
- Officer Baker saw Oswald pass by on the second floor through the window in the door of the vestibule at a time this door had been closed for at least five seconds. It is inconceivable that Oswald was walking in circles in the small vestibule for five seconds while the door was closing and Truly rushed past, only to then walk past the window of the door from right to left. And why, as an assassin on the run, would he calmly walk to the lunchroom? He knew the building and knew how he could leave easily by simply walking straight ahead to the stairs in the southeast corner. Moreover, it is certain that Oswald was not out of breath, and not even nervous, a fact that is difficult to combine with the immediately preceding events of which he stood accused.

There is therefore no real concrete evidence that Oswald was effectively in the sniper's nest. If we look at the facts objectively, the logical conclusion is that Oswald was not at the crime scene at 12.30 p.m., the time of the assassination.

WHERE WAS THE ASSASSIN AFTER THE ATTACK?

Yet even if Oswald may not have been in the sniper's nest, the sniper did shoot from there. This alternative gunman must have entered and left the building, and must have had Oswald's Carcano. Entering the building and getting ahold of the Carcano in Ruth Paine's garage doesn't seem like an insurmountable problem. A bigger problem is remaining invisible within the building. No strangers were spotted in the building before the shooting took place. In the JFK movie, Oliver Stone has several workers carrying out a renovation of the floor in the book depository, but there is absolutely no objective indication of this.[276] There is only an eighty-year-old man[277] with kidney problems. Ten minutes before the motorcade passed by, this man asked to briefly use the toilet. He left the building shortly afterwards and drove away in a black car. As far as I am aware, no serious researcher suspects this old man of any involvement.

After the shooting, the assassin also had to get away again unseen. Several people have been reported allegedly leaving the book depository immediately after the assassination. James Worrell saw a man in a sports jacket leave the book depository through the back door three minutes after the shooting.[278] This man was in his late twenties or early thirties, weighing about 155 to 165 pounds and 5'7" to 5'10" tall. Another witness, Richard Randoph Carr, was heard for the first time in the trial that District Attorney Jim Garrison conducted. He was a rather lousy witness, but claimed that he had seen a man in a sports jacket get into a Rambler station wagon after the shooting. He allegedly also saw this man at a window on the seventh floor, diagonally above the sniper's nest, before the shooting.[279] Helen Forrest also told historian Michael Kurtz that she had seen a man leave the school book depository through the back door and board a Rambler station wagon.[280] The man Forrest saw strongly resembled Oswald. Witness James Elbert Romack, on the other hand, claimed that, apart from a brief interruption, he had kept an eye on the rear of the building immediately after the shooting. He had not seen anyone leaving the building.[281] The final witness was Deputy Sheriff Craig. In his very first statement on the day of the assassination, he himself said: 'I heard a shrill whistle and I turned around and saw a white male running down the hill from the direction of the Texas School Book Depository building and I saw what I think was a light colored Rambler station wagon.'[282]

None of those witnesses can really convince me. Even more important is that the time schedule that applies to Oswald applies even more, of course, to the alternative gunman. He also had to get past Dorothy Garner unseen. The only logical explanation for getting away unseen after the shooting seems to me – but this is purely speculative – to take advantage of the general confusion, and use a police uniform.

Another question is, of course, who the alternative gunman could be. There is no shortage of potential candidates. 'Mac' Wallace, a man who took care of Johnson's shady deals, is often mentioned. The assertion that his fingerprint was allegedly found in the sniper's nest is probably not true, as the only unidentified imprint in the sniper's nest was a palmprint, and not a fingerprint.[283] This does not alter the fact that Wallace was a dodgy character who didn't shrink from committing murder. However, someone like Eladio del Valle probably qualifies better for the position of candidate assassin. This fervent anti-communist Cuban hated Kennedy so intensely that getting himself hired as a hitman would probably have seemed like an added bonus to him. Del Valle was brutally murdered on February 22, 1967, the same day that David Ferrie also died under suspicious circumstances, and this at precisely the time that both men had attracted the full attention of Jim Garrison's investigation. Del Valle was an excellent shot, he suddenly had plenty of money after the assassination and he is claimed to have been in Dallas on November 22.[284] Looking at it objectively, del Valle qualifies ten times more as Kennedy's assassin than Oswald. Only the so-called presence of Oswald at the crime scene, and the discovery of his rifle turn him into the obvious suspect, but without these arguments, Oswald would never have made it onto the shortlist of would-be assassins of Kennedy. If it is then also established that Oswald did not shoot with the Carcano, and was not even in the sniper's nest, men like del Valle immediately move to the top of the list. But there are many more candidates.

It would not have been difficult for a professional killer to get ahold of the weapon and smuggle it into the unguarded book depository in the night of Thursday to Friday. The chaotic building offered sufficient opportunities to hide a man and a weapon. It is perhaps even relevant that the owner of the building was David Harold Byrd, a business tycoon and member of the infamous Dallas Petroleum Club. Some of his friends are not unknown to us: George de Mohrenschildt, Clint Murchinson, Haroldson Hunt, CIA man David Atlee Phillips, Lyndon Johnson, George H. Bush, General Edwin Walker …

As the owner of the Temco company, Byrd was also the employer of the aforementioned 'Mac' Wallace. To be clear, there is no evidence whatsoever to suggest that Byrd was in any way involved, but it is striking how the same names always pop up all through the file.

Our goal, however, is not to try and find out who the potential alternative gunman could be. In order to make a huge step forward in the file, we should establish whether it was Oswald who fired the shots. Let us therefore once again review our three initial questions regarding the sniper's nest, the weapon and the perpetrator.

A BRIEF RECAPITULATION

We started from the indisputable observation that the following three assumptions must be correct if Oswald was Kennedy's assassin as a 'lone nut':

1. There were shots from the sniper's nest;
2. The shots were fired with the Carcano;
3. The shots were fired by Oswald.

We are hereby only interested in the truth. If Oswald is guilty, we should be able to endorse this with as much conviction. Based on the analysis of the facts, we can confirm the first two items. There were indeed shots from the sniper's nest, and they were more than likely fired with the Carcano. But, objectively speaking, we must conclude that the claim that Oswald was the gunman is contrary to the findings. All the objective elements we have investigated point in the same direction: Oswald did not fire the Carcano himself, and he was not at the crime scene. The fact that this assumption is quite outrageous is not a valid counter-argument. Anyone who wants to disregard this conclusion must rebut, in detail and with reference to the source, the answers we have provided to the seven questions in the section headed 'Could Oswald have shot with the Carcano?' in Chapter 2, and must demonstrate that Oswald did shoot the Carcano, and that he was at the crime scene at the time of the assassination. The problem with the believers is that they are inclined to refute every argument, while Oswald only needs one element that proves beyond reasonable doubt that he is innocent.

The most surprising finding is the answer to question 2 above: the shots were fired with the Carcano. This answer interrelates with the assumption that the Carcano was brought into the building assembled and perfectly adjusted. This cancels out the otherwise insurmountable questions regarding the precarious reassembly, the lack of fingerprints, the questionable accuracy of the weapon and the insufficient length of the package Oswald had with him that morning. The above leads to the unexpected conclusion that the Carcano was indeed used for the shots, but that it was not Oswald who took the shots. This possibility has never before been considered by the conspiracists. Those who don't believe in Oswald's guilt felt compelled to run with the pack and cry out that the Carcano is an unreliable weapon, but the facts contradict this. Oswald was at best a mediocre shot, but the Carcano is not that bad if it is properly adjusted. That precludes that the Carcano entered the building dismantled. If the Carcano was indeed smuggled into the building in twelve pieces, the conspiracists are right in saying that the weapon was unusable for the assassination. But, properly mounted, the Carcano was suitable for firing a pretty accurate shot from 80 yards, provided the shooter was aware that the weapon shot slightly over the top and to the right, a deviation that was actually more of an advantage than a disadvantage, given the route of the limousine.

This does not mean, of course, that there were no weapons around that were much better suited to successfully killing the president. The main intention behind the use of the Carcano could then have been to point directly towards Oswald, the scapegoat.

We started this first part of the investigation on the basis of a logical analysis of the question as to whether Oswald could be a lone nut. We have systematically examined every component of this analysis, building exclusively on facts arising directly from the file.

Based on this examination, we can formulate a solid, substantiated working hypothesis:

— the shots were fired from the sniper's nest;
— not by Oswald, but by a member of a conspiracy;
— and with Oswald's perfectly adjusted Carcano;
— which the sniper brought into the book depository fully assembled;
— with the intention of pointing out Oswald as the perpetrator after the assassination.

Chapter 4 – A murder of pure opportunity

Always approach a case with an absolutely blank mind.
Form no theories, just simply observe and draw
inferences from your observations.

Sherlock Holmes in Arthur Conan Doyle's
The Adventure of the Cardboard Box

We can propose logical and objective arguments to determine whether Oswald may have been the culprit. Many believers are impervious to this. They belong to the 'I don't want to know' group. They have often based their opinion once and for all on a single decisive argument. They deem this one argument to be irrefutable, and the whole debate is therefore closed for them.

It was the same kind of reasoning that almost led to Galileo Galilei being burned at the stake in the 17th century. Everyone was able to see for themselves that the sun revolved around the earth, and not vice versa. His intricate theoretical explanation was the devil's handiwork, and only meant to mislead you. Even Galileo could do little about this without making his situation even more precarious, so he chose to remain silent. It's hard to go against a seemingly irrefutable and, moreover, populist argument.

Things are not much better in today's television and visual culture. The 'I don't want to know' argument can even get a grip on the best informed and most critical observer. Chris Matthews, the anchorman of the political talk show *Hardball* on MSNBC, is a man whose opinion I regularly accept with full confidence. He has also written a good book about Kennedy,[285] but he refuses to hear the word *conspiracy* and the name *John Kennedy* in the same sentence. That makes him quite prickly. Matthews dismisses all the arguments of the conspiracists with a single question. Oswald was already working in the school book depository when Kennedy's route through Dallas was still unknown. How could he then have been placed there as a *patsy* of conspirators?

The question of how Oswald ended up in the TSBD is indeed relevant and deserves an answer. To find this answer, we must start with a benevolent teacher who wanted to learn Russian.

(NOT) AN EVERYDAY COUPLE

Ruth Paine, with maiden name Ruth Hyde, was only 31 years old in 1963, but she already acted old. She laughed sparingly and with her mouth turned downwards. She was an intelligent and socially conscious woman, self-confident, punctual, altruistic, and was an advocate of equal rights for African Americans. Ruth was a member of the Quaker faith. In 1957, industrious as ever, she opted for the difficult Russian language lessons at school. Folk dancing was her form of frivolity, and that was how she met her future husband Michael Paine.

Figure 37.
Ruth and Michael Paine in 1964.

Michael came from a wealthy family with important connections. His father was an architect and peace activist. His mother was a Forbes, a niece of Rosemary Forbes, the mother of John Kerry, the Democratic presidential candidate in 2004 and Secretary of State under Barack Obama since 2013.[286] But Ruth Paine mockingly said that her mother-in-law must have come from the modest branch of the Forbes family. Nothing special. Yet James Douglas in his book *JFK and the Unspeakable* mentioned some even more striking connections. Allen Dulles, a member of the Warren Commission and former CIA director, also happened to be descended from a Forbes. Michael's mother was also a lifelong friend of Mary Bancroft, an American spy and novelist. Bancroft was active in Switzerland during the Second World War. She was not only a patient of psychiatrist Carl Gustav Jung there due to her compulsive sneezing,[287] but was also the mistress of her boss Allen Dulles.[288] It was a shock to him when he realized during the Commission's questioning[289] that

Ruth's mother-in-law was actually the bosom friend of his lover. Michael's stepfather was also no gray mouse: as an engineer, he had designed the Bell helicopter. The Bell Helicopter company counted the army among its best customers. Michael followed the footsteps of his stepfather, and went to work as an engineer.

There's also a story to tell about Ruth's family. Ruth's sister Silvia Hyde had been on the payroll of the CIA for eight years in 1963. This emerged from documents disclosed thirty years later. It was not discussed in 1963. Silvia's husband John Hoke worked for the international aid organization Agency for International Development (AID), a not-so-innocent NGO. AID helped the CIA to inconspicuously infiltrate agents into developing countries. Ruth's father, William Averell Hyde, suddenly received a three-year contract at AID in October 1964, the month after the completion of the Warren Report. He became the regional advisor for insurance throughout Latin America. This means that Ruth's sister worked for the CIA, and both her brother-in-law and father worked for an international organization that acted as a front for the CIA. Researcher Steve Jones also refers to an FBI document of December 2, 1963, in which two friends of the Paines put their hands in the fire to prove their total innocence. But these friends were Fred and Nancy Osborn, and Fred's father, Fred Osborn Snr., happened to be 'a friend and colleague of Allen Dulles'.[290]

AN EXTRAVAGANT FRIEND

The Paines were also friends with the eccentric geologist Baron George de Mohrenschildt, a man of the world. He was a personal friend of George Bush, later CIA director and the 41st President of the US, who was an informer in the Kennedy case on November 22, 1963. Bush made two attempts to convince the FBI that Castro exiles could be involved in the assassination. Four months before the presidential elections of 1988,[291] when Bush was a candidate, evidence emerged of his role as an informer. Without blinking, Bush lied that it was a case of a 'namesake'. Once Bush was president, the White House responded that 'it wouldn't give dignity to this matter with additional comments.'[292] George de Mohrenschildt was also once a family friend of Jackie Kennedy's mother. The future first lady sat for a photo with him as a toddler in his lap.

Baron de Mohrenschildt was into his fourth marriage in 1963, and lived in grand style, without a clearly identifiable source of income. Professor Joan

Mellen described him as follows: 'He was never very good at finding oil or dealing with oil. He was really a person that is for sale, very cosmopolitan, very charming very good looking not very capable in any of the business ventures that he went into. A perfect person to be taken up by the intelligence services of a variety of countries especially CIA.'[293]

This animated, extroverted aristocrat with multiple university degrees[294] also became very good friends with Lee Harvey Oswald. The non-conformist de Mohrenschildt found a kindred spirit in a maverick like Oswald. But the left-wing Oswald was still an exception in the otherwise very right-wing circle of friends of the baron, who investigator Lee Forley described as 'bitterly anti-Communist and in some cases extreme right-wing fascist'.[295] The Bolsheviks had expelled de Mohrenschildt from his home country, Belarus, as a child. The chance that he would develop sympathy for a communist later in life therefore seemed very small. And in any case, de Mohrenschildt first asked permission from the CIA before he moved closer to his friend. He contacted J. Walton Moore, the head of the *Domestic Contacts Division* in Dallas. The baron apparently became Oswald's *handler*, his CIA watchdog. De Mohrenschildt closely followed the life of the Oswalds. The next leg of his endless journey brought him to Haiti in April 1963. Just as he disappeared from the lives of the Oswalds, Ruth Paine appeared in it as if by magic. Ruth spent a few months of frantic efforts to penetrate into the private lives of the Oswalds. In early September 1963, she visited her sister with the CIA connections.[296] Immediately after the contact with her sister, Ruth took Marina into her home. All these links to the CIA may be explained away as coincidents but the contacts of de Mohrenschildt and the Paines with Lee and Marina were not innocent. That is evident from a letter from Hoover to General Counsel Rankin of the Warren Commission. In October 1964, Hoover gave Rankin the urgent advice to not disclose the FBI reports about Michael and Ruth Paine and George and Jeanne de Mohrenschildt. Hoover wrote: 'Making the contents of such documents available to the public could cause serious repercussions to the Commission.'[297] Hoover had good reason to be nervous. There was already a worrying leaked document. The FBI apparently had a telephone tap on the Paines' line on November 23, 1963, the day after the assassination.[298]

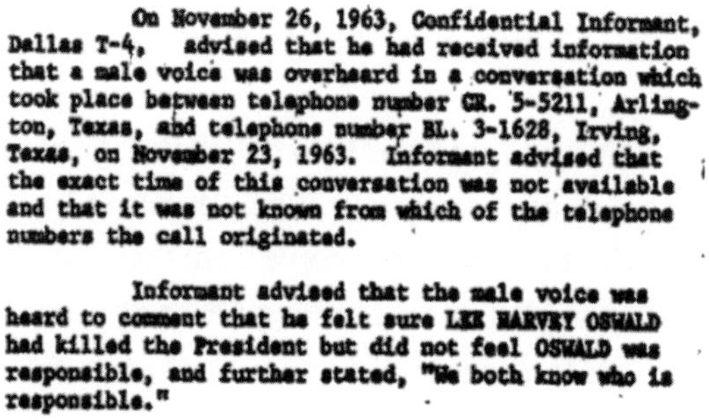

On November 26, 1963, Confidential Informant, Dallas T-4, advised that he had received information that a male voice was overheard in a conversation which took place between telephone number CR. 5-5211, Arlington, Texas, and telephone number BL. 3-1628, Irving, Texas, on November 23, 1963. Informant advised that the exact time of this conversation was not available and that it was not known from which of the telephone numbers the call originated.

Informant advised that the male voice was heard to comment that he felt sure LEE HARVEY OSWALD had killed the President but did not feel OSWALD was responsible, and further stated, "We both know who is responsible."

Figure 38. Ruth and Michael Paine on the phone: 'We both know who is responsible.'

Ruth called her husband in his office at Bell Helicopter at 1.00 p.m. on Saturday using a *collect call*, a telephone call that is paid by the person called.[299] The confidential informant, i.e. an FBI agent, heard Michael say that he was sure that Lee Harvey Oswald had assassinated the President, but that he did not feel that Oswald was 'responsible'. And then he continued: 'We both know who is responsible.' Michael Paine afterwards emphatically denied the content of the conversation. The Commission Counsel asked: 'Did you make any remark to the effect that you knew who was responsible?' Paine answered: 'I don't know who the assassin is or was; no, so I did not.' To be sure, Commissioner Liebeler asked a second time: 'You are positive in your recollection that you made no such remark?' Michael Paine answered: 'Yes.'[300] The FBI therefore lied, according to Paine. But why would the FBI invent the tapped phone call? It is, of course, Paine who lied here, and the FBI was concerned that more would leak out about Michael and Ruth Paine.

At the time of Hoover's letter, the Commission had already completed its work several months before, and was busy with the annexes, which would amount to 26 volumes. What did Hoover actually mean? What information about the Paines could have serious repercussions for the Commission?

THE FIGHT FOR MARINA

Despite their origins, Ruth and Michael Paine led an unremarkable life in a small suburb of Dallas. The Bell Helicopter factory where Michael worked was located in Fort Worth, and that had brought the Paines to Irving. Ruth was teaching in a Quaker school in 1963. She had two children, and had lived more or less separated from her husband since September. Ruth and Michael were still friends, but no longer lived under the same roof. They finally divorced in 1971.

The path that finally brought Oswald to the book depository began in February 1963. Ruth was invited to an evening with Baron George de Mohrenschildt.[301] He had invited a number of people from the Russian community to his house, and Ruth was also invited through Everett Glover, the only guest in the company whom she knew. Ruth and Everett sang medieval madrigals in an amateur choir. Glover knew that Ruth was very interested in Russia, and therefore arranged a place for her on de Mohrenschildt's guest list.

During the dinner, Ruth first met Lee and Marina, two good acquaintances of the host. Lee had lived in Russia for almost three years, from October 1959 to June 1962. He was married to the beautiful 20-year-old Marina Prusakova. Together with their baby June, Marina had accompanied her husband on his return to the USA. Because they spoke Russian, the Oswalds felt somewhat at home in the colorful company around the eccentric nobleman. But they nevertheless remained the odd ones out. Most of the members of the Russian community in the US were, like de Mohrenschildt, refugees who had left their homeland to escape the tyranny of the workers' paradise. They were therefore mostly upper class, rather conservative and fiercely anti-communist.[302] Marina, on the other hand, had been a member of Komsomol, the communist youth movement. The uncle with whom she had lived was a colonel in the security service.[303] Oswald even openly enthused about communism that evening. Happy as a child that finds itself at the center of attention for a while, he openly declared himself to be a Marxist. He claimed that the economic system of the Soviets was superior to Western capitalism.[304]

The other participants were shocked, but listened politely. It was not every day that they met someone who had taken the exceptional step to flee *to* Soviet Russia. The taciturn Ruth didn't get much chance to participate in the conversation. Politics was not really in her nature, and her knowledge of the language was still too limited. But she did notice Marina, who also said little and was mainly concerned with her baby. The idealist in Ruth popped up and she asked the address of the young woman. She afterwards explained that she had seen it as an opportunity to meet someone who spoke 'modern' Russian. The best way to learn a language is, of course, to also speak it. The conspiracists believe that, after his hard day's work as a Marine, Oswald set about successfully learning Russian all on his own. But the truth is that Oswald only had a good command of the language after having lived in Russia for three years. 'Just a trace of an accent', [305] was how de Mohrenschildt assessed the quality of his pupil's Russian. But before he went to the Soviet Union, Oswald's learning process was as slow as that of any other student. He only picked up some basic knowledge during his military service in Japan. On his transfer from Japan to California, he took a language test. His knowledge of Russian then was still very deficient and passive. He scored +4 for reading, +3 for writing, but -5 for comprehension of spoken Russian. Some stories made the rounds. Marine Dan Powers met Oswald in Japan outside the base with a Eurasian woman who, according to Powers, spoke Russian.[306] Maybe Oswald picked up his first sentences there as *pillow talk*. Intimate conversations between lovers are also conducive to learning a foreign language quickly. In any case, Oswald only really mastered the language by speaking it daily.

Ruth therefore had a point when she thought that help from someone who really spoke the language was not to be missed. She did not waste any time; she wrote to Marina and quickly arranged a first appointment. A few more visits followed in the subsequent weeks. Ruth made sure that she could always be alone with Marina. Marina knew almost no one in the US, and certainly no one who could speak Russian, however poorly. Lee prevented her from learning English. The approach that Ruth sought was therefore very welcome. Marina soon laid bare her whole heart to her new friend. She confided in Ruth that she was unhappy, and asked for advice because she was pregnant again, but really had no idea how she could prevent pregnancy without abortion. In early April, after she had known the Oswalds for only six weeks, Ruth undertook a first attempt to persuade Marina to move in with her in the fall, towards the end of her pregnancy. Marina was welcome in Irving, but without Oswald.[307] In Lee's eyes, this was not a welcome friendly act, and he felt that Marina should really know better, even though she felt lonely and neglected: in practice, accepting Ruth's proposal was tantamount to an actual separation. The uncertain Lee could hardly interpret the proposal other than the start of the end of his marriage. But the young, self-indulgent Marina thought it was just fine.[308] This was yet another humiliating blow for the headstrong Lee: an intrusive Quaker teacher questioning his performance as head of the family and provider. We know that Lee did not take this lightly, because Marina had already briefly moved in with Katya Ford, another friend, in 1962. She described to Ruth Paine Lee's facial expression when he heard that she had temporarily sought shelter with this friend: 'She described his face as she left as shocked and dismayed and unbelieving.'[309] Yet he responded quite stoically this time, maybe because the threat was still far off, and, frugal as he was, he perhaps saw the advantages of the situation. So Ruth won her first battle in the fight for Marina.

A second chance soon arose. On Wednesday, April 24, Ruth visited Marina in the Oswalds' unkempt rental premises in Neely Street. (It was in the backyard of this miserable place that Marina took the famous photographs of Oswald with the Carcano.) To Ruth's astonishment, Oswald was about to leave for New Orleans. He had packed three suitcases and two large duffel bags from his time in the Marines. Lee had just been sacked by the Jagers Stovall photo company, and wanted to seek new employment in New Orleans, the city where he had spent his youth. Maybe he also left so suddenly because of a failed attack on the extreme right-wing, retired General Walker he allegedly committed on April 10. The arrival of Ruth offered Oswald a chance to save on a taxi, because she gave them a lift to the bus station. There, Oswald bought two tickets, one for him and one for Marina, who would join him later when he had found work. Ruth suggested that Marina could perhaps temporarily move in with her until then. This seemed like a good idea, because what was Marina, who spoke no English, to do on her own with a baby in Dallas? The proposal received the approval of all, and Oswald traded Marina's ticket in again, because Ruth was also willing to take Marina to New Orleans by car as soon as Oswald asked for her. Oswald stored his luggage at the bus station. In anticipation of his departure for New Orleans later that evening, the trio went back to Neely Street in order to load the Oswalds' entire possessions into Ruth's station wagon. This is how the pregnant Marina and the one-year-old June found themselves in Irving, a suburb of Dallas, for the first time on April 24. Ruth immediately tried to persuade Marina to stay longer than just temporarily. 'I made [...] an invitation for her to stay with me, past the time of the baby's birth, if she wished to.'[310] But Oswald did not yet give up the fight for Marina. He already found work in New Orleans on May 9, as a maintenance man at the Reily Coffee Company. He rented a shabby apartment the next day, and called Marina. She was elated. '*Papa naslubet!* Papa loves us', she happily told her little daughter.[311] Ruth also kept her word, and brought Marina all the way to New Orleans. On May 11, the young Russian woman was again under the conjugal roof, at least temporarily.

Not long afterwards, Marina sent several letters to Ruth complaining about Lee. He had even threatened to send her back to the USSR. Ruth wrote back to her protégé on July 11: 'Dear Marina, If Lee doesn't wish to live with you anymore and prefers that you go to the Soviet Union, think about the possibility of living with me.'[312] It was not really fair of Ruth to suggest this as help in an emergency, as she had clearly aimed at living together permanently with Marina for some time, and Oswald's threat was actually helpful for her. Ruth shifted the battle to Oswald's weak spot: it was impossible for him to give Marina the luxury that she desired so much. She knew that Marina was very susceptible to this, and began to tempt her relentlessly. At first, she told Marina that she herself had also received money from her parents for a long time, and that it was not shameful to accept help from the family. But she and Marina would, of course, first have to become a family, so she wrote: 'I would be happy to be an aunt to you and I can. We have sufficient money. Michael will be glad. This I know. He just gave me $500 for the vacation or something necessary. With this money it is possible to pay the doctor and hospital in October when the baby is born, believe God. All will be well for you and your children.'[313] Ruth played the financial argument as much as possible to lure Marina. She also stated that, from a taxation point of view, Marina could be considered to be a person dependent on Michael, and that the related tax benefit would be large enough to allow her to live with them. But that last suggestion was wrong. Ruth later explained the lie as merely 'bad arithmetic', but also said the following to the Commission: 'But I think that in fact this reference to the tax reduction did not encourage her, as I had hoped.'[314] Because Ruth was well aware that Lee would feel very hurt if Marina came to live with her, and wanted to avoid Marina's bad conscience thereby becoming an obstacle, she already anticipated this in her letter: 'I don't want to hurt Lee with this invitation to you. Only I think that it would be better that you and he do not live together if you do not receive happiness.' She also tried to tone down any moral objections by Marina by arousing pity, and by implying that non-cohabiting spouses were quite normal: 'I understand how Michael feels. He doesn't love me and wants a chance to look for another life and another wife. He must do this, it seems, and so it is better for us not to live together.'[315] Later, towards the end of the very long questioning by the

Commission, Ruth briefly forgot her role of good Samaritan, and explained why she wanted to bring Marina into her home. 'I was tired of living alone and lonely' and 'I enjoyed her company'. Only then did she mention that the chance of learning Russian 'added a wider dimension to my rather small and boring life as a young mother'.

But despite her lures, Ruth failed to land Marina. Things were temporarily going relatively well between Marina and Lee. Marina also proved to be smarter than Ruth in the field of tax benefits: she immediately realized that she could only be fiscally dependent on Michael if she was no longer dependent on Lee, in other words, if she was divorced from him. That was still a bridge too far for her: 'Lee would not agree to a divorce.'

On July 19, Lee lost his job at the Reily Coffee Company. For him, the mysterious period in New Orleans now began, about which Jim Garrison would agonize in 1968. Oswald committed himself to the pro-Castro camp, and at the same time offered to help Carlos Bringuier in his struggle against Castro. After a skirmish during the distribution of pamphlets for the FPCC, or *Fair Play For Cuba Committee*, Oswald ended up in jail as a left-wing activist. He also appeared in the newspapers and on radio and television. Proof of this surfaced later in the Cuban consulate in Mexico City, in order to strengthen Oswald's pose as a pro-Castro militant and as an argument to explain the application for a visa for Cuba, or even for the creation of incriminating evidence in order to prove that he was an accursed left-wing extremist. This period of striking Castro activism lasted only six weeks, and ended on September 20 with Oswald's intention to go to Mexico. Ruth again saw her chance, and drove once again all the way from Irving to New Orleans. She finally achieved her goal on September 23. Marina and June went with her to Irving. On September 24, Oswald left for Mexico on a bus. During the last two months of his life, he only saw his wife and daughter on weekends, in Irving. Ruth Paine had found her roommate and Oswald acquiesced to the new circumstances, but he did not give up on Marina. Ruth had to admit that he did his best on the weekends to make the reunion with his family possible: 'In this brief period during the time that he came out on weekends, I saw him as a person who cared for his wife and his child, tried to make himself helpful in my home, tried to make himself welcome although he really preferred to stay to himself.'[316]

Ultimately, Ruth was not able to enjoy her victory in the struggle for Marina for very long. After the assassination, Marina was taken to a secure location where she was screened from the outside world. James Herbert Martin, the manager of the Six Flag Inn where Marina was staying, immediately pushed himself forward as her manager in exchange for a fee of 10 percent of her receipts.[317] He also began a relationship with the beautiful Russian woman.[318] This fee was not bad: on December 5, Marina had already received 7,525 dollars in gifts,[319] and the checks from compassionate Americans kept flowing in.

Ruth still sent a series of desperate letters, but they left Marina ice-cold. She disdainfully rejected the pleas for friendship. The two women would briefly meet each other again just once. During the trial in New Orleans, a member of the jury asked Marina if she still saw Ruth. Marina said that the Secret Service had advised her against keeping in touch with Ruth. 'Seems like she had friends over there [at the CIA] and it would be bad for me if people find out connection between me and Ruth and CIA.' The jury member then asked: 'In other words, you were left with the distinct impression that she was in some way connected with the CIA?' Marina replied: 'Yes.'[320]

OSWALD IN THE TSBD

Ruth Paine was also responsible for Oswald taking a job at the TSBD. On October 14, 1963, she was drinking a cup of coffee with some neighbors. Their conversation would have far-reaching consequences. Ruth was not crazy about Lee,[321] but she also bore him no ill will.[322] Always looking for a good deed, she raised the issue of Oswald's problem in finding work. With a second baby on the way, being unemployed was an unpleasant situation. One of the four neighbors, Linnie Mae Randle, told Ruth that her younger brother, (Buell) Wesley Frazier, 'thought they needed another person at the Texas School Book Depository.' [323] That is at least Ruth's version of the events. At the hearings, Linnie denied that they had really discussed a vacant job in the TSBD,[324] but she had said that her brother had found work in the book depository. Ruth had then asked her to call if there was a vacant position, but Linnie declined because she didn't know anyone in the TSBD.

Ruth then called herself, and explained Oswald's difficult situation: 'I have a fine young man living here with his wife and baby, and his wife is expecting a baby – another baby, in a few days, and he needs work desperately.'

Roy Truly, the superintendent of the depository, reacted positively to the appeal: 'We could possibly use him for a brief time.'[325] Ruth brought Lee to the interview by car a day later. Truly found Oswald to be a decent guy. Above all, the fact that the young man addressed him politely as *Sir* pleased him. He gave Oswald the job, and he could already start work the next day, on October 16, 1963.

Unfortunately, nobody asked Ruth Paine or Roy Truly at what time the interview took place on October 15. That is important because Ruth had another telephone conversation on the same day, with Robert Adams of the Texas Employment Commission. The employment agency had a job for Oswald in the luggage department of Trans Texas Airways. The wage was $310 per month, much more than in the TSBD, and it was steady work. Truly had explicitly stated that the job in the book depository was temporary, until the busy period was over. The woman who answered Robert Adams's call in the Paine home told him that Oswald was not there, and that she would pass on the message. Adams himself called back again the next day: 'The following morning at 10:30 o'clock I again called the BL3-1628 Irving Texas number and learned from the person who answered that Oswald was not there and that he had in the meantime obtained employment and was working.'[326] It is difficult to imagine that a woman who answered the phone in Ruth's home in English could be anyone other than Ruth herself. Nevertheless, she remembered nothing about the two phone calls from the employment agency. The fact that Oswald appeared to have *meanwhile* found work when the second call came in indicates that this was not yet the case during the first telephone conversation with Adams. Ruth Paine thereby deliberately sent Oswald to the TSBD, and not to any other job.

Despite her good memory of all the details of her efforts, Ruth no longer knew about two job offers on the same day when she appeared before the Commission. When she was asked the question a second time, she responded: 'No, in Dallas?' The third repetition of the question still didn't ring a bell: 'No, I do not recall that. 310 dollar a month?' She still couldn't believe it: 'And he definitely offered such a job?' The Commission spelled it out for her once again: 'He might have been able to secure a job through the Texas Employment Commission as a cargo handler at $310 per month.' Then Ruth suddenly vaguely remembered something: 'I do recall some reference of that sort, which fell through – that there was not that possibility.'[327] She had heard something about it, but through Lee. That is a flagrant lie. Adams was told twice by an English-speaking woman that Oswald was not there. And the fact that Lee did not get the job at Trans Texas Airways is solely due to Ruth.

Oswald therefore ended up in the school book depository five weeks before the assassination. There is certainly some coincidence involved here. The employment of neighbor Buell Wesley Frazier cannot, of course, be part of a conspiracy to assassinate the president. But there was apparently still more to it. Both Ruth and Michael Paine had CIA contacts. So what information about them had Hoover so worried?

Ruth made sustained efforts to persuade Marina to stay at her home. Her motive of philanthropy mixed with opportunism need not be at odds with an information contract for the CIA, on the contrary. The friendship could exist without CIA instructions, but the watchdog contract could not exist without the friendship. A semblance of friendship and altruism was also de Mohrenschildt's official motive for approaching the Oswalds. The timing of Ruth's approach is too obvious: it looks suspiciously like the changing of the guard when de Mohrenschildt left for Haiti. Ruth followed the rules of her undercover assignment. She lied smoothly under oath. She stated, for example, that Linnie Mae Randle had suggested applying to the TSBD, while she herself had taken the initiative. More importantly, she deliberately lied about the fact that she had sabotaged a much better job offer for Oswald. Did she want to prevent him giving up his job in the book depository? If so, why did she do it, and on whose behalf?

Michael Paine also lied. This is especially evident from his denial of his mysterious statement on the phone, the day after the assassination. And what did Michael mean when he said to Ruth that they both knew who was responsible for the assassination of Kennedy?

There is another indication that the Paines knew more than they admitted. When the police rang the doorbell shortly after noon on November 22, Ruth received them with open arms and, even before the officers could identify themselves, said: 'I've been expecting you all.'[328] She let the officers in, who didn't even have a search warrant with them, and explained her clairvoyance about their arrival as follows: 'Just as soon as I heard *where* the shooting happened, I knew there would be someone out.' Ruth did not even know that Oswald had a weapon, but it was enough to hear *where* the attack was carried out in order to predict the arrival of the police? Almost immediately, Michael also turned up in Irving. 'We had only been there a few minutes and we were in plain cars', said police officer Gus Rose regarding the time of Michael's arrival. Michael turned to Ruth: 'Just as soon as I heard *where* it happened, I knew you would need some help.'[329] It is clear that Ruth and Michael possessed inside information that allowed them to complete the bits of information that trickled through the media. The fact that they were silent about it, confirms the supposition that they were thinking and acting within their role as CIA informants at that moment. Yet we shouldn't overestimate the role of the Paines. To make Ruth into a co-conspirator who went into action in February 1963 by cunningly writing letters in bad Russian is taking things too far. Even though something may have been up with the Paines, we would then have to involve Roy Truly and Buell Wesley Frazier in the plot in order to maintain that Oswald was deliberately steered towards the book depository. Ruth and Michael Paine were not the type of schemers that would knowingly provide help in order to bring an assassin into position. They probably helped the CIA with information about possible communist infiltrators in good faith and out of patriotism, and were only indirectly involved in the employment of Oswald in the TSBD. They knew what information they had to pass on about Oswald: Oswald was a subversive element, a Marxist. They assumed, of course, that the CIA would pass this information on to the police after the assassination. Oswald's background and his presence at the crime scene were enough to put him on the list of possible perpetrators. Consequently, the arrival of the police was no surprise for Ruth, and Michael knew as much as she did. As soon as he learned *where* the attack had taken place, he immediately knew that the police would visit Ruth, and he rushed to her aid in case the police would be difficult to deal with.

KENNEDY ON DEALEY PLAZA

The route of the presidential motorcade only became widely known on November 19. The newspapers reported the route for the first time on that day. The *Dallas Times Herald* wrote: 'The motorcade will then pass through downtown on Harwood and then west on Main, turning back to Elm at Houston and then out on Stemmons Freeway to the Trade Mart.'[330] According to the believers, potential conspirators therefore only knew on Tuesday that the president would drive past the window of the book depository on Friday.

That's perfect timing for an opportunity killer such as a temporary insane Oswald, but it's much too short to plan a coup or a retaliatory conspiracy. On October 15, nobody could organize to bring Oswald into the right position on a route that was only known on November 19. The argument of the MSNBC anchorman Chris Matthews that Oswald's employment in October proves that he was not part of a conspiracy seems valid. But there are theoretically two ways to bring Oswald and the president together. You could bring Oswald to the place where Kennedy would drive past, but you could just as well bring the president to where Oswald was located. Who therefore determined the route the presidential motorcade would take, and how did that happen?

Governor John Connally was the main instigator of the presidential visit. Connally was a smooth operator who had made a career as a political subcontractor for Lyndon Baines Johnson. He had served the vice president slavishly for decades in the hope that he could move up a place in the ranking with every career leap of LBJ. Connally's nickname was also LBJ, but in his case this stood for *Lyndon's Boy John.* Nevertheless, Connally knew to appeal to the rich people in Texas, and fund raising was important for the upcoming elections. If anyone could use some reflection from the presidential charisma, it was the colorless congressman Al Thomas. Kennedy liked Thomas, but needed him primarily because he was involved in determining the NASA budgets. The president had made a political stunt out of the race to the moon, and therefore wanted to keep Thomas as a friend. And all was not hunky dory between the Democrats in Texas. Texan Democratic senator Ralph Yarborough, who, as a progressive, was no longer *on speaking terms* with the rather conservative Connally, also sat in this snake pit. The extreme right-wing General Walker, one of Connally's rivals for the Democratic nomination for the governor's post, openly aired his neo-Nazi sympathies, and Kennedy had therefore dismissed him from the army. Nevertheless, Walker received 138,000 votes[331] in the Democratic primary. This gives an indication of how conservative Democrats were in Texas in 1963. (Johnson, who, as president, would later approve the laws for equal civil rights for black Americans, thereby sighed that this would lose the South for the Democrats for fifty years. A prophetic statement. Connally saw the storm coming, and immediately became a Republican when Johnson disappeared from the scene in 1968. Yarborough was the only Southern senator who would vote for all civil rights laws from 1957 to 1970.) And then there was Earl Cabell, the mayor of Dallas, whose brother Charles was sacked by Kennedy as deputy director of the CIA.

The ideological spread within the Democratic Party was therefore embarrassingly wide. The feud between Connally and Yarborough became acute during the presidential visit in 1963. Like two small children, the Governor and the Senator refused to sit in the same car. Kennedy had to bang his fist on the table, and oblige the two fighting cocks to maintain at least the appearance of unity during his campaign tour. Kennedy also saw the visit as an opportunity to restore some unity to the Texas Democratic Party. Texas was too important in the race to win half the electoral votes. A divided party usually wins few elections. Kennedy also granted the embattled Vice President Johnson a place in the spotlight of his home state. Johnson had become depressed and bored by the political impotence entailed by the office of Vice President. He saw with sorrow that his once unassailable position in the Lone Star State was eroding, and there were also a number of serious scandals in which there was the threat of his name being mentioned. Here also, his powerlessness to intervene decisively presented him with a serious problem, and as time passed, the chances increased that the media would display the whole mess on their front pages.

Kennedy not only came to Texas to patch together the Democratic Party, he also wanted to feel the mood on the ground. He knew his charisma and the sympathy with Jackie after the loss of their premature son had the political value of gold. How far could Kennedy go with the call of the black population for equal citizenship? How far could Kennedy seek a detente in the Cold War? There was no better method to find out than to drive through Dallas in an open car. Adlai Stevenson, Kennedy's UN ambassador, had been taunted and spat at in Dallas not too long before, however, after General Walker had incited a mob. But Kennedy was not Stevenson. The President was naturally inclined to take on any challenge, and to emerge victorious from the battle. He could almost smell his second term. Kennedy had grown into his role and was more ambitious than in 1960, when it was above all the fortune and the dream of his father Joe Kennedy that had ensured Kennedy's momentum. The trip to Texas was the kickoff of a campaign that would last an entire year. Kennedy was – by his own standards – physically okay, and, as always, mentally ready for battle. He was excited, even though he knew only too well that he was not going on a picnic outing.

The presidential visit to Dallas was first mentioned in the press in late September. Connally was officially the host, and he was allowed to define the outline of the program. But he did this in consultation with Johnson. Jerry Bruno, the *advance man* of the Democratic Party who prepared the political travels of the President, had to submit the concrete agreements with the White House to Walter Jenkins, an employee of Johnson. Bruno met Connally in Dallas on October 29. The Governor quickly made it clear that he alone was in charge. The location of the lunch in Dallas led to a showdown. Connally and his followers wanted the Trade Mart, while Yarborough was in favor of the *Women's Building*. In politics, it is, of course, very important to give your followers the chance to meet the president. The Women's Building could accommodate 4,000 spectators, and would therefore be open to a much broader and more multicultural audience. Connally wanted the Trade Mart, where only 1,500 guests could attend an exclusive lunch with a price tag. The Trade Mart was also the wrong place for security reasons: above all, the large number of entrances and exits constituted a risk. On behalf of the Democratic Party and in consultation with the Secret Service at the White House, Bruno resolutely opted for the alternative, the Women's Building. From both the political and security point of view, this was the only right choice. But security in 1963 was not as all-important as it is now. A group of surprised tourists who had become lost in the corridors once stumbled into the office of Attorney General Bobby Kennedy while he was in a meeting. And even in the presidential office, the *Oval Office*, security was minimal. The President was surprised one day by a visitor who proudly showed him a Belgian machine gun. Nobody had thought it necessary to keep the man with the gun away from Kennedy.

The actual preparations for the trip started on November 12. Agent Winston Lawson from the Secret Service was sent to Dallas to prepare the visit. After a background game of political arm wrestling, the Democratic Party pushed Jerry Bruno aside and replaced him with Jack Putterbaugh. According to Lawson, Putterbaugh was responsible for the parade.[332] It was also Putterbaugh who finally recommended the Trade Mart for the lunch. In the meantime, Connally also pressured the local Secret Service into stating that they would be able to secure the building. Although not yet official on November 14, only the Trade Mart was mentioned in a report on the preparations.[333] It was clearly already final behind the scenes. Once the Trade Mart was the destination, the route passed unavoidably by Dealey Plaza, the only passage under the railway line with access to the highway interchange in the direction of the Trade Mart.

Connally cannot be suspected of leading the limousine, in which he would travel himself, into an ambush. But he could certainly have been influenced to first reduce the venues for lunch to two sites, and to then push for the Trade Mart as the final decision.

The believers assume that potential conspirators in search of a *patsy* had settled on Oswald, and no one else. In their scenario, the conspirators would have to set up Oswald on Kennedy's route, or vice versa, and that is clearly no sinecure. But their hypothesis is not accurate enough. The conspirators only had to have 'someone' on the route who could take the blame for the assassination of the president. Whether this was Oswald or some other scapegoat made no difference to them. For this wider hypothesis, it is sufficient that there were a number of candidates for Oswald's role, and that the plotters knew where they would be. The route was thereby not determined depending on where Oswald was, and Oswald was not employed in the TSBD as a result of the route. Because there is, in fact, a third possibility: Oswald was picked to cover *one* route, but if another route or even another city brought another patsy into play, the assassination could also take place somewhere else. That means that the perpetrators would have anticipated more than one potential patsy, and would patiently wait for the president to drive past one of the potential patsies under "favorable" conditions. This may seem far-fetched, but this is the Kennedy file. Never think anything is too far-fetched without examining the facts.

FOILED ASSASSINATION IN CHICAGO

Three weeks before the trip to Texas, Kennedy was supposed to visit Chicago and attend a sporting event. On Saturday, November 2, the presidential plane Air Force One was due to land at O'Hare Airport at 11.40 a.m. On Wednesday, three days before the visit, the FBI received a call from an informant code-named Lee: four snipers planned to assassinate Kennedy during his passage through Chicago.[334] In addition to this information, the local FBI received a second disturbing phone call on Thursday. A lady reported that four lodgers were staying in her rented rooms. They had four guns with a telescopic sight with them, and a map of Kennedy's route through Chicago.

What did the FBI do with these two tips? Hoover sat back. In his opinion, an attack on the president was not a federal crime and was therefore outside his jurisdiction. Guarding the president was the exclusive domain of the *Secret Service*, and that settled it for the FBI.[335] A potential communist in a troupe of amateur actors was important for Hoover, but an attempt to murder President Kennedy had nothing to do with him!

The information came to the Secret Service in the form of a rattling telex without any further commentary, and ended up on the desk of their agent Martineau in Chicago. The Secret Service had the reported lodgers of the rented room shadowed. At some point, Agent Stocks of the Secret Service was discreetly following a car in which two of the four suspects were traveling. With Stocks in their wake, they mistakenly drove into a dead-end street, and were forced to turn back. On their way back, they passed Stocks's police car, which just happened to be receiving a message over the radio at full volume. The two immediately realized that he had followed them, and tried to flee, but were arrested. The problem with this unexpected arrest was that their accomplices were still at large. As the arrested men didn't say a word, there were still possibly two heavily-armed strangers planning an attempt on the president's life. One of the suspects was allegedly Miguel Casas Saez – also known by the name of Angel Dominguez Martinez – a dangerous Cuban who knew how to handle weapons. In his work *Ultimate Sacrifice*, historian Lamar Waldron refers to a CIA document[336] according to which Saez was spotted near the presidential parade in Chicago.

On Saturday morning, at 10.15 a.m. Washington time, the presidential visit to Chicago was canceled at the last minute. The official reason was the brutal assassination of the Vietnamese President Diem. According to the press release, Kennedy remained in the White House to closely monitor the situation. That decision really was taken at the last minute; the press plane that would accompany the president to Chicago had already left. The names of the two detainees and those of their non-arrested roommates remained unknown. Martineau seized all the information his agents possessed. In violation of the usual rules, they were ordered to not create a single document about the incident. They only passed their information on verbally, and then dutifully handed over their notebooks. James Rowley, the head of the Secret Service, gave Martineau a special number for the case by phone, a COS number (*Central Office Secret*). Only Martineau wrote a report on the incident in Chicago, and he delivered it directly to Rowley. When Kennedy was assassinated three weeks later, Martineau immediately put a stop to any discussion among his agents, despite the new developments. He firmly assured them that there was no link whatsoever between the foiled assassination in Chicago and the assassination in Dallas. 'Forget 2 November in Chicago', he ordered, 'Lee Harvey Oswald was a lone gunman.'

Lamar Waldron[337] assumes that this secrecy arose on the initiative of the Kennedys themselves. A *Cuba contingency plan* was supposedly in place, a plan drawn up to prevent unforeseen incidents with a link to Cuba (such as the presence of the dangerous Cuban Miguel Casas Saez) quickly leading to diplomatic escalation. The political climate was such that any attempted attack in which a pro-Castro militant was involved could be misused, and could trigger a call for an invasion of the island. That would bring the Cubans into a state of alert, and the government would be politically obliged to take action at a moment that was not of its own choosing. The Kennedys wanted to avoid this. In the short-term, there was a secret plan on the table for Cuba. This was not the time to alert the Cubans, and even less to allow the opposition to set the timetable. This could explain the strict secrecy. The cover-up operation was working anyway.

But there was the threat of a leak after the assassination in Dallas: Special Agent Bolden of the Secret Service had seen and heard what had happened in Chicago on November 1 and 2, and was sure that this was related to what happened three weeks later in Dallas. The parallels were too obvious, and Bolden felt called upon to be a whistleblower. He tried to contact the Warren Commission on May 17, 1964, in order to inform them of the earlier attempt to assassinate Kennedy in Chicago. His 'indiscretion' turned sour on him. A few days later, his boss Martineau suddenly accused him of serious criminal offenses. Bolden was accused of having tried to sell Secret Service records to a counterfeiter. Although Bolden stated that the accusation was ridiculous, he found himself on trial on July 12, 1964, before he had even recovered from his astonishment. Judge Perry, who presided over the trial, urged the jurors to convict Bolden, but the jury found the case left a lot to be desired. There was no decision on guilt or innocence, and the trial had to be repeated. On August 12, at the second trial, a new witness appeared out of nowhere: Joseph Spagnoli, who, coincidentally, also had a pending trial with Judge Perry. He worked for the ruthless gangster Sam DeStefano, an accomplice of godfather Giancana from Chicago.[338] Through the incriminating testimony from Spagnoli, Agent Bolden was convicted this time, and ended up in jail. Spagnoli later admitted that the district attorney had forced him to lie. His incriminating statement against Bolden was perjury. Nevertheless, Bolden was never given a review of his trial. In prison, Bolden ended up in the psychiatric ward. 'You won't know who you are any more when we get through with you', threatened his guards. During his imprisonment, Bolden's family was also the target of a failed bomb attack, arson, a shot through the window and a brick through the windshield of the car. Bolden was only released after six years, in 1971. A few years later, the commotion following the Watergate scandal offered some hope for a new climate of openness and integrity. Despite his first hard collision with reality, Bolden undertook a second attempt to disclose the foiled attack in Chicago, which nobody in America knew about yet. He became the discreet informant of investigative journalist Edwin Black, who wrote for the little-read newspaper the *Chicago Independent*. The reporter had been working on this story for a while, but had come up against a wall of silence everywhere. In the hope of a major breakthrough, the journalist followed the new tracks that Bolden had showed him. What was happening in Chicago three weeks before the Kennedy assassination? Black went to work thoroughly, and ended up tracing Agent Stocks. Had this guy really messed up the surveillance of two of the four suspects in that dead-end street? Stocks apparently could not remember anything: 'I just can't remember one way or the other. You'll have to call Washington for more information.'[339] But if indeed nothing had happened, why did he not answer that question with a simple no? The enterprising journalist didn't give up, and he went on to question other secret agents, who were also curiously affected by collective amnesia. Nobody flatly denied the story, but everyone kept a low profile. 'No comment', was the most commonly heard reply.

Black then searched through the FBI files in the archives of the Warren Commission in Washington. He was amazed to find how seriously the FBI in Chicago had taken the investigation. The federal agents, who are generally praised by the believers, showed an admirable zeal in the Kennedy case. When someone stated that a homosexual from Chicago had slept with Oswald, they examined it thoroughly: 'An agent worked day and night, tracking the source of the rumor, from homosexual to homosexual, until seven persons later, he located the source, a bisexual male who claimed he agreed that he had remarked: "Wouldn't it have been nice to sleep with Oswald".'

Black also found the report of an investigation that started with a girl who had a friend who worked in a bookstore. The bookstore had a strange customer who was supposed to have explained that the Kennedy assassination was part of a plot by Martians to eradicate all world leaders. The FBI naturally also had to investigate this down to the core: the agents questioned no less than twelve people to eventually end up at a science fiction fanatic. He admitted that he had said that such a scenario would be an interesting plot for a science fiction book. Yes, the zeal of the FBI agents was admirable, yet Black could find no trace of hearings or reports related to four heavily armed men who aimed to assassinate the president, two of whom were arrested and interrogated. His investigation in Washington didn't get him any further, and he eventually wrote an article that dealt mainly with the story of his persistent quest.

Another three years later, Bolden appeared as a witness for the HSCA in 1978,[340] but he also failed to convince the parliamentary inquiry commission. There was no evidence that something special had happened in Chicago on November 2, 1963: 'The committee was unable to document the existence of the alleged assassination team. Specifically, no agent who had been assigned to Chicago confirmed any aspect of Bolden's version. One agent did state there had been a threat in Chicago during that period, but he was unable to recall details.'[341] Acute amnesia must have been a veritable epidemic in Chicago.

In his article about his investigations, Black chronicled the denials in their initial, uncoordinated phase, and a great deal could be read between the lines in these collective denials. Unfortunately, the *Chicago Independent* only had a small circulation, and disappeared from the market shortly after the article was published. As a result, the very detailed report remained largely unnoticed. It only received the attention it deserved 25 years later, but, by then, the final assessment of the HSCA that there was absolutely no evidence of four snipers and two arrests in Chicago on November 2, 1963, had already been written into the history books.

The story about the alleged foiled assassination was intriguing enough in itself, but Black found out that more disturbing things had been going on in Chicago. In the fall of 1963, Lieutenant Berkeley Moyland of the Chicago Police sat in a cafeteria on Wilson Avenue in civilian clothes. The manager, who knew him, pointed out a man who seemed to be expressing threatening language against the president. The police officer went to the table where the young man was sitting and immediately saw that the young man had severe personality problems. He also suspected that the man was armed. Moyland identified himself as a police officer and, in a fatherly manner, advised the young man, who was called Thomas Arthur Vallee, to watch his words a little in the future when he was talking about Kennedy. Lieutenant Moyland then dutifully contacted the Secret Service by telephone, who promised to take the necessary steps. Moyland soon received a return call from the Secret Service with clear instructions:[342] 'Don't write anything about it. Don't tell anything about it. Just forget about it.'[343]

As the day of Kennedy's visit to Chicago approached, the Secret Service had meanwhile already figured out that Thomas Arthur Vallee was indeed a fanatic, obsessed with the threat of a communist takeover. Vallee was a paranoid, schizophrenic loner and a gun freak – in short – someone with the perfect profile of a 'lone nut.' It seemed sensible to the Secret Service to monitor him during Kennedy's visit. Two agents from the service raided Vallee's apartment on November 1, and found an M1 rifle, a carbine and ammunition. That was enough indication for them, and they asked the Chicago police to put Vallee under surveillance around the clock, and to arrest him if necessary. Two police officers, Daniel Groth and Peter Schurla, were assigned the task.

On the morning of the presidential visit, when Vallee left in his car, Groth and Schurla unobtrusively gave chase. At 10.15 a.m., the news that the presidential trip had been canceled was announced in Washington. This means that the decision was probably taken there at around 10 a.m., or 9 a.m. Chicago time. The police officers, who until then had done nothing against the potentially dangerous Vallee, suddenly forced him to pull over his car at 9.10 a.m., claiming he had not used his signal. When they saw a hunting knife lying on the passenger seat, they arrested Vallee for the illegal possession of weapons.

He remained in custody for the rest of the day, and was only released in the evening.

No one disputes the existence of Vallee and his arrest on November 2. Like Lee Harvey Oswald, this unstable young man had the perfect profile to be passed off as a lonely, dangerous nut in the right circumstances. Besides the fact that the name Thomas Arthur Vallee has eleven letters in common with Lee Harvey Oswald, the two men shared more than that. Vallee was also a former Marine and, like Oswald, had joined the service before he reached the legal age to do so. He was also stationed at a Japanese military base, Camp Otsu, while Oswald had been stationed in Atsugi. Both bases were known for their links with the CIA. Camp Otsu housed the *Joint Technical Advisory Group*[344] in a twenty-building complex, and was, in fact, one of the main CIA bases in Asia. Because Vallee was arrested in his car, a nosy reporter from CBS News was able to inquire about the license plate (31-10RF). It turned out to be a number with a secret registration, 'reserved for the intelligence services of the United States'.[345] Agent Groth apparently also had a connection with the intelligence service. According to an investigation by Professor Daniel Stern of Northeastern Illinois University, he was probably an undercover CIA agent. Groth's colleague Schurla also appears to have been involved in intelligence work. When investigative journalist Black tracked him down years later, he had already been promoted to the powerful intelligence service of the Chicago Police. It was also Schurla who finally gave Black the much needed confirmation on the Vallee story. When he heard what Black already knew about the events on November 2, he sighed and finally said: 'Okay, if you got all that information, you've got the Vallee story. Go ahead and print it.' Black also succeeded in tracing Vallee himself later. The man was then living in abject conditions. He told Black how he had been active in the early sixties in a training camp organized by the CIA on Long Island. Cuban exiles were trained there for the revolt against Castro.

Here again, Vallee had something in common with Oswald. They were both identified in a similar camp at Lake Pontchartrain near New Orleans.[346] Vallee found a job in the printing industry with IPP Litho-Plate, while Oswald obtained a similar job at Jaggers-Chiles Stoval. Are these similarities too striking to be based only on coincidence? The address of Vallee's workplace was 625 West Jackson Boulevard, Chicago, precisely on the route of the presidential motorcade. The prominent Kennedy author James Douglas visited the spot and referred to the view from the roof of the building as 'strikingly similar to the view from the Texas School Book Depository'. In Chicago, the presidential parade also had to make a slow turn in order to drive from the Northwest Expressway onto West Jackson, and this was then followed by a slow drive past the building where Vallee was working.

The link between Vallee and the CIA was not officially recognized anywhere, of course, but his existence, his arrest in connection with a possible attack in Chicago and his perfect profile as a lone nut were. All traces of the four snipers have been erased. If Kennedy had been assassinated in Chicago, it is highly likely that the name Thomas Arthur Vallee would now be commonplace, and that the world would never have heard of Lee Harvey Oswald. There would also have been no proof of a conspiracy, or of four snipers. Only the hypothesis of the lone nut would have been supported by an abundance of evidence. The assassination of Kennedy by Thomas Arthur Vallee would then probably also have been purely a 'crime of opportunity' in Bugliosi's and Matthews's. By chance, a deranged young man had access to an open window along the presidential route. He seized his chance to make history and to finally mean something. It is a foolish, inevitable act, an unfortunate combination of circumstances. Investigator James Douglas sought out Vallee's sister in 2004. She said the following about the involvement of her brother: 'My brother probably was set up. He was very much used.'[347] Unlike Oswald, Vallee was fortunate that two informants reported the presence of four snipers independently of each other, and that the President's visit was therefore canceled. Only after that had been decided did the two officers who had closely shadowed Vallee – one of whom had CIA connections – arrest him.

JOSEPH MILTEER, PROPHET OR WINDBAG?

Joseph Milteer was an assertive white supremacist. He inherited a tidy fortune from his father and concentrated on his life's purpose: the promotion of his racist ideology. Because of this, he was in close contact with numerous radical right-wing groups in the United States. People like Milteer attract attention, and William Somersett, an undercover agent from the Miami Police, therefore kept him under observation. On November 9, two weeks before the assassination in Dallas, Somersett made a recording of a telephone conversation with the extremist. In this, Milteer boastfully announced that Kennedy would be assassinated: 'From an office building with a high-powered rifle ...

He knows he's a marked man.' Puzzled, Somersett asked: 'They are really going to try to kill him?' Milteer's answer was: 'Oh yeah, it is in the working …' The undercover agent let Milteer know that he had doubts about this: the assassination of Kennedy would shake up the whole country, and was a reckless initiative. 'We've got to know where we're at', he added. But Milteer himself was not worried about what would happen after the assassination: 'They will pick somebody up within hours afterwards, if anything like that would happen. Just to throw the public off.'[348]

According to the audio recording, Milteer made it clear on November 9 that he knew what was awaiting Kennedy. But maybe he was just daydreaming, with a bit of boasting? If you read the full transcript of the recording, the latter hypothesis seems the most likely. For example, before he mentioned that Kennedy knew he was doomed, he said that the President had fifteen doubles who took his place in dangerous situations. This cannot be a serious statement from someone who was involved in the basic facts of a political liquidation. And after he said that it was in the working, he mentioned, by name and first name, the man who, according to him, would carry out the assassination: a certain Jack Brown. Nobody has subsequently heard anything about Jack Brown, although the FBI did not actually search for him intensely – in contrast to the talkative homosexual and the ambitious SF fanatic. Milteer also didn't limit himself to the scenario of a shot from an office building. He also said that Kennedy could easily be shot from a hotel across from the White House if he went out onto the balcony on a sunny day. Milteer did make another statement, however, which may sound prophetic in retrospect. According to him, the weapon could best be brought to the location in pieces: 'Sure, disassemble a gun. You don't have to take a gun up there, you can take it up in pieces. All those guns come knock down. You can take them apart.'

If you read the whole text, the picture is rather different than just lifting the most striking passages out of context. Milteer is just a conceited idiot, a rabid, right-wing loudmouth. Yet he clearly demonstrates that it doesn't need exceptional imagination to come up with a scenario in which Kennedy is shot from an office building, and a scapegoat is then arrested to take the blame. If Milteer could invent this, there is no doubt that kindred spirits could also come up with such a scenario, and with more concrete plans. Milteer is also said to have been spotted in New Orleans with private detective Guy Banister. Banister had an office at the address that was shown on Oswald's pro-Castro pamphlets. That's strange, because Oswald was actually far-left and pro-Castro. Banister was radical right, anti-Castro, and a former FBI man with CIA connections. How did his address then get onto Oswald's pamphlets? There is no hard evidence of any contact between Milteer and Banister,[349] but they were in any case kindred spirits, so a meeting in New Orleans is not entirely inconceivable. Milteer could have heard something about an imminent attempt on Kennedy's life in this way.

FOILED ATTEMPT IN TAMPA

Kennedy was expected in Tampa, Florida, on November 18. There too, the Secret Service had heard wild rumors about a possible attack. Only after the assassination in Dallas did a very small article appear about the case in the *Tampa Tribune* on November 23, and an even smaller article in the *Miami Herald* on November 24.[350] One of these articles referred to 'a memo from the White House Secret Service dated Nov. 8 [that] reported: "Subject made statement of a plan to assassinate the President in October 1963. Subject stated he will use a gun ... Subject is described as white, male, 20, slender build, etc."'[351] This description rings a bell for us, of course.

After the modest press coverage, things became quiet about the case. The fact that we can only now find anything about it in two local newspapers does not mean that the threat was not serious. The clippings are virtually the only remaining evidence that something was going on. Years later, in its search for Kennedy documents, the ARRB found that the Secret Service, in violation of the JFK Records Act, had destroyed all the documents relating to the threat in Tampa. Only in 1996 was J.P. Mullins, head of the Tampa Police in 1963, ready to confirm the newspaper reports to author Lamar Waldron. The threat in Tampa had indeed been very serious. A rare file from the Secret Service that had not been destroyed, and that emerged in the late seventies 'made it clear that the threat on Nov. 18, 1963 was posed by a mobile, unidentified rifleman shooting from a window in a tall building with a high power rifle fitted with a scope.'[352] A parliamentary investigator confronted the Secret Service agent who had written this memo with its contents. The man claimed to suffer from 'virtually complete loss of memory'. He remembered nothing of the case, even though the text of his own memorandum had just refreshed his memory.

According to the newspaper article, the white, slender-built, 20-year-old man the police were looking for in Tampa was Gilberto Policarpo Lopez, a potentially violent individual with a Cuban-American background. Once again, Policarpo also had all the characteristics of a dangerous lone nut. He was 23, practically the same age as Oswald, and had also just left his wife. Oswald had communist sympathies, had defected to the Soviet Union and then returned. Policarpo also had communist sympathies, had defected to Cuba and had returned to the US a few years later. Just like Oswald, Policarpo was involved in the *Fair Play For Cuba Committee*. Both were involved in clashes with anti-Castro demonstrators as a result of the pamphlets they handed out. They had also both appeared in the local newspapers after the incident, so that there was ready proof of their extremism and tendency towards rowdiness. Both Oswald and Policarpo happily announced that they were communists at a time when communism was loathed in the USA. But neither of them was a member of a communist party, or was part of an organization with a communist nature. Both men tried to go to Cuba via Mexico City in the fall of 1963. They both apparently had contacts with one of the national intelligence services, and these organizations kept an eye on their day-to-day activities. According to Waldron, Policarpo also had 'a job in the vicinity of an upcoming JFK motorcade'.[353] Once again, no one remembered anything, and the files were destroyed through an oversight.

We therefore know little or nothing about Policarpo. Why was he suspected of plotting an attack on the President? Were the similarities with Oswald so striking that all data about him had to be thoroughly erased, both in recollections and in the files? The presidential parade in Tampa drove past the Floridan Hotel, a building that, according to Police Chief Mullins, could not be secured from a safety point of view. It was the highest building in Tampa, with lots of open windows as the President passed by. Even more important was that the building looked out over a point where the presidential motorcade would have to make a sharp left turn. For safety reasons, the motorcade had to slow down to an unacceptably low speed there. Kennedy, who was a fatalist in such matters, refused to be intimidated by the threat. He considered the risk of an attempt on his life to be part of his job as president. After not showing up in Chicago, he couldn't cancel a visit yet again at the last moment. A soldier always runs the risk of a bullet, so why should Kennedy, as commander-in-chief, try to evade it?

Kennedy was lucky on November 18. There was no attempt on his life in Tampa. Yet something was clearly seriously wrong. The indiscreet ramblings of Milteer had perhaps – very temporarily – saved Kennedy's life. Security measures were tightened after the intercepted phone call, and additional precautions were taken. According to Police Chief Mullins, Policarpo – like Vallee in Chicago – was kept under lock and key for the duration of the presidential visit. It is perhaps for this reason that the conspirators decided to call off the attack in Tampa. Also Gilberto Policarpo Lopez would therefore not go down in the history books as Kennedy's assassin. According to the CIA, however, another illustrious figure was on the loose in Tampa: the dangerous Cuban Miguel Casas Saez.

The fact that the police in Tampa had not received any information about what had happened shortly before in Chicago is also worth a mention. Police Chief Mullins certainly supplied the FBI with all the information about what had happened in Tampa. Up to now, however, these documents have not yet surfaced in the FBI files. But even worse was the fact that the Dallas police also did not receive any information on the recent incidents in Chicago and Tampa, with the all too familiar consequences.

MIGUEL CASAS SAEZ

As far as the FBI and the Secret Service were concerned, Chicago, Tampa and Dallas were three completely separate events, and Vallee, Policarpo and Oswald were completely unrelated. We are leaving a fourth person, Richard Case Nagell, aside due to some credibility problems.[354] But we can link all three – Vallee, Policarpo and Oswald – to a plan to assassinate Kennedy. The three plans had the same modus operandi: a shot out of a window as the presidential limousine was passing by at low speed. The three incidents occurred within a span of three weeks.

There are enough similarities between the three cases to be able to claim with reasonable certainty that they were part of one common plan. We have already mentioned that Miguel Casas Saez turned up near the presidential route, both in Chicago and in Tampa. The 23-year-old, dangerous Cuban also appeared in Dallas. His aunt told a CIA informant that 'Miguelito' left Dallas in the direction of Mexico immediately after the assassination, and went to Cuba from there.[355] He had this in common with Policarpo Lopez, who also left for Mexico on November 22.[356] The CIA informant also added that Saez 'had firing practice and capable of doing anything'. Anthony Summers believes that this is a curious detail. Because, on September 25 or 26, three strangers called on Silvia Odio, a young woman of Cuban descent. One of the three was called 'Leon' and, after the assassination, Silvia identified him as Oswald. During a phone conversation on the day after the strange visit, Silvia heard that this 'Leon' was an ex-Marine. He was also 'a good shot and capable of doing anything.' That's as good as the same wording used in the CIA report on Saez, as if the same script was used for both. According to another informant, Saez was 'a militiaman from the worst type'. The CIA investigated the case further, and heard through the grapevine[357] that Saez was always penniless, until he disappeared a few weeks before the Kennedy assassination. On his return, he was well dressed, had lots of money and was wearing American jackets and shoes. To complete the picture, Saez was also learning Russian. It looks very much as though Saez was the selected Cuban who had been groomed for taking the blame if Vallee, Policarpo or Oswald no longer qualified for the role of scapegoat.

A CRIME OF OPPORTUNITY?

Was Oswald an opportunity killer? An opportunity killer is someone who does not shrink from committing murder under certain circumstances, or if a special opportunity occurs. The number of potential opportunist assassins among us is fortunately limited, as is the chance of the president happening to drive by your window in an open car. The combination of the two elements is extremely rare.

In this chapter, we nevertheless came across four people who met this exceptional double condition: over a period of three weeks, the president drove in an open car past three lone nuts at a speed that was much too slow to be safe. In addition, a dangerous Cuban also popped up at each of these locations. Is this statistically possible, or did these four eccentrics fit into a broader plan aimed at assassinating Kennedy?

The employment of Oswald in the book depository on October 15 does not necessarily exclude the assumption that he was already involved in a conspiracy in October. It is enough to accept that the range of action of the conspirators was larger than Dallas, and that they had made a number of provisions at different times and locations in order to be able to strike as soon as conditions turned out favorably. If the attack was called off, all the evidence would disappear. If the operation succeeded, however, the evidence would also disappear, except for the traces that led to the one scapegoat. It was not by chance that Oswald ended up in a favorable position to shoot Kennedy, it only *seems* to be a coincidence. Believers assume that it made no sense to maneuver Oswald into the book depository before the Trade Mart was selected as the definite lunch location. But the location of the lunch is but one of the many risks. It could also have rained cats and dogs in Dallas on November 22. A Plexiglas roof would then have been fitted to Kennedy's limousine, and Oswald would probably have remained unknown – like Policarpo, Vallee and Saez. The unavoidable risks (rain, moving the lunch to a different location, etc.) were reduced by increasing the number of opportunities. It is then enough that the conditions turned favorable only once. Things went wrong in Chicago and Tampa, but the sun shone in Dallas and, as expected, the Trade Mart was the destination of the motorcade.

FILE 2

THE MURDER OF J.D. TIPPIT

Chapter 5 – Death of a police officer

It is of the highest importance in the art of detection to be able to recognize, out of a number of facts, which are incidental and which vital.

Sherlock Holmes in Arthur Conan Doyle's
The Adventure of the Reigate Squires

Less than three quarters of an hour after the assassination of the President, Police Officer Tippit was brutally gunned down in a suburb of Dallas. The suspect was once again Oswald, who, after General Walker and President Kennedy, thereby purportedly committed a third assassination attempt. His alleged guilt in the murder of Tippit often serves as a stepping stone to the evidence of his involvement in the Kennedy assassination. Who else but a fleeing felon would shoot a cop? Assistant Counsel Belin of the Warren Commission even called the murder of Officer Tippit the 'Rosetta Stone' for solving the assassination of Kennedy. On this 2,200-year-old granite stone, the same text is written in three different ways: once in Greek and twice in Egyptian, in both the demotic script and in hieroglyphics. This provided the golden key to the deciphering of the mysterious hieroglyphs. Writings that had remained incomprehensible for thousands of years suddenly became readable. The reference to the Rosetta Stone is a cliché in the Kennedy mystery, but it is not the only echo of Dealey Plaza in the Tippit murder investigation.

THE TIME OF THE MURDER

The most important, recurring phenomenon is the problem of getting Oswald to the crime scene. Officer Tippit was murdered on 10th Street, 1,320 meters away from the rented room where Oswald was last seen around 1.00 p.m. Tippit's murder took place at 1.14 p.m. at the latest.[358] We know this because a witness contacted police headquarters at 1.16 p.m. using the car radio of the murdered policeman.[359] The murder took place a few minutes earlier. The man who informed police headquarters was T.F. Bowley. He was not a direct witness of the attack, but had driven his car down the street immediately afterwards. Bowley saw the stationary police car and the motionless officer lying in a pool of blood on the asphalt. The perpetrator was already out of sight by that time, and other witnesses were already on the spot.[360] So at least thirty seconds would already have passed since the attack. Bowley parked his car and initially looked after the victim, the heavily bleeding Officer Tippit. Meanwhile, another witness, Domingo Benavides, unsuccessfully attempted to inform the police headquarters with Tippit's patrol car radio. Bowley saw that the officer was beyond any further help, took the microphone over from Benavides and successfully sent a message. This message arrived at 1.16 p.m. But how much time had passed at this point since the shots were fired? This is an important question. With every extra second, the presence of Oswald at the crime scene becomes more problematic. The actions of Bowley, from the moment he drove into the street until he took over the microphone, must have taken at least two minutes to complete. The murder had therefore already happened at 1.14 p.m. at the latest. But there is a problem with the lower limit of the timing. Bowley was a solid witness, and had instinctively looked at his watch when he realized that something was seriously wrong. According to him, the time was then 1.10 p.m. If that is true, and the murder happened immediately before, Tippit was not killed at 1.14 p.m., but around 1.09 p.m. That is very important, because, in this case, Oswald would not have had enough time to walk to the crime scene from his rented room.

Was T.F. Bowley really at the crime scene at 1.10 p.m.? Bowley's timeline starts with a fixed point. He had picked up his daughter from her school in Singing Hills at 12.55 p.m. They drove together along Marsalis Avenue and 10th Street to the place where Bowley would pick up his wife from her work. According to the route description of Google Maps, the drive from Singing Hills to 10th Street East is almost 11 kilometers long, and takes 12 to 13 minutes. Taking into account a few minutes to pick up his daughter, it is therefore logistically possible that Bowley drove into 10th Street at 1.10 p.m., but 1.15 p.m. is just as well possible.

We need to determine the exact time of the murder more accurately. Another witness might be able to help us here. Helen Markham was a waitress in the Eat Well restaurant. In her own words, she left her home on 9th Street shortly after 1.00 p.m. and walked to the bus stop via Patton Avenue, where she wanted to get on the 1.15 p.m. bus that would take her to work. In my investigation on site, I found that the construction of new school grounds and the removal of a street had changed the situation compared to 1963, but it can still be reconstructed sufficiently. The distance from Helen's house, at number 328, 9th Street, to the bus stop is exactly 300 meters. She crossed 10th Street, the crime scene, about halfway along that route. She stopped at that intersection to let traffic pass. A man was walking on the other side of the street, from right to left, seen from where she was standing. A police car then drove into the intersection. The car slowed down and followed the walking man at a snail's pace. They stopped a little farther on. The police officer may have called out something, but, if so, Helen had not heard it. The unknown man walked slowly towards the car. He leaned into the open window of the door on the passenger side and had a conversation with the police officer. Nothing pointed to an abnormal situation, according to Helen Markham. After a while, the man stood upright again and calmly took two steps back. The police officer also showed no sign of panic whatsoever. 'The policeman calmly opened the car door and I still just thought, a friendly conversation,'[361] Markham recalled. The policeman stepped out of the car. 'He was just calmly walking to the front of the car' and then it happened. '... when he got even with the wheel on the driver's side, front you know, that man shot him.'[362]

Figure 39. The crime scene on 10th Street[363]

What can we learn from this about the time of the murder? Markham stated that she left her home 'a little after one'. She lived on 9th Street, about 30 meters from the corner of Patton Avenue. There she turned right, onto Patton Avenue. The distance between the corner of 9th and the corner of 10th Street is 130 meters. When she saw the unknown man, Helen had therefore already covered a distance of 160 meters, and was still 140 meters from the bus stop. At four kilometers an hour, she could cover the 300 meters from her house to the bus stop in about 4.5 minutes. If she didn't want to miss her bus, she should have left her home at the latest between 1.08 and 1.09 p.m. That gave her about two minutes extra, and was more or less 'a little after one'. At four kilometers an hour, she covered the 160 meters to the corner of the crime scene on 10th Street in about 2.5 minutes. According to this hypothesis, she reached the place from where she could see the unknown man and the police car at around 1.11 p.m. The murder happened shortly afterwards. How much afterwards? In her statement before the Commission, Helen Markham repeatedly mentioned a period of 'a few minutes'. That is certainly an overestimate. If we reasonably estimate the duration of the scene from the intersection to the shot at one minute, the murder took place at 1.12 p.m., at least if Helen left her home between 1.08 and 1.09 p.m. Could she have left home later than 1.09 p.m.? This seems unlikely. Helen's demeanor at the intersection of Patton Avenue and 10th Street was very relaxed. She unhurriedly watched the interaction between the unknown man and the police officer. She still believed at that time that it was a 'friendly conversation'. Why would she risk missing the bus to work for the sake of a trivial encounter between a policeman and a civilian? Helen therefore apparently still had plenty of time if she continued to watch the whole encounter. She had to walk another 140 meters to the bus stop, and therefore still needed more than two minutes to catch the 1.15 p.m. bus. Consequently, the encounter between the unknown man and Tippit must have taken place around 1.12 p.m. at the latest. This also corresponds with other data. Helen could then have left her home at 1.09 p.m., still just about 'a little after one'. T.F. Bowley, who drove into the street at 1.13 p.m., could just about see this as ten past one from a quick glance at his watch. When Bowley parked his car and got out, he still had 2.5 minutes before he established the connection to the police station. According to our analysis, Tippit was murdered between 1.12 and 1.13 p.m.

OSWALD AT THE CRIME SCENE

Given the fact that the perpetrator had a conversation with the police officer first, he must have been at the crime scene at around 1.12 p.m. at the very latest. Was this feasible for Oswald after the assassination on Dealey Plaza?

The first shot from the sniper's nest occurred forty seconds after 12.30 p.m.[364] Oswald encountered Police Officer Baker in the lunchroom on the second floor ninety seconds later. Oswald could have been on the sidewalk in front of the book depository at the earliest one minute later. He then walked seven blocks to the east, to the bus stop at the intersection between Murphy and Elm Street. During the investigation, the FBI took an average of 6.5 minutes for this distance.[365] Oswald then caught a regular-service bus, but that moved too slowly for him. Due to the chaos on Dealey Plaza, the bus had hardly traveled two blocks in four minutes. Oswald got off the bus at the intersection of Poydras and Elm Street. He then went to the northwest corner of the intersection of Lamar with Jackson Street. The FBI estimated this at three minutes. Oswald then stepped into a taxi for a ride to his rented room across the wide Trinity River. He sat next to the driver. A middle-aged lady also wanted to get in at the same time. She had presumably not seen that the taxi was no longer free because Oswald was sitting in front. There was a brief conversation and Oswald even offered the taxi to the lady.[366] When the lady turned down the friendly offer, the taxi drove off. We should allow at least an additional thirty seconds for this interaction. According to his statement to the Warren Commission, the taxi driver encountered hardly any hindrance from the traffic chaos after the assassination. Oswald preferred not to get out at the address of his rented room, and let the taxi driver drive 580 meters beyond his actual destination. Only then did he dare to get out. According to the initial tests by the FBI, the taxi ride would have taken on average between 7 and 8.5 minutes, depending on the predetermined maximum speed and the number of red traffic lights.[367] But the FBI apparently drove a little too far. The taxi driver had noted the address that Oswald had given him on his driving sheet: North Beckley 500. But, before they reached that point, Oswald said: 'This'll do fine right here' The taxi driver stopped 7 meters in front of the intersection with Neely Street. This point is 580 meters past Oswald's rented room. In the second reconstruction, the FBI did take the place where Oswald had actually got out of the taxi into account. They also stopped at every traffic light that had gone to red during the ride on November 22.[368] Commission Counselor Belin and taxi driver Whaley agreed that, under those conditions, the taxi ride took 5 to 6 minutes.[369] Because Oswald had deliberately made the taxi drive too far, he had to walk all the way back to his room. FBI agent Barrett required 6 minutes for this route in the reconstruction. That timing is broadly in line with the statement by Commission Counselor Belin, who covered the distance in 5 minutes and 45 seconds according to a stopwatch.[370]

According to the official calculation,[371] Oswald entered his rented room therefore shortly before 1 p.m. at the earliest.

Oswald's actions	Duration	Time
Last shot on Dealey Plaza		12:30:40
Meeting with Officer Baker	1:30 min	12:32:10
Oswald leaves the TSBD	1:00 min	12:33:10
7 blocks to bus stop on Murphy Street	6:30 min	12:39:40
Bus drives 2 blocks to Poydras in heavy traffic	4:00 min	12:43:40
By foot to taxi-stand NW-corner Lamar and Jackson	3:00 min	12:46:40
Getting in and conversation with lady and taxi driver	0:30 min	12:47:10
Taxi drives 2.6 miles to 500 block of North Bleckley Ave.	5:30 min	12:52:40
Arrival at rooming house N-Beckley	5:45 min	**12:58:25**

This timing generally agrees with the statement of Oswald's landlady, Mrs. Earlene Roberts. She placed his arrival at 'around 1 o'clock, or maybe a little after'.[372] Oswald arrived just before one o'clock, but we can say that he was in the building at the time specified by the landlady. In his room, Oswald quickly changed his pants and, according to his own account, also his shirt. He also put a gray jacket on, which he zipped up. He then put his pistol in his pocket and hurriedly left the room. 'You sure are in a hurry', said his surprised landlady, but Oswald did not respond, and left. How long was Oswald in the building? According to Mrs. Roberts 'maybe not over 3 or 4 minutes – just long enough, I guess.' Three or four minutes seems a lot for someone who was in a rush. A minimum estimate of two minutes seems acceptable for the whole visit to the rented room.

Oswald then waited a while at the bus stop outside the house. Had he taken the bus, he would actually have returned towards Dealey Plaza. But he apparently changed his mind, and quickly left in the opposite direction on foot. The delay at the bus stop took at least thirty seconds. It was therefore around 1.01 p.m. when Oswald started his walk to the crime scene. The distance from the rented room to the scene of Tippit's murder is 1,320 meters. When the FBI walked the route, the officers took 12 minutes at the first attempt. In the second attempt, 'at a brisk pace', FBI agent Barrett covered the distance in 10 minutes. Based on my personal experience locally, 10 minutes to me seems very tight. In the Discovery Channel documentary *Unsolved History*, historian David Perry put this to the test with Gary Mack, once a critic of the Warren Commission, but who converted to become a believer after his appointment as manager of the 6th Floor Museum. We can therefore assume that Mack was looking for the minimum time necessary. The reconstruction of the walking test from North Beckley 1026 to the crime scene at 10th Street was clocked off in *Unsolved History* at 11 minutes and 10 seconds.[373] If we take that timing into consideration, Oswald was at the crime scene 5 seconds after 1.12 p.m.

Oswald's actions	**Duration**	**Time**
Arrival at rooming house N-Beckley 1026		**12:58:25**
Changing clothes and pocketing gun	2:00 min	13:00:25
Waiting for bus in front of rooming house	0:30 min	13:00:55
1,320 meters to crime scene "at brisk pace"	11:10 min	**13:12:05**

Here again, it's just about possibility. Oswald could have reached the crime scene within one minute of the time of the murder. Once more, it all comes down to a second.

We can summarize the timeline as follows:

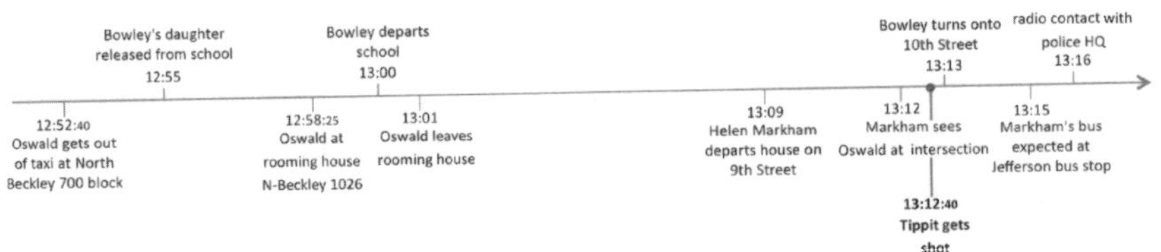

It's not impossible, but the timeline is so tight that the conspiracists could easily also argue the opposite. Note, for example, that the Commission and the FBI did not include any time at all for intermediate occurrences in their timing. For example, a journalist who was looking for a phone spoke to Oswald on the doorstep of the book depository. The FBI did not allow for the time this cost. And when Oswald left the bus after only two blocks, he asked the bus driver for a transfer ticket for later use. This also took additional time. Did the FBI measurement of the taxi ride also take account of the time Oswald needed to settle his bill and get out? Oswald allegedly also urinated on his way to the crime scene. We can no longer ascertain whether that is true, but the FBI walking test certainly did not consider any loss of time. Why would Oswald have hurried? He had no interest in standing out, that much is sure. The direction in which Oswald proceeded on 10th Street also poses a problem. According to witness Jimmy Burt, the killer walked from east to west on 10th Street. In that version, the police car therefore drove towards the perpetrator. In Barrett's reconstruction, Oswald was walking to the east when Tippit's police car overtook him – which corresponds with the statement of Helen Markham. But what if Markham was mistaken, and Burt was right? Dale Myers assumes that the hypothesis in which Oswald walked from the east to meet the police car would require at least an extra 90 seconds.[374] This time is simply not available.

A thorough analysis quickly reveals that the data was adjusted to the detriment of Oswald in the official investigation. In the initial reconstruction, the taxi ride took 7 to 8.5 minutes and the journey on foot to the crime scene took 12 minutes. This ultimately became 5 to 6 minutes for the taxi ride, and 10 minutes for the walk. The taxi ride actually became shorter because a material error had been put right. The error itself is a fact. The address in the 500 block of North Beckley was noted in the driving sheet of the taxi driver. But Oswald got out of the taxi slightly earlier. There is something fundamentally wrong with the calculation, however. The ride in the second reconstruction was only 155 meters shorter than the original route.[375] Yet this reduced the taxi trip by 1.5 to 3 minutes ... was the taxi suddenly driving at between 3 and 6 kilometers an hour along the broad Beckley Avenue? According to the taxi driver, the traffic was normal. The average speed over the three attempts carried out by the FBI was 33.7 kilometers an hour.[376] The shortening of the trip by 155 meters could therefore only save approximately 20 seconds, in comparison with the original FBI measurement of 7 to 8.5 minutes. Oswald would then have walked along North Beckley Avenue faster than the taxi could drive. In order to shorten the walk from the rented room to the crime scene, Oswald's speed was increased significantly. At the start of the investigation, FBI agent Barrett covered the distance in 12 minutes at a normal speed. When it appeared that Oswald could not have arrived at the scene of the murder in time, a 'brisk pace' was suddenly needed. And so, 12 minutes became 10 minutes, as if by magic. I'm not claiming that Oswald did not walk briskly, but, it is clear that the FBI changed the parameters during the proceedings to what suited them better.

But, ultimately, on the basis of the analysis and the investigation on the spot, it is possible that Oswald could just have reached the crime scene before Officer Tippit's murder took place.

THE SHELLS

There was a big problem in the sniper's nest with the identification of the shell cases found and the markings made on them.[377] The Tippit case is no different. Shortly after the police had started the inspection of the scene, witness Benavides handed over two shells he had found to Officers Barnes and Poe. Both officers claim they scratched their initials on the shells. But there was subsequently nothing to be seen. When asked by the Commission to identify the shells, Barnes indicated Q74 and Q75.[378] His colleague Poe believed that he had added shells Q77 and Q75 to the evidence.[379] The officers therefore only agreed about Q75. The Warren Commission then summoned Barnes again in order to clarify the disagreement. He now pointed to shells Q74 and Q77 as the shells that he had marked... [380] Q75, the only shell about which the officers had agreed, was now left out. Instead of solving the problem, the manipulation once more only made it worse. Fortunately for the Warren Commission, both the 16-year-old Barbara Davis and her sister-in-law each found a shell in their front yard a few hours after the murder. It's a riddle why the shells were not found immediately. The perpetrator had reloaded his weapon during his flight, and the witnesses had seen where he had thrown the empty shells. How difficult was it to examine this location afterwards? Half of the witnesses had heard three shots, while some heard more. So there was good reason to continue the investigation of the crime scene after only two shells were discovered. Nevertheless, the evidence chain for the third and fourth shells is fairly intact. But then a new problem popped up. Two of the four shells were found to be of the Winchester brand, while the other two had the brand name Remington. But three Winchester bullets and only one Remington bullet had been found in the body of the unfortunate police officer. The bullets therefore did not match the shells.

FINGERPRINTS

The timing and the shells are not the only similarities in the problems with the evidence for the attack on Dealey Plaza and for the murder of Officer Tippit. If we go down the list, we come to the fingerprints. There were no fingerprints from Oswald on Tippit's patrol car. The killer, however, leaned against the door on the passenger side in order to have a conversation with the officer through the open window. According to witness Jimmy Burt, he thereby placed his hands on the body of the vehicle.[381] There were fingerprints at this place, but they were not Oswald's.

LINKING THE BULLETS TO THE GUN

A murder that has been carried out with a revolver can usually be easily resolved if the suspect has the weapon. The investigation then only has to link the bullets in the victim to the suspect's weapon, to the exclusion of all other guns. Oswald had a pistol with him when he was arrested. But Oswald's .38 pistol had been modified to fire .38 Special bullets, which are slightly smaller than the standard .38 bullets. Consequently, according to weapon expert Cunningham, there was no certainty that the bullets in the victim came from Oswald's weapon.[382] His colleague Nicol was willing to go a little further, and ascribe one of the four bullets to Oswald's gun. But the fact remains that the most obvious evidence of Oswald's guilt or innocence is beyond our reach due to misfortune.

INVISIBILITY

Another recurring phenomenon is Oswald's special gift of becoming invisible. From the place where he left the taxi to his rented room, and from there up to the crime scene, he walked at least two kilometers on foot, but nobody noticed him at all. Lots of people were obviously sitting glued to their television sets waiting for more news about the fate of the president. Oddly enough, there were suddenly at least 26 witnesses once Oswald appeared close to the crime scene.[383] The shots would, of course, have attracted attention. But obviously not everyone was sitting in front of a television set that Friday afternoon at around 1.00 p.m., yet nobody noticed Oswald between the moment when he left the taxi, at 12.53, and the time immediately before the murder, 1.12.

Why in heaven's name did Tippit stop a pedestrian who wasn't breaking any law at that time? The Warren Commission did not literally say that Tippit considered the man to be a suspect in the Kennedy assassination. It simply stated that Oswald matched the description of the suspect.[384] That description read as follows at 12.43 on Channel 2 of the police radio: 'slender white man of about thirty, 1,78 meters, 75 kilogram'.[385] There was no mention about the clothing of the suspect. 'That is all we have,' added dispatcher Murray Jackson to the concise physical description. The report was based on information that Inspector Herbert Sawyer had received about a white man who was neither old nor young.[386] Sawyer referred to a witness 'who claimed to have seen the barrel of the rifle on the fifth or sixth floor of the building and claimed to have been able to see the man.' This was probably Brennan, the man who was sitting on the low wall in front of the book depository and looked up. In his first statement, Brennan indeed reported a nice looking, slender, white man in his early thirties and weighing about 75 to 80 kilograms.[387] But he also said: 'I could see this man from about his belt up.' How did the police know how tall the suspect was? It's also strange that the anonymous informant gave no description of the clothing, while Brennan – remember his confusion regarding the brown shirt – claimed to have seen that the suspect was wearing a light-colored to khaki shirt and pants of a similar color. When he met Tippit, Oswald was wearing black pants and a dark brown shirt.

Whatever the origin of the description, Officer Tippit must certainly have heard the vague description, because it was repeated no less than five times via the radio communication. Oswald was 24 and weighed 68 kilograms.[388] That is six years and seven kilograms too few, but, on the whole, Oswald more or less fit the 'general' description in the report – just like thousands of other men in Dallas. Did Tippit speak to the man as a result of the vague description? Why would Tippit assume that the president's assassin would be quietly walking around in the residential suburb of Oak Cliff ? In retrospect, we can think of one reason: Oswald rented a room near 10th Street, and David Belin pointed out that 10th Street is located four blocks from a stop for a Route 55 bus. With this bus, Oswald could travel to Lancaster Road, where he could have caught a Greyhound bus to Monterrey in Mexico with his very last 17 dollars. This does not sound illogical, but Belin pondered over this for a year, and it's therefore difficult to believe that Tippit figured this out within half an hour, and he could not have known that Oswald was the suspect and where he lived. He had, in fact, every reason to assume that the killer of the president would not boldly amble along 10th Street on foot. And even if he had assumed this, what was his plan? To politely ask every man who answered the vague description whether he was Kennedy's assassin? The only way in which Tippit could have recognized an arbitrary male pedestrian as the suspect from the radio message would be a flash of clairvoyance. The official version of the assassination of Kennedy resorts more than once to paranormal phenomena to explain a bold twist in the story, and that is also the case in the murder of Tippit.

DEMATERIALIZATION OR TELEKINESIS?

Evidence that appears and disappears, or inexplicably pops up at a place other than where it should be according to the laws of physics, is a normal phenomenon in the Kennedy assassination case. In the Tippit investigation, Oswald's wallet was an early and very incriminating piece of evidence of his guilt, because, for unexplained reasons, the wallet contained false identity papers in the name of Hidell. The murder weapon was bought under this name. Yet again, the wallet is the subject of a surrealistic controversy. In a news clip from WFAA,[389] we can see how three policemen hold a wallet at the scene of Tippit's murder. This happened before Oswald was arrested in a cinema a bit farther on. According to the WFAA reporter, this was Tippit's wallet, but that is incorrect. The police immediately knew the identity and the address of the murdered officer and therefore didn't need to check Tippit's identity papers. Tippit's wallet was only removed from his trouser pocket at the hospital.[390] Moreover, Tippit's wallet was black, and the found wallet was brown.[391] In his book, Agent Hosty wrote that it was Oswald's wallet.[392] But according to the official story, Oswald had his wallet with him when he was arrested in the cinema. How could Oswald's wallet then be found in the pool of Tippit's blood? The question is whether this was actually Oswald's wallet. The similarities between Oswald's wallet and the one that we see in the news clip are striking. Dale Myers published the photos of both wallets in his book *With Malice*.[393] According to him, it is not Oswald's wallet, despite the striking similarities. For example, he sees a slight difference in the rounded corners of the front edge of Oswald's wallet and the more rectangular edges of the wallet that was found at the crime scene.

Figure 40. Left: Oswald's wallet, right: the wallet at the crime scene.

Myers is convinced that he is right. He undoubtedly has a point when he says that 'Anyone with a brain knows that if Oswald's wallet had been found at the crime scene it would have been printed in every newspaper and broadcast on every radio and television station in America before the end of the day, Friday, November 22, 1963.' But if the wallet was neither Tippit's nor Oswald's, whose was it then? And where was this evidence later? Nobody knows.[394] And why was this second wallet completely ignored later? This piece of evidence does not appear in the inventory of the evidence, and everyone who had had the wallet in their hands remained as silent as the grave. The existence of the second wallet only came to light through the old news clip.

Was Oswald's wallet found in 10th Street? It was, according to FBI agent Barrett, because he said that, following the discovery of the wallet, Captain Westbrook asked him at the crime scene whether he knew a certain Oswald or Hidell.[395] Barrett also claimed that a witness had seen how Oswald had handed over something to Tippit through the window of the police car. It seems not illogical that the officer asked the unknown man for his papers, and found that the wallet contained two different identity papers. Tippit then stepped out of the car in order to investigate the matter further. Another witness confirms that the police knew Oswald's name before the arrest. On February 28, 1964, cinema cashier Julia Postal stated to the FBI that 'the officers arresting Oswald had identified him, Oswald, to her by calling his name.'[396] When the Commission questioned the cashier four weeks later, on April 2, she said the opposite: 'When I said 'Oswald', [I meant] that man, because I didn't know who he was at that time ....'[397] Her correction of her statement was not very subtle. The discovery of the wallet disappeared from the case, and any knowledge of Oswald's identity disappeared with it. Only years later, when the old news clip emerged, was the second wallet discussed again. What was the Commission trying so hard to hide?

Let's examine the evidence chain of the second wallet. It begins once again completely anonymously. Officer Kenneth Croy was given the wallet at the crime scene by an 'unknown person'. In turn, Croy handed it over to Sergeant Calvin Owens.[398] Ultimately, the evidence ended up with Captain 'Pinky' Westbrook. Westbrook is one of the men standing around the wallet in the news film. He was normally responsible for internal police investigations. The captain was therefore aware of the weaknesses of each of his officers.[399] Westbrook was present at two relevant scenes: both on 10th Street and at the arrest of Oswald in the Texas Theater cinema. In the meantime, the first wallet had disappeared from the face of the earth, and from the memories of all the officers.

Let's therefore examine the evidence chain of the other wallet. Officer Paul Bentley pulled Oswald's official wallet from his back pocket while he was being brought to the police station.[400] He is also one of the officers who claimed that Oswald was about to shoot at the police during his arrest.[401] Luckily, someone managed to insert their thumb between the hammer and the firing pin, and the weapon didn't fire. It was a close thing, because the bullet 'was already hit by the firing pin, but not enough to go off.' After an examination of the weapon, firearms expert Eisenberg rejected this, based on technical reasons: 'We found nothing that would indicate that the firing pin of this weapon had touched the ignition charge of one of these bullets.'[402] Bentley had therefore invented an important element in the early public condemnation of Oswald or had at least exaggerated. But precisely this officer is the first step in the evidence chain of the wallet in Oswald's back pocket. Was Bentley speaking the truth?

FBI agent Barrett denied this during the ABC *News Story* program on the fiftieth anniversary of the assassination: 'They said that they took the wallet out of his pocket in the car? What hogwash! [Captain] Westbrook held the wallet in his hand.' It's always advisable to be cautious with statements that only emerge after half a century, but this belated statement from Barrett is actually the only one that respects the laws of nature, and I'm therefore more inclined to believe it. Let's try to soberly set the record straight: 1) Oswald obviously didn't have two identical wallets with him; 2) a wallet with certain characteristics was in the hands of Westbrook in 10th Street; 3) Westbrook moved from 10th Street to the cinema for the arrest of Oswald; 4) during the arrest, a wallet appeared with the identical characteristics; 5) there was no longer any trace of the first wallet. In the real world, this means that Westbrook only added the wallet that was found on 10th Street to the evidence material after the arrest. But why is it better that the wallet was found on Oswald's possession? Dale Myers is right to say the discovery of the wallet in 10th Street was sure to be trumpeted around because it was so incriminating for Oswald. But perhaps, for some reason or other, the wallet in Oswald's back pocket was even more incriminating. Let's keep this in the back of our minds.

Logic dictates that we must assume that there is only one wallet. But according to Dale Myers, there were certainly two wallets. His whole book is a campaign to declare Oswald guilty of the murder of Tippit. If Oswald's wallet was found at the crime scene, Myers would certainly have confirmed this. But he remains convinced that there are small differences between the two wallets. We can also follow the inevitable consequence of that assertion. If there were indeed two different wallets, both with papers of Oswald and Hidell, then there is a false Oswald wallet in circulation. That would, of course, upset the whole story of the lone nut. It is strange enough that the lone nut Oswald would have a wallet with the Hidell ID with him. Two identical wallets is completely crazy. FBI agent Barrett and cashier Postal must have been mistaken when they claimed that the name Oswald was mentioned even before his arrest. The wallet is then just any lost wallet. But then why does everyone seem to suffer from collective amnesia about the innocent finding of a wallet? And where is that wallet? And what a coincidence that the wallet so closely resembles Oswald's wallet ...

The following chart can help us to determine what the most probable hypothesis is:

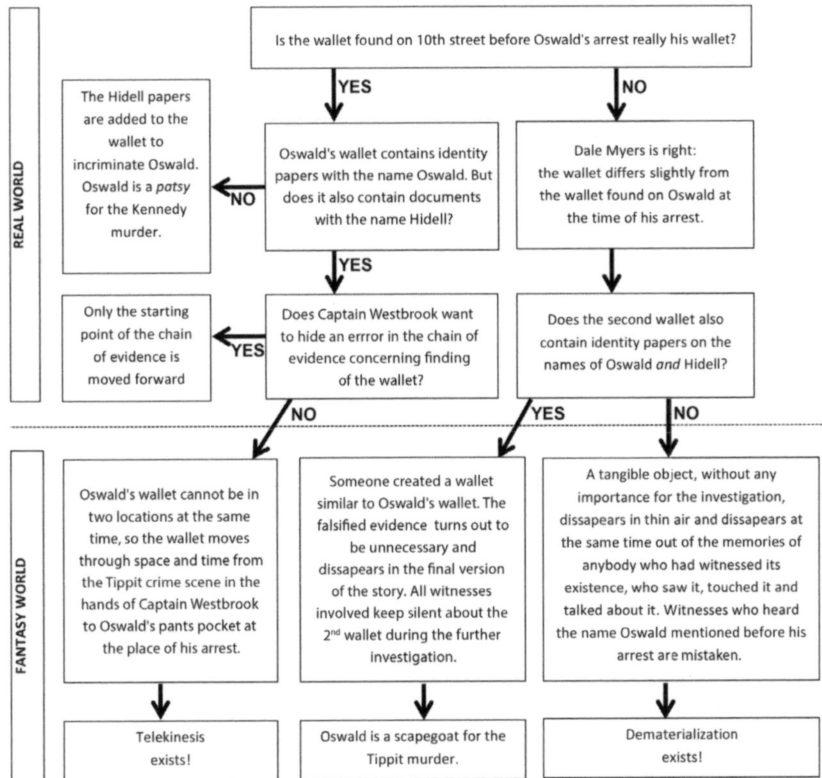

There are only three possibilities within the known laws of physics:

1. Oswald voluntarily handed over his entire wallet to Tippit. (Why did he not just hand over his identification as Oswald?) The wallet did contain both Oswald's and Hidell's papers. (Why would Oswald carry the incriminating Hidell papers with him?) After the murder, Oswald forgot to take the evidence with him. (Why would Oswald not do that?) The wallet later ended up with Captain Westbrook, who had already had the evidence with him for some time, in the cinema. Oswald's pants pocket seemed to be a better idea as a new starting point of the chain of evidence. (Why would Westbrook think that?)
2. Oswald voluntarily handed over his entire wallet to Tippit. The wallet only contained Oswald's ID. Tippit would then allegedly have added the very incriminating Hidell papers to the wallet, and would afterwards state that Oswald had handed the wallet with the Hidell papers over to him. But Tippit could no longer explain anything, because he

was dead. It therefore seemed a good idea to the police to put the 'supplemented' wallet immediately back into the possession of Oswald as direct evidence.

3. Someone copied Oswald's wallet, including the double identity papers, the photo of his little daughter and everything in it. If Oswald managed to escape, this reserve wallet would be added somewhere to the evidence to brand him as the perpetrator. When Oswald escaped after the murder of Tippit, the crime scene seemed to be the best place to bring the second wallet into circulation. But when Oswald was then caught in the cinema, the second wallet was no longer needed, and was removed from the evidence as quickly as it had appeared.

Admit, every one of these hypotheses sounds implausible, but one of the three assumptions above has to be correct, as the remaining possibilities are in conflict with the laws of nature:

4. One wallet with incriminating documents was simultaneously on 10th Street and in Oswald's back pocket in the cinema.
5. One wallet without incriminating documents existed at a specific moment and then suddenly disappeared into thin air. At least five police officers had seen and touched this harmless piece of evidence, and had discussed the contents at a very dramatic time in their lives. Nevertheless, they all subsequently suffered from collective amnesia and no-one could remember the wallet from 10th Street anymore. The true owner, an innocent man who lost his wallet at a murder scene, never claimed his property back.

The believers implicitly settle for one of the last two statements. They never add whether they chose the telekinesis option or the dematerialization option, including the associated loss of memory.

TWO STEPS ARE ENOUGH

In the Kennedy case, we continually come up against a web of interrelationships that always involve the same names. The person who comes into the picture seems quite normal in the version of the Commission, but when we examine the direct connections, we quickly find ourselves in remarkable company after only two steps. Officer J.D. Tippit is no exception. At first glance, he seems to have a spotless reputation. The Warren Commission pretended to make an effort to investigate Tippit's background, but we are served up with a very polished version of the police officer. According to those who knew him, Tippit was 'appreciated by his colleagues', 'used good common sense', was 'deeply religious' and 'a fine and ideal policeman, of good morals and who was conscientious and did a good job.'[403] He liked to drink a beer, but was never seen drunk. The man had a sense of humor, loved his wife and was the perfect family man. His wife stated that whenever he was not working, 'he would spend all of his time at home, either working in the yard, playing with his children or having friends over.'[404] His hobbies were water-skiing, fishing and hunting. One of Tippit's colleagues also declared to the FBI that he believed 'that Officer Tippit stopped Oswald to check him because of the similarity in appearance.'[405] (A new clairvoyant confirms Tippit's clairvoyance ...)

Only good things are said about the deceased, of course, but if something sounds too good to be true, it usually involves deception. The details about Tippit's private life do not matter – which is also why we call it private – but let's take a closer look at his working life. The man had apparently three jobs. He was a full-time police officer, in itself not a bad day job that provided him with 490 dollars a month[406] – around 3,800 dollars, or 3,000 euro in today's money. That's not bad for someone with a 'limited education'[407] who had only attended school up to the eighth grade[408] and was 'not clever enough to pass the end-of-year exams'[409] In the weekend, he earned money carrying out security work at Austin's Barbecue restaurant, and he also kept order at the Stevens Park Theatre cinema on Sundays.[410] Despite these three sources of income and his flawless lifestyle, Tippit had a lot of trouble making ends meet. In his investigation, Dale Myers put his hand in the fire for Tippit: he was not a man to involve himself in dubious activities. That may be the case, but before accepting it we prefer to have a closer look.

The restaurant where Tippit worked was the property of Austin Cook, a self-declared member of the ultra-right John Birch Society.[411] According to the official version of his biography, Tippit was a supporter of Kennedy. Yet he worked with someone who was a member of a club of fanatical Kennedy-haters. General Edwin Walker was also a leading member of the John Birch Society.

In Austin's Barbecue, Tippit was also said to have had an affair with waitress Johnnie Maxie Witherspoon, who gave birth to a baby seven months after the murder.[412] According to investigator Professor Bill Pulte, restaurant manager Austin Cook was also a friend of Ralph Paul,[413] who, in turn, was a good friend of Jack Ruby, who murdered Oswald. Tippit was also said to have personally known Ralph Paul. Tippit's second part-time job, providing security at the Stevens Park Theatre cinema, even provides a direct link between Tippit and Ruby's partner Ralph Paul. One of Ralph Paul's restaurants was the Miramar, a business that was located near the Stevens Park Theatre.[414] That's not too disturbing on its own, but the name of the manager of the Stevens Park cinema really does open up a Pandora's Box in Tippit's background. Before he came to Dallas, Manuel Avila was the CBS correspondent in Mexico, and was afterwards a correspondent for the Voice of America. The CIA is never far away there.[415] In addition to his cinema, Avila also ran a nightclub, and worked as an interpreter for fervent anti-Castro activists.[416] He maintained direct contacts with CIA-sponsored organizations such as DRE and Antonio Veciana's Alpha-66 group. Avila was an acquaintance of Alpha-66 member Aurelio Pino, who was questioned by the FBI in the context of the Kennedy assassination because he was a friend of Sylvia Odio.[417] A lot of prominent names emerge when we investigate the last months of Tippit's life. There was also a direct connection between Avila and Jack Ruby. Avila's cinema also apparently housed less innocent activities. Historian Larry Hancock wrote the following about this: 'It was said that, in addition to the screening room downstairs, a prostitution business also made use of the facilities associated with the cinema.'[418] As a fellow nightclub owner and a trader in fornication, Avila undoubtedly knew his colleague Jack Ruby.

The official picture looks neat:

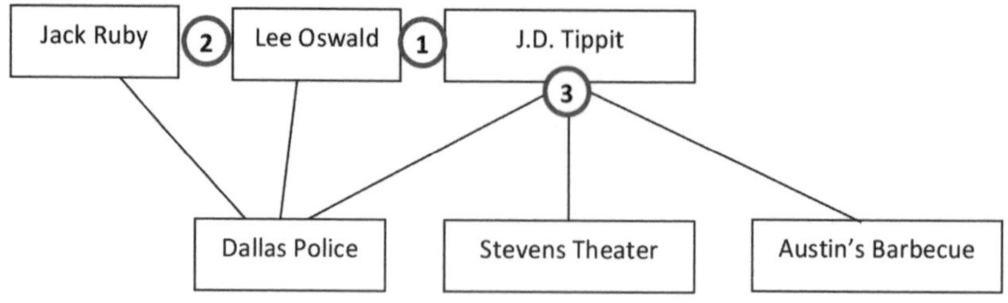

Lee Oswald murdered Officer Tippit purely coincidentally (1); Jack Ruby murdered Lee Oswald purely coincidentally (2).

J.D. Tippit happened to work for the police, Stevens Park Theatre, and Austin's Barbecue.

But by digging a little deeper, we can add the following links:

- **Former general Edwin Walker**, the man whom Oswald allegedly wanted to assassinate, was a member of the John Birch Society, an organization that was often mentioned in the same breath as Walker. Austin Cook, Tippit's employer at the restaurant, was also a member;
- **Ralph Paul**, Ruby's silent partner in the Carousel, the man with whom Ruby phoned intensively the day before he shot Oswald. Tippit was said to have known Ralph Paul personally;
- **Mexico**, the country to which Oswald traveled in the penultimate stage of his life. The Oswald-Mexico chapter was an important stage in the run-up to Dealey Plaza. Mexico is the CIA's intermediate station for Cuba, with 47 percent of the embassy's telex reports concerning Cuba operations;[419]
- **DRE**, a militant anti-Castro organization. Oswald got into trouble with DRE member Bringuier in New Orleans, thereby ending up in jail, and was later involved in a radio debate and a WDSU-television interview. These facts counted later as important proof that Oswald was a communist and a Castro sympathizer. The CIA amply financed DRE, and Avila worked together actively with the DRE.
- **Antonio Veciana**, the dictatorial leader of Alpha 66, an organization of Cuban militants. Avila also provided assistance to Alpha 66 via the Cuban halfway house in Harlandale Avenue, Dallas. Veciana later testified that he had met Oswald in Dallas together with David Atlee Philips.
- **David Atlee Phillips**, propaganda specialist and head of the Cuban operations of the CIA in Mexico. Just after Kennedy's assassination, he was closely involved in the manipulation of the evidence about Oswald's movements in Mexico.
- **Sylvia Odio**, the woman to whom Oswald is said to have paid a visit (more on that later in chapter 16). Avila's contact person at Alpha 66 was Aurelio Pino, who also knew Sylvia Odio.

- **Jack Ruby**, nightclub manager and murderer of Oswald: Ruby and Avila were colleagues, and probably knew each other through the nightlife scene.

Let's also not forget that Tippit's main employer was the Dallas Police. Jack Ruby was the preferred friend of the police in Dallas – although he probably did not know Tippit personally – and Oswald was murdered in the basement of the police station, with or without help from the inside. It is also striking that Cuba never fails to appear when we dig deeper than the Warren Commission was prepared to do.

If we add all of this to the chart, the nice picture of the Warren Commission already looks quite different:

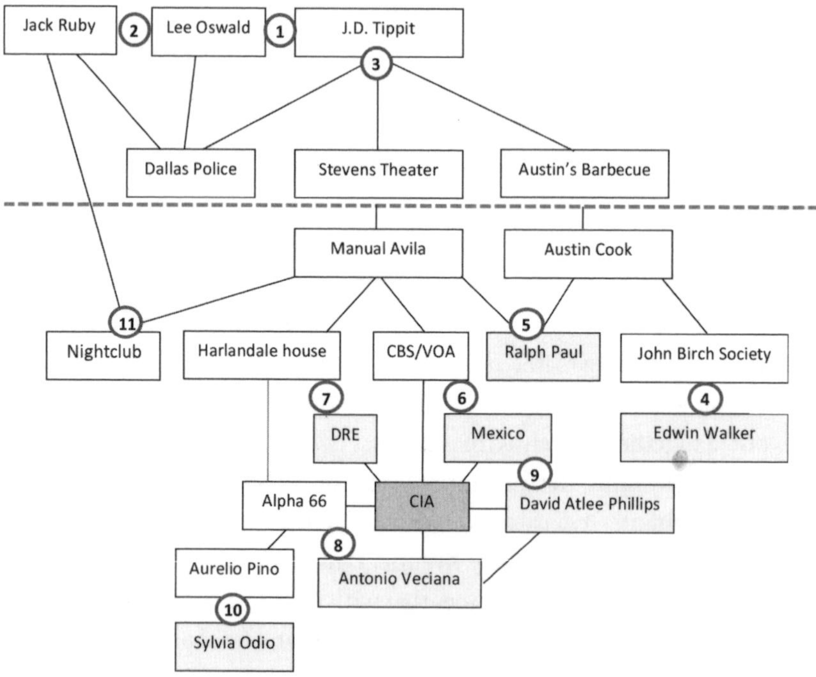

Is it again simply a coincidence that Tippit was barely a few steps removed from so many of the protagonists in the case? Is it again a coincidence that the Warren Commission noticed nothing special in the investigation into the background of Tippit? Let's leave the answer to these questions for the moment, and restrict ourselves to being aware of the recurring phenomenon.

A SECOND OSWALD

A second Oswald repeatedly appears in the Kennedy case. In the run-up to November 22, all kinds of people impersonated Oswald and conspicuously brought an Italian rifle into a shooting club, had a sight mounted onto a weapon that had already had a sight when it was bought, wanted to buy a car stating that they would soon receive a large sum of money, or wanted to hire a small plane that could reach Mexico on the afternoon of November 22. The question of whether several persons were impersonating Oswald will arise repeatedly in the further investigation.

The Tippit case did not want to lag behind: here also, a second Oswald had to emerge. According to this scenario, an Oswald-double killed the police officer. In the eyes of the public, the shooting of a policeman is undeniable proof of Oswald's guilt. After Oswald had been arrested in the cinema, his double vanished from the face of the earth. Once the real Oswald was suspected of the murder of the policeman, he had very little chance of surviving the arrest. That scenario is quite far-fetched, however.

SUSPICIOUS WITNESS DEATHS

Finally, the Tippit case also made a substantial contribution to the list of mysterious attacks on the lives of witnesses. The fate of Warren Reynolds thereby attracts the most attention. Reynolds worked in his brother's garage, one block away from the place where Tippit was murdered. He saw the killer running by, and followed the man up to the parking lot of the Texaco tank station. On November 22, the FBI noted that Reynolds 'would hesitate to definitely identify Oswald as the individual.'[420] More explanations from Reynolds were apparently unnecessary, and the Warren Commission also did not hear him. Two months after the murder, on January 21, 1964, Reynolds wanted to lock up the garage at 9.15 p.m. When he tried to switch on the light, it remained dark. As he was walking to the fuse box in the dark, he was shot at, and was hit in the head. There is no doubt that the shot was intended to kill him. Reynolds had no enemies, however, and nothing was stolen from the garage. The only reason he could think of for this reckless attempt on his life was his role as a witness in Tippit's murder case, but there was, of course, not a shred of evidence of that connection. A certain Darrell Wayne Garner was suspected of the attack on Reynolds. But the man had an alibi for the moment of the attack. Nancy Jane Mooney willingly provided the alibi. She was also known as Betty McDonald, a former stripper in Jack Ruby's Carousel nightclub.[421] On February 13, three weeks after the attack on Tippit-witness Reynolds, this young lady was arrested after a brawl with another woman over a man. In the same night, the police found her dead in her cell, hanged with her toreador pants.[422] The conspiracy story also reports an attempt to abduct Reynolds's 9-year-old daughter, following which the terrified man was suddenly ready to identify Oswald beyond any doubt as the man he had seen running away on November 22.

Witness Domingo Benavides was also convinced that someone tried to kill him because of his involvement in the Kennedy case. His brother, who looked very much like him, was shot dead in a bar in February 1965[423] without any apparent reason.

A third witness, Harold Russell, also feared for his life, and did in fact die three years later ... as a result of a heart attack after a police intervention in a brawl.

SIMILARITIES WITH THE KENNEDY CASE: CONCLUSION

We could continue for quite a while with peculiarities that appear in the Tippit case and ressemble similar occurances in the Kennedy case:

- At Dealey Plaza, the Carcano was initially incorrectly identified as a Mauser. On 10th Street, the murder weapon was at first incorrectly described as a .38 automatic pistol on the basis of the shells that were found. The shells of an automatic pistol and those of a revolver are, however, very easy to distinguish from each other.[424]
- The man who fled from the Tippit crime scene hid his jacket under a parked car in a Texaco station parking lot. That's good news with a view to the evidence, because Oswald had left his rented room wearing a jacket,[425] and was no longer wearing a jacket at his arrest in the cinema. But the jacket that was found had an identification label from a laundry. No other item of clothing of Oswald had a label from a laundry. There is no doubt that Oswald never had his clothes cleaned externally. He was just too poor and too stingy for that.

- Oswald's landlady saw a police car stop in front of her house at the time Oswald was changing his clothes. According to her, this was police car 207 (or perhaps 107 or 106).[426] Two officers sat in the car. There were two brief signals with the horn, and the car then slowly drove forwards in the direction of Zangs Boulevard.[427] This story obviously excites the overheated imaginations of many conspiracists. The true facts have never been clarified.
- As in the Kennedy case, the line-ups to identify the killer were organized in such a way that the result was completely worthless. That was partly Oswald's own fault, because he had conspicuously protested about the line-up. It was also partly inevitable because important witnesses such as Benavides admitted that they had recognized Oswald on the basis of the television reports that they had seen before they were asked to identify him. But all this does not alter the fact that the confrontations were worthless as evidence.
- For inexplicable reasons, the police considered it unnecessary to record the identities of the 24 other patrons in the cinema.[428] According to some sources, this did, in fact, happen, but the list disappeared afterwards. It's hard to say which situation is worse. It's not completely inconceivable that Oswald had an appointment with an accomplice in the cinema. Among others, John Martino, an associate of mobster Johnny Roselli, claimed that Oswald 'had agreed to meet his contact person in the Texas Theater.'[429] It's strange, for example, that, in a cinema with more than 800 seats, he sat down next to one of the 23 other visitors, only to move a little later and sit down next to someone else. Oswald possibly thought that he would be less conspicuous if he gave the impression that he was accompanied. I believe that Oswald did not have an appointment in the cinema. To just give one argument: If that had been the case, he was walking in the wrong direction on 10th Street.
- Just as they did with Dorothy Garner, the key witness for the timing of Oswald's movements in the book depository, the Warren Commission completely ignored key witness T.F. Bowley. Apart from his statement immediately after the murder, no single hearing of him is known. The reason is probably because Bowley said in his statement that, according to his watch, Tippit already lay bleeding on the ground at 1.10 p.m.

- This case also has eyewitnesses who contradict one another. The witnesses once again provided a wide range of statements about the number of shots, the descriptions of the persons and the direction in which the killer(s) fled.
- An incredible coincidence cannot be missing in the list: both Oswald and Tippit sometimes took breakfast in the Dobbs House Snackbar. According to waitress Mary Dowling, they were even there at the same time the day before the murder.[430] As if there were not enough eateries in Dallas to prevent a murderer and his victim, who did not know each other, calmly eating breakfast together the day before the murder.

If the official version of events is correct, the murder of Tippit should be a simple matter. Oswald was on the run, was on the point of being arrested and cold-bloodedly murdered the police officer. A quarter of an hour later he was arrested, had the weapon with which the crime was committed with him, and was recognized by witnesses. However complex the whole Kennedy case is, the murder of Tippit should be an exception. But that is clearly not the case. The strange findings that are so typical for the whole file are undiminished in the Tippit chapter. It is difficult to interpret this observation other than as an indication that the Tippit chapter is strongly intertwined with the complete case at a deeper level.

WHY DID TIPPIT SPEAK TO THE PEDESTRIAN?

The chapter began with a quote from Sherlock Holmes: in the maze of information, we have to separate the main items from the side issues, the essential from the incidental. To me, the vital question seems to be the following: Why did Tippit stop an arbitrary pedestrian on 10th Street? If we can figure that out, we could probably also answer many other questions with reasonable certainty.

Whatever the reason was for him to speak to the man, it was certainly not the similarity with the description of the suspect after the assassination of the president. The Commission knew perfectly well why it chose its words carefully, and only insinuated a connection. Nothing indicates that Tippit suspected that he was confronting a killer. For example, Tippit did not warn the dispatcher, which was not only the mandatory procedure, but is also what every sensible person would do if he thought he was dealing with a murder suspect on the run. The police officer also did not have his gun ready. Walt Brown asked the legitimate question: 'Why would Tippit be so careless?'[431] Tippit had a leisurely chat and stepped out of the car calmly and slowly. It therefore does not appear that, at that moment, he suspected that Oswald was dangerous. We can therefore also exclude the possibility that Tippit was sent to kill Oswald as part of a conspiracy. If that was the case, he would certainly have kept his gun at the ready. I also agree with Dale Myers that a cold-blooded murder was not in Tippit's nature. Neither the official version (agreement with the description) nor the common conspiracy hypothesis (Tippit was sent to murder Oswald) seem to offer the answer to our question. So we again have to dig deeper into the known facts about the murder.

Tippit was on 10th Street, 4.5 kilometers outside his normal district. At 12.44 p.m., radio dispatcher Jackson gave him the order to 'go to the area of Central Oak Cliff.'[432] That was not Tippit's normal patrol area, but just happened to be the district where Oswald's rented room was located. Why would the police send someone to this god-forsaken place with priority? The president of the United States has been assassinated less than a quarter of an hour earlier. Nobody knew precisely what had happened, or whether the President was still alive. There was still no mention whatsoever of Oswald. And yet it was the first concern of the police to move an officer from one quiet residential district to another quiet residential district just at the moment when all other officers were in the highest state of alarm. The instruction to Tippit – and to a colleague who did not respond to the instruction – is unique in the transcript of the radio communication. The Warren Commission asked three policemen and Police Chief Jesse Curry whether they knew the reason for the strange instruction to Tippit. No one could think of an answer.[433] But even stranger is that the instruction to Tippit to go to Central Oak Cliff is completely missing on the original copy of the radio communications of December 5, 1963.[434]

		rifle - no further description or information at this time. Then rebroadcast. 12:45PM KKB364 Dallas
12:45PM		Some squad asked, what is he wanted for?
	531	Signal nineteen involving the President.
	233-531	He's thought to be in this Texas School Book Depository here on the northwest corner of Elm and Houston. Many squads checking out to the location.
12:48PM	531	Information broadcast again on the shooting of the

It states: 'Many squads checking out to the location.' There were officers who reported that they were heading for Dealey Plaza. But that did not affect Tippit, who the dispatcher had given the instruction to go to another location. The instruction appears (or reappears after being left out in the first version) in the version from the logbook[435] of March 23, 1964 (Number 87 is Tippit):

	rifle. No further description or information at this time.
Disp	12:45 KKB-364, Dallas.
Unknown	What is he wanted for?
Disp	Signal 19, involving the President.
233	233.
Disp	233.
233	He is thought to be in this Texas Book Depository on Northwest corner Elm and Houston.
102	Out this location.
Disp	10-4. 102 and 233.
81	81.
Disp	81.
81	I'll be going north on Industrial from Corinth.
Disp	10-4. 81.
Disp	87-78 move into Central Oak Cliff area.
93	93 to 531. I'm clear, where do you want me to go?
Disp	Report to old School Book Depository, Elm and Houston area.
Disp	Unit clearing?
95	95, clear
Disp	95 clear 12:46.

Either the instruction to Tippit was omitted from the first copy for one reason or another, or no instruction was given at all. This may have then been added to the later copy in order to provide, after the facts, a sensible explanation for Tippit's presence at the place where he lost his life. In any case, there was no reason for sending Tippit to Oak Cliff, because he was already there. Five credible witnesses[436] saw Tippit at the most northerly point of Oak Cliff at around 12.45 – where he was not supposed to be. He had parked his car in the grounds of the Gloco Benzine Station at 1502 North Zangs Boulevard. For ten minutes, he kept a sharp eye on the traffic coming from Houston Street Viaduct.[437] According to the witnesses, he suddenly drove off with screeching tires at around 12.55. That is approximately the moment when Oswald drove by in his taxi. The route that Oswald's taxi driver Whaley indicated did indeed run via the Houston Street Viaduct.[438] Moments later, the dispatcher asked Tippit where he was. The officer said: 'I'm more or less at Keist and Bonnie View.'[439] But he wasn't there at all at that moment. At 1.00, Tippit stormed into the Top Ten Record Shop at 338 West Jefferson Boulevard. Louis Cortinas, the clerk in the record shop, stated the following in 1981 in an interview with Earl Golz of the *Dallas Morning News*: '[Tippit] rushed into the store and asked me whether he could use the telephone on the counter. [...] Tippit said nothing on the phone as he apparently received no answer. He stood there long enough to let the phone ring seven or eight times. Tippit hung up the phone and ran quickly away, he was upset or worried about something [...] Tippit hurried in his car along Jefferson, via Bishop, to Sunset, where he drove past a stop light and turned right into Sunset. [...] Maybe 10, not more than 10 minutes after Tippit had left, I heard on the radio that he had been shot.'[440] The owner of the shop also said that Tippit 'departed hastily and did not say a word. He had just enough time to reach the place where he was shot down.' When the dispatcher called Tippit at 1.03, the officer was trying to reach someone by phone in the record shop, and could therefore not respond to the call because he was not in his car.[441]

After leaving Jefferson Boulevard at high speed, Tippit stopped a car on West 10th Street in a very unusual manner by brutally cutting off its path. This happened eight or nine blocks from the place where he would die. James A. Andrews, the surprised driver of that car, told investigator Greg Lowrey that Tippit 'seemed very upset and agitated and was acting crazy.' Lowrey summed up what Andrews told him as follows: 'A police car suddenly appeared driving in a westerly direction on West 10th Street, behind Andrews' car, overtook him and made a sharp curve in front of Andrews' car so that he had to stop. The police car turned sideways in front of Andrews' car at an angle to the curb in order to stop him. The officer jumped out of the patrol car, motioned Andrews to stand still, went to the back of Andrews' car and looked at the space between the front and rear seats. Without saying a word, the officer went back to his patrol car and then drove quickly away. Andrews was stunned by this strange behavior, and looked at the nameplate of the police officer, where 'Tippit' could be seen.'[442]

The next witnesses to notice the police officer were Helen Markham and taxi driver Scoggings. Both of them stated officially that Tippit, who had previously been in a hurry, now drove extremely slowly, at around 15 kilometers an hour. At that moment, the police officer saw the unknown man who was walking on the sidewalk along 10th Street. In the last half hour of his life, Tippit was clearly looking for someone. It is also clear that this person was Lee Harvey Oswald, because, as soon as the agitated policeman saw the man, he suddenly switched to a very quiet form of driving. Tippit was specifically looking for Oswald at exactly the right place. He was looking for him at a time when no one could have known who Oswald was or where he could be located. Very shortly after the Kennedy assassination, someone must have given Tippit information about Oswald, and the specific task of locating him.

TIPPIT'S REAL MURDERER

Despite all the controversy, we need have no doubt that Oswald murdered Officer Tippit. At time A, 1.01 p.m., Oswald stood at location A, the sidewalk in front of his rented room at North Beckley Avenue 1026. At 1.36 p.m. (time B), shoe salesman Brewer on Jefferson Boulevard observed how Oswald clearly ducked into the doorway of a shop as a police car drove by. Brewer thought this was suspicious, and followed Oswald. Shortly afterwards, he saw him sneak into the Texas Theatre cinema (location B) without paying. This led to a dramatic police operation in which Oswald was arrested. The murder took place halfway between location A and location B, and halfway between time A and time B. Oswald had a pistol on him at the time of his arrest, which was loaded with three bullets of the Remington brand and three bullets of the Winchester brand.[443] The bullets in Tippit's body were compared with test bullets that were fired with Oswald's pistol. There was a technical problem here, because the barrel was slightly too wide for the .38 Special bullets that were used, but expert Nicol was still able to assign one of the bullets with certainty to Oswald's gun.[444] The paraffin sampling test was positive for Oswald's hands. Although this test sometimes incorrectly yields positive results, the traces that were found also form a pattern that indicates that Oswald had fired a gun. Unlike the President of the United States, humble police officer Tippit did receive a careful autopsy. Not a single element of the medical findings was inconsistent with the hypothesis that a man had shot the officer four times at close quarters. Solutions are conceivable for the riddle of the three Winchester bullets for only two Winchester shells. It is sufficient, for example, that the police did not find one of the Winchester shells at the crime scene and that the weapon already contained one empty Remington shell before the attack. Furthermore, a shell was found in the estate of witness Louis Davis. The man had probably withheld the piece of evidence as a souvenir. Maybe that was the missing Winchester shell? The fact that witnesses go souvenir hunting should not surprise us any more than the fact that they contradict each other on many points. People are not robots.

The absence of fingerprints on the exterior of the car does not mean that Oswald was not the person who had a conversation with Tippit through the open car window. Witness Jack Tatum was driving past the police car at the moment that Oswald spoke to Tippit. According to him, Oswald kept his hands in the pockets of his jacket. That might explain the absence of fingerprints. The timing is indeed very tight, but not impossible. Traveling 2.6 miles in a car in normal traffic in a time of 5.5 minutes corresponds to an average speed of 42 kilometers an hour. That is realistic. Jimmy Burt is the only witness to claim that the perpetrator was walking west on 10th Street. He could have been mistaken. And covering 1,320 meters on foot in eleven minutes is still only 7.2 kilometers an hour. That's a brisk pace, but not impossible for a 24-year-old ex-marine.

It seems unlikely that possible conspirators deliberately tried to eliminate witnesses. Witness Warren Reynolds was shot in the head. However bizarre his story may be – and it certainly is, if only because of the link to Jack Ruby and the Carousel – the chance is small that there is a connection to the murders on November 22. The alleged perpetrator, Wayne Garner, was, in fact, a mentally ill fringe figure. Despite her youth (24 years of age and the mother of four children over whom she no longer had custody), Nancy Jane Mooney, who provided him with an alibi, had fallen on hard times in all respects. She had made several suicide attempts in the weeks before her death. And how could the conspirators have been able to influence the testimony of Domingo Benavides in 1964 by carrying out an attack on his brother a year later? And why would they wait three years to eliminate Harold Russell as a witness? Moreover, the attack on Reynolds is said to have been carried out because he had not been willing to identify Oswald as the murderer with 100% certainty, while the two others were killed precisely because they had done so.

I can therefore state in good conscience that, if I were a member of a jury, I would deem Oswald guilty of the murder of Tippit, because that has been proven beyond reasonable doubt. This was also the conclusion of the HSCA in 1979: 'Based on Oswald's possession of the murder weapon shortly after the murder and the identification of Oswald as the killer by eye witnesses, the Commission concluded that Oswald shot and killed Officer Tippit.'[445]

But there are strong indications that Tippit was not an accidental victim. The image of a conscientious cop who recognized a passerby as the suspect in the assassination of Kennedy is nonsense. Tippit was actually looking for Oswald a quarter of an hour after the assassination. He not only knew who to look for, but also where to look. Someone had given him information and a specific assignment.

Regardless of which hypothesis we retain in connection with the unsolved mystery of the wallet, this remains an abnormal and suspicious situation that is clearly directly related to the murder.

Through his three working environments, Tippit had direct contacts with a whole range of individuals and organizations that turn up again and again in other chapters of this case.

Oswald's very violent reaction with regard to Tippit shows that he was very emotional and angry. For a fugitive at large, it would normally be enough to shoot down the police officer. But, even after three deadly shots, Oswald walked to the other side of the police car and shot the policeman one more time at very close range. If he had simply been on the run, this shot to finish him off represented an unnecessary risk for Oswald. There was clearly something personal for Oswald. The extent of the trap, of which Tippit, in his eyes, was a part, was gradually permeating Oswald's mind.

Our working hypothesis for the murder of Tippit is as follows:

- Only after the assassination did Oswald realize that he was being made responsible for the assassination of Kennedy. He fled in panic, fetched his weapon from his rented room and went to a bus stop in order to reach the long-distance bus station for Mexico from there.
- Less than fifteen minutes after the assassination, and on behalf of the conspirators, Officer Tippit watched out for Oswald near the area where his lodgings were, where they expected him to emerge.
- Whatever Tippit tried to get Oswald to do, it is clear that Oswald no longer trusted anyone, and therefore brutally shot down the police officer. His extremely violent reaction shows that he was very upset about the situation in which he had become entangled. We can completely forget the official motive – that Oswald shot Kennedy out of a need for recognition. If

Oswald had simply acted in order to get himself into the history books, he could have voluntarily surrendered himself to Officer Tippit.

This is no speculative theory, but a logical deduction based on the facts. We can therefore retain this working hypothesis as a basis for further investigation.

FILE 3

THE MURDER OF OSWALD

Chapter 6 – Hired killer or buffoon?

THE IMPORTANCE OF RUBY FOR THE CONSPIRACY HYPOTHESIS

The third assassination in the Oswald case is the murder in which he himself was the victim. Nightclub operator Jack Ruby shot Oswald down in the basement of the police headquarters in Dallas. Did someone want to brutally silence Oswald? The Warren Commission didn't think so. The Commission was sure that Ruby was a lone nut, and that he killed Oswald as a pure murder of opportunity. The believers still stubbornly defend that view.

According to reports from his school, Jack Ruby was not very bright. He scored 94 in an IQ test in 1922. He was not stupid, wrote Bugliosi, but 'no one would have ever accuse him of being bright either'.[446] Bugliosi was wrong once again: after Ruby's arrest in 1963, he had an IQ of 109 according to intelligence tests in prison. The assessment also indicated that he could have achieved a score between 115 and 120 without the hindrance of his limited education.[447]

Before he Americanized his name, Jakob Rubinstein, the son of a Polish immigrant, grew up in unenviable circumstances. When Ruby's father was not unemployed, he made a living as a carpenter. He was above all an alcoholic, a womanizer and had a highly flammable nature, according to a report based on Ruby's truancy.[448] His mother Fannie was an illiterate, mentally disturbed woman. Ruby left school without a certificate, and, as a teenager, ended up in jail for a while for selling sheet music without copyright. Not a felony, but typical of him. Peddling activities perhaps constitute the only common thread in Ruby's life. He was never short of sweet talk and commercial ambition. He always had grandiose plans, and tried selling linoleum, newspaper subscriptions, lottery tickets and candy door-to-door ... nothing was beneath him when it came to earning a dollar. But he never did any real work. His Carousel club fits well into the picture. Outside the opening hours, Ruby only worked on his business one hour a day. The club was open five hours in the evening. Everything that Ruby ran, and in which others invested, was doomed to fail. The Carousel was the highlight, but also marks the end point of a hopeless series of attempts by this scatterbrain to keep his head above water. The S & R Inc. company had paid the modest purchase price for the Carousel. Ruby was not a shareholder, and therefore not a (joint) owner of the bar. Only when he paid off his debt to his friend Ralph Paul could he become the half-owner.[449] But the chance of him doing this seemed small. Nevertheless, Ruby acted as if the Carousel was his own business. He also considered the Vegas Club, which was run by his sister Eva, as his own property. Ruby took the decisions in both cases, cashed the revenues and paid the bills fairly regularly. Barman Andrew Armstrong, who had a good overview of the revenue, described the financial situation as follows: 'We was making most of the payments. We was never behind on the rent or anything. We didn't get the lights cut off.'[450]

Figure 41. The Carousel, above a delicatessen. Not exactly a classy place.

In addition to his personal loans, Ruby also had a tax debt of 44,413.86 dollars[451] – this translates to 300,000 dollars in 2015 – an amount that inevitably increased with interest, penalties and new, unpaid assessments. He could not expect to pay off his debts with the Carousel. At best, the bar broke even. When the club generated $1,400 revenue once over a weekend, this was the highest takings ever. In August 1963, the gross margin (after the purchase of liquor and the payment of 10 per cent tax) was 1,237 dollars per week on average, for example, 1,351 dollars in September. Just the wage costs for four strippers, a few other statutory, more dignified attractions in-between, and a four-member band amounted to $1,160 each week. Less than $200 a week remained after paying these expenses. With this limited income, he had to pay rent for the first floor at the Commerce Street number 1312, all utilities, pay the maintenance and kitchen staff, a bartender, and also pay himself. The eight girls who acted as waitresses, sold cigarettes and provided the animation for the customers were not even on the payroll. Ruby barely knew their first names, and the girls themselves had to scrape by with tips. According to his predecessor Paul Roland Jones, Ruby apparently had to pay bribes to the police. The FBI noted Jones's statement: 'In order to operate in the city, Ruby must have been paying off the police department, just as he himself (Jones) had done years earlier.'[452] The stripper union AGVA (American Guild of Variety Artists) – actually an extortion mechanism of the Mafia – was also an additional cost. From the testimonies presented to the *Senate Rackets Committee* in the summer of 1962, it appears that the trade union collected approximately one million dollars in contributions each year, but did nothing for its members.[453] If the owner of a club refused to pay, remarked National Secretary Jackie Bright to the Saturday Evening Post, a phone call to 'a few people who were friendly disposed towards the AGVA' was enough. The money would be received the next day.[454] Ruby also had to pay the union a contribution for each girl. It is not inconceivable that the greed of the AGVA and the police was an important part of his financial worries. The police force in Dallas did not have the reputation of being trustworthy and incorruptible. 'Historically, the department was corrupt from top to bottom [...] You never knew which side your boss or your partner was on. There was a lot of money in circulation,' said a retired police captain.[455]

In any case, Ruby's business future was yet again anything but rosy in November 1963. Hugh Aynesworth of the *Dallas Morning News* was undoubtedly right when he wrote: 'Jack Ruby was the quintessential wannabe but never was.'[456] Reporter Toni Zoppi, a personal acquaintance of Ruby, stated: 'He'd be the worst fellow in the world to be part of a conspiracy, because he just plain talked too much.'[457] Police inspector Revill, who was intensively involved in the internal investigation after the murder of Oswald, had known Ruby for ten years in 1963, and called him 'an obnoxious bungler.' He immediately laughed off the notion that Ruby was a member of the Mafia: 'If Jack

Ruby was a member of organized crime, then the personnel director of organized crime should be replaced.'[458]

Ruby undoubtedly only knew the gangsters as customers of the striptease bar[459] or as figureheads of the stripper union AGVA. He was a serial failure in great financial difficulty, without any rank or position in the Mafia hierarchy, and in no way had the profile of a gang member. But the coin also has a flip side. The conspirators would be crazy to have Oswald murdered by someone who was directly connected to their organization. Furthermore, Ruby's hopeless situation, and the fact that the Mafia there was well aware of this (as if they hadn't caused it themselves through AGVA), made him useful for an assignment. Ruby had one indispensable asset for the murder of Oswald: he regularly walked in and out of the police station without anyone finding it abnormal. He brought the law enforcement officers sandwiches and soft drinks, genuinely looked after the men in uniform, and occasionally provided free admission tickets to the Carousel. If Ruby killed Oswald on someone's instructions, it was a task that was only imposed on him *after* Oswald was arrested alive because gangster Jim Braden and Officer Tippit had failed to eliminate the scapegoat Oswald. With his unlimited access to the police station, Ruby was the perfect man to solve the problem of the conspirators with a single belly shot.

THE OFFICIAL STORY

On May 29, 2007, ninety years after JFK's birth, Vincente Bugliosi debated with David Talbot about the Kennedy assassination and Oswald in the MSNBC talk show Hardball. Bugliosi considered the timing to be the proof that Ruby acted alone and impulsively: Ruby only arrived in the police station just seconds before Oswald. A professional assassin would never go to the crime scene at the last minute, and take the risk of being late. That's a strong argument, but does it stand up to closer examination?

According to the official story, the timing looked like this:

— The day before, Police Chief Curry had announced: 'You better be around here about 10.00 a.m.'[460] Chief Inspector Fritz assumed that the hearing of Oswald would finish around 10 a.m.[461] The transfer of Oswald to the jail could then take place at any moment that Sunday morning.

— On Sunday, November 24, Ruby showed no interest at all in the police operation surrounding Oswalds's transport and decided to stay at his apartment.
— But then, at 10.19 a.m., Ruby received a call from one of his girls, Karen Bennett, who needed money urgently. The Carousel was unexpectedly closed following the assassination, and she had not received the usual advance on her wages. Ruby said he would send her $25 by telegram as soon as possible.
— Ruby waited another 45 minutes before leaving his apartment, around 11 o'clock he drove downtown.
— At 11.17 a.m., Ruby sent the *moneygram* from a Western Union office that was – by pure coincidences – 104 meters from the police station from where Oswald should have been transferred to prison more than one hour earlier.
— Ruby was outside the Western Union office again at 11.18 a.m.
— The distance to the police station was timed to be one minute and 13 seconds. Ruby then needed another 22 seconds to reach the underground garage.[462] At exactly the same moment Oswald appeared in the basement from the elevator.
— Ruby murdered Oswald at 11.21.

If Oswald had been brought outside one minute earlier, he might still be alive today. The tight timing actually raises serious doubts about Ruby's status as a hired assassin. The questioning of Oswald was unexpectedly extended by the presence of Postal Inspector Harry D. Holmes from the US Postal Service, who took part in the interrogation. At the last minute, Oswald also demanded the right to put on his own sweater. He was allowed to do this. If the arrogant and stubborn Oswald had not won this small victory over his interrogators, he would have left the building a few minutes earlier, before Ruby was there. "Is Oswald himself perhaps also an accomplice in his own murder?" suggested Bugliosi sarcastically.[463]

The improbably tight timing of Ruby's presence does not say everything, however. We're sure that Gavrilo Princip assassinated Archduke Franz Ferdinand of Austria on June 28, 1914, as a member of a conspiracy. But the first attempt with a bomb failed. Princip went off to buy a sandwich in a café. Nobody could have foreseen that the Archduke's chauffeur would drive the wrong way shortly afterwards. It was impossible to plan the time at which the armed Princip came out again with his sandwich just as the Archduke's open car drove by. The assassination nevertheless took place, and Princip was a member of a conspiracy. Planning and luck do not necessarily exclude each other. But here, it certainly does appear that Ruby came face to face with Oswald purely by chance and on impulse.

Journalist Seth Kantor slept slightly longer than intended on Sunday morning. He was convinced that his arrival at the police station at 10.40 a.m. would be much too late.[464] But Ruby, the supposed assassin, started out even later than Kantor: he remained in the shabby rented room he shared with bachelor George Senator until nearly 11 a.m. Ruby began the most important day in his life rather unspectacularly: he hung around aimlessly in his underwear until Karen Bennett phoned him at 10.19 a.m. to ask for money. Ruby promised to quickly send her 25 dollars. The phone call lasted till 10.21 a.m.[465] Ruby then dressed, which was always difficult. He wanted to look elegant and was worried about his weight and his thinning hair. Shaving off his heavy beard – twice a day – also took time. What's more, he was not a morning person. When he was finally finished, he grabbed hold of the money from the receipts and his Colt. He drove to downtown Dallas – a drive of about 15 minutes.[466] Ruby therefore left at around 11 a.m., which is 40 minutes after the call from Karen. He was clearly not in a hurry, and that's strange. Reporter Toni Zoppi, who knew him well, said the following: 'He had to be where the action was. He was like horseshit, all over the place, wherever anything exciting was happening. That's why the President's assassination and all the follow-up activity at the jail with Oswald and the press attracted Jack like a magnet.'[467] It would have been almost impossible for the Ruby from this description to stay away from the vicinity of the police building at 10.00 a.m. At 11.15, however, he was quietly standing waiting his turn at the counter of the Western Union office.[468] A black lady in front of him wanted to send a telegram. This took less than a minute. But they might just as well have had to carry out a transaction that was more time consuming, or there could have been two customers in front of Ruby in the queue. The timing within the Western Union office was therefore beyond his control. Ruby did not seem abnormally rushed or stressed. He dutifully waited his turn. The receipt for the money was stamped at 11.16 a.m.,[469] and the order to send the money at 11.17 a.m.[470] The transaction was therefore completed in the first half of the 17th minute,[471] and Ruby was on the street again at around 11.18 a.m. at the earliest. He then walked towards the police station. Ruby only arrived at 11.20 a.m., more than an hour after the scheduled departure of Oswald. It seems that it really was a coincidence that Ruby and Oswald stood eye to eye on Sunday, November 24, at 11.21 a.m. In an interview on his deathbed, Ruby said that a single traffic offense determined his fate. 'The ironic part of this is had not I made an illegal turn behind the bus to the parking lot, had I gone the way I was supposed to go straight down Main Street, I would have never met this fate because the difference in meeting this fate was 30 seconds one way or the other.'[472]

There is another curious element: Ruby shot Oswald in the stomach, not in the head or the heart. This points to an unprepared, impulsive action. Oswald came within an inch of surviving. He died in Parkland Hospital two hours after the attack. He could still have regained consciousness in those two hours, and could have made a statement at a time when he had nothing left to lose. From the point of view of the conspiracy hypothesis, that would have been disastrous for the conspirators.

Figure 42. Ruby took a resolute step forward, and only revealed his gun as he shot, so that bystanders could not immediately disarm him or deflect the shot. The shot with the middle finger, with his index finger directed at the victim, is unusual.

There are also some elements that might cast doubt on the purely impulsive character of Ruby's act:

- Detective Archer said to him immediately after the attack: 'Jack, I think you killed him.' While looking Archer in the eye, Ruby is said to have answered: 'Well I intended to shoot him three times.'[473] That seems a clear indication of premeditation, and is therefore contrary to the story of the miraculous timing.
- The Warren Commission portrayed Ruby as a grief-stricken, pathetic loser. But was Ruby crushed by grief, and surprised at what he had done after murdering a man on an emotional whim? If that were so, he doesn't seem to have lost his sense of humor. On arriving at the prison, Ruby underwent the usual rectal examination. The medical student on duty noted the following: 'Jack Ruby laughed and stated that "he had been given better massages."'[474] This is not the only incident confirming Ruby's good humor. The FBI noted that when they took Ruby's fingerprints and pictures for the police file, he 'exchanged pleasantries' with Detective Carlson from the identification division of the Dallas Police.[475]

The official story refers to a combination of Ruby's story: the depressive Ruby, the serial loser burdened with tax debts, the bruiser who was desperate for recognition, the emotional scatterbrain, and the outraged patriot who, through a coincidental set of circumstances, was able to carry out an impulsive act. The matter is clear for the conspiracists: Ruby silenced Oswald on the instructions of the real assassins of Kennedy. Both stories focus on the question of *why* Ruby killed Oswald. But the motives are open to multiple interpretations. It is a subject of debate, and thereby also a discussion without end. The question of *how* Ruby killed Oswald can be answered objectively. We can make a precise analysis of the available facts. Maybe this could lead to a better answer to the question of why he did it. The timing is the key to the riddle. We must first examine whether the encounter with Oswald was as tightly timed as was claimed.

Chapter 7 – Three crucial minutes

THE CRIME SCENE

The front of the police building in Dallas consists of a large neoclassical building in Harwood Street. It's built in gray hardstone, and has an imposing facade with ten Greek columns. Behind this building is a more recent complex in yellow brick. That part has two facades, one on Main Street and one on Commerce Street. Underneath this building is a large car park.

Figure 43. The entrance to the garage of the police building on Main Street and the exit on Commerce Street.

The entrance to the car park is situated on Main Street, and the exit on Commerce Street. They are aligned to each other, thereby forming a kind of tunnel connection between Main Street and Commerce Street. The police offices are situated on the third floor of the building on Harwood Street. This is where Oswald was interrogated. The basement can be reached directly using the elevator, with a short corridor leading from the elevator to the underground car park.

AN INGENIOUS PLAN

The police had been warned three times that night that Oswald would be murdered during his transfer to jail. Yet access for the media was given priority over safety.[476] The decision to allow more than fifty press representatives[477] into such a confined space demonstrates an incomprehensible stupidity. The final number of journalists would rise to 150.[478] To make matters worse, more than seventy members of the police force were also milling around in the basement,[479] dozens of whom undoubtedly had no specific task at that point in time. It was quite easy to circumvent the checks in such a large group of people.[480] All you needed was a camera or another attribute to create the impression that you were a journalist, and you were inside.[481] The Dallas Police

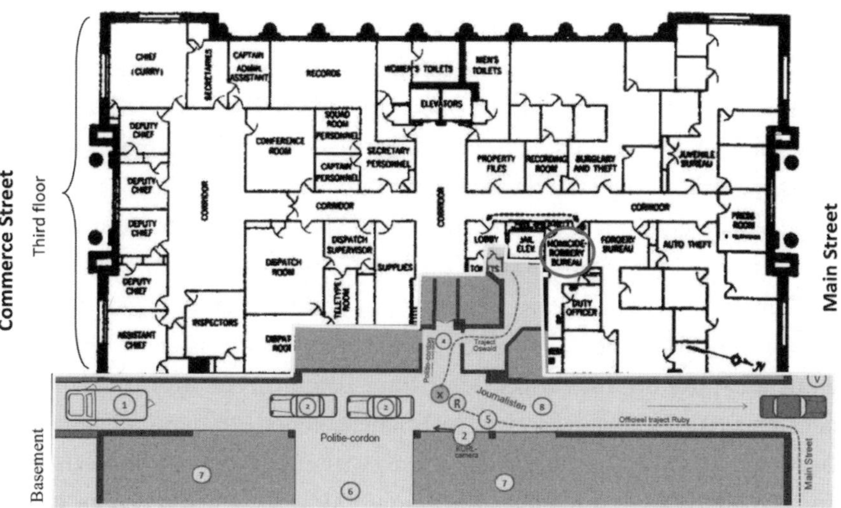

Figure 44. Connection between the building in which the elevator and the office of the homicide squad, where Oswald was interrogated, are situated and the basement car park underneath the adjacent building where Ruby (R) killed Oswald (X).

once again lived up to its reputation for slapstick justice. Somebody had, however, come up with the brilliant idea of protecting Oswald against the threatened assassination attempt by transporting him in an armored light truck. The truck was scheduled to enter the car park through the exit on Commerce Street. The national channels were to broadcast the maneuver on live television.

The armored truck was not in fact a police van, but a vehicle for money transportation. Nobody informed Captain Fritz of the plan, however, or put much effort into its practical development. Harold J. Fleming, Managing Director of the private firm Armored Motor Services Inc., only received a request for an armored truck between 9.30 and 9.40 a.m.[482] The police were not familiar with the rental firm, and could consider itself lucky that Harold Fleming could be reached, because he was just about to leave to attend Sunday service with his family.[483] Although Fleming was the managing director of the company, he was not the right man to arrange the practical side of the transaction. He first tried in vain to reach his local deputy manager, Mr. Hall. Operation Manager Leonard could also not be reached. Finally, he managed to get Mr. Mastin, the manager of the Fort Worth branch, on the phone. This was not an obvious choice, because Fort Worth is 35 miles away from Dallas.

Fleming asked Mastin anyway whether he knew where to find the key of a truck that was situated in Dallas. Mastin couldn't answer that question, but he told his managing director that Mr. James, a former vice president of the firm on early retirement, was living near the church where Mr. Hall was probably going to attend mass. James could get Hall out of the church. This idea actually worked, and Hall[484] could jump into action. He, in turn, contacted Deputy Manager Goin and driver Dietrich.[485] The latter was able to start work immediately. With regard to all these phone calls, Fleming stated to the Warren Commission that this was all a matter of 'getting organized and there was no time for conferring [...] This was an instantaneous decision.'[486] The whole affair was pure improvisation. After three death threats against the president's assassin had been received by phone, someone thought up a plan for Oswald's transportation to jail at 10 a.m. without any prior consultation – and the police started haphazardly contacting at least seven people at 9.35 a.m. The driver of the truck was picked by chance, and nobody had any information about his background. As soon as Captain Fritz heard of this foolish plan, he scrapped it.[487] The money-transport vehicle was only to serve as a distraction. While the armored vehicle was to draw all the attention, Oswald would be transported in a normal automobile. But this was obviously nonsense. The TV was continuously airing the events live. Everyone would therefore know that Oswald was not in the armored truck, but in the private automobile. Despite Fritz's opposition and the change in plan, the police continued to make preparations to get the truck. This also was fraught with difficulties. Managing Director Fleming suddenly came up with a practical realization: Would the truck fit through the gateway? After Assistant Chief Batchelor measured this, the truck turned out to be too high, because a pipe was in the way. The driver then drove the truck as far backwards as possible, but was not able to drive inside. To make matters worse, the vehicle also had starting problems, which were caused by a low battery.[488] It could only be started up with much difficulty, and it wasn't at all sure that it would be able to drive away from the police basement without problems. 'We were afraid the truck might stall on the ramp,' stated Fleming before the Commission without a hint of shame, and the Commission didn't consider this any further.

This whole vaudeville demonstrates that the police force in Dallas consisted of a gang of idiots who didn't have a clue about minimal security or about organization and planning at even a basic level. But there is still another aspect. The armored money-transport truck eventually managed to take up its desired position at the exit on Commerce Street between 11.10 and 11.15 a.m. This means that a whole series of insiders knew that the transport could never take place at 10 o'clock. When the vehicle for the official transportation of Oswald in a rather eye-catching manner was in the position from where the transport was to start, it was already later than 11.11 a.m. The police then still had to thoroughly search the vehicle, and that took more than five minutes. By then it was already 11.16 a.m. For those who knew the time of arrival of the money-transport truck and the duration of the search, it was clear that Oswald would not be transferred before 11.20 at the earliest.

Other outsiders were aware of this timing too. Lawyer Tom Howard came forward as Ruby's lawyer immediately after the shooting. Police Officer McGee saw the lawyer enter the police building through the column building immediately before the assassination of Oswald.[489] He walked to a position from where he could overlook the elevator. As soon as the lawyer saw Oswald leave the elevator, he said to the police officer: 'That's all I wanted to see.' The shot came immediately afterwards. The fact that Howard was able to come so close to Oswald in the police building at this crucial moment is significant. It gives an idea of the shockingly inadequate security, but also of the alleged ignorance with regard to the exact time of Oswald's transfer. Or was Howard's perfect timing another incredible twist of fate?

A UNIVERSAL CLOCK

We know with certainty that the armored vehicle only took up its position at 11.11 a.m. KDRL TV handed the continuous live recording of November 25 over to the FBI.[490] This recording lasts 31 minutes and 35 seconds. The images alternate between two cameras, one outside in front of the building on Commerce Street, and one in the basement. But the soundtrack of the broadcast is continuous.[491] The camera transition does not create a gap in the timeline. The shot, which occurred at 11.21 a.m.,[492] corresponds to the time indication of 13 minutes and 7 seconds on the KDRL film. The live broadcast started at 11.08 a.m. – which is nine minutes before Ruby wired 25 dollars in the Western Union office. We witness how the police thoroughly inspect the police van for several minutes. After the inspection, the broadcast had already been on the air for 9 minutes and 53 seconds. It was therefore 11.18 a.m. at that time. Ruby finished his transaction in the Western Union office on Main

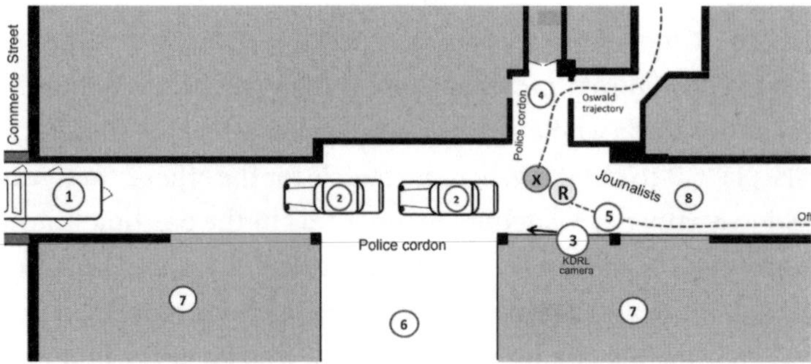

Figure 45. Floor plan of the crime scene.

Street. The countdown of the three crucial minutes on the KDRL clock can start.

Most journalists are behind the camera (3) in the car park that is situated slightly lower (7).[493] Ten to twenty privileged journalists are situated at the exit to Main Street (5). They block the ramp to Main Street (8). Ruby (R) jumps forward from this group to shoot Oswald at location (X). Two cars (2) are behind the money-transport truck (2). One of them was to be used for Oswald's transfer.

THE BLACK CAR

We hear a horn blast twice in the live broadcast. Twenty seconds after these horn blasts, Officer Blackie Harrison asks the journalists to make way. Next, a black car drives across the picture from left to right. This is Lieutenant Rio Pierce leaving the building from the lower car park on the right towards Main Street, i.e. using the driveway. This is because the money transporter (1) is blocking the exit.[494] Also seated on the rear seat are Sergeants Putnam and Maxey.[495] Half a minute later, the car disappears from the picture. There are 52 seconds to go before the shot.

Officer Roy Vaughn[496] was guarding the open gate on Main Street. He saw the car driving up and stood aside to allow it to pass. Officer Vaughn stated later: 'The first thing I noticed the car – still standing inside the ramp [...] As it come on up the ramp, I stepped to my right, and it came up the ramp.'[497] According to Vaughn, the car therefore initially stood still. This is correct, because we can hear the characteristic squeak of tires braking on smooth concrete 47 seconds before the shot in the KDRL film. Twelve seconds later, we again hear a car honking, but the sound is not coming from the black car, but probably from one of the two cars behind the police van. We know this because there are also horn blasts while the rear car reverses immediately before the shot.

In order to let the black car through, Officer Vaughn had to briefly leave his post at the gate. He took two steps onto the sidewalk to the right, with his back to the building, past the driveway lined with low walls, towards the east. This was also where the Western Union office was situated. The officer waved the black car on when it was clear to join the traffic: 'I stepped out on the sidewalk somewhere between the sidewalk and the curb, I believe it was right around the curb, and I glanced [...] to see that traffic was clear, and then motioned them on and I turned around and walked back.' Commission examiner Hubert also explicitly asked: 'You did not go into the street at all?' The reply was brief: 'No.' Hubert continued: 'You did not pass the curb?' Vaughn replied: 'No, sir; not that I recall. I don't believe I did at all.'

QUICK RUBY

The police officer briefly glanced at the traffic and then turned back to return to the gate he was guarding. According to the official story, Ruby used this brief moment to slip inside. None of the three occupants of the car saw Ruby walk towards the gate and swiftly jump over the low wall.[498] Ruby then walked unhindered and unnoticed across the entrance to the basement car park. This ramp is more than thirty meters long.[499]

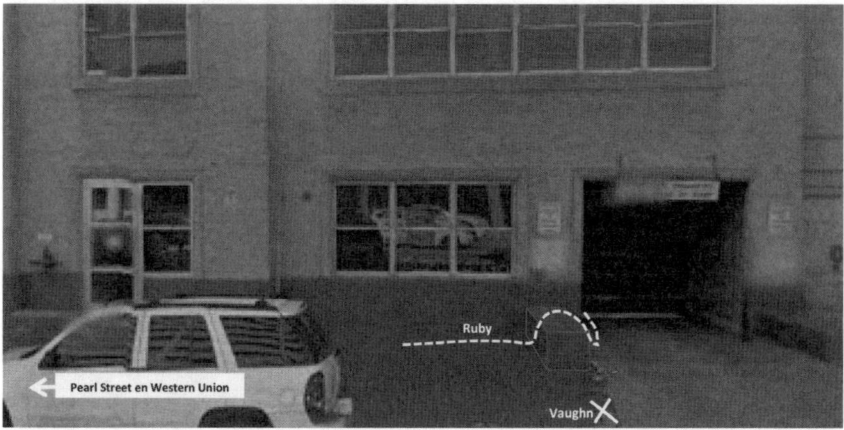

Figure 46. The gate in Main Street. Take a look at the wall Ruby had to cross unseen.

Thanks to the KDRL movie, we can calculate to within a few seconds precisely when Ruby stepped into the police building. The last indication of the presence of the black car in the car park was the squealing of the tires. This can be heard at time frame t-47, 47 seconds before the shot. Assuming that Pierce had already driven out completely ten seconds after standing still, and that Ruby slipped inside within the subsequent 5 seconds, then, at that time, Ruby had no more than 32 seconds for his appointment with world history. According to the Warren Commission, Ruby required 22 seconds to come down the entrance ramp.[500] This puts Ruby at the crime scene at t-10, ten seconds before the shot.

Seventeen seconds before the shot, there is a sudden movement in the hall, clearly the harbinger of the long-awaited convoy. At that time, Ruby was still walking down to the basement. Seven seconds before the murder, we see Captain Fritz usher the small procession inside. Ruby and Fritz therefore arrived on the spot at the same moment. Fritz's full attention is on the reversing car in which Oswald was to take his place. He is standing with his back to Ruby, who jumps forward at that point and shoots. There is a skirmish, and Ruby is easily disarmed. Reporter Bob Huffaker pronounces the historic words: 'Lee Oswald has been shot!' Ruby is taken into custody.

Figure 47. Captain Fritz is looking at the car that will transport Oswald. Ruby shoots.

Chapter 8 – Ruby at the crime scene

RUBY'S FIRST STATEMENT

How did Ruby get into the police station? The answer to that question may also provide the answer to two other important questions: Did Ruby act with premeditation and did he have help from third parties within the police station.

The most reliable information is usually the first statement after the facts. After his arrest, Ruby ended up on the sixth floor of the police station. He spoke with Sergeant Patrick Dean of the Dallas Police. According to Dean, Ruby explained that he had entered the building through the driveway on Main Street. He saw the black car driving out, and slipped inside the building at that moment.[501]

During the investigation, major doubts arose as to whether Ruby had indeed said that to Dean. Burt Griffin, a Commission staffer with integrity, was responsible for the Ruby investigation. He was convinced that Dean had lied. He tried – cautiously – to move the witness to a more truthful version, but the Warren Commission promptly whistled him back, and asked him to not approach the Dallas Police anymore. Above all, the Commission did not want to provoke controversy. There is another interesting detail: Dean was a good acquaintance of Joseph Civello, a famous Mafioso[502] who was a top figure in organized crime. In Dallas, Civello was known to be the manager of Carlos Marcello and, of course, he also knew Ruby.[503]

The first indication that Dean lied is Ruby's first official interview by the FBI. He refused to explain how he had entered the basement garage. The only thing that FBI agent Ray Hall could note down was: 'Ruby did not wish to say how he got into the basement or at what time he entered.'[504] Why would Ruby obstinately refuse to repeat to the FBI the statement he had already made two hours before in the presence of the police and the Secret Service? Dean had two witnesses of his first conversation with Ruby, Police Officer Archer and Special Agent Sorrels.[505]

In his first written statement, Archer made no mention of a statement by Ruby.[506] His memory only improved in his second statement, on November 30: according to Archer, Ruby had made a statement that could be summarized in three points. Point 1: The crowd in front of the police station on Main Street attracted Ruby's attention. This is already a lie: there were a maximum of five people[507] at the police station on Main Street, certainly no crowd, because there was nothing going on on the Main Street side of the building. Point 2: Ruby slipped inside while Vaughn and Pierce were talking to each other.[508] That is also a lie. Neither of them ever mentioned that they had had a conversation. Point 3: Immediately after his arrest, Ruby stated that he was in the basement three minutes before Oswald.[509] This cannot be true, of course, not even approximately. Three minutes before the shot, Ruby was leaving the Western Union office, more than a hundred meters away. The Commission heard Archer on March 25, 1964. He was not asked a single question about the first interview with Ruby or about how he entered the building.[510]

Special Agent Sorrels of the Secret Service, the second witness of Dean's conversation with Ruby, formally denied that Ruby had said anything at the time about how he had entered the building. Sorrels is the most reliable witness of the conversation. He was 62 years old at the time, and had more than forty years' experience in the job.[511] In contrast to Dean and Archer, he took careful notes.[512] In its report, the Commission said nothing at all about Sorrels's formal denial of Dean's version of the facts. We gradually get an idea why commission staffer Griffin was so sure that Dean had lied about Ruby's first statement. Another indication in this direction is the fact that, while the HSCA was looking deeper into the case in 1968, Dean refused to submit a written statement under oath about the events at the police station on November 24.[513]

Two other officers were also with Ruby after his arrest: McMillon and Clardy.[514] McMillon also confirmed the story of Dean. When Griffin questioned him, he was very careful: 'Let me see. Let me see those notes there. I believe I have it in them. Refresh my...'[515] Why had he said nothing in his first statement about Ruby's explanation of how he had entered the building? McMillon could only stammer: 'I didn't think anything about it being important at all at the time.' The report was only submitted to Chief Commissioner Curry three days after the murder of Oswald.[516]

Officer Clardy again dished up the story about the brief conversation between Vaughn and the driver of the black car. In Clardy's version, somebody had even seen Ruby entering. Ruby allegedly said: 'When I got approximately halfway down the ramp, I heard someone holler, "Hey, you!", but I don't know whether he was hollering at me or not, but I just ducked my head and kept coming.'[517] No-one else had heard this explanation from Ruby.

Later that day, McMillon and Clardy were also present at the first official questioning of Ruby by FBI agent Hall. When Ruby obstinately refused to disclose how he had got inside the building, McMillon and Clardy did not find it necessary to inform Hall that Ruby had already answered that question in their presence. McMillon reluctantly admitted to Griffin that any sensible policeman would have informed the FBI agent about Ruby's earlier statement.[518] The logical conclusion is that Ruby never made this earlier statement. There is yet another indication that Clardy lied.

The FBI, the Secret Service and the Commission staffers were unanimous: Ruby said nothing on November 24 about how he entered the building.[519] Yet Dean persisted in his lies, and found three policemen who were willing to lie with him.

THREE MORE WITNESSES

The Warren Commission predictably concluded that Ruby came into the building through the driveway on Main Street.[520] They thereby relied on three witnesses who had seen Ruby enter the basement. Two of them were again police officers in the Dallas Police. The first was Reserve Officer William Newman. Reserve officers are citizens who occasionally work for the police as volunteers. They were also keen to see Oswald in person on November 24. Newman saw Ruby coming in just after Oswald's arrival was announced with 'Here he comes!'[521] But that can't be right: the photo evidence proves that Ruby was already down there at that moment. The second witness was Reserve Officer Croy, but this spectator didn't notice anything special on November 24, or at least nothing he could remember on November 26.[522] Fortunately, his memory cleared around December 1. One week after the murder, Croy remembered that he had seen Ruby, and had even spoken to him. But his Ruby was wearing a 'dark maroon coat with a black thread woven into it' and 'wearing a brown hat.'[523] It's just too bad that Ruby was not wearing a jacket and that his hat was gray. On April 2, Croy stated that 'Ruby ran past him, burst through the line in front of him and shot Oswald.'[524] This is without doubt another lie. The photos prove that Ruby was standing quietly among the attendees five seconds before he sprang forward to shoot. The two testimonies are totally worthless as evidence that Ruby entered the building via the driveway. The Commission nevertheless mentioned the policemen as witnesses of its position, but wisely kept silent about their names and also that Burt Griffin, the Commission's own adviser, had labeled both of them as liars. We now have six lying police officers. Dean, Archer, McMillon, Clardy, Newman and Croy. The Commission did name the third witness of Ruby's entry: television producer Jimmy Turner. He saw Ruby coming in through the driveway.[525] But Turner was certain that Ruby was wearing a sort of bowler hat with a very broad rim: 'It was a felt hat, had a pretty large brim on it, and it was a – round on top, which you seldom see.' He remembered that the man who came in through the driveway also wore an overcoat and appeared 'much heavier'[526] than Ruby.

Apart from the two lying police officers, the Commission had only this one, rather doubtful witness of Ruby's descent into the garage. That's not very much when you remember that there were more than 120 people present in the basement, including many professional policemen standing with their eyes on Main Street, and who had to hermetically seal the garage against unauthorized people. The Commission nevertheless concluded that its evidence 'tends to support Ruby's claim'.[527] We cannot share this view. Dean whispered the statement about the driveway into Ruby's ear. Ruby himself refused to take a position in the early phase. In the basement, only two witnesses who lied and one very weak witness saw Ruby arrive. But there were in fact dozens of witnesses in the basement – and three in the black car – who did *not* see Ruby in the driveway. There can only be one explanation: Ruby was not there. Besides the one weak witness who saw Ruby, there is also at least one strong witness who did not see him: Officer Vaughn.

VAUGHN DEFENDS HIMSELF

The scapegoat in the story about the driveway is Police Officer Vaughn. His only assignment was not to lose sight of the 2.5 meters of the driveway to the garage. According to the official version of the story, he failed miserably, with the death of Oswald as a result. But Vaughn did not simply accept that version of the facts. According to him, Ruby did not come into the building through the entrance gate. The agent always remained formal in his statement. He also took a lie detector test, and passed it – in contrast to Dean. Vaughn was asked the following questions:

— Did you see Jack Ruby near the Main Street entrance?
— Answer: No.

— Did you allow Jack Ruby to enter the basement?
— Answer: No.
— Did you lie to Chief Fisher regarding this incident?
— Answer: No.
— Have you told Chief Fisher the complete truth regarding this incident?
— Answer: Yes.

The investigation ended with the clear conclusion of Detective Bentley: 'It is the opinion of this Examiner this person answered each of the questions with the truth.'[528] Police Inspector Revill was part of the internal commission of inquiry that had to investigate how things could have gone so fundamentally wrong. Revill was always careful in his statements, but he had no doubts about Roy Vaughn: 'I am satisfied that Roy Vaughn did not see Jack Ruby nor did he knowingly permit him to enter the basement.'[529]

Vaughn was also a good officer as evidenced by a review of his efficiency, where he scored 90 percent. He feared disciplinary consequences if he was made to bear the full responsibility for Ruby's unauthorized entry into the building, and he was obviously not happy with this. Vaughn had therefore every interest in finding witnesses who could confirm that Ruby did not come through the garage door. He remembered the presence of Officer Daniels near the driveway. Colleague Napoleon Daniels had indeed had a good view from the building of the situation at the driveway on Main Street. Vaughn called him on Monday to find out what he had seen. Daniels had seen the black car drive out. Had he seen someone walking down afterwards? Daniels answered: 'No, definitely not; there was nobody.'[530] Vaughn's relief was only short-lived. Four days later, Daniels said something completely different. He had indeed seen a man coming down past Vaughn, even before the black car drove out.[531] But that's impossible, of course. In that case, the driver and the two passengers in the car would have also noticed the man. Daniels changed his statement once again three weeks later, on December 18: he now accused Vaughn of having knowingly let Ruby inside.[532]

He stated it only took VAUGHN about 15 or 20 seconds to return to his position at the head of the ramp. He recalled wondering why VAUGHN let the man walk by him and assumed that he must have known the individual.

But this statement is also inadequate. It does not give Ruby enough time for the 30 meter descent.[533] Ruby would have had to jump forward and shoot immediately after his descent. That is contrary to his statement to the FBI on November 25, where he stated that 'he was standing among the other media representatives'[534], and with a photo[535] of Captain Fritz seven seconds before the attack. We can see Ruby standing among the journalists on the right of the photo.

Figure 48. Seven seconds before the attack, Ruby was already standing among the press representatives.

Daniels was already in his third version. Only the first statement is credible: Daniels did not see Ruby on the driveway. Daniels's lie detector test[536] was also devastating for his credibility. He scored 'false' on all questions. The difference to Vaughn who had 'Answered Truthfully' to all questions,[537] could not be greater. Even the Warren Commission had to admit that Daniels was lying.[538]

SOMEONE WHO SEES NOBODY IS ALSO A WITNESS

- Terrance McGarry was a UPI reporter. In the five minutes before the shot, he was standing in the basement on the ramp by Main Street. He saw noone come down.[539]
- Taxi driver Harry Tasker was parked with a view of the driveway. He was waiting for a journalist in the basement, and thereby carefully kept an eye on the driveway in case his customer came out and wanted to follow

Oswald in the car. Tasker saw the black car drive out, but he did not see Ruby going in.

- In addition, Sergeant Flusche had also parked his car on Main Street, and kept his gaze fixed on the driveway. He was waiting for instructions to escort the Oswald convoy, and was standing next to his patrol car. Flusche had known Ruby for years. He is also certain that he did not see him enter through the driveway on Main Street.[540] It is also remarkable that Flusche immediately gave his important testimony to his superior Lieutenant Knox, but that no trace of it has ever been found. His story only became known fifteen years later, during the HSCA procedure and through the intervention of a journalist.
- Sergeant Putnam was a passenger in the black car. If someone had to have seen Ruby, it would have been him. Putnam said there was not a single spectator five meters to the left and to the right of the car.[541] According to him, the attention of Vaughn was on the traffic on Main Street for a maximum of three or four seconds. 'We didn't even stop the car. It would be very few seconds,'[542] he stated.
- Officer Harrison – precisely the man next to whom Ruby appeared in order to shoot Oswald – had also known Ruby for twelve years, and stood at the ideal position to see the slope of the driveway. He asked the reporters to clear away from the exit to Main Street to let the black car through. He was therefore looking in the right direction at the crucial moment. Harrison was very clear in his first statement: 'He said he glanced up the ramp several times and was looking toward the Main Street ramp when Lieutenant Pierce's auto made a left turn into Main Street. He also said he did not observe anyone coming down the ramp on Main Street.'[543] But on March 25, 1964, Harrison stated before the Commission that he had *not* looked in the direction of the ramp until the car turned left into Main Street. We may add Daniels and Harrison to the list of lying policemen. That makes eight of them now.

If we take Harrison's first statement to be the correct one, there are then five strong witnesses who should have seen Ruby, but who are certain that this was not the case. With Vaughn, there are six. There were, of course, more than one hundred other witnesses in the basement who did *not* see Ruby enter through the driveway on Main Street. It's always dangerous to rely on witnesses who had seen nothing. Maybe many of them were looking in the wrong direction, but it's a known fact that people are well able to detect movement in the corner of their vision, and then respond by turning their head in that direction. The fact that most attendees did not see Ruby coming down the ramp proves nothing, but if more than one hundred people do not see anyone, this is still a strong indication.

TOO LITTLE AND TOO MUCH TIME

Ruby could not enter the building before the black car was completely outside. He then had to climb over the small wall before he could descend into the basement garage. This causes yet another anomaly in this scenario. We know that Ruby was on the sidewalk of the Western Union office three minutes before the shot. He was walking at a normal speed, according to the clerk at the Western Union.[544] The exact distance from the farthest exit of the Western Union office to the center of the ramp is 104 meters.[545] According to the timing, Ruby walked to the garage door half a minute before the shot. There then remain 2.5 minutes to walk a distance of 100 meters ... that requires a speed of only 2.5 km/h. On December 29, 1963, the police repeatedly tested the distance at a normal walking pace: 1 minute and 13 seconds.[546] Twice that time is therefore *not* normal. The only thing that the Commission could think of was that Ruby 'could have consumed this time (1) in loitering along the way, (2) at the top of the ramp or (3) inside the basement.'[547] The first possibility is already excluded. Why would Ruby deliberately procrastinate en route from the Western Union office to the police station? The second possibility is also excluded: none of the three occupants of the black car saw Ruby 'dawdling' at the top of the driveway. The third possibility is technically impossible. Ruby could only sneak in once the black car had driven out. There is no get-out: not only does Ruby not have enough time in the basement according to the official scenario, he also has too much time, more than one minute, on Main Street.

AN ALTERNATIVE ROUTE

If Ruby did not come into the basement through the garage door, how did he get in? Gary Mack,[548] curator of the 6th Floor Museum, knew the situation in the police station very well. According to him, anyone could enter the building through the glass doors of the main hall on November 24. Police Chief Curry confirmed that the double glass doors of the entrance hall on Main

Street were never locked in 1963.[549] Once you were in the hall, you could get to the basement garage via a staircase. There was a door at the bottom of the stairs. According to Sergeant Dean, this was definitely locked on the garage side. Reserve Officer Worley confirmed this.[550] But was the door also locked on the side of the stairs? Because of the fire regulations, the door had a large horizontal handle so that it could always be opened. Dean himself "believes," however, that the door was locked on both sides.[551] He also believed that, on the orders of Sergeant Putnam, the maintenance man, John Servance, had locked the door on the staircase side. Dean used the terms "I believe" and "I think" three times in two sentences. That is certainly cautious. The Commission spoke to Sergeant Putnam immediately afterwards, but carefully avoided asking a question about locking that door. John Servance was certain that the door was not locked on the staircase side, simply because it couldn't be.[552] His two colleagues Edward Pierce and Louis McKenzie confirmed this. So, once again, we know what Dean's 'belief' is worth. There is no doubt: Ruby could reach the basement via the hall and the stairs.

We can therefore outline Ruby's alternative route as follows:

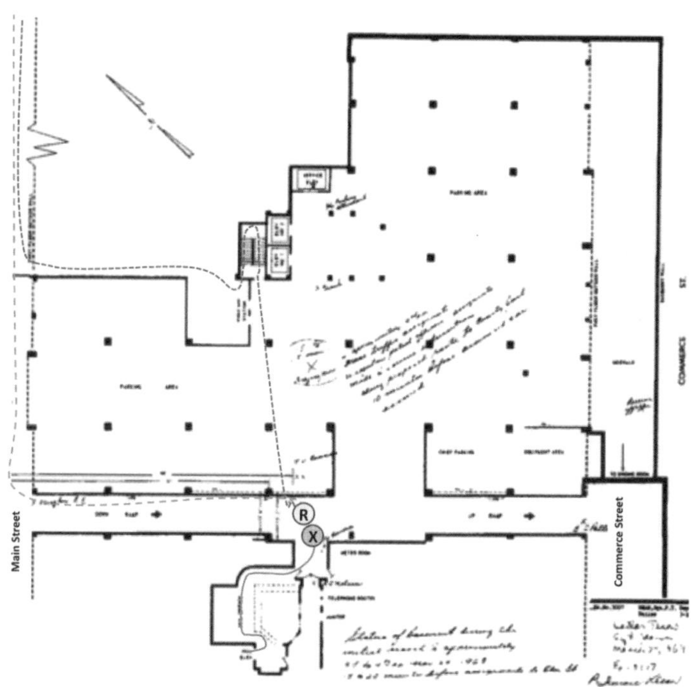

Figure 49. Alternative route that Ruby could have followed to get to the basement.

There is indeed an alternative option (by the stairs) and there is still the official version (by the driveway) for the diehard believers. On the basis of the lapse of time in the recorded TV program, we can now compare the timing of the scenarios to see which of the two is the most credible.

THE TIMELINE OF THE TWO HYPOTHESES

Now that we know the objective facts, we can compare the two timeframes:

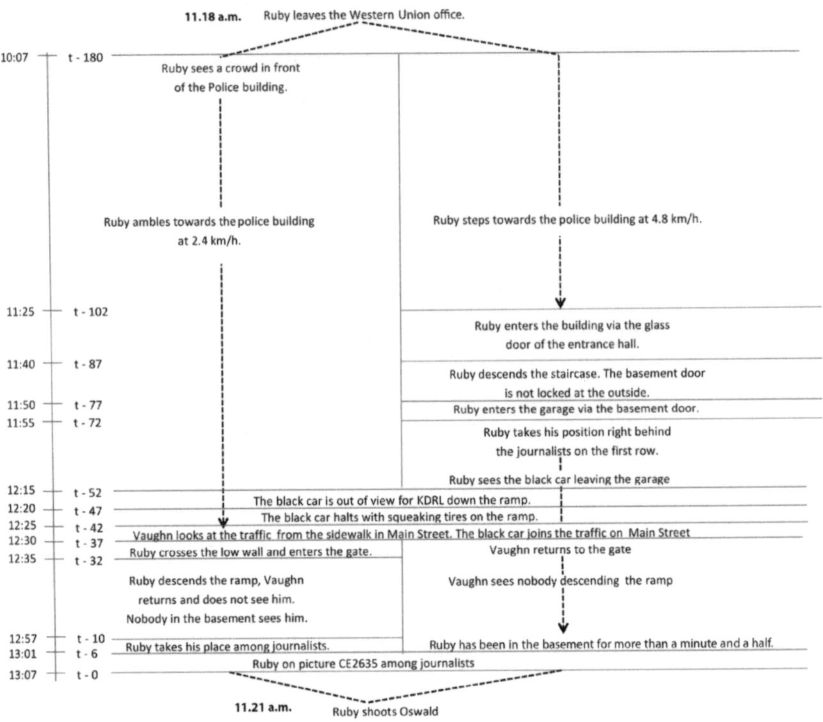

Figure 50. Which of the two scenarios is the most likely?

There is no doubt that Ruby came into the basement via the stairs, and not through the driveway. There are too many illogical elements in the official story, while everything falls neatly into place in the alternative scenario. The entrance via the stairs is also less conspicuous, and gives a reasonable explanation for all the witnesses who did *not* see Ruby.

Does it make a difference which route Ruby eventually took? Yes, because entering the basement behind the back of Roy Vaughn at the moment that a car happened to drive outside purely by chance could not be planned in advance by Ruby. If Ruby took the alternative route via the stairs, advance planning was not only possible, but also necessary.

THE ROLE OF THE POLICE

Ruby lied about how he entered the police building. He came down the stairs, not through the driveway of the garage. He also lied about the preparation that preceded the attack. He didn't get there by accident, but knew well in advance how he could enter. These lies could have been part of his attempt to plead "temporary mental incapacity." Ruby had sufficient experience in criminal law, and realized how important it was that his act should seem unprepared and impulsive. But more important is that all the police officers, with the exception of Vaughn, lied. Perhaps the explanation for these lies has nothing to do with the murder itself. Dean was responsible for the security of the basement. It is possible that he made up the alternative entrance in order to place the blame for his error on Vaughn. After Dean had kindly told him, Ruby saw the advantages of the scenario through the garage door. Pure chance played a much greater role in supporting this version of the facts, and when the cops showed themselves willing to support the story, Ruby had no objection to this. The true facts about how he came into the garage are not necessarily a deathblow to the official hypothesis.

If Ruby came into the basement via the stairs, this makes the tight timing slightly less tight. Ruby then had leeway of about ninety seconds, and that is much more than 'a few' seconds. But even if Ruby entered ninety seconds before Oswald, this still remains an incredible coincidence. We should actually consider how "accidental" Ruby's presence in the Western Union office was, because if Ruby was there *by chance*, he would also be in the police station basement *by chance* four minutes later.

Chapter 9 – The 25 dollar question

Ruby's tight timing is a crucial clue that points towards a purely impulsive act, and is closely related to the payment of 25 dollars to Karen Bennett through a Western Union office.

LITTLE LYNN

The 19-year-old striptease dancer Karen Bennett – with stage name Little Lynn – who asked for Ruby's help early on this particular Sunday morning was living with Bruce Carlin. Karen had already been legally married before, when she was fourteen.[553] In 1963, she had no idea of her parents' whereabouts, and made no secret of her debauched life. The Warren Commission – with hypocritical courtesy – addressed her as Mrs. Carlin. We will stick to Karen.

The core of the official story is true. It is a fact that Jack Ruby wired 25 dollars to Karen Bennett Carlin at 11.17 a.m. from the Western Union office on Commerce Street, at less than one minute's walking distance from the police station where Oswald was being interrogated. Deeper down, however, the story becomes rancid and unclear.

Figure 51. Jack Ruby and the 19-year-old Karen Bennett Carlin.

In November 1963, Karen had been working for Ruby for three months.[554] Being pregnant, she was in a rather uncomfortable situation for a stripper. She would not be a star anymore. Despite her young age, the chances that things would ever turn out well for Little Lynn were very limited. She was a stripper, a prostitute, a drug addict and a crafty, unreliable police informant. On May 15, 1963, telltale Karen made a statement to the Dallas police. G.T. Cox, an officer of the narcotics squad, recognized the informant. She had also been providing – not very useful – information for two or three years. Officer Cox painted a rather unflattering picture of Karen: 'a prostitute, which (sic) he knows went on the Circuit, which is a group of prostitutes who travel from place to place over the United States.' Further we read: 'Officers do know this subject is addicted to narcotics, and has told conflicting stories.'[555] Not a fine reputation for a teenager.

Exactly one hour before Oswald's murder, Ruby promised Karen by phone that he would wire her 25 dollars through Western Union. A little later, Karen and her 'husband' Bruce, along with millions of Americans, witnessed Oswald's murder live on TV. When it appeared that Jack Ruby was the perpetrator, it seemed unlikely that he would have taken the time to wire the money to Karen. She stated in this regard: 'After I saw the thing on television, I said I bet Jack didn't send the money, so my husband dialed the number and he asked if they had a money order for me, and they said: "Yes."'[556] The local Western Union office had therefore already confirmed before 12 noon that they had received the 25 dollars in good order. Karen had put pressure on Jack by saying she needed the money urgently, so it could be expected that the couple would pick up the money immediately after this welcome news. But when this was investigated at Western Union, it appeared that Karen only picked up the money at 3.25 p.m.[557] Apparently it was not quite so urgent, and this leads us to the first element of doubt.

BROKE OR NOT?

There are serious contradictions against Karen and Bruce being in need of quick money. The police in Fort Worth recorded in December 1963 that an informant had made the following comments about where they lived: 'Several characters going and coming from this location who he suspects as being prostitutes, and pimps. That they are in and out of there all hours and their dress is not becoming at times.'[558] If it is true that Bruce was running a private brothel in their house in December, it seems unlikely that he was unable to think of a way to get hold of a few dollars for shopping at the end of November.

On January 10, 1964, Karen's grandmother reported her as missing. The search warrant stated the following additional information: 'Money carried – Unknown – Subject usually carries large amounts.'[559] Three weeks later, Karen turned up again:

ADDITIONAL INFORMATION
Jewelry worn-wrist watch-make unknown
large diamond ring on left hand
Money carried-Unknown-Subject ususally carries large amounts

Is it really possible that Karen and Bruce didn't have a penny between them on November 23? The official storyline is that Bruce was unemployed. That turned out to not be the case at all. Bruce Carlin was the permanent assistant of Jerry Bunker, who had set up a trade in boxes with medicines, hair spray, razors, cosmetics and everything else hotel guests could need. Those boxes were available in hotel lobbies for the guests. Incidentally, Bunker was also an ex-boyfriend of Karen.[560] Bruce helped Bunker to sell the products, find new customers, take down orders and distribute the products in hotels across Texas and Louisiana. Together with Bunker, Carlin was on the road for deliveries from at least Thursday, November 21, to Saturday, November 23. Carlin didn't recall much of the trip because it was so busy: 'When we took these trips, it was a mad trip – we worked all day and would drive all night.' On Thursday, they finished with the motels around Houston, and then drove on to New Orleans. There, they heard that Kennedy had been shot on Friday afternoon, but that didn't stop them from continuing to work diligently. Carlin couldn't remember whether they had slept in New Orleans on Friday night. It was also possible that they had driven back to Fort Worth, where they had then arrived on Saturday morning.[561] It's very likely that they caught up on some sleep on Saturday. If they did stay overnight in New Orleans, Bruce was back in Fort Worth on Saturday afternoon at the earliest. The strange thing is that Bruce claimed that he was doing all this hard work for Bunker for free. Bruce accompanied Karen to Dallas on Saturday night. Perhaps Ruby would open up the Carousel anyway that evening, and then Karen could go to work. According to the official story, Bruce and Karen only had 50 cents on them.[562] Strange that a man who felt tough enough to hit his pregnant girlfriend[563] was shy about asking for a few dollars for 60 hours of work. Even if it's true that Bruce was not compensated for his efforts, it still provides food for thought. Someone who is willing to work free of charge is not in urgent need of money. There are other indications that Bruce had more means than he wanted to make out. At the end of his hearing by the Commission, Carlin actually complained about the problems this whole ado about Ruby had caused in his life. He said unsolicited: 'I was making good money up until this started.'[564] Bruce Carlin, who had worked for free and started into the weekend without a dollar, suddenly appeared to have been earning well before the affair with Ruby turned everything upside down. The statements about the financial situation of the couple are very shaky indeed. On closer inspection, that's not the only thing that's more than a little shaky.

A TRIP TO DALLAS

According to the official story, Karen was not sure whether the Carousel would open on Saturday night or not. She made her way to the Carousel by 9 p.m., the usual opening hour. Why Bruce accompanied her to her work is not clear. The third person in the company, the driver of the three, was stripper Nancy Powell – who went by the stage name of Tammi True. She had also danced in the Carousel, but Ruby had fired her on Thursday night. She went to the Carousel on Saturday night to claim her unpaid wages from Ruby. Tammi was also broke, it seems. The Carousel turned out to be closed, and there was no trace of Ruby anywhere. Karen suddenly realized that Bruce and herself didn't even have enough money to take the bus home. All they could do was to contact Ruby by telephone. 'I wanted some money on my pay to get back home,'[565] Karen stated before the Commission. Money for the bus – that is consistent with her first statement. On November 26, the FBI recorded: 'She asked Ruby for enough money for transportation.'[566] Tammi happened to have Jack Ruby's private phone number on her, and Karen phoned him at 8.30 p.m. Ruby promised to meet her at the club within the hour (according to her first statement) or within half an hour to forty minutes (according to her second statement) to give her the money.[567] Tammi, Bruce and Karen could only wait for the arrival of their generous money lender.

At 10.30 p.m., Ruby still hadn't shown up. Karen called a second time, this time from the office of the car park next to the club. Tammi was not present during this second phone call. The second conversation with Ruby was still only about money for the bus. Bruce took the receiver from Karen. Ruby claimed he didn't owe Karen anything, and Bruce replied: 'I realize that, Jack, but we need the money to get back.'[568] In the end, they came up with a practical arrangement: at 10.33 p.m., the car park attendant advanced Karen 5 dollars,[569] and Ruby would pay him back later.[570]

Karen erroneously situated the time of the second phone call between 9 and 9.30 p.m.[571] That is impossible. At that time, Jack was quietly drinking a Coke in the Empire Room, an establishment on Riverside Boulevard. He could easily have reached the Carousel in five minutes by car to fulfill the promise he made during his first phone call. But Ruby preferred to bore the pianist in the Empire Room. The chat lasted at least half an hour.[572] 'Maybe about 30 or 40 minutes, because he talks a whole lot – you know how fast he talks,' the pianist said later. Ruby did not make the impression that he was depressed, and did not once mention the assassination of the president and the so-called intense feelings this caused him. He even seemed in good spirits and gave three people a tip of five dollars each.[573] The five dollars for Karen's bus ticket could therefore not have been a big problem for him. Even after he left the Empire Room just before 10 p.m.,[574] Ruby did not drive to the Carousel. He calmly went back to his flat on the other side of the Trinity River, and simply left Karen, Bruce and Tammi, who had been waiting for him for hours, in the lurch. The drive to his flat only took fifteen minutes. Ruby was therefore back home by 10.15 p.m. at the earliest, where he had the second telephone conversation with Karen. But he first called his sister at 10.20 p.m. with the earth-shattering news that he had eaten liver with onions.[575] Ruby then phoned Lawrence Meyers[576] and arranged to meet him for a meal on Sunday night.[577] When the phone call with Karen took place, it was just before 10.30 p.m. This timing is consistent with the time stated on the receipt for the five dollars, i.e., 10.30 p.m. During this phone call, Jack said that he could not possibly come downtown, because he himself was expecting a visit or a phone call. That's just another lie. Ruby didn't receive any visitors and was not expecting a phone call. On the contrary, he told his roommate Georges Senator that he had some unfinished business in the Carousel, and then left immediately.[578]

With the five dollars they had received from the car park attendant, Karen and Bruce were able to return to Fort Worth. Karen remembered it well: she used some of the five dollars to pay for the bus. 'We didn't have enough money to get back on the bus, so we had to take some of it and go back on the bus.'[579] But Bruce recalled the same return trip as somewhat different. According to him, Karen and himself simply returned to Fort Worth the same way they had come: as passengers in Tammi True's car.[580] This was also confirmed by Tammi.[581] Strange that they needed five dollars to get home, while they could have a free ride with Tammi True. Why did Karen lie about how they returned home?

And why did Tammi come to Dallas? She no longer worked for Ruby, and didn't demand money at any time that night. It would be expected that Tammi would be standing angrily beside Karen during both phone calls, inquiring about Ruby's payment plans. But Tammi didn't speak to Ruby during the first call, and she wasn't even around for the second one. She seemed not to worry too much about her empty wallet. She resurfaced in the company of Karen and Bruce again after the second phone call, and the trio made a good night of it. In Fort Worth, they got smashed in The Three Twelve Club, where they arrived at 11 p.m. and stayed until the club closed its doors.[582] Any financial worries were obviously temporarily resolved.

RENT OR SHOPPING?

On Saturday night, Karen only asked for money for public transport. When asked by the Commission whether she also talked to Jack about the rest of her salary, Karen replied concisely and clearly: 'No.'[583]

Assistant Counsel Leon Hubert, the examiner for the Commission, quickly realized that this reply did not fit in with the official story. If only the money for the bus had been discussed, then why was the phone call on Sunday morning necessary? Despite the clear answer from the witness, the Commission Counsel immediately asked the question once again, but in different words. This time, Karen had her mind on the matter, and she responded: 'Just enough money to get back home on, and I happened to mention I would need money for rent tomorrow, and he said to call him.' During her second hearing in Augustus, Karen worded it as follows: 'I asked him for enough money to get home, at least.' And, about more money than necessary for the bus, she stated: 'He told me to call back some time the next day.'[584] The extra money was needed for the rent. This corresponds to what the FBI recorded on November 26: 'She needed money to pay her rent.'[585] But this story also needs some adjustment: the landlord had not urgently asked for the rent. 'Had your landlord been pressing you for the rent?' Leon Hubert asked. Karen's reply was clear again: 'No.'[586] The money was not for the rent, but for some groceries they urgently needed. This may be plausible, but why did Karen state something different initially?

The story of the urgent shopping also lacks credibility. How come Karen and Bruce hadn't realized on Saturday morning that they only had 50 cents to get through until Sunday or Monday evening? Why did Bruce start into the weekend on a budget of 50 cents, after having worked free of charge for 60 hours? Bruce was well aware that Ruby wasn't under any obligation to pay Karen's weekly wages before Sunday night, even if the Carousel had been open on Saturday night. The Commission asked Armstrong, the Carousel bartender, when the girls were paid. His reply was clear: 'Every Sunday night.'[587] Ruby sometimes only paid on Monday. During her deposition before the Commission, Karen indicated that she had been paid on a Monday twice, but couldn't quite remember whether her normal salary payments were due on Saturdays or Sundays. The Commission's examiner prompted the memory of the witness with a leading question: 'Wasn't your salary due that Saturday night?' The truth is that Ruby didn't owe her anything on Saturday,[588] and he also clearly said this to Bruce: 'She works for me and she is to get paid at a certain time and I don't owe the girl anything.' From the above, we already know that Bruce was also aware of this. Only Karen apparently knew nothing of it. In response to the question of the Commission, she could only stammer: 'I think it was; yes.'[589] The fact that she did not respond with 'yes' speaks volumes. Clearly, she knew perfectly well, like Bruce and Jack, that the salaries were not paid out on Saturdays. Who wouldn't know when their salary is due, particularly if they're short of money anyway?

AFTER THE MURDER

All these strange contradictions demonstrate that there was quite some lying going on about the 25 dollars. Karen's further reaction confirms that suspicion. On November 24, the day Oswald was murdered, she was questioned by Special Agent Warner of the Secret Service. When talking to Burt Griffin, an investigator of the Warren Commission, he let slip that Karen was 'extremely nervous and afraid' during the questioning. Warner later explained this in an affidavit: 'At the beginning of the above interview Mrs. Carlin was highly agitated and was reluctant to make any statement to me. She stated to me that she was under the impression that Lee Harvey Oswald, Jack Ruby and other individuals unknown to her were involved in a plot to assassinate President

Kennedy and that she would be killed if she gave any information to the authorities. It was only through the aid of her husband that she would give any information at all. She twisted in her chair, stammered in her speech, and seemed on the point of hysteria.' [590]

Little Lynn had presented proof on a silver platter that Ruby's act was purely impulsive. But she became terrified as soon as the consequences of her assistance had sunk in. She explicitly suspected Ruby of complicity in a conspiracy, and feared for her life. This only makes sense if she knew something that was extremely dangerous. Tammi True and Larry Crafard, a boy who was helping out in the Carousel, had meanwhile also left Dallas head over heels. There was clearly a sense of panic. When Karen had to appear as a witness in a hearing preceding Ruby's criminal case on December 23, she was carrying a gun in her purse. 'She had forgotten the gun was in her purse,' is what she had recorded.[591] This statement is also not an example of credibility. Another bizarre incident occurred during this hearing. Several prisoners escaped in the courthouse, and Karen screamed out in fear: 'Oh, my God, they're after me.'[592] Karen had clearly been living in fear for her life for a full month. She then went missing from January 10 to at least February 2.[593] She apparently went into hiding for three weeks, but from whom? Shortly afterwards, Karen went into hiding again, this time for the rest of her life. She died as Karen 'Block' on August 16, 2010, in Montgomery, Michigan.[594] Karen's sister stated to Shaw that Karen had 'basically lived in fear after the assassination and kept her windows barred and covered.' Karen's son described it as follows: 'He and his mother moved around a lot and lived in more states while he was growing up than he passed through later in life as a truck driver.' After her brief involvement in the events of November 23 and 24, 1963, the once fearless teenager lived in terror for the rest of her life.

When we examine the facts in detail, not much of the original story can be upheld. We can consolidate the bare facts in a diagram that inevitably demonstrates that Karen didn't need 25 dollars at all. The money transfer was part of a carefully prepared plan.

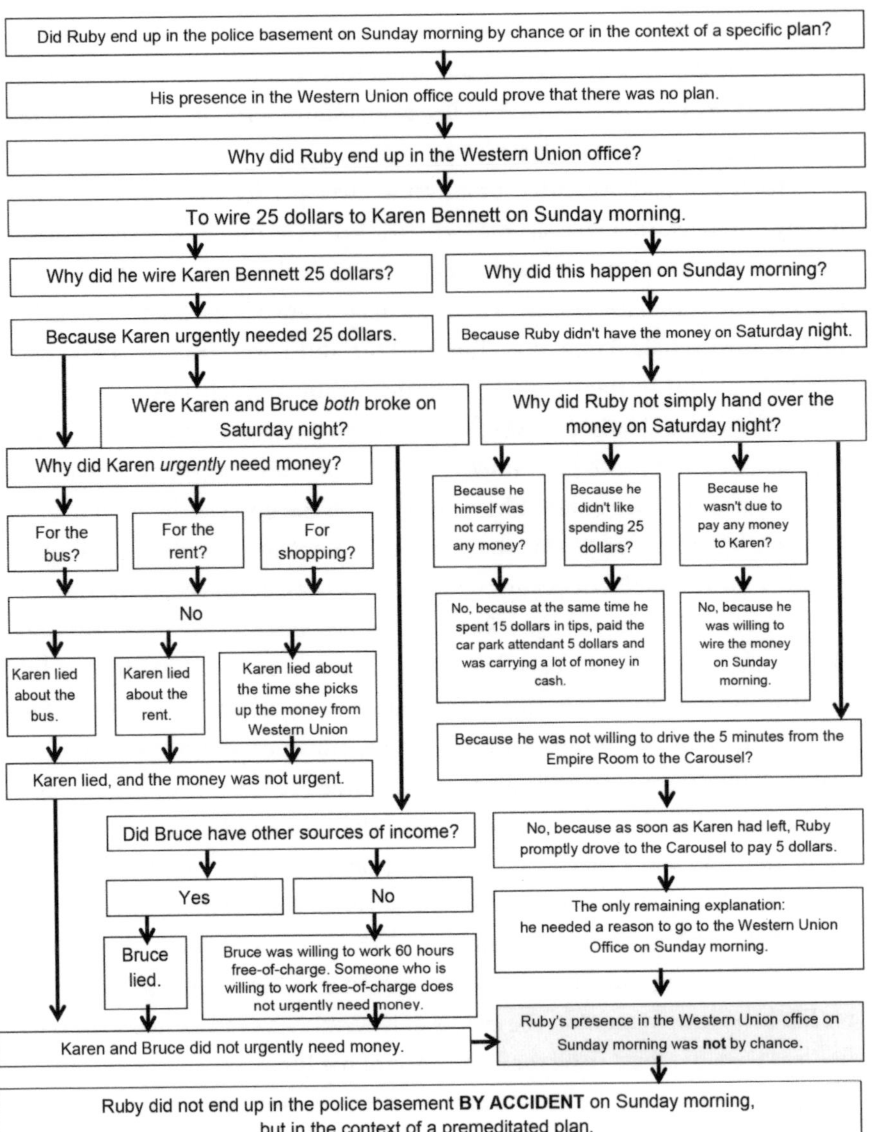
Did Ruby end up in the police basement on Sunday morning by chance or in the context of a specific plan?
His presence in the Western Union office could prove that there was no plan.
Why did Ruby end up in the Western Union office?
To wire 25 dollars to Karen Bennett on Sunday morning.
Why did he wire Karen Bennett 25 dollars?
Why did this happen on Sunday morning?
Because Karen urgently needed 25 dollars.
Because Ruby didn't have the money on Saturday night.
Were Karen and Bruce both broke on Saturday night?
Why did Ruby not simply hand over the money on Saturday night?
Why did Karen urgently need money?
For the bus?
For the rent?
For shopping?
No
Karen lied about the bus.
Karen lied about the rent.
Karen lied about the time she picks up the money from Western Union
Karen lied, and the money was not urgent.
Because he himself was not carrying any money?
Because he didn't like spending 25 dollars?
Because he wasn't due to pay any money to Karen?
No, because at the same time he spent 15 dollars in tips, paid the car park attendant 5 dollars and was carrying a lot of money in cash.
No, because he was willing to wire the money on Sunday morning.
Because he was not willing to drive the 5 minutes from the Empire Room to the Carousel?
No, because as soon as Karen had left, Ruby promptly drove to the Carousel to pay 5 dollars.
Did Bruce have other sources of income?
Yes
No
Bruce lied.
Bruce was willing to work 60 hours free-of-charge. Someone who is willing to work free-of-charge does not urgently need money.
The only remaining explanation: he needed a reason to go to the Western Union Office on Sunday morning.
Karen and Bruce did not urgently need money.
Ruby's presence in the Western Union office on Sunday morning was not by chance.
Ruby did not end up in the police basement BY ACCIDENT on Sunday morning, but in the context of a premeditated plan.

Chapter 10 – On the trail of Jack Ruby

The fact that Ruby entered the police building well prepared, and that the money transfer was also part of a careful plan, only says something about the premeditation of the murder, but does not rule out that Ruby committed the murder as a lone avenger. To obtain more clarity, we must again follow the trail of the perpetrator.

FRIDAY EVENING

At least five witnesses claimed that Ruby tried to get near to Oswald on Friday at 7.00 p.m.[595] The Commission claimed that all these witnesses were mistaken.[596] Ruby attended the Friday service at his synagogue, and then devised a new plan to get close to Oswald. He bought eight corned beef sandwiches at a delicatessen, and proceeded to the police station at 10.30 p.m. in a good mood. He greeted an old friend in the elevator 'and jokingly asked if he had been arrested.'[597] He left the elevator on the third floor, but a police officer stopped him from going any farther. Ruby lied that he had to bring the sand-

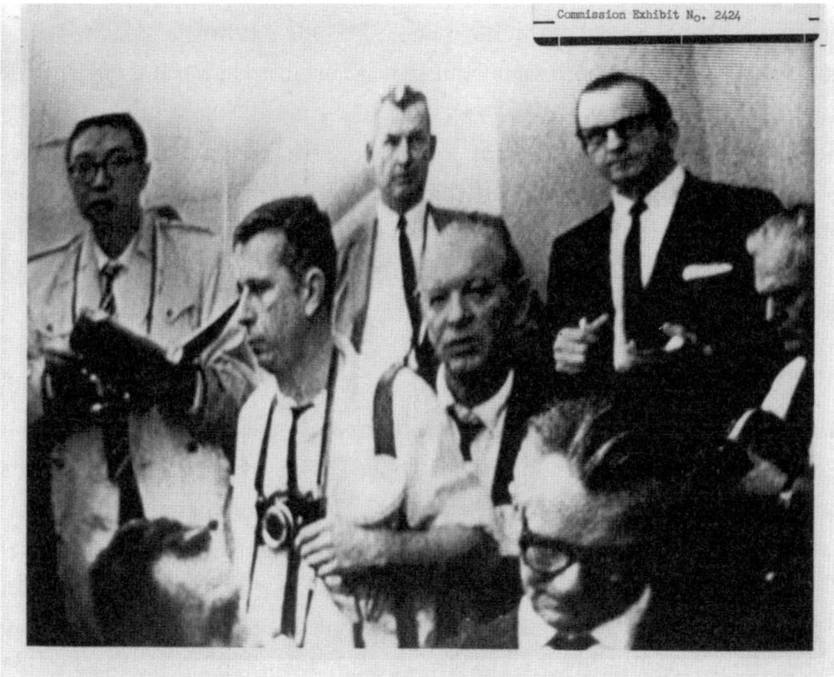

Figure 52. During the press conference, Ruby corrected the District Attorney: it was not the Free Cuba Committee, but the Fair Play For Cuba Committee!

wiches to Joe Long of the KLIF radio station. Just then Police Chief Curry and district attorney Wade appeared in the corridor. Wade announced that Oswald would appear at a press conference in a room in the basement. Ruby simply joined the crowd, and walked downstairs unhindered.[598] During the press conference, Ruby stood at the back, at a table among the journalists. He interrupted the District Attorney when he said that Oswald was a member of the *Free Cuba Committee* (FCC). Ruby called out that it was the *Fair Play for Cuba Committee* (FPCC). This is a detail that eluded even the District Attorney at the time.

Ruby was beaming after his small triumph. He shook the hand of foreign reporters and handed out tickets for the Carousel. He introduced Russ Knight, a radio reporter for KLIF, to District Attorney Wade. The journalist was able to ask Wade some exclusive questions. A smug Ruby enjoyed his role as a vital link between the police and the press, and did not look in the least like a murderer who could not get close enough to his victim to carry out his attack. Ruby went to the KLIF radio station around 1.45 a.m., where he finally was able to hand out his sandwiches. The 2.00 a.m. news started with 'Through a tip of a local nightclub owner…'[599] This was music in Ruby's ears, and it made his day. Radio man Duncan was certain: 'He was not grieving. If anything – if anything, he was – well, I use the word "happy" guardedly.'[600] Still, according to Duncan, Ruby took some satisfaction from his involvement in the events. When he left the radio station[601] at around 2:15 a.m., he still did not seem to be an assassin who has just missed his target. But his attempts to get near Oswald had, of course, been instructive for what would follow.

A NOCTURNAL CONVERSATION

There was a small parking garage at the back of the block of the Carousel, on Commerce Street.[602] After midnight, Police Officer Harry Olsen parked his car there.[603] Olsen also had his girlfriend, Kay Helen Coleman, with him, better known as Carousel dancer Kathy Kay. Olsen and Kathy had been in a relationship for one year.[604] They were both divorced, but a relationship between a police officer and a stripper is obviously not something you flaunt. 'You know, the police department, the wives couldn't work in a place like that,'[605] explained Kathy to the Commission. Kathy Kay had two daughters, Susan and Sheri, nine and seven years old. This did not prevent the couple from going out together at night. 'We went out. We, you know, got nervous sitting there,' said Kathy.[606] They were ready for a strong drink in a bar, and later ended up in the parked car, where they also drank a few beers.[607]

After the experiences at the police station and at the radio station, night animal Ruby was much too excited to sleep. After leaving KLIF, he drove past the parking garage and got into Olsen's car, where a long conversation took place. In his testimony before the Commission, Olsen claimed that the conversation lasted from two to three o'clock.[608] That's strange, because he talked about ten minutes in his first statement[609] – quite a big difference. According to the couple, four people took part in the conversation: Ruby, officer Olsen, dancer Kathy and night watchman Johnny. That latter is a lie.[610] Everything indicates that the couple were looking for some privacy in the car. They didn't need night watchman Johnny-no-name there. When Ruby joined them in the car at around 2.30 a.m., they were three people, not four. The lack of conversational topics is also quite strange. Police officer Tippit was killed on 10th Street. His colleague Olsen was working as a private guard on 8th Street, a stone's throw from the site of the murder, and Ruby was always the best friend of every man in uniform. You would therefore expect that the murder of Tippit would be the topic of conversation, if only indirectly. But when the Commission asked Kathy if she had talked about Tippit, she denied it. The only thing that Olsen could remember about the conversation was: 'We were all upset about the President's assassination, and we were just talking about how we hated it, that it was a tragedy.' Ruby also behaved quite normal according to Olsen's first statement in early December: 'He did not appear to be any more upset over the tragedy than the average individual.'[611] But when Olsen appeared before the committee on August 6, 1964, the official story of Ruby's "impulsive" act was now widely known. And the Ruby who Olsen then remembered suddenly became 'very nervous' that Friday night.

Ruby himself claimed that he had driven directly from KLIF to the editorial office of the *Dallas Times Herald*. He made no mention of the conversation in Olsen's car, despite having stopped for more than one and a half hours. All those concerned therefore initially lied about the encounter, and gradually adapted their story.

Between three and four o'clock that Saturday morning, Olsen and Kathy Kay drove back to her apartment. Ruby got Carousel-sidekick Larry Crafard and his roommate George Senator out of bed for a strange journey through nocturnal Dallas. Ruby was very agitated about a billboard that said 'Impeach Warren.' The design of the poster reminded him of an advertisement in a local newspaper that had criticized Kennedy heavily, and that on the very day of his visit to Dallas. These anti-Kennedy and anti-Warren initiatives annoyed Ruby immensely. According to him, they harmed the reputation of Dallas. The trio took a Polaroid photo of the billboard, and then, in the post office, tried unsuccessfully to find out the identity of the owner of the mailbox that was mentioned on the poster. Meanwhile, it was almost morning, and the three men went to a cafeteria for a cup of coffee.

At first, Senator told a very different story. In his first statement, he claimed that Ruby woke him at 3.00 a.m., that they talked about the death of Kennedy and that Jack was so inconsolable that he asked him to join him for a coffee. That time is wrong by one and a half hours, as if the conversation with Olsen had been cut from the timeline. The statement also says nothing about Larry Crafard and the reason for the strange nocturnal journey. Senator made a statement under oath about the events of November 23 the next day.[612] Instead of telling the truth, he served up an image of an inconsolable Ruby: 1) 'Jack was taking the President's death hard,' (2) 'he felt sorry for the President's family,' (3) 'Jack was too sad,' (4) 'he acted like he was stunned and shocked,' (5) 'That was the first time I ever saw tears in his eyes,' (6) 'He was still sad and very sorry for the President's family,' (7) 'I could tell Jack was brooding and still shock up,' (8) 'Jack kept repeating about the President's family and how sorry he felt for Mrs. Kennedy.' More than any other statement, it is this first testimony of Senator that convinces me that the whole story of a grieving Ruby is a joke. Ruby was not depressed when he left the police building. He was not depressed in the car with Olsen, and even less so when he excitedly got Senator out of his warm bed for a nightly ghost tour through Dallas. Even the Warren Commission admitted that Senator proved unreliable as a witness, and the HSCA found his statements "extremely vague" and "not coherent."[613] But why in heaven's name would Senator lie?

SATURDAY

On Saturday morning, Larry Crafard woke up Ruby by phoning him with a question about food for the dogs. Ruby scolded him so aggressively that the black boy packed his bags and fled from Dallas. Ruby slept on peacefully for most of the day. Only towards evening did he become active again. Ruby's timeline on Saturday night was pretty full:

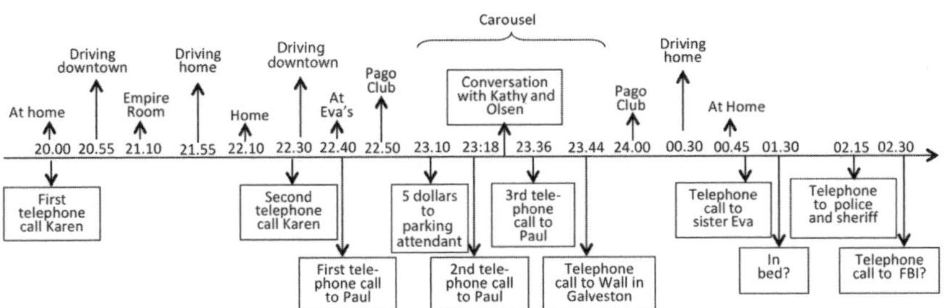

Despite all these pursuits, Ruby did not find time for a short detour to the Carousel to bring Karen the money he had promised her. It's clear that Ruby knowingly did not want to meet Karen on Saturday evening. Was Ruby in his apartment by chance when Karen called the second time, or was he there deliberately in order to register the call? Because as soon as Karen hung up the phone, Ruby drove back to the city, where he visited his sister Eva. At 10.44 a.m., he had a nine-minute long telephone call[614] from her apartment with his business partner Ralph Paul.[615] According to Paul, the phone call was a lachrymose affair: '... his sister was crying and he cried with her on account of the President...'[616] Based on Ruby's behavior earlier that evening, we can conclude that Paul was lying about Ruby's inconsolable condition. In any case, Ruby went to the Pago Club after the conversation with Paul. There, he spoke calmly and quietly with manager Bob Norton.[617] Ruby drank his Coke and finally went to the Carousel around 11.15 p.m. In the meantime, Karen was already on her way to Forth Worth.[618] Ruby paid the parking attendant back the five dollars he had advanced to Karen. The good man was now a reliable witness of Karen's urgent request for money. Ruby carefully kept the receipt as future proof of Karen's money problem.

At 11.18 p.m., Ruby made a call from the Carousel to the Bull Pen drive-in hamburger restaurant belonging to his business partner Ralph Paul. The manager had already left, so Ruby immediately called the home phone number of Paul.[619] Three telephone calls between Ruby and Paul were registered. The FBI extensively questioned Paul about these at 9.30 p.m. on November 24. The reason why this only took place at 9.30 p.m. is a story in itself,[620] a tangle of lies. What is certain is that Paul spent part of the afternoon with attorney Howard and Tammi True, and called in accomplices to lie about his use of time. The FBI eventually got hold of Paul, and a sound and thorough interrogation took place that lasted more than two hours. In his first statement, Paul shamelessly claimed that the last time Ruby had called him was on Saturday afternoon at 3.00 p.m. That was their last contact.[621] Ralph Paul, Ruby's best friend and business partner, lied. Imagine this situation for a moment:

— Your best friend calls you three times on Saturday night;
— This friend then commits a murder on Sunday morning;
— The police interrogate you for more than two hours on the same day;
— You make no mention of the nocturnal calls.

The further investigation, naturally, brought the calls to light. During his interrogation by the Commission on April 15, 1964, Paul's memory therefore had to be restored, be it only partially. He stated that Ruby only phoned him twice: at 10.30 p.m. and again at 11.30 p.m.[622] He continued to deny the third call. According to Paul, Ruby was heartbroken and crying together with his sister during the second phone call at 11.30 p.m. This is not true: Ruby only made the first call from his sister's apartment. The other calls were made from the Carousel, where he also remained all the time between the calls. Paul also continued to lie about the topic of the conversation: "He told me that no one was doing business downtown." That was apparently the only topic. But why would Ruby call Paul three times to share the same meaningless message?

After the second phone call with Paul, Ruby went to arrange the pictures in the window of the closed Carousel, surely an urgent activity late on a Saturday night. Just at that moment, quite by accident, Kathy Kay and Officer Harry Olsen drove by. Olsen said he had last met Ruby on Friday night. He thereby failed to mention that he also briefly spoke to Ruby on Saturday night in front of the Carousel.[623] The entrepreneurial duo then drove around aimlessly, as far as we are to believe them, for more than three hours. On Sunday morning, they heard the news that their close friend Ruby had murdered Oswald. Kathy, Olsen or both also lied about their further activities on Sunday.[624] Let's therefore examine Harry Olsen's whereabouts in more detail.

Due to a broken kneecap, Police Officer Olsen was off duty on the day on which President Kennedy visited the city.[625] This did not prevent him from helping out a colleague, whose name escaped him, by carrying out his side-job as a security guard at a villa. 'I was working at an extra job guarding an estate,' explained Olsen to the Commission. The policeman on sick leave worked as a private security guard from 7.00 a.m. to 8.00 p.m. on November 22. But in Karen's version, Olsen was already home at 4.00 p.m. Unfortunately, Olsen could not remember the owner's name or the exact address of the property. We must therefore also include Olsen in the select club of people who do not remember where they were when they heard the news of Kennedy's assassination. Kathy had brought Olsen his lunch at midday, remained on the spot for an hour and phoned the Carousel from there. But she also could not remember the exact address of the mysterious estate. Eventually, however, Olsen recalled that it was actually on 8th Street. [626] Coincidentally or not, that is only a stone's throw from 10th Street, where Officer Tippit was murdered. Tippit was himself on 8th Street at 12.54,[627] at the moment when Kathy brought Harry his lunch.

Olsen therefore had no alibi for the time of Kennedy's assassination. He was at an unknown address near Oswald's rented room, close to where his colleague Tippit was feverishly looking for someone immediately after Kennedy's assassination. Olsen met Ruby on Friday evening and on Saturday evening. The true content of those conversations will remain a mystery, and the only thing that is clear is that all those involved have lied about it. If Olsen's amnesia about November 22 had something to do with the plot against Kennedy, and the reason for his presence on 8th Street was in connection with his colleague Tippit, who was nearby, then this police officer was closely involved in the three murders of that weekend.

After the brief conversation with Kathy and Olsen, Ruby called Ralph Paul a third time. Once he had hung up, he suddenly remembered an urgent problem with amateur strippers in the establishment of his competitor, Weinstein. He took the spirited initiative to thereby call Breck Wall, the chairman of the stripper's trade union, AGVA, in Dallas at 11.44 p.m.

According to the official story, Ruby wanted to persuade the stripper union to prohibit his competitor from using unpaid amateurs. AGVA was a front organization of the Mafia. Even Bugliosi[628] and Posner[629] agree about this. It is not inconceivable that Ruby had a serious problem with his payments to the AGVA. This is why he was in regular telephone contact with the union just before the murder, and not about the amateur strippers, a small problem that had dragged on for more than two years. Ruby had already complained about it in March 1961,[630] and this problem could therefore not have been the reason for an urgent phone call to Wall in the night from Saturday to Sunday. Incidentally, Wall was with some childhood friends in Galveston, 500 kilometers away from Dallas, at the time. Although Ruby did not know these friends, and nobody actually knew where Wall was,[631] Ruby's call reached him barely a few minutes after his arrival in Galveston.[632] At exactly the same time, the very skilled pilot David Ferrie arrived in the seaside resort. Ferrie had had a meeting with Carlos Marcello on Friday and, following the news about the assassination of Kennedy, had left New Orleans in a hurry, despite a heavy storm. There was an airfield in Galveston, the perfect starting point for flying a small plane to South America or Mexico. But back to Ruby: he miraculously managed to reach Breck Wall at the right place and at the right time.[633] The call lasted only two minutes. The chances of them meaningfully discussing the amateur strippers in that time is nil. The official story therefore makes no sense.

Jack re-emerged in the Pago Club[634] at midnight, where he sipped a Coke for half an hour – he rarely drank alcohol. Three witnesses confirmed his presence. Ruby then called it a day, and drove back to his apartment. He called his sister again at a quarter to one in the morning.[635] Ruby himself claimed that he finally went to bed at 1:30 a.m.[636] There are no witnesses of this.

There were three more mysterious phone calls that night: one to the sheriff, one to the Dallas Police and one to the FBI. A man called the sheriff's office at 2.15 a.m. Deputy Sheriff C.C. Mc Coy picked up the phone. The unknown man said that a committee had decided that Oswald was to be killed during his transfer from the police station to jail.[637] At about the same time, Superintendent Glen King of the Dallas Police also received a call with the same message.[638] It was the turn of the FBI at 2.30 a.m. A man said: 'I represent a committee that is neither right or left wing and tonight, tomorrow morning or tomorrow night, we are going to kill the man that killed the President.' He then added: 'We wanted to be sure and tell the FBI, Police Department, and Sheriff's office.'[639] We can thus assume that the three calls came from the same source. Superintendent Frazier of the Dallas Police received the report from the FBI and alerted Captain Fritz, who referred him to Police Chief Curry. Unfortunately, Curry had put his phone off the hook in order to be able to sleep undisturbed.[640]

There is no evidence to figure out who informed the three police authorities of the intention to shoot Oswald. But in any case, someone warned about the attack three times, almost like a biblical invocation to turn away evil. It takes little imagination to recognize the confused mind of Ruby here. The man who called the officers was undoubtedly a very troubled person. A prankster does not call three different authorities, and someone who is planning an attack must really be mixed up to attempt to thwart his own plans and increase the risk of arrest. But, in the light of his life story, something like this could be expected of Ruby. It looks very much as though the three phone calls in the night originated from Ruby. That is also what Captain Fritz believed: 'I have always felt that that was Ruby who made that call.'[641]

SUNDAY

Karen had been asked to call Ruby on Sunday morning around ten o'clock. The phone call took place at 10.19 a.m.[642] and lasted two minutes and twenty seconds.[643] All the objections from the night before about sending the money had disappeared like snow in the sun. Ruby made no objection whatsoever to the 25 dollars that Karen asked for: 'Well, I have to go downtown anyway, so I will send it to you by Western Union.'[644]

Ruby sent the money at 11.17 a.m. Karen and Bruce collected it at 3.25 p.m.[645] from the Western Union office in Fort Worth. They also lied about this. At 11.00 p.m. on the same day, Karen said she picked up the money ten minutes after Ruby had shot Oswald.[646] The FBI noted: 'Mr. and Mrs. Carlin *immediately* went to the Western Union Office, Fort Worth, Texas, and waited.'[647] Bruce was also present at that statement, and it was therefore not an innocent mistake. Their memory could not have been so bad that they no longer remembered at 11.00 p.m. that they had only collected the money at 3.25 p.m. Bruce and Karen therefore deliberately lied. They then adjusted their statement: they meant 'ten minutes after Karen knew the money had indeed been sent.' But this confirmation came almost immediately: 'My husband dialed the number and he asked if they had a money order for me, and they said, "Yes."'[648] Karen therefore knew at around 12 noon that the money was available, and they therefore did not collect it 'ten minutes later.' In reality, the couple took their time. This is shown by the third version of their story: 'We ate and washed dishes, and I cleaned up the house, and it took me a while to get dressed.'[649] There were apparently sufficient provisions present in the Carlin household to calmly cook. This is again contrary to the story of the urgent grocery shopping. A quiet meal, washing the dishes, cleaning, and taking time to dress themselves were all more important than collecting the money.

Why did Karen and Bruce lie about the timing of the collection of the money? They wanted to maintain the impression that they really needed the money urgently. But, all too quickly, Karen, who was certainly not easily intimidated, remained terrified of the consequences of those lies for the rest of her days. That only makes sense if Karen knew that the story of the 25 dollars extended beyond Ruby.

THE COMPLICITY OF THE POLICE

All this leads to a clear conclusion: the murder of Oswald has been carefully staged. The money transfer to Karen was fabricated, and there was careful thought about how the security in the police basement could be bypassed. But there remains one unsolved mystery: How did Ruby know so accurately when he had to "accidentally" emerge?

Lieutenant Revill was part of the internal inquiry commission of the police in 1963. He stated before the HSCA in 1978 that if the money transfer was a setup, 'then Ruby had to have had assistance from someone in the police department. To know exactly what time Oswald was to be transferred.' Fourteen years earlier, Ruby himself also expressly stated before the Warren Commission: 'If it were timed that way, then someone in the police department is guilty of giving the information as to when Lee Harvey Oswald was coming down.'[650]

The man who stands out most as a possible accomplice is a policeman, Blackie Harrison. He was the man behind whose broad back Ruby hid before his lunge at Oswald. He was also one of the police officers who lied about how Ruby entered the basement of the police building. Harrison had known Ruby for twelve years.[651] But, at the crucial moment, he had not seen or recognized Ruby behind or next to him, he claimed. Ruby became very angry when the name Harrison was discussed at a hearing.[652] He did not want to embarrass his old policeman friend. But why would Harrison get into trouble if he had indeed not seen Ruby before the attack? Interrogator Revill had serious doubts about Harrison. He explicitly demanded that Harrison underwent a lie detector test. The test took place on December 13, 1963, but Harrison sabotaged it by taking tranquilizers in advance.[653] The test that was carried out by Detective Bentley was assessed as 'not conclusive.' Lieutenant Revill subsequently preferred not to provide an official statement to the Commission about Harrison, a colleague who he met on a daily basis: 'If this is being recorded, then I'd rather not state an opinion as to his [Harrison's] truth and veracity.'[654] That certainly says enough. If Revill was convinced that Harrison had told the truth, he would have said so.

The fact that Ruby hid behind Harrison's back before he lunged at Oswald is actually not the only indication of the involvement of that officer in the scenario. Blackie Harrison went to have a coffee outside the police building with his colleague Louis Miller on Sunday morning at around 8.00 a.m. They tarried in the coffee shop for about half an hour until they were called back to the station by telephone.[655] That may seem perfectly normal, but we are on our guard, because, thanks to Revill, we know that not too much credence should be placed on Harrison's statements. On March 24, 1964, Commission Counsel Griffin wanted to question Louis Miller about the coffee break. That should have been a standard procedure, but Miller acted extremely difficult. He refused to take the oath and was unreasonably suspicious. The hearing started at 3.55 p.m., and Miller had the commission counsel explain for twenty minutes what the interview was to be used for. After the incident with Dean, Griffin had become quite cautious. He patiently explained the procedure, but Miller kept asking stupid questions and, at 4.15 p.m., remembered that he had to collect his children at 4.30 p.m.[656] Griffin tried to schedule the hearing for later that evening, but it was ultimately postponed to the following day. Miller now did take the oath, but his whole statement suffered from persistent amnesia. His story consisted of variations on the same theme: I don't recall, I don't remember, I wouldn't have any idea, it is possible, I couldn't say, I'm not sure, the best I remember ...[657] Miller did not know the exact time of the coffee break, and also forgot who had called Harrison. These are, however, two concrete facts about which there is no dispute: the timing of the coffee break was between 8.00 and 9.00 a.m., and it was Goolsby who had called Harrison with the request to return to the station as soon as possible. But even about this, Miller was extremely cautious and careful in his statements.

When Harrison came to testify, he brought a lawyer with him. Commissioner Griffin noted in his memorandum that Harrison 'was somewhat slow in revealing the coffee-break [...] and had to be prodded to talk about the telephone call he received there.'[658] But another hole in Harrison's activities was more important. 'About, I would say, 3 or 4 or 5 minutes to 11, I went down to the subbasement to get me some cigars.'[659] There is a strong implication here that Harrison phoned Ruby from the police building shortly before 11.00 a.m. That would perfectly match Ruby's timing. The trip to the Western Union office took about fifteen minutes.[660]

We have already stated more than once that the police force of Dallas was not a good example of integrity and sense of duty, and that there were lies, blunders and bungles, even by 1963 standards. But fumbling and the blurring of moral standards are not proof of complicity, even though the whole story points in this direction. 'The problem with falsified stories is that inconsistencies frequently occur. As opposed to the truth, which is compatible with its environment,' wrote Bugliosi on page 882 of his opus magnus.[661] What makes the whole Ruby story so suspicious is the fact that so many lies and inconsistencies are needed to keep it afloat. Ruby was not overcome by grief, Karen was not in need of money, the AGVA was not a trustworthy trade union, policemen who were supposed to protect Oswald influenced Ruby, gave him access, provided information, ignored death threats aimed at Oswald, and lied constantly. The official story of Ruby as a troubled misfit who coincidentally got the chance to shoot Oswald is nonsense. The image of the not very bright Ruby is also not correct. Ruby seemed to be very well capable of devising plans, and of adjusting his strategy when they took a wrong turn. We must also qualify whether Ruby was an inveterate chatterbox. Ruby was a man with a lot of secrets. The people around him knew very little about his doings.

A WORKING HYPOTHESIS FOR THE MURDER OF OSWALD

The facts only fit together in the following scenario:

1. Ruby did not see himself as part of Kennedy's assassination. That explains his responses during the lie detector test. According to the machine, he answered truthfully when he said he was not part of a conspiracy. He indeed had nothing to do with the assassination of Kennedy, and was only involved in the murder of Oswald.
2. Ruby was only involved in the plot as the executor of a separate contingency plan. He was not a Mafioso nor an ice-cold assassin. That is precisely the point: the conspirators would have to be crazy to give the murder of Oswald the signature of a professional liquidation.
3. Only the scenario of an impulsive act by an unstable man was suitable. The investigation then stops at the perpetrator. Oswald was never left alone. His killer would certainly be arrested and put on trial afterwards. It was therefore necessary that he should be convinced that the murder was carried out on his own initiative and with his own motive. Otherwise the murder would be a waste of time and, once in custody, the assassin would perhaps be a greater danger than Oswald.
4. Officer Olsen was near Oswald's rented room just after Kennedy's assassination. Tippit also popped up there moments later. Whatever the plan was, it failed, and ended with the death of Tippit.
5. The same evening, Olsen primed the impressionable Ruby by spooning into him that killing Oswald would be a heroic act, a mission of honor. Maybe Olsen shared responsibility for the failed attempt to intercept Oswald in Oak Cliff. In any case, Olsen took this part of the preparation of Ruby upon himself. Afterwards, in his testimony before the Commission, he no longer recalled what he had said during the late-night conversation with Ruby. He did remember, however, what Ruby had said: 'It's too bad that a peon, or a person like Oswald, could do something like that.' Olsen remembered the following words from his girlfriend Kathy Kay: 'In England they would have Oswald by his

toes and drag him through the street.'[662] A legitimate civil retaliation against Oswald was certainly the topic of conversation.

6. Once Ruby seemed susceptible to the basic idea, he could be put under pressure on Saturday, probably through the AGVA, to carry out the murder of Oswald. Olsen and Kay had already handed him a ready-made motive. He was assured that the murder of Oswald would relieve him of his financial worries. As a bonus, he could count on the recognition and appreciation he so craved. If they played the game smartly, Ruby would be quickly released and, in addition, would gain the status of a national hero.
7. Ruby could no longer resist the tempting offer. He also knew that he would definitely become an outcast if he refused, and that the AGVA would tighten the noose around the neck of the Carousel. He actually did not have much choice.
8. Then arose the problem of the practical approach. Ruby knew how justice worked in Texas. Given an acceptable reason, such as a (white) perpetrator who briefly lost his mind out of moral indignation, the verdict of the jury would be mild.
9. Ruby had already stood face to face once with Oswald that weekend. He knew that he could get close to him, and was assured that the police would help him in staging a new encounter.
10. In order to camouflage the premeditated nature of the act, Ruby looked for a reason for being near the police station by 'pure chance.'
11. Karen *Little Lynn* and her Bruce had always been willing to support Ruby in his shadowy plans, and wouldn't shrink from making another false statement. The plan that Karen urgently needed money from Ruby was thereby concocted. This would be sent by Western Union in order to be near the police station 'by coincidence.'
12. Officer Harrison would ensure that Ruby would be at the right place, neither too early nor too late. That is the strong – and at the same time the weak – point in the plan. The tight timing would indicate chance, but it also meant that Ruby, the disaster tourist par excellence, could not be in the police station at ten o'clock. That is a strong indication that he knew quite well that nothing would be happening there at that time.

13. With the help of the police, Ruby entered the building through the entrance hall and the stairs to the garage. He was not in the basement for 'a few seconds,' but actually more than a minute before Oswald was brought out.
14. The plan still nearly went wrong when Ruby warned the legal authorities about the planned attack at least three times on Saturday night. A hopelessly contradictory attempt to frustrate his own plans seems just the thing for Ruby. It's almost as if he felt the need to submit the terrible act he was about to commit to a trial by ordeal. If the murder still took place despite his warning, it would not be his fault, but the fault of those who did not prevent the pre-announced murder. But there is also another possible explanation: Ruby was put under pressure to commit the murder, and saw only one way to escape it, namely by increasing the security around Oswald. If the police drastically changed their plans because of the telephone threats, the persons ordering the attack could hardly blame Ruby for not bringing it to a successful conclusion.
15. Ruby's attack was the third attempt to eliminate Oswald. Olsen, who was partly responsible for the failed attempt by Tippit, set Ruby up. Dean ensured that he could enter the crime scene undisturbed. Harrison informed Ruby about the right time.
16. The conspirators themselves were careful to remain in the background.

FILE 4

L.H. OSWALD, NUTCASE OR AGENT?

It was a journey into a maze that had grown,
over the years, to bewildering proportions. Yet what emerged
were similar images along many of the pathways,
an indication – often only gossamer – of a concealed thread
emanating from a common spool.

Gaeton Fonzi, 'Who Killed JFK?,' *Washingtonian*, November 1980

Chapter 11 – Worse than mistaken

We have determined that Oswald could not have been the sniper in Dealey Plaza. This means that there were accomplices. There is no single innocent explanation for the fact that Tippit was specifically looking for Oswald in the right place less than fifteen minutes after the assassination. Ruby was also no lone nut. But who were the other parties involved?

If the perpetrators involved Oswald in the plot, they must have been in touch with him before the assassination. If we follow Oswald on his journey to Dealey Plaza, we must come close to the perpetrators at some point. But it's useful to first sketch a picture of Oswald himself. He remains an elusive figure. Every time we think we're getting closer, he eludes us once again with some new contradiction. The report of the Warren Commission dedicated a full 50-page chapter to 'Lee Harvey Oswald: Background and Possible Motives.' There is still some room for nuance where the report deals with Oswald's youth, but he then gradually becomes a caricature. Certain aspects are purposefully magnified, while others are omitted. The Commission concludes the chapter as follows: 'Out of these and the many other factors which may have molded the character of Lee Harvey Oswald there emerged a man capable of assassinating President Kennedy.' This conclusion is not surprising, because everything that could contradict it has been omitted. Yet it is premature: Oswald's background and personality do not sufficiently explain the assassination of Kennedy. In the weeks before the assassination, the FBI was 'unanimous in the opinion that Oswald did not meet the criteria for the Security Index.'[663] In their eyes, he did not constitute a danger for the visit of the president to Dallas. Hoover did not agree with this. 'They are worse than mistaken,' he wrote outraged across the page. 'No one in full possession of all his faculties can claim that Oswald didn't fall within this criteria.'[664] Was the FBI director right – or were his agents? Was Oswald a crazed fanatic or a tragic nutcase? Or was there another explanation for his involvement in the assassination of President Kennedy?

The real Oswald was an intelligent but rather headstrong young man. He had unusual political views, and a very anti-authoritarian attitude. Oswald always hid his true feelings, and preferred to remain silent, which some have confused with arrogance. He defected to the Soviet Union when he was twenty. He had not yet come to terms with his troubled youth when he launched himself headlong into a marriage with a woman who cared little about him. He could barely feed his family after his return from the Soviet Union. These unfavorable conditions provided anyone who wanted to put Oswald in a bad light with enough opportunities to do so.

But the few people who knew Oswald better are remarkably positive about him. I met two of his friends in person at the ARRC conference in 2014. Both continue to defend Oswald against what they call an endless series of baseless slanders during his stay in Russia, in 1960. If Oswald differed from his contemporaries, then it was only because he was funnier and friendlier than most others, Ernst Titovets assured me. Buell Frazier, Oswald's friend who gave him a lift to work on November 22, confirmed this. He is now a spirited seventy-year-old with a soft voice and a modest and friendly disposition, who gives you his full attention. Because of his great significance as a witness in the case, I was very curious to find out what kind of person Buell Frazier was. He has been standing firm for 51 years, and has not changed even one letter of his very first statements. He was arrested on the day of the assassination, and was rather harshly questioned as a possible accomplice. It was clear that Oswald's guilt had to be established at all costs, and the pressure on Buell to adjust his views on the length of the paper bag must have been enormous. But he insisted that the bag was only two feet long. In this matter, a lot

Figure 53. From left to right: Buell Frazier, Ernst Titovets and myself. It was a strange experience to stand next to two of Oswald's friends.

depends on whether you believe Buell or not. During our chat, it quickly became clear to me what kind of person he is.

Our brief encounters during the conference convinced me that Buell is telling the truth about his friend. Buell has no hidden agenda, and he is definitely not the type of witness who puts together a story to make an impression. This gentle, straightforward man with great self-respect would not tolerate anyone putting words into his mouth, or being put under pressure to change his opinion. If Buell Frazier says that Oswald was a fine and amusing friend, I believe it. Ernst Titovets is also a solid witness. He was a medical student at the time, and wrote an enlightening and intelligent book in 2010 about Oswald's stay in Russia. He had the advantage that he knew the people involved, spoke the language, and had become a good judge of character in his capacity as a physician. Titovets doesn't make Oswald a saint, but his positive character traits prevail: 'He was a good man' and 'he had a good sense of humor'.[665]

It appears that, for those who knew him, Oswald was not the deranged psycho freak the Warren Commission presents. Zack Stout, who served as a Marine together with Oswald, said the following about his army buddy: 'He was absolutely truthful, the kind of guy I'd trust completely.'[666] James R. Persons also provides a positive description of Oswald: 'He was easy to get along with. He was quiet... not one of those animals.'[667] When he was in 8th grade, his peers chose Oswald as their class representative.[668]

The Warren Commission portrayed a completely different image of Oswald: 'It is apparent that Oswald was moved by an overriding hostility to his environment. He does not appear to have been able to establish meaningful relationships with other people. He was perpetually discontented with the world around him. Long before the assassination, he expressed his hatred for American society and acted in protest against it.'[669] Even if this were the case, there is no indication whatsoever that this person would be willing to kill for his convictions. Oswald's most striking commitment was his pro-Castro position on the Cuba issue. Kennedy had not overrun Cuba. There was no reason to assume that the liquidation of Kennedy would lead to a more favorable policy towards Cuba, and Oswald was aware of this.[670] He was intelligent enough to realize that the assassination of Kennedy would probably lead to an invasion of Cuba and the end of the Castro regime. In the absence of a rational motive, the believers turn Oswald into an irrational personality. Posner described Oswald as 'humorless,'[671] and had witnesses summoned who considered him to be 'arrogant and cold,'[672] 'brutal and cruel,'[673] 'a mental case,'[674] 'selfish and aggressive'[675] and 'a complete idiot.'[676] Isn't it a little strange that this complete idiot without any education was able to hold a lecture before a group of Jesuits at Spring Hill College in Mobile, Alabama, in July 1963? His highly educated listeners were convinced that he had enjoyed 'at least higher education.'[677] Posner completely lost it when he wrote: 'his rebellious convictions against government and authority were slowly evolving toward violence and revolution.'[678]

Could this unsociable man mutate into a revolutionary terrorist without any apparent reason? Once again, we let the facts speak for themselves.

DETACHMENT ISSUES

Two months before Lee's birth, on October 18, 1939, his father died. Oswald's mother, Marguerite, felt she would be better off without her third child. She tried to put him in an orphanage even before his third birthday, but the toddler was refused because he was too young. Marguerite didn't give up, however, and she succeeded when Lee was four. Gerald Posner calls this a happy childhood: 'The atmosphere was relaxed, and Lee's older brothers watched out for him during his stay there, which was quite uneventful.'[679] Perhaps this particular orphanage was the exception to the rule, but the opposite seems rather more likely. Marguerite recalled that Lee cried and said: 'Mother, I want to get out of here. There are children here who have killed people, and smoke. I want to get out.' When Lee finally got used to the situation and became attached to the people who surrounded him, Marguerite unexpectedly took her children away from there in 1944. She had found a new husband, Edwin Ekdahl. The five-year-old Oswald adapted, and enjoyed the presence of a father figure. But the relationship soon began to suffer from persistent quarrels, and Ekdahl gave up on it in 1946. He gave the marriage a second chance in 1947. Lee was clearly relieved when his stepfather returned, but Marguerite finally showed her husband the door in January 1948. A series of chaotic moves, and as many boarding schools, followed for Lee. He was also lagging behind at school. When Lee was twelve, Marguerite relocated to New York. From then onwards, Lee was extremely reluctant to form new emotional bonds. He skipped school, didn't need any friends, and hung around aimlessly in the Bronx, museums and the subway all day. The incorrigible truant ended up in the Youth House juvenile detention center. This is where Evelyn Siegel made the initial psychological evaluation of the obstinate boy. She clearly felt sorry for the sensitive and intelligent boy who was never really given the chance to find his feet in a more or less stable environment. She puts her finger on the problem in the very first paragraph: 'Lee Oswald is a seriously detached, withdrawn youngster of thirteen, remanded to Youth House for the first time on a charge of truancy. There is no previous court record. Laconic and taciturn, Lee answered questions, but volunteered almost nothing about himself spontaneously. Despite the fact that he is very hard to reach, Lee seems to have some ability to relate, which, in view of the solitary existence he has been leading, is somewhat surprising. There is a rather pleasant, appealing quality about this emotionally starved, affectionless youngster, which grows as one speaks to him, and it seems fairly clear that he has detached himself from the world around him because no one in it ever met any of his needs for love.'[680] The psychologist continues: 'He was not a mentally disturbed kid... He was just emotionally frozen. He was a kid who had never developed a really trusting relationship with anybody. From what I could garner, he really interacted with no one. He made his own meals. His mother left at around 7:00 a.m. and came home at 7:00 p.m. and he shifted for himself. You got the feeling of a kid nobody gave a darn about.'

When he was only twelve, Lee was already a child with serious detachment issues. He survived, but avoided the pain of new emotional disappointments by adopting a very detached attitude towards the outside world. Intelligent and sensitive children are often most susceptible when it comes to detachment disorders. Oswald was highly sensitive. 'I think Lee was a lot more sensitive than any of us realized at the time,' his brother Robert testified later.[681] He was also very intelligent, and even the Warren Commission had to admit it: 'Lee scored an IQ of 118 on the Wechsler Intelligence Scale for Children. According to Sokolow, this indicated a "present intellectual functioning in the upper range of bright normal intelligence."'[682] He added that 'although Lee was presumably disinterested in school subjects, he operates on a much higher than average level.' Doctor Hartogs wrote: 'This 13 year old well built boy has superior mental resources and functions only slightly below his capacity level in spite of chronic truancy from school.'[683] But, despite his intelligence, Lee could not find his place in the world, and, in the end, he gave up on it. He told his probation officer 'that he liked to be by himself because he had too much difficulty in making friends.'[684] We may assume that his unusual philosophy was an attempt to compensate for an inner sense of emptiness. Due to his detachment problems, Lee seemed predestined to become a victim. He was not a psychopath or a pervert. The inner struggle with emptiness, fear and anger absorbed all his energy. This always ended in willful or antisocial behavior with negative consequences, mainly for the child himself. This was apparently also the impression journalist Priscilla Johnson obtained after her interview with Oswald in Moscow, when he was ready to renounce his American citizenship. She wrote: 'I have suggested that nothing about Oswald was more striking than his burial of the emotional factor – a denial, almost, that he had any feelings at all. And yet, looking back, I have two conflicting recollections. One is that he was struggling to hide his feelings from himself. The other is of emotion that would not be hidden. It was the counterpoint between the two, I suppose, that gave me a sense that there were gaping chinks in his armor and that he was too frail, psychologically, for what he had set out to do.'[685]

Chapter 12 – I led three lives

Based on the character traits of the young Lee, it's no surprise that he became hooked on the television series *I Led Three Lives*, a series about the fascinating life of a spy with multiple identities. The believers see this as the cause of Oswald's later penchant for pseudonyms and innocent secrecy. In their eyes, Oswald wanted to escape the tedious banality of reality by leading an exciting secret life. This helps them to explain a whole series of strange elements in Lee's life. But one could just as well argue that Lee's taste for adventure and his fascination for an exciting TV series demonstrate that he was an ordinary American boy. The truth lies somewhere in between. Lee grew up with a minimum of emotional bonds, and his imagination was very probably the only thing that could fill this gap. He also filled this gap with reading. He built up his personal views on the world from the difficult books he browsed through. This was the time when Ethel and Julius Rosenberg were sentenced to death for passing on top secret information to the Russians. In the aftermath of this affair, Oswald was captivated by the communist pamphlet literature, and seemed to have found a mission. His philosophical choice was authentic. Palmer E. McBride, a childhood friend, testified about the 16-year-old: 'Lee Oswald was very serious about the virtues of Communism and discussed these virtues at every opportunity. He would say that the capitalists were exploiting the working class, and his central theme seemed to be that the workers would one day rise up and throw off their chains.'[686] For this emotionally abandoned boy, a brotherhood of all mankind seemed irresistible. He told Priscilla Johnson: 'I was looking for a key to my environment and then I found socialism.'[687] Does this sound like an unscrupulous opportunist, let alone a dangerously disturbed individual? He was merely looking for a way to escape from his social handicap, but his views may not always have been mature, or perhaps he didn't always interpret the philosophical treatises correctly. Addressing the Commission, George de Mohrenschildt conveyed a harsh judgment on Oswald's intellectual efforts: 'His mind was of a man with exceedingly poor background, who read rather advanced books, and did not understand even the words in them. He read complicated economical treatises and just picked up difficult words out of what he has read, and loved to display them.' For a teenager without any qualifications, however, this was quite an unusual and serious effort on Oswald's part.

Figure 54. Lee Harvey Oswald as a child, a young recruit and a young adult.

His childhood definitely came to an end when he was barely seventeen. The frail, emotionally starved Lee joined the tough guys of the Navy. This was an obvious attempt to find a place within a community, and he apparently succeeded in fitting in reasonably well. His asceticism was again an outstanding character trait. He never complained about physical discomforts or poor living conditions. Three months after the start of his military service, he achieved a score of 212 on the sharpshooter test, two points above the minimum needed to put him in the average marksman category. His further evaluations also place him in the middle group. But he surprised everyone in his exams by finishing seventh in his class.[688] In 1957, Oswald was even given limited command over other recruits, and a position that gave him access to sensitive and secret information. He was given 'confidential security clearance.' Oswald attended a training program as a flight controller and radar operator, and, in August, set off to the air force base in Atsugi, Japan. There were a few incidents during his further army service. Lee contracted a venereal disease, and once injured himself with a gun. But the army heads seemed to judge him mildly on the facts time and again. The most striking feat of 'Oswaldkovitch,' as his fellow recruits called him, was his seemingly unrealistic ambition to learn Russian, an extremely difficult language, on his own. If Lee managed to gain a basic knowledge of the language during his military service, this was done with at least some collusion from the army. The quality of this knowledge was not so high, incidentally. Even when he had been living in the Soviet Union for a while, his knowledge of the language was still relatively limited. He only learned to master Russian quite well over the years, and thanks to the daily interaction with Marina.

James Botelho, Oswald's roommate in the army, also provided a description that begins to sound rather familiar by now: 'He was unusual in that he generally would not speak unless spoken to, and his answers were always brief. He seldom associated with others.'[689] Corporal Thomas Bagshaw felt sorry for the frail Oswald. He considered him one of the few with whom one could have an intelligent conversation, but 'Oswald was honest and blunt, and that's usually what got him into trouble.' He was the perfect laughing stock for the rougher Marines. 'They called him Mrs. Oswald, threw him in the shower fully dressed and hassled him in every other conceivable way. Oswald would not fight back; he would just turn away from a provoker and ignore him.'[690] Oswald succeeded in being temporarily accepted by the group of Marines, but eventually withdrew into himself again. He seemed bitter, consciously stopped mixing with the group, and referred to his fellow Marines as 'you Americans.' The words 'exploitation' and 'imperialism' reappeared in his accusatory monologues.[691] In the end, he had no choice but to look for a 'normal' life among other people elsewhere. It is not illogical that, in view of all this, he set his sights on the Soviet Union. If he did not fit into American society, and all Americans were against the Russians, the idea that he would be able to put down roots there could have been very attractive. After all, wasn't brotherhood elevated to a doctrine in the worker's paradise?

GHOST DRIVER IN THE MIGRATION FLOW

Defector Oswald left for the Soviet Union in September 1959. This was, of course, extremely exceptional during the Cold War. According to Posner, there were eleven cases between 1958 and 1960. But even among these rare cases, Lee was unique. Most of his fellow defectors were running away from their marriage and/or other problems.[692] Oswald was apparently the only 'ideological' defector. He went to the Soviet Union in the belief that life would be more pleasant there. The idea was so crazy that there was a lot of speculation in finding an explanation for it. The believers consider this as proof that Oswald hated American society. The conspiracists, on the other hand, are sure that Oswald was part of an American plan to infiltrate the countries behind the Iron Curtain.

The argument of the believers can easily be refuted: Oswald did not hate American society. But he was strongly opposed to some of the excesses of capitalism. In his talks with Ernst Titovets, he denounced overt racism. The US degraded the black population to second-class citizens in order to be able to better exploit them economically. They could do the harder and dirtier work for lower wages. Oswald also denounced the fact that studying in America was too expensive, and that becoming ill was actually unaffordable. Yet while he indeed criticized the Western model quite severely, he also defended the American system while in Russia. His criticism of the communist model was also quite harsh. He considered the planned economy a stupid idea, the bureaucracy insufferable and the living conditions desolate. Oswald was irritated by the lack of personal freedom and of freedom of opinion. He mocked the mindless indoctrination during the compulsory collective gymnastics, and found the personality cult with regard to Lenin downright ridiculous. Oswald therefore did have critical ideas about the ideal model society, but they were not biased against the United States, and even less so against Kennedy. His criticisms were actually largely valid, and are now widely accepted shortcomings of the American model.

The conspiracists' assumption that Oswald was a secret agent who was dropped behind the lines does not seem to be illogical. Every empire tries to have eyes and ears in the enemy camp. But it's not obvious to use someone like Oswald for this purpose. On the one hand, it seems logical to recruit someone for such a mission who has barely any ties to the motherland. It is therefore quite possible that Oswald's overt communist sympathies and his social isolation made him a suitable candidate. But what could the Americans expect from a one-man 'fifth column' behind the Iron Curtain? Victor Marchetti,[693] the USSR specialist of the CIA, might provide an answer to this question: 'In the late 1950s the *Office of Naval Intelligence* (ONI) operated in Nag's Head, North Carolina, a training base for intelligence candidates to be sent to the Soviet Union.' He explained that the CIA was looking to recruit 'young men who were made to appear disenchanted, poor American youths who had become turned off and wanted to see what communism was all about.' After the training, these young men were sent to the Soviet Union 'as defectors, when in actuality the ONI was hoping they would be picked up as agents by the KGB.'[694] Oswald fitted perfectly into this frame. He could not find his place in America, and longed to escape to another country where brotherhood seemed to be the rule. He was a Marine with a strange curriculum, who suddenly became a defector to the Soviet Union. Richard Helms, former CIA Director, repeatedly insinuated that the intelligence department of the Navy was responsible for Oswald on his return from the Soviet Union.[695] There are other indications that the army's intelligence department had recruited Oswald as a Marine, but the Soviets did not take the bait. And the story ends there.

After his return, neither the Americans nor the Russians took Oswald seriously. The failed 'doubling' role of Oswald was too insignificant for the Americans to worry about, and the Russians also could not turn it into a propaganda stunt, because they were expecting nothing but trouble with the defector, and preferred to avoid a diplomatic incident. Initially, Oswald didn't even obtain a residence permit, and it looked as if he would soon have to take a return flight to America. Lee was heartbroken, and attempted to commit suicide. The Russians almost had a dead American on their hands, and therefore quickly changed tactic: all in all, it couldn't do much harm if Oswald were to settle down somewhere in their territory. Oswald took up residence in Minsk. He was employed there as an unobtrusive worker in a radio factory, and was living in an apartment that, by Russian standards, was luxurious.

MINSK

In Russia, Oswald also came across as a self-willed and uncommunicative personality, but not as stupid, unfriendly or humorless. He caused astonishment, because he was the only one to still rave about the superiority of communism over capitalism. He was a pacifist and, in some ways, truly believed in the idealistic principles of the Soviet ideology. This surprised his fellow workers, because they were numbed by the constant propaganda, which nobody paid attention to or believed in any longer. The superiority of the Soviet system was not noticeable on the shelves in the shops, and that was ultimately what mattered. The proclaimed equality was also far from apparent in real life. The bureaucracy was a caste system where everyone was wary of those who were higher or lower in the pyramid. Oswald also quickly realized that he had not landed in paradise, and his dissatisfaction gradually increased. He slowly became aware that the problem was in his head, and that it wouldn't be solved by trying to change the whole outside world. If that was the case, he ultimately preferred American society, and he started making his preparations for a quiet retreat. In the meantime, he tried to pick up girls from time to time, and made the best of his status as an expat in a city where foreigners were still something of an attraction. He was bored in Minsk, and couldn't even spend the little money he earned, because there was nothing to buy. Oswald was also often irritated by his Russian colleagues, who didn't understand the American. Titovets described a typical incident: the radio factory where Oswald worked had only one press available, and the rule was that the worker who started using the press could continue to use it until the job was finished. Oswald didn't like this lack of efficiency in the production. When a colleague left the press, the machine was free in his opinion, and he refused to wait. His colleague Max was tired of Oswald ignoring the rules, grabbed him by the collar and pushed him roughly against a steel pillar. 'He was all ready to give Oswald a punch or two when he suddenly realized that he could not hit the man,' testified Titovets. 'That damned American offered absolutely no resistance. He stood propped against the steel pillar with his arms dangling limp along the sides of his body, looking quietly at Max.'[696] Oswald was apparently not a violent person himself, but the willing victim of his own asocial initiatives. The same masochistic trait drove him into an unhappy marriage shortly after. Oswald was crazy about Ella Germann, but she had scornfully rejected his wedding proposal and had hurt him deeply in the process. Marina Prusakova was a very superficial girl who only dreamed of marrying a foreigner. The two met, and married soon afterwards. Lee believed that this would repay Ella Germann 'tit for tat.' But he was now stuck with Marina, who was soon scornful of him because of his poor performance in bed. Matters soon turned violent between Lee and Marina. She sometimes took a hit from the otherwise unflappable Lee, but she knew how to defend herself. According to Titovets, Lee was also sometimes covered in scratches. Even before his marriage, he had already told his friend that he could live with a woman who didn't love him, as long as he loved her enough – a train of thought that makes sense for someone with detachment issues. Oswald quickly brought such a disaster upon himself by marrying Marina.

Priscilla Johnson McMillan gave us a clean version of Marina in her bestseller *Marina and Lee*. We have McMillan to thank for this portrait of her as Lee's victim, which has entered into the official mythology surrounding the assassination of Kennedy. Others see Marina as a former prostitute who had been chased from Leningrad shortly before she met Lee.[697] Marina was probably a very different person altogether.

MARINA

Yuri Merezhinsky, the son of prominent party members, introduced Lee and Marina to each other. His mother was Lydia Cherkasova, a professor of biochemistry and chairman of her department at the State University of the Soviet Republic of Belarus. She was also the head of the Laboratory of Radiation Research of the Science Academy,[698] and, in that capacity, had access to top secret information. Her husband was also a professor. Both were members of the Communist Party, of course. Cherkasova accompanied Soviet President Khrushchev and the Minister of Foreign Affairs to the 15th General Assembly of the UN in New York – the one where Khrushchev hit the table with his shoe. She also saw Jack and Jacqueline Kennedy pass by only a few meters away from her in the midst of the campaign for the presidency. Cherkasova later gave a lecture on her trip to the United States in the Trade Union Palace in Minsk. Oswald and Ernst decided to attend it. The KGB had meanwhile installed listening devices all over Oswald's flat, and were therefore well aware of the type of women Oswald preferred. Before the lecture started, Yuri asked Oswald to give him a hand with projecting the slides his mother wanted to show. As a result, Oswald remained near him for a large part of the evening. When the pretty Marina Prusakova entered the hall at some point in a striking red dress and a lascivious hairdo in the style of Brigitte Bardot, she walked over to Yuri and greeted him as an acquaintance. He introduced her to Lee. It was immediately clear that Oswald could easily fall for her.

After the lecture, Professor Cherkasova had a party at her home. Friends of Yuri were, of course, welcome. The lovebirds therefore had several hours to get to know each other. Oswald accompanied Marina to her flat afterwards. She lived – by pure coincidence again – near Oswald's flat. Professor Cher-

Figure 55.
Marina on her wedding day, April 30, 1961.

kasova was very friendly to Lee in the following weeks, and, for a while, Lee was a regular guest in her home. When Titovets interviewed her on this many years later, she made it no secret that she was in close contact with the Russian secret service, the KGB, at the time.[699] It was also very unlikely that the professor would receive an American dissident in her home without prior consultation.

All of this therefore indicates that Marina and Lee did not meet by chance. During his private investigation, Titovets interviewed everyone who was involved in this first meeting, but nobody was willing to take the responsibility for having brought the couple together. They all lied about the reason for the very first contact, but their statements were unanimous about what took place afterwards. For Titovets, there is no doubt that the Soviet authorities sent Marina to Lee. They were well aware that the live-in niece of a colonel of the security department was looking for a foreigner, and that the time was right, because her loose morals had caused her reputation to deteriorate rapidly. She was therefore offered her American on a silver platter. Lee was immediately captivated by the beautiful Marina. Her friends Yuri and Kostya carefully shielded her from other admirers. Six weeks after they first met, wedding bells were ringing for Marina and Lee. The spouses barely knew each other, and also had little affinity for each other's sensitivities. Lee appreciated hygiene and cleanliness, for example, and didn't care about material luxuries. Marina hated housekeeping, was sloppy and lazy,[700] but demanded a better standard of living than was possible in the Soviet Union. She was also a chain smoker. Lee was a non-smoker, and also preferred to stay away from alcohol. Marina had also had casual sex with several men. Titovets heard from Yuri that sex was one of her hobbies: 'She had a pretty face. Nothing else. She was mostly after men.' The marriage was also a letdown when it came to sex, but Marina was nevertheless soon pregnant. Lee had meanwhile started the bureaucratic Calvary of collecting money and the necessary paperwork to return to the United States. June was born on February 15, 1962, and, four months later, Oswald, Marina and their little girl were on American soil. They were welcomed by Spas T. Raikin of the *Travelers Aid Society*. According to Raikin, this was just because he spoke Russian. In 1993, however, it appeared that Raikin did indeed have CIA connections. In his autobiography *Rebel With a Just Cause*, he moreover described how he had specialized in the recruitment of students for revolutionary brigades in Bulgaria. He thereby made intensive use of false identities, tricks and deception. He argued that this was necessary, because the communists also used the same tactics.[701] The first man to shake Oswald's hand upon his return to the US therefore had the same characteristic background as several of Lee's later contacts.

The government obviously kept a discreet eye on Oswald – and perhaps even more on Marina – during the period following his return. Not so much because they were suspected spies, but as a result of the mutual paranoia that dominated relations between Russia and the US. Counterintelligence was at least as important as espionage. The purpose of counterintelligence was to expose the spies of the enemy country. The KGB had assumed that the strange American had not landed in Moscow by accident. The CIA now assumed that Marina was perhaps a communist agent. The Americans were well aware that their attempt to turn Oswald into a double agent had failed miserably. Oswald seemed just a little too much of a liability, and that had kept the Russians from recruiting him. They hadn't bothered to have Oswald return to the US as a covert communist spy who would become active later, but they had linked him to Marina. But they couldn't do much with her either in the end.

Despite this being the heyday of paranoia, American interest in the eccentric Oswald dried up pretty quickly. The first year in the United States was not easy for the Oswalds. Finding work was not easy, and the marriage bounced from crisis to crisis. There was no money for anything, but they managed to keep their heads above water. Oswald managed to repay his debt of 435.71 dollars for his repatriation within eight months, and also repaid his brother Robert, who had loaned him 200 dollars. That was an almost impossible effort for someone who earned barely more than a dollar an hour, if he was working, that is. From June 1, 1962, to January 28, 1963, Oswald had an income of 1,516 dollars, including the 63 dollars he still had in his pocket when he arrived in the United States. He paid 377.13 dollars in rent and utilities and 226.21 dollars for the trip from New York to Fort Worth. Together with some other expenses, such as a typing course and subscriptions to magazines, he spent a total of 654.41 dollars. Of the remaining 861 dollars, Oswald therefore used 635.71 dollars for repaying his debts.[702] This means that the family of three only had 225 dollars available for food, clothing, transport and the like during a period of eight months. That's less than a dollar a day. Oswald could be accused of many things, but not that he didn't promptly repay his debts. In any case, this was very thoughtful of someone who, at the same time, was allegedly becoming radicalized. As soon as his debts had been paid off, he bought a carbine and a pistol. On March 31, 1963, Marina took the famous photographs of Oswald with his weapon in the backyard.

FILE 5

THE ATTACK ON E.A. WALKER

Chapter 13 – Hunter of fascists

In an adversary system, guaranteed by the sixth amendement of the constitution, everyone is entitled to a day in court before a free, impartial, and independent judge. An accused is allowed to develop and present his own evidence and arguments.The judge or jury must be an impartial fact finder who is not involved in the presentation of arguments so as to avoid a premature decision.[703] None of these elementary principles were respected in Oswald's case. And so it is possible that – without any adversarial process – the Warren Commission came to the conclusion that Oswald had a criminal past. On April 10, 1963, he was supposed to have carried out an attempted assassination with his Carcano on the ultra right-wing ex-general Walker.[704] The self-proclaimed Marxist had at least a motive for the attack. Edwin Walker was a right-wing agitator. He had close connections with the John Birch Society, a political action group that spread its ultraconservative ideas with a cocktail of religion and patriotism. As a major general, Walker was obviously very prominent. President Eisenhower posted him on to Augsburg in Germany. There, the rebellious general continued to vent his neo-Nazi political views, and this led to some incidents. In the end, Walker took the honorable way out, and resigned. Although he thereby lost his pension, he gained a publicity springboard, and rich and powerful friends who shared his political views. Walker emerged as an enthusiastic mouthpiece for the far right. He organized mass rallies, firmly opposed the doctrine of racial integration, the Supreme Court, the United Nations and, of course, Kennedy, who, in his opinion, would not take action against the communist threat. Walker and Kennedy despised each other. In 1962, the southern United States were still in the grip of racism. The Law Faculty of the University of Mississippi refused to accept the courageous African-American James Meredith on two occasions, based on the color of his skin. Meredith appealed against his rejection to the Supreme Court, and asked for a court order enforcing his registration. White supremacists, with the support of the Governor of Mississippi, were eager for a confrontation and were able to count on the clear support of the wider population. Kennedy sent five hundred federal agents from the US Marshals Service to ensure that Meredith could enroll safely. There was heavy rioting, in which two people were killed, a journalist and a chance passerby, and 75 people injured. Members of the Ku Klux Klan stirred up the crowds, who, armed with iron bars and Coke bottles filled with gasoline, frantically chanted 'Lynch the nigger!' The president finally sent in the army to restore peace. The situation was very explosive and could turn into a mini civil war at any moment if the president had to use the army against its own citizens. When Kennedy learned that Walker was personally inciting the demonstrators with his racist demagogy, he was filled with disgust. 'Imagine that son of a bitch having been commander of a division up till last year!' he grumbled. Attorney General Bobby Kennedy had Walker arrested, and imprisoned him in a lunatic asylum. Walker was, however, delighted with his victim role. It allowed befriended politicians to describe him as the first political prisoner of the Kennedy dictatorship. His constitutional rights to free speech had been violated. (He said nothing about those of the student James Meredith.) But it was indeed an unworthy action of an Attorney General to lock someone up in a mental institution, regardless of how reprehensible he was, and Bobby Kennedy had to back down. Kennedy again lost some of his popularity with white southerners, and Walker triumphed. His supporters thought he was a hero who stood far above the dimwit in the White House. From then on, pestering Kennedy was a permanent source of income and popularity for Walker. He drew as much as he could from this keg, including on November 22, 1963. A hateful, black-rimmed 'Welcome Mister Kennedy' ad from one Bernard Weissman, a young man who had served under Walker in Germany, appeared in the *Dallas Morning News*. The ad was funded by right-wing extremists. When Weissman learned that Kennedy had been assassinated, he reacted as follows: 'First, what was said, like, I hope he is not a member of the Walker group – something like that – I hope he is not one of Walker's boys.'[705] Someone who knew Walker closely therefore considered it quite possible that the general was involved in the Kennedy assassination. It all shows how irreconcilable the political differences were between Walker and Kennedy.

Oswald was also the opposite of Walker in every respect. He saw through the tactics of hateful troublemakers such as Walker, who goaded on the impressionable crowd solely because of the self-interest of a small privileged minority. Intellectual pacifists like the Rosenbergs were sentenced to death, but cynical windbags like Walker were applauded. The true warmongers remained safely in the background, and financed the agitators. Oswald therefore certainly had a motive to qualify as a suspect for the attack on Walker. But that led to a paradoxical situation: if Oswald hated Walker, he could not logically hate Kennedy. But this contradiction eluded the Warren Commission completely. They conveniently circumvented this difficulty with regard to the attack on Walker by only considering what suited them. The Commission reasoned that if Oswald had already made an attempt on the life of a public figure before November 22, this was a strong indication that he had taken the step to violent action. Just like the murders of Tippit and Oswald, the attempt to assassinate Walker was often called the Rosetta Stone by believers.

APRIL 1963: THE ATTACK

For a while, the controversial general feared an attack on his life. On April 8, his associate [706] Robert Surrey saw two suspicious figures 'walk up the alley and onto the Walker property and look into the window of the Walker house.'[707] Surrey went to investigate. The car of the suspicious men had no licence plate. He opened the car door and searched unsuccessfully for identity papers. In any case, Oswald was not one of these men, Surrey stated later. He did report the fact to the police immediately.[708] The general's fears were confirmed two days later. On April 10, shortly after 9.00 p.m., the general sat bent over his tax return with the office light on.[709] A bullet missed him by a hair's breadth.

His 14-year-old neighbor 'Kirk' Coleman and his 19-year-old friend Ronald Andrew heard the shot. Kirk first thought it was an exhaust backfire, but Ronald was sure it was a rifle shot. Kirk immediately ran outside and climbed the fence at the back of the garden. From there, he could see the parking lot of a small Mormon church building. A medium-sized man with long black hair got into a green or blue 1949 or 1950 Ford, and drove away in a hurry. Another man also got into a car, but Kirk didn't see the make and model. The man was bending over, and seemed to put something on the floor of the car. He also drove away, but seemed in less of a hurry.[710]

General Walker himself first went upstairs to fetch his gun, and then went outside with his gun drawn. He walked through his garden and along the garden path to the parking lot. He arrived just in time to see a car leaving the car park.[711] He could therefore only have seen the second, unhurried man driving away.

Walker's neighbor Ross Bouve had a hyper-alert border collie, Toby, who incessantly barked when strangers came near their backyard. He also barked 'at anyone or anything on the Walker property.' Because he had barked and growled at a group of passing boy scouts on April 10, Mrs. Bouve had locked Toby in the laundry room for a while. The shot happened while he was still serving his sentence there, but Toby did not sound an alarm. He was very sick the next day. 'Toby [...] vomited extensively,' said his owner. She was convinced that '...someone had given him something to quiet him or drug him or poison him.'[712]

The police from Dallas quickly arrived at the scene of the attack. The bullet had flown through the wood and glass of the window, past Walker's head and right through a stone wall. The police found a 'mushroomed bullet' in the adjoining room. In two police reports, the bullet was described as 'with a steel hull.'[713] A murder attempt on a prominent person appeared, naturally, on the front page of the *Dallas Morning News*. According to the article, Detective Ira Van Cleave described the bullet as a 30.06.[714] In the local newspaper the next day, it was still a 30.06, and the *New York Times* also printed that information. The perpetrator of the attack was not found, and things went quiet about the case – until the end of November.

Curiously enough, the man who first insinuated a connection between the Kennedy murder and the attack on Walker was none other than Walker himself. The story of the Oswald-Walker connection popped up a few days after the assassination of the president[715] in the *Deutsche Nationalzeitung und Soldatenzeitung* newspaper in Munich. Walker must have known that newspaper from when he was stationed in Germany, but initially answered very evasively when the Commission asked him about it. But the FBI discovered that he had carried out intercontinental calls with a journalist from the German newspaper on the evening of November 22, and at 7.00 a.m. in the morning of November 23. When confronted with this, Walker no longer denied that he was an informer of the newspaper, but he did deny that he had made the link between the attack on himself and the assassination of Kennedy. That is unlikely. No one was interested in Walker on November 22 but Walker himself. Nevertheless, the Commission believed the general. The link between the attack on Walker and the attack on Kennedy therefore officially became an accidental guess of a foreign journalist to whom Walker had passed some general information about the JFK murder.[716] But the source of the information was not in Germany, it was definitely in Dallas. That became clear on Saturday afternoon, November 23. At that moment – when the German newspaper had not yet appeared – a reporter from the WFFA television channel asked Police Chief Curry whether Oswald could also have been involved in the attack on General Walker.[717] Surprised, Curry could only answer: 'That I don't know.' That the question was raised proves that someone was also spreading the rumor in Dallas.

Around the time that Police Chief Curry gave his TV interview, a second search was being conducted in Irving, at Ruth Paine's house. Marina was already under the care of the Secret Service at the time. The agents searched through Paine's books in a remarkably thorough manner, as if they were looking for something specific. Ruth explained: 'Before they left they were leafing through books to see if anything fell out but that is all I saw.'[718] When the officers were outside, Ruth realized that two books in her cupboard, including a Russian book with cooking and sewing advice for housewives, actually belonged to Marina. She thought that, after the arrest of her husband, Marina would certainly need to have these useful domestic and cooking tips, and she went to the police in Irving that same Saturday evening. She handed the books over to Captain Paul Barge, with the request to see that the book was returned to Marina via the Secret Service.[719] At least that's the version from the police, who noted November 23 as the day of receipt. In her statement of December 6, Ruth Paine indicated the date of transfer of the book as "a week after the attack."[720] The book remained quietly at the police station for a number of days, depending on the exact date on which Ruth gave it to the police. Agent Kunkel of the Secret Service noted down that the police in Irving only handed the book over to him on December 2, together with two letters, postcards and 'one unsigned page taken from a writing pad, written in pencil, giving various instructions concerning a post office box [...] and where he could be located in the event of his arrest.'[721]

Ruth and Marina received a telephone call about this on December 2.[722] Agent Gopadze of the Secret Service came by to show her the message written in Russian that was found in the book. The letter seemed to have been written by Oswald, and was supposedly addressed to Marina. It was apparently a mini emergency plan with some guidelines. The writer of the note did consider the possibility that he would be arrested or killed. In that case, the addressee of the note did not have to worry: the bills were paid, she had $60 in cash, and his paycheck would follow. The writer's clothes should be thrown away, but not his papers. The last point was: '11. If I am alive and taken prisoner, the city jail is located at the end of the bridge through which we always passed on going to the city.'[723] This letter would seem to constitute definitive evidence that Oswald had carried out the attack on Walker. But there were some problems: there was no date and no direct reference to an attack on Walker. Even stranger was that fingerprints of no fewer than seven people were found on it, but not those of Lee and Marina.[724]

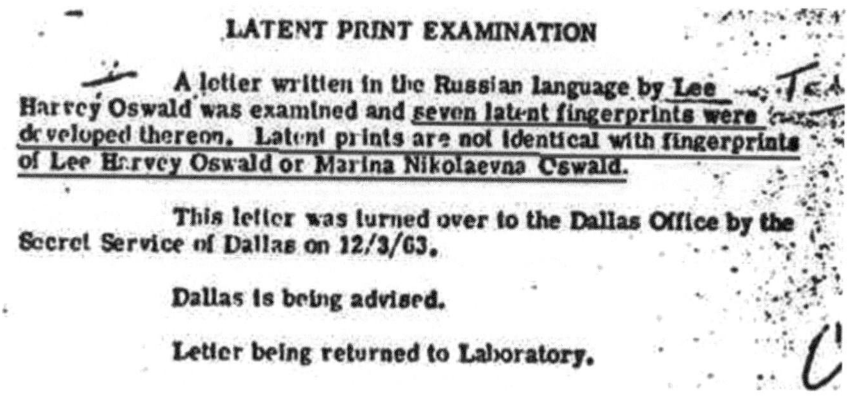

LATENT PRINT EXAMINATION

A letter written in the Russian language by Lee Harvey Oswald was examined and seven latent fingerprints were developed thereon. Latent prints are not identical with fingerprints of Lee Harvey Oswald or Marina Nikolaevna Oswald.

This letter was turned over to the Dallas Office by the Secret Service of Dallas on 12/3/63.

Dallas is being advised.

Letter being returned to Laboratory.

Figure 56. The letter does not show fingerprints of Oswald and Marina.

The Commission did not include the fact that their fingerprints were missing in their 27 volumes, and also not in the commission documents. They also didn't ask FBI fingerprint expert Latona anything about it during his hearing. There are, however, several good questions that could have been asked: Were there any fingerprints from Ruth Paine, did Lee write with gloves on, and did Marina use tweezers to read messages from her husband? And another one: Had Marina actually read the message?

After the telephone call with Ruth and Marina on December 2, 1963, the Secret Service noted: 'She disclaimed any notice of such note.'[725] But Marina changed her statement the next day: 'The note was written by her husband, Lee Oswald, prior to his attempted assassination of former General Walker, the head of the fascist organization. [...] the note, together with a post office key, was left on a dresser of their bedroom.'[726] Contrary to that, she declared in February that she had found the letter in Lee's tiny little study.[727] Why would Lee leave a message for Marina in a room that he had explicitely prohibited her to enter?[728]

The letter was very incriminating for Oswald, but Walker's neighbor Kirk Coleman was questioned again, and according to him, Oswald was not one of the men who had left the scene shortly after the attack. Coleman's first statement, recorded immediately after the incident, was buried deep down on half a page in the annexes.[729] The new hearing on June 3, 1964, had to adjust the original statement. The FBI agent made use of the dangerous process in which he described what the witness had said. In his first statement, Kirk was in a room at the back (1) and walked outside (2) after a brief conversation with the boy who was with him (3). In the new version, the bedroom became 'the door opening'. And subsequently, this door became an outside door. The conversation with the friend went missing. There now only remained a short and immediate sprint from the outside door to the fence. The FBI estimated the distance between the door and the fence as 4.3 meters.[730] Kirk only needed two seconds for this, according to a reconstruction. The perpetrator of the attack had to cover 10.66 meters to reach the parking lot, however.[731] That would require around five seconds, and the fugitives then still had to walk a few meters across the parking lot to their cars. According to the FBI, the persons Coleman had seen two seconds after the shot could therefore not have been the perpetrators.[732] Their whole argument fails miserably, however, if Kirk needed seven seconds before he could look over the fence. The seconds that were 'cut out,' for example, during which his friend Ronald said that he thought it was a shot, were already enough for that. The seconds it took to go from the back room to the outside door were also enough. The hasty departure of the first car also had to be left out in the adjusted statement. According to the FBI, Kirk was better able to remember this fourteen months after the facts than on the day itself: the man drove away at a normal rate of speed. He did not speed down the driveway.[733]

The credible testimony of Coleman was ignored and distorted. Even Walker was indignant about this, and felt he had a right to know who wanted to murder him. According to him, someone had silenced Coleman: 'The boy has been told not to say anything.'[734] The General was also convinced that Oswald was *not* the perpetrator. He told the Commission: 'I had no way of knowing that Oswald attacked me. I still don't. [...] In fact, I have always claimed he did not.'[735]

DID OSWALD SHOOT AT WALKER?

If we disregard the letter that appeared on December 2, and look at the hard facts, it's difficult to find a direct connection between Oswald and the attack on Walker. Everything points to the contrary. Kirk Coleman was an impeccable witness and had no reason not to tell the truth. He was not seeking attention; on the contrary, he even begged the police to keep his name out of the public eye. His friend Ronald Andries was able to confirm that Coleman looked at the parking lot over the fence, and also when he did it. Regardless of whether Kirk stood there two or thirty seconds after the shot, or whether the first car left the parking lot in a hurry or normally, the following points remain as facts:

1. According to the police, the shot came from behind the back fence,[736] therefore from outside Walker's garden. Walker confirmed this: 'There wasn't any doubt the shot was fired [...] outside the lattice fence';[737]
2. After the shot, the gunman was on the garden path to the parking lot, and could only leave the crime scene by that route;[738]
3. Kirk Coleman was already at the fence before anyone who left the garden path would have had the time to leave the parking lot. The FBI even claimed that Coleman was already there after two seconds;
4. Kirk only saw two men, who each got into a car and left the area;
5. Neither of these men was Oswald,[739] who, moreover, did not have a driver's license;
6. Walker went through his garden and along the garden path to the parking lot, and met no one. Consequently, the gunman was no longer on the garden path at that time.
7. Coleman and Walker both saw the second car drive onto Turtle Creek Boulevard. There was therefore no unguarded moment when Coleman was no longer looking and before Walker reached the parking lot.

The logical conclusion is that one of the people who Coleman had noticed had to be the perpetrator. But according to Marina, Oswald laughed at the folly of the Americans who assumed that you could only flee by car. You'd be less obvious on foot, he said. There is certainly strong evidence that several offenders were involved in the attack. Besides the two cars that left the parking lot just after the attack, there was still the odd duo that had explored the grounds two days earlier.

The Commission nevertheless concluded that Oswald was the only person to shoot at Walker, and gave four reasons for it:[740]

(1) the contents of the note that Oswald left for his wife on April 10, 1963;
(2) the photographs found among Oswald's possessions;
(3) the testimony of firearms identification experts; and
(4) the testimony of Marina Oswald

We will now examine the four arguments, in reverse order.

THE TESTIMONY OF MARINA OSWALD

Bugliosi wrote: 'Since we know that Oswald attempted to murder General Walker because he confessed to his own wife that he did, nothing is further required to make the point.'[741] This argument is only valid, of course, if Marina was a reliable witness. Bugliosi knew that she was not, but referred to the obvious grounds of excuse for this: she was only 22, wanted to protect Lee as a wife, did not speak the language, had had to make an almost endless number of statements (45 statements already before she appeared before the Commission), was afraid of being deported, and so on.[742] These reasons do indeed provide a moral ground for excusing Marina's actions, but do not take away the fact that her statements are largely lies. Commission staff lawyer Norman Redlich wrote the following in a memorandum for the Warren Commission: 'Marina Oswald had lied to the Secret Service, the FBI and this Commission repeatedly on matters which are of vital concern to the people of this country and the world.'[743] They were not lies to exonerate Oswald. At some point, perhaps not coincidentally while she was negotiating the sale of her memoirs with *Life Magazine*,[744] Marina even claimed that Oswald wanted to murder former Vice President Richard Nixon. Marina had locked Oswald in the bathroom on that day to prevent it. Unfortunately, Nixon was not even in the vicinity on the date that she made up. When it also turned out that the bathroom door could only be locked from the inside, the whole story fell through. That was not a lie to protect her husband. Marina stated this herself in 1988 in an interview with *Ladies' Home Journal*: 'When I was questioned by the Warren Commission, I was a blind kitten. Their questioning left me only one way to go: guilty. I made Lee guilty. He never had a fair chance … But I was only 22 then, and I've matured since; I think differently.'[745]

That Marina was also unreliable in her final version of the Walker assault, which she made in 1964, can be seen from her very cautious appearance before the HSCA.[746] The main witness of the Warren Commission, and of Bugliosi, was only prepared to confirm the following about the connection between the letter and the assassination attempt on Walker:

> Question: Where was this note left?
> Answer: I don't remember.
> Question: Did you find it before he returned?
> Answer: I think so.
> Question: What did you do with the note when he returned?
> Answer: I don't remember.

Marina's statements, which the Warren Commission made such grateful use of, were actually very weak arguments. Maybe two other direct witnesses could increase her credibility. According to Marina, Oswald buried his weapon after the attack, and only dared to retrieve it three days later, on Saturday, April 13. On that particular evening, George and Jeanne de Mohrenschildt turned up at the apartment in Neely Street, very late and totally unannounced. They had bought a large pink rabbit in New York for little June. It was the day before Easter. Lee and Marina were already sleeping, and Lee opened the door 'half undressed, maybe in shorts.'[747] The baron was in an elated mood. Marina showed Jeanne around the shabby apartment. She also opened the door to Lee's tiny study, where the gun stood clearly visible against the wall. Jeanne called to her husband: 'Look, George, they have a gun here.' The baron said that he then jokingly asked: 'Are you then the guy who took a pot shot at General Walker?' According to de Mohrenschildt, Oswald was startled by this question, which he had intended as a joke. 'He sort of shriveled, you see, when I asked this question.' Jeanne remembered the whole thing as being much more relaxed: 'It was just a joke.'[748]

Marina's version of the conversation is again the most incriminating for Lee. According to her, de Mohrenschildt asked the crucial question as soon as Oswald opened the door: 'Lee, how is it possible that you missed?'[749] There was certainly something serious going on, in any case. We know that for sure because immediately after that nocturnal visit, George and Jeanne left the country in a hurry. They only returned from Haiti in April 1967. Only then – at least according to their statement – did they find a copy of backyard photo 133-A among the objects they had stored before their departure. Oswald had written the following on the back of this photo on April 5, 1963:[750] 'To my friend George from Lee Oswald.' Whatever he may have claimed, this dated dedication makes it hard to believe that George de Mohrenschildt had never seen that picture. Someone had also added the Cyrillic text: 'Hunter of Fascists – Ha ha ha!!!' This contempt for Lee leaves little doubt that Marina was the author of this. George and Jeanne de Mohrenschildt also confirmed this.[751] In his very last interview, a few hours before he committed suicide in suspicious circumstances, de Mohrenschildt claimed that he only received the photo after the attack on Walker. But Epstein rightly adds that, at that moment, Marina was no longer in the mood for jokes about Oswald as a hunter of fascists.[752]

There is no reasonable doubt that de Mohrenschildt received this photograph on April 5, five days before the attack on Walker. He knew that Oswald had a rifle, and Marina had shown them what he planned to do with it: to hunt fascists. In early February, Oswald had met the German geologist Volkmar Schmidt at the de Mohrenschildts. He became involved in a political debate with Schmidt that lasted hours, so de Mohrenschildt must have been aware of it. During this conversation, Schmidt had compared Walker to Hitler, and Oswald had eagerly snapped up the comparison. When the attack on the former general became front page news only a week after having received the incriminating photo with Marina's address, which left not much room for interpretation, it was only natural for de Mohrenschildt to ask whether Oswald had something to do with the assassination attempt. The baron had only returned from New York on Saturday evening. The pink rabbit for June was just an excuse for calling on the Oswalds so late at night. George and Jeanne de Mohrenschildt were clearly not on a friendly visit, but on a fact-finding mission to find out whether Oswald had carried out the attack. They were so shocked by the result of their mini-investigation that they definitively disappeared from the lives of the Oswalds fifteen minutes later, and even left the country. Everything suggests that George and Jeanne de Mohrenschildt came to the conclusion that Oswald was involved in the attack, and that it was better to stay away from him before someone had the idea of ex-

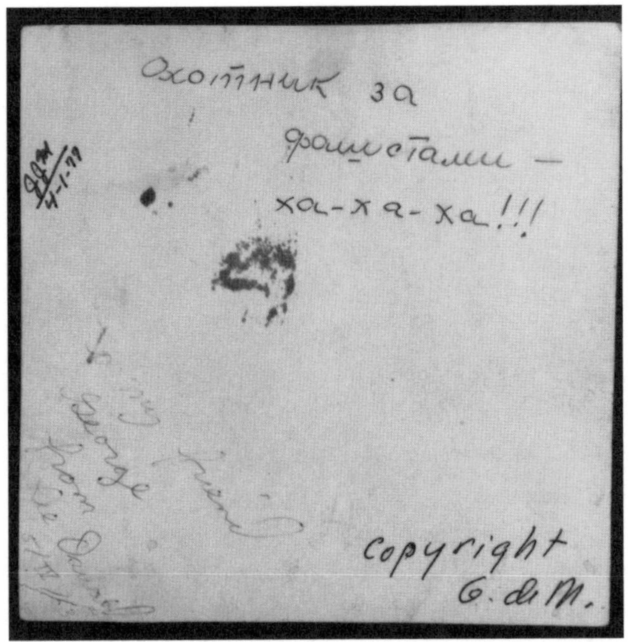

Figure 57. Marina's sarcastic remark on the back of de Mohrenschildt's copy of the backyard photo.

ploring their possible involvement. Regardless of the fact that Marina is credible as a witness or not, the behavior of the de Mohrenschildts leads to the conviction that Oswald was indeed in some way involved in the attack on Walker's life.

THE BULLET FRAGMENT

Initially, according to the press, the bullet in Walker's house was a 30.06. On April 10, it was clearly noted on two occasions that it was a 'bullet with a steel jacket.'[753] The bullet could not be linked to a specific gun due to the lack of a suspect and a weapon. This changed on November 22. Was there a connection between the bullet fragment in Walker's house and the Carcano with which the president was assassinated?

Robert Frazier, the FBI expert, did not want to come to that conclusion. The bullet was too heavily damaged. There was also no contradiction and the bullet was ultimately identified as a 6.5, but it was impossible to attribute it to the Carcano 'to the exclusion of all other weapons.'[754] Frazier's reluctance led to an academic discussion about the forensic need for full certainty.

Joseph D. Nicol, the supervisor of the *Illinois Bureau of Criminal Identification and Investigation*, carried out his own investigation,[755] and had less hesitation. He concluded 'that there is a fair probability' that the Walker bullet fragment was shot with the Carcano.[756] Spectroscopy expert Heiberger, on the other hand, stressed that the lead of the Walker bullet and the lead of the Kennedy bullet were different alloys, and that usually meant that they were a different type of ammunition.[757] The Commission didn't want to hear this, and did not summon Heiberger as a witness. Even the HSCA could not conclusively link the Walker bullet fragment to the Carcano. 'The panel concluded that the Walker Bullet was too damaged to allow conclusive identification of the bullet with a particular firearm.'[758] There are also fascinating discussions on the Internet about the NAA tests that were carried out on the fragment.[759]

But before we can answer the question of whether fragment CE573 was fired with a Carcano, there is, of course, still the question of whether CE573 is actually the fragment that was found in Walker's house on April 10.

The photo on the left shows CE573, the bullet fragment from the attack on Walker; the photo on the right shows the 'magic bullet' of the Kennedy assassination. The resemblance is striking.

But the resemblance also applies for the copper color of the bullet. Conse-

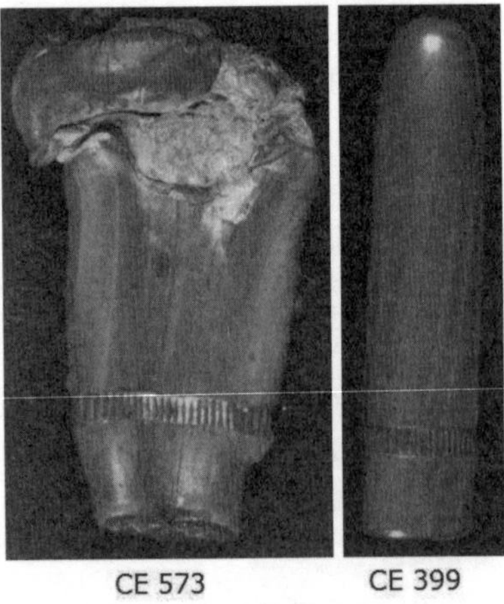

Figure 58. The Walker bullet and the magic bullet.

quently, nobody who saw a color photo of CE573 would say that the fragment had a steel sleeve. The Commission also put the question to weapons expert Frazier:[760]

Question: Is this a jacketed bullet?
Answer: Yes, it is a copper-alloy jacketed bullet having a lead core.
Question: Can you think of any reason why someone might have called it a steel-jacketed bullet?
Answer: No, Sir; except that some individuals commonly refer to rifle bullets as steel-jacketed bullets, when they actually in fact just have a copper-alloy bullet.

The Commission therefore already had prima facie reasons in 1964 to doubt the authenticity of the bullet fragment in the evidence. The true extent of the problem only came to light in 1978. G. Robert Blakey, the Chief Counsel of the HSCA showed fragment CE573 on the television in 1978. Walker, who was watching the program at home from his armchair, was stunned by what he saw. This was *not* the fragment that was found in his house on April 10, 1963. Walker should know. Immediately after the attack, he had held the bullet in his hand. He would certainly have paid attention to an object that nearly killed him. He immediately sent a telegram: 'The bullet before your Select Committee called the Walker Bullet is not the Walker Bullet that is fired at me and taken out of my house by the Dallas Police on April 10, 1963.'[761]

On February 17, 1979, Walker also wrote a letter to the Attorney General Griffin Bell, in which he called CE573 'a ridiculous substitute.' He was sure of his facts: 'I saw the hunk of lead, picked up by a policeman in my house, and I took it from him and I inspected it carefully. There is no mistake. There has been a substitution for the bullet fired by Oswald and taken out of my house.' As a military man, Walker had experience with bullets, and had carefully examined the bullet when it was found. Walker was certainly not inclined to help a supposed anarchist like Oswald. The right-wing general must have been very sure before to challenging the evidence against a communist. His lawyers also exchanged letters with the ministry on the issue. An assassination attempt was a serious matter. If Oswald had been falsely accused, the real perpetrator was still at large. For once, Walker was right to be angry with the government.

But, then, by whom and when was the fragment switched? The chain of custody of the Walker bullet is once again – we have become used to it – a complete mess. Police officers argued about who had found the fragment, and recorded contradictory statements full of gaps.[762] But we can reconstruct the chain of custody of CE573 as follows:

1. General Walker and Officers Norvell and McElroy saw the fragment at the scene on April 10;
2. The fragment then ended up with B.G. Brown, a subordinate of Lieutenant Day;
3. Brown gave the fragment to Lieutenant Day;
4. On April 25, Day handed the fragment over to Alexander from the Municipal Crime Laboratory;
5. On December 2, when Oswald suddenly became the suspect in the case, Day picked up the fragment from the crime lab;
6. The fragment then went to FBI agent Odum;[763]
7. Odum sent the bullet to the FBI lab by registered mail. There, the bullet became specimen Q188;
8. The experts Frazier, Cunningham and Nicol examined Q188.

Before December 2, nobody had any interest in distorting the evidence in the obscure Walker case. We can consequently ignore the first four links in the evidence chain. On April 22, 1963, Lieutenant Day testified before the Commission that CE573 was indeed the fragment that was found at Walker's house.[764] The experts Frazier, Cunningham[765] and Nicol[766] confirmed that CE573 was the fragment they had examined. This means that the bullet fragment had not yet been swapped up through swapped up through Link 4, and that it was no longer substituted from Link 5 onwards. If Walker's allegation about the substitution is correct, then it was Lieutenant Day who carried it out. Day again.

The Commission relied on the bullet fragment as proof of Oswald's guilt. It had to prove that fragment CE573 was found at the crime scene, and could only do so by having the evidence authenticated by someone who had seen it on April 10. These persons were Officers Norvell and McElroy, and the general himself. The Commission did not hear the two police officers, and carefully avoided confronting Walker with the evidence. Expert Alexander had examined the fragment at the time for the Dallas Police, but was also not consulted. The Commission knew very well that there was a problem, however, because two police reports had separately described the bullet as 'with a steel jacket.' The further procedure also clearly shows that the Commission deliberately circumvented the problem.

CE573 appeared as Commission evidence on March 31, 1964. Commission Counsel Eisenberg gave expert Frazier a pillbox with a bullet fragment. He then said to the witness: 'I would like to state for the record that this bullet was found in the Walker residence after the attempted assassination of General Walker.'[767] Commissioner McCloy reacted alertly: 'As far as you know, we have no proof of that yet?' Eisenberg had to admit that there was indeed no proof that fragment CE573 was found at the crime scene. Expert Cunningham was heard on the very same day. Eisenberg already started giving an unsubstantiated statement about the location at which the fragment was found. He changed his mind, hesitated and finally said that the fragment 'is believed to be the bullet found in the Walker residence.' But, a few days later, the alert McCloy was not present at the hearing of expert Nicol about CE573. Allen Dulles was flustered for a moment, and asked: 'Would you refresh my memory as to this other exhibit – I don't remember – is 573 the actual bullet that was fired and mutilated in the Walker attempt?'[768] Eisenberg answered: 'Yes.'

In the three interventions by Eisenberg, CE573 made the transition from not authenticated to authenticated. On April 22, the Commission was able to go a step further with the witness hearing of Lieutenant Day. Day claimed that CE573 was indeed the bullet fragment that he had received from his subordinate Brown on April 10. When Edwin Walker was finally heard on July 23, the authenticity of CE573, albeit fraudulous, had already been accepted. Consequently, nobody deemed it necessary to ask the general to confirm that CE573 was the fragment that had been found in his house. Through that omission, it took fifteen years before Walker realized that the evidence in the file on the attempt on his life had been tampered with. For Oswald, it was too late to become angry.

PHOTOS

The Commission's third argument to prove Oswald's guilt are photos of Walker's house taken by Oswald. According to Marina, Oswald kept a notebook about the preparations for the attack on Walker. He had destroyed it at her request. But not everything was destroyed. Four photos were found among Oswald's possessions: three of Walker's house and one of the nearby railway. The photos seem to have been taken on March 9 or 10 with Oswald's Imperial Reflex camera. The FBI concluded this from the state of a construction site that could be seen in the background.[769] That was just a month before the attack and, perhaps even more telling, two days before he ordered his Carcano. On one photo with a parked car, Oswald had obscured the license plate by making a hole in the photo. Whose car it was and why the license plate was cut out remains a mystery, but in any case, the photos confirm that Oswald was involved in the attack in one way or another.

THE LETTER

But participating in an assault is something else than committing it all by himself. Even the Commission realized that all the evidence against Oswald as sole perpetrator was weak. But there was still the trump card, the famous letter. The Commission assumed that it was authentic. Their expert James J.

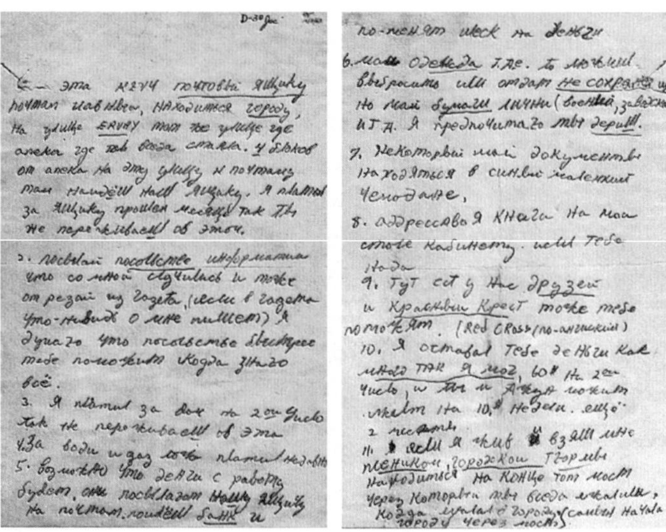

Figure 59. Oswald's letter.

Cadigan[770] confirmed that it was Oswald's handwriting, and so did Marina.[771] The HSCA was more cautious for a technical reason. The experts did not want to analyze the letter (item 57 of the 63 examined documents) because the document was written in a language that the handwriting experts did not know.[772] But this document is certainly authentic. A forger would probably have considered it sufficient to write a short, clear confession in Oswald's handwriting. Each of the eleven items in the letter could be checked; a forger would not only have to imitate the handwriting, but also the style and the poor Russian of Oswald. The financial details are also typical of Oswald. There are too many elements in the letter that a forger would have wisely avoided. We need have no doubt that the letter is genuine. The conspiracists point to all kinds of errors in the letter,[773] but they are Oswald's errors. Not every error proves that it is a falsification. It is not true that, by definition, a forger would make more errors than Oswald himself.

In the last point, Oswald also stated that, if he was taken alive, he would probably end up in the City Jail of Dallas. He was therefore planning a criminal act in Dallas. The content of the letter also allows it to be dated to within the very short period when the Oswalds lived on Neely Street. Oswald lived there from March 2 until April 24, 1963. He no longer lived under the same roof as Marina after leaving Neely Street, and the letter can therefore not date from that period. Oswald also wrote: 'I paid the house rent on the 2nd.' He only paid rent twice while living on Neely Street: a month in advance at the start of the rental, and on April 2 for the second month. The letter was therefore written between April 3 and April 24. The date of the attack on Walker, April 10, falls perfectly within this time period.

There are still a lot of open questions, but the letter certainly reveals enough about Oswald's involvement in the attack. The following elements also point in that direction:

1. From an ideological perspective, Oswald had a motive for wanting to kill Walker;
2. The evidence contains photos of Walker's backyard on March 9 and 10, 1963. The photos are taken with Oswald's camera;
3. Walker's telephone number was in Oswald's notebook;

4. Oswald had had his gun since March 25, 1963, and the attack followed less than three weeks later;
5. Before April 5, Marina wrote 'Hunter of Fascists' on the copy of the backyard photo that was found among the possessions of George de Mohrenschildt;
6. Lee lost his job at Jagers Stovall on April 6. This heavy setback may have sparked his inferiority complex, and could have led to an abnormal increase in his assertiveness;
7. George and Jeanne de Mohrenschildt fled as far away as possible after their nocturnal visit to the Oswalds on April 13;
8. Lee fled Dallas on April 24, two weeks after the attack.

It is therefore as good as certain that Oswald was involved in the attack on Walker. The following elements also point to the involvement of third parties:

1. Shortly before the attack, Walker's associate Surrey saw two men who were examining the area;
2. If Oswald was the perpetrator, he would have been on the garden path or in the parking lot. The testimonies of Coleman and Walker show that he was at neither of these places;
3. Coincidentally, there were two unknown figures present at that moment who apparently had nothing to do with the attack;
4. Walker did not think that Oswald was the gunman;
5. The original bullet fragment from Walker's apartment seems to have been substituted by a Carcano bullet.

The evidence is very contradictory, but the question of whether Oswald acted alone or not, and whether he was the gunman or not, ultimately makes little difference for the Kennedy case. There is another aspect that seems to be more important. The dubious honor of giving Oswald the idea of carrying out an attack on Walker goes to Volkmar Schmidt, the German oil geologist who had intensely talked with Oswald for three hours at the party at the de Mohrenschildts. Just like Ruth Paine, Volkmar Schmidt came to the get-together at the de Mohrenschildts as an acquaintance of Doctor Everett Glover. He was also very interested in the study of the Russian language. In 2008, researcher William 'Bill' Kelly recorded an excellent telephone interview with Schmidt.[774] The German proved to be no ordinary figure. During the Second World War, Schmidt was very friendly in Germany with Professor Kuetemeyer,[775] who, in turn, was a good friend of Graf von Stauffenberg, the colonel who tried to assassinate Hitler with a bomb in a briefcase. Kuetemeyer was also a good acquaintance of psychiatrist Carl Gustav Jung. Is it too far-fetched to remind you that Allen Dulles was the head of the Swiss branch of the OSS, the forerunner of the CIA, in 1943, and, in that position, had contacts with the initiators of the attack on Hitler? We also know that Dulles's former mistress, Mary Bancroft, was being treated by Jung for compulsive sneezing, but that this went further than a mere relationship between patient and doctor. In his intelligence work, Dulles made use of Jung's brilliant insight into human motives. He commented on these later: 'Jung's verdict really helped me to gage the political situation.'[776] Among other things, Mary Bancroft acted as an intermediary between Dulles and Jung before the assassination attempt on Hitler.

Just as was the case with Ruth Paine, Schmidt's background also very quickly brings us close to Allen Dulles. As an oil geologist, Schmidt also had the same vague profession as de Mohrenschildt, and could visit developing countries that were interesting for the CIA without raising suspicions. Speaking Russian was an important condition to qualify as a potential watchdog for Lee and Marina. Even in this point, Schmidt met this expectation pattern. In many ways, Schmidt, Paine and de Mohrenschildt seemed to be three cats from the same litter. The differences are great, but the basic pattern is very similar. All three were closely involved in Oswald's role in the attack on Walker. Schmidt was incidentally also completely in agreement with the CIA in his description of Oswald as an irrational, bitter and dangerous man who was capable of doing anything out of pure desire for recognition. He was also one of the few who claimed that Oswald was fervently opposed to Kennedy. According to Schmidt, this was just the reason to make him aware – with the very best intentions – of the despicable, neo-fascist ideas of Walker. Could Oswald not focus his anger better at someone like that instead of at a man like Kennedy? Schmidt described it as if he had only wanted to waken Oswald from his unreasonable anger and to start him thinking: 'When I heard how hateful he was towards Kennedy and Cuba, which was kind of irrational, I tried to say "hey, there's something much more real to be concerned about," because I don't know about Castro, but I know about this Walker, he's kind of a Nazi, yea?' Schmidt admitted that his three-hour conversation with Oswald could have led to the attack on Walker. Years later, Schmidt still burst into tears when he drove past Dealey Plaza, purely because of the realization of his 'terrible responsibility.' The responsibility is undeniable, but not because Schmidt gave Oswald the idea of focusing his aggressiveness on Walker instead of Kennedy, fourteen months before the attack. Schmidt is responsible because he failed to inform the police of the possible involvement of Oswald after the attack on the general. If Oswald had been arrested in April for the failed attack, his name would at least have been added to the security list. It seems most unlikely that he would ever have been given the opportunity to get close to Kennedy on November 22. Not only Schmidt, but also de Mohrenschildt knowingly held back important information about Oswald and his possible involvement in the attack on Walker. Schmidt and de Mohrenschildt must have had a very good reason to keep quiet about it. The most innocent explanation for this is that they did indeed pass on the information, but not to the Dallas Police or the FBI. They fulfilled their civil duty by keeping the CIA informed of the state of affairs. The heavy responsibility for withholding the information then ultimately lies exclusively with the CIA. Dulles told his fellow Commission members that if the CIA had to choose between reporting a crime or protecting its secrets, it would not hesitate for a second. What secret or which agent(s) did the CIA protect in April 1963 by not informing the FBI and the Dallas Police about an armed eccentric, a stray extremist?

FILE 6

L.H. OSWALD, AGENT PROVOCATEUR

Chapter 14 – New Orleans

The CIA was never far from where Oswald was. In 1978, Senator Richard Schweiker headed a Senate committee that investigated the operation of the intelligence services. He had no doubt that there was a connection between Oswald and the CIA: 'We do know Oswald had intelligence connections. Everywhere you look with him, there are fingerprints of intelligence.'[777] There are never more than indications, but that is inherent to good intelligence work.

When did the CIA's interest in Oswald first arise? The opinions on this are divided. According to the official story, the CIA had, in fact, not the least interest in Oswald after his return from the Soviet Union. J. Walter Moore of the CIA's *Domestic Contacts Division* considered that Oswald was no more than 'a harmless lunatic.'[778] The prodigal defector was not even officially interviewed. According to the HSCA investigation of the files on known defectors to the Soviet Union, 'the fact that Oswald was not interviewed (was) more the rule than the exception according to procedures followed by the CIA at that point in time.'[779] But in spite of these denials, we know for sure that the intelligence service did keep an eye on Oswald after his return to the United States. A CIA memorandum pointed towards the use of 'suitable channels' to approach Oswald, but without applying too much pressure: 'Don't push too hard to get the information we need, because this individual looks odd.'[780] De Mohrenschildt and Ruth Paine, in their capacity of friends who discreetly but closely monitored Oswald and Marina, fitted perfectly into this picture of 'suitable channels.'

On Wednesday, April 24, two weeks after the attempt on Walker's life, Ruth Paine gave Oswald a lift to the Greyhound bus station in Dallas when he left for New Orleans. There, Lee[781] moved in with his aunt Lilian and his uncle Charles 'Dutz' Murret, who was active in gambling circles and, according to the HSCA, even had contacts with 'significant organized crime figures affiliated with the Marcello organization.'[782] Oswald already found work on May 9, as a maintenance man for coffee machines at the Reilly Coffee Company. Wages were 1.5 dollars per hour. His employer, William B. Reilly, was an ardent anti-Castro militant.

New Orleans was abuzz with anti-Castro activities, most of which were financially supported by the CIA. The central pivot of these activities was private detective W. Guy Banister, described by Glenn Fleming as 'a racist, anti-Castroite and an alcoholic, wrapped tightly within a raging temper.'[783] Banister was a former FBI agent, and had meanwhile joined the CIA. He was also a member of the John Birch Society and the paramilitary *Minutemen*, two organizations who had General Walker as their figurehead. One of Banister's memorable statements was that the world's problems could be better solved '*with a bullet than with a ballot.*'[784] Anthony Summers assumes that Banister was mainly useful as a circuit breaker or 'cutout' for the CIA, a bit like a switch aimed at preventing the occurrence of legal short circuits. The CIA only had jurisdiction outside US territory. Any activities in New Orleans therefore had to be carried out indirectly. In this respect, Banister was a suitable buffer guy, despite his alcoholism and his quick temper.[785]

One of his employees was pilot David Ferrie, a strange guy with a wig and false eyebrows. He had been involved as a pilot in the spectacular air operations in the period before the Bay of Pigs operation. But Ferrie is probably also the pilot who clandestinely flew godfather Carlos Marcello into the country again after Robert Kennedy had banned him from the United States. Ferrie and Carlos Marcello were working very closely together in the week before the assassination of the president. Ferrie also drove hundreds of miles headlong to Texas through a heavy storm on the day of the assassination. He stopped at every payphone along the way and had animated discussions, but, on the following Monday, he was unable to recall what these had been about. On the Sunday, Ferrie's hectic trip ended in Galveston, a seaside resort on the Gulf of Mexico, and the perfect base for reaching Mexico with a small airplane. (Breck Wall of AGVA was also in Galveston when Ruby phoned him around midnight on Saturday night.) As soon as Ferrie heard on Sunday that Oswald had been killed, he drove back to New Orleans without stopping.

We've come full circle: Lee Oswald, Dutz Murret, Carlos Marcello, David Ferrie, Guy Banister and back to Oswald ... David Ferrie also happened to be an old acquaintance of Oswald. When he was 16, Oswald participated in a paramilitary youth camp of the *Civil Air Patrol* (CAP). Ferrie was one of the youth leaders there. Because of his predilection for boys and planes, Ferrie was an enthusiastic helper.

The same conspicuous Ferrie also often turned up in Banister's building in Camp Street.[786] Others who had an office in the same building were Sergio Arcacha Smith, the local representative of the *Cuban Democratic Revolution-*

ary Front, and his companion Carlos Quiroga.[787] In a report in April 1963, the Cuban secret service also linked the following people at Camp Street no. 544 to the CIA: Orlando Bosch, Antonio Cuesta, Antionio Veciana, Luis Posada, Eladio del Valle, Manuel Salvat and Manuel Villafana.[788] Carlos Bringuier, the leader of the anti-Castro group DRE, which was financed by the CIA, was also seen there. Bringuier was the man with whom Oswald had a significant fight later. The above explains why the building was also dubbed the *Cuban Grand Central Station*. The mix of Cuban exiles, CIA, Mafia and frustrated patriots was an endless source of contradictions. But there was one thing they all agreed on: Kennedy was to blame for everything that was going wrong. All the anti-Kennedy lines therefore converged in New Orleans, and more specifically in Guy Banister's ramshackle office building. One block away was the Reilly & Co. Coffee Inc. If Oswald really was an ingrained communist, he had picked a very strange place to look for work in New Orleans. Despite the political preferences of his boss, however, he seemed quite happy with his new job, and he soon managed to rent a flat on Magazine Street. He called Marina to come and join him. As she had promised, Ruth Paine drove the pregnant Marina all the way from Dallas to New Orleans. On May 11, Marina found herself back under the conjugal roof in New Orleans. After her comfortable stay with Ruth, however, she was deeply disappointed with the poor surroundings Lee was able to offer her. The arguments started again on the very first day they were reunited.

THE FPCC OFFICE

Oswald didn't throw in the towel and outed himself intensively and openly as pro-Castro, unhindered by the Castro-haters in his immediate vicinity. On May 26, he wrote a letter to the Fair Play for Cuba Committee (FPCC)[789] to inform the FPCC chairman that he planned to rent a small office to form a local branch. Three days later, he received a reply from the concerned chairman, who strongly advised against a local office due 'to the lunatic fringe in your community.'[790] Oswald disregarded this good advice: he opened an office at Camp Street 544, thereby not hiding from from the 'lunatic' anti-Castro activists but boldly venturing into the lion's den. He had one thousand pamphlets with the heading *Hands Off Cuba!* and five hundred membership forms printed in early June. The FPCC branch of New Orleans was born. The believers see this as proof that Oswald was a communist, but there is an alternative explanation. The CIA had previously also urged Court Wood, a student who had returned from Cuba shortly before, to start up an FPCC branch. This happened under the supervision of David Atlee Phillips,[791] a CIA man who continually emerged in Oswald's proximity from then onwards. In a memorandum dated September 26, the FBI also reported on the CIA attempts to infiltrate the FPCC in the fall of 1963: 'This will be done by distributing propaganda through appropriate cut-outs. CIA is also giving some thought to planting deceptive information which might embarrass the Fair Play for Cuba Committee (FPCC) in areas where it does have some support abroad.'[792]

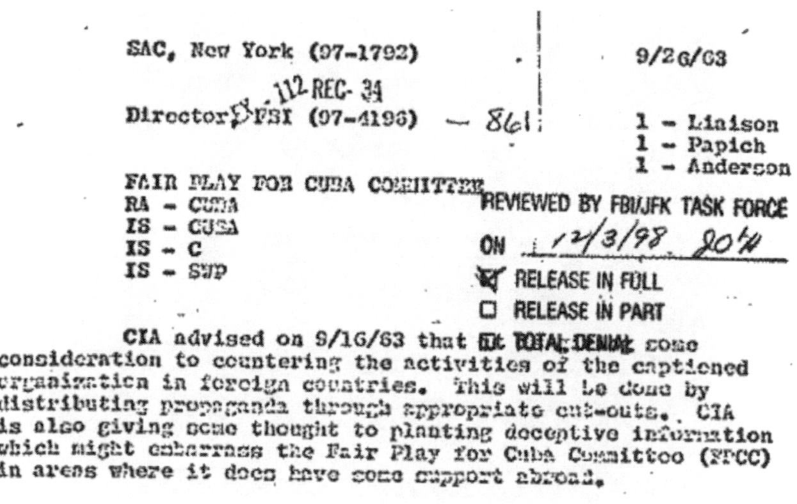

SAC, New York (97-1792) 9/26/63

112 REC- 34

Director, FBI (97-4196) — 861

1 - Liaison
1 - Papich
1 - Anderson

FAIR PLAY FOR CUBA COMMITTEE
RA - CUBA
IS - CUBA
IS - C
IS - SWP

REVIEWED BY FBI/JFK TASK FORCE
ON 12/3/98
☒ RELEASE IN FULL
☐ RELEASE IN PART
☐ TOTAL DENIAL

CIA advised on 9/16/63 that it is giving some consideration to countering the activities of the captioned organization in foreign countries. This will be done by distributing propaganda through appropriate cut-outs. CIA is also giving some thought to planting deceptive information which might embarrass the Fair Play for Cuba Committee (FPCC) in areas where it does have some support abroad.

Figure 60. FBI memorandum about the infiltration of the CIA into the FPCC.

Oswald's one-man branch in New Orleans fitted perfectly into the CIA's plans and tactics. Guy Banister was, of course, an expert in this type of operation. He hired the brothers David and Allen Campbell, for example, two former Marines who pretended to be pro-Castro at the university in order to identify the Castro sympathizers among the students. This is how Allen Campbell was able to report to Banister that Oswald was distributing pro-Castro pamphlets in New Orleans. Banister initially laughed this off, until he learned that an address was printed on the pamphlets. The mentioned address was Bannister's own, 544 Camp Street.[793] This provided evidence of direct contact between Oswald and himself, and that was highly undesirable. Banister preferred to stay in the background. There are many testimonies about contacts between the two men,[794] but, on the other hand, Banister's subordinate, Jack Martin, who was constantly in his vicinity, had never seen Oswald.[795] Banister was therefore very discreet in his contact with Oswald. That's not very surprising in the context of an undercover operation. But there's enough circumstantial evidence to assume that he was monitoring Oswald's FPCC initiatives. The CIA, Banister's main employer, had asked for such an infiltration, and Oswald's FPCC approach perfectly mirrored Banister's style: a fake pro-Castro militant recruiting kindred spirits in order to take down their details.

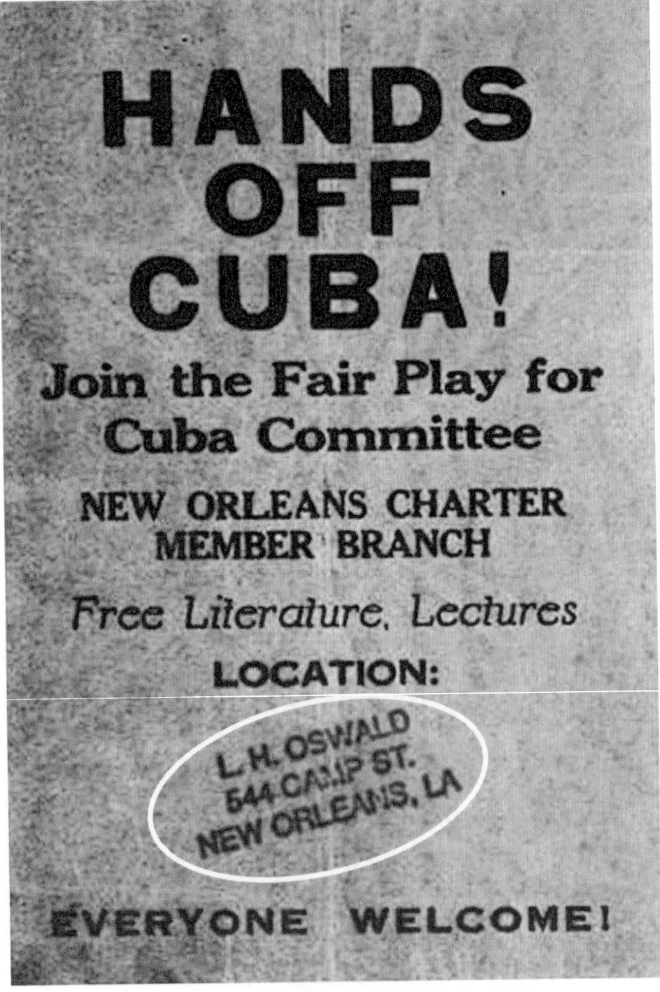

Figure 61. Oswald's FPCC folder with Banister's address.

Oswald's pro-Castro activities did not go unnoticed in any case. In mid-June, he conducted a one-man demonstration at a shipyard, where he distributed pamphlets, which soon ended up on Hoover's desk. But the most remarkable incident was a clash with an anti-Castro group. Carlos Bringuier was the local representative of the *Directorio Revolucionario Estudantil* (DRE), an organization that organized raids against Castro's Cuba. The DRE was 'conceived, created and funded by CIA.'[796] The student organization received no less than 50,000 dollars from the CIA every month,[797] and its activities were monitored by the highest level of the CIA administration. Propaganda Specialist George Joannides, head of the CIA Psychological Warfare department, was the permanent contact person for DRE, reporting directly to David Atlee Phillips, the head of the *Cuban Operations* of the CIA station in Mexico City. If Oswald's FPCC branch was also an idea of Phillips, he controlled both Oswald and Bringuier from the background. According to the official story, Oswald walked into Bringuier's clothing store in early August to join his anti-Castro organization. Bringuier played for time. But, much to his surprise, he saw the same Oswald distributing pro-Castro pamphlets in Canal Street on Friday, August 9. Furious, he attacked Oswald, who smiled imperturbably and said: 'OK Carlos, if you want to hit me, hit me.' It is unlikely that Bringuier was not aware that Oswald had been disseminating such pamphlets for over six weeks already. Canal Street is in the immediate vicinity of Bringuier's clothing store.[798] But there is even irrefutable proof that this whole scene was staged. On August 1, Oswald wrote a letter to the national chairman of the FPCC, which he posted on August 4.[799] Strangely enough, Oswald mentioned how his street demonstration had been attacked and reprimanded by the police. But the skirmish and arrest only actually took place eight days later. The incident had therefore been planned in advance, and both Bringuier and Oswald played the game. The judge gave Oswald a fine of 10 dollars for disturbing the peace. When he left the courthouse, a WDSU TV crew just happened to be in front of the building, purely by chance, of course. Four days later, Oswald was once again distributing pamphlets, this time right in front of the International Trade Mart. He had even hired two extra people in order to raise the credibility of his FPCC branch to three members.[800] The media were again surprisingly well-informed. Oswald was invited to a radio interview with William Kirk Stuckey, a journalist now known for helping the CIA.[801] In the end, the interview only received 4.5 minutes of airtime. But when the anti-communist Edward Butler informed Stuckey of the fact that Oswald was a Soviet defector, Oswald's news value increased. On August 21, he participated in a real radio debate, in which Bringuier and Butler confronted him with his anti-American past. Butler was another right-wing provocateur by nature. He was the head of the private propaganda service INCA, an organization that aimed to fight communism with propaganda and deception. Butler explained his method to a journalist at some point: 'The conflict manager will infiltrate troublemaking groups, try to divert them from their goals, break up their structure, create internal dissension.'[802] Discrediting the FPCC through Oswald seems to fit perfectly with this strategy. Oswald, scorned by believers such as Posner for his limited intelligence, did surprisingly well in the hefty debate, which lasted 25 minutes. He played his role of hardened Marxist brilliantly.

Thanks to all the fuss, Oswald's pro-Castro commitment had already received extensive coverage in the media and in police reports by the end of August. If anyone was ever to ask the question who Oswald was, the answer would be readily available and apparent to everyone who listened to the debate. His contacts with the CIA, on the other hand, remained well-hidden. Fortunately, there was one crack in the wall of lies and silence. There was a witness of a meeting between Oswald and a CIA agent: Antonio Veciana. This ardent anti-Castro activist was the leader of the terrorist organization Alpha 66. His contact person at the CIA was one Maurice Bishop. The now very old Veciana admits these days that Maurice Bishop was, in fact, David Atlee Phillips.[803] Among other activities, Alpha 66 attacked several Russian vessels that sailed to the island, and didn't even stop this kind of nonsense when the world was tottering on the brink of nuclear war. The fact that Phillips urged Veciana to provoke Russia at a time when Kennedy was trying to improve the dialog with the Soviet Union was outright mutiny. Phillips did not agree with the sweet talk of the president. He told Veciana: 'You have to put Kennedy against the wall in order to force him to make decisions that could remove Castro's regime.'[804] Phillips had a meeting with Veciana every month. During one of these meetings, Veciana saw his contact person talk to 'a pale, slight and soft featured young man.'[805] On November 22, Veciana immediately recognized Oswald on the photographs in the news: it was the man he had seen talking to Phillips early in September. Gaeton Fonzi, a member of the Church Commission and later investigator of the HSCA, asked him whether he could possibly be mistaken, and whether this young man possibly only resembled Oswald. Veciana replied: 'Well, you know, Bishop himself taught me how to remember faces, how to remember characteristics. I am sure it was Oswald. If it wasn't Oswald, it was someone who looked exactly like him. Exacto, exacto.'[806]

Barely three weeks after this meeting, Oswald turned up in Phillips's home base, Mexico City. It is therefore very likely that the topic of the conversation Phillips had with Oswald was this visit to Mexico. Did Phillips mislead Oswald into believing that he would be able to enter Cuba without problems on the basis of his FPCC track record? Did Oswald believe that the bus trip to Mexico meant the start of an exciting new life as a double agent on the paradise island? Oswald was naive enough to believe such a thing. He was open for this, and even looked forward to it. He applied for his tourist visa for Mexico on September 17. The visa number was 24085.[807]

ESTADOS UNIDOS MEXICANOS
SECRETARIA DE GOBERNACION
ORIGINAL Nº 24085
VALIDA POR 15 DIAS
BUENA PARA UN SOLO VIAJE POR DIAS
Apellidos y nombre LEE, HARVEY OSWALD
FOTOGRAFO
Sexo H M Edad 23 AÑOS Estado Civil S C
Documento con el que acredita su nacionalidad
ACTA NACIMIENTO
Menores que lo acompañan
MEXICO, D. F.
NUEVA ORLEANS, LA., EUA.,
17 SEPTIEMBRE DE 1963.
ENTRADA SET 26 1963
SALIDA
OCT 1963

ESTADOS UNIDOS MEXICANOS
SECRETARIA DE GOBERNACION
DUPLICADO Nº 24085
VALIDA POR 15 DIAS
BUENA PARA UN SOLO VIAJE POR DIAS
Apellidos y nombre LEE, HARVEY OSWALD
FOTOGRAFO
Sexo H M Edad 23 AÑOS Estado Civil S C
Documento con el que acredita su nacionalidad
ACTA NACIMIENTO
Menores que lo acompañan
MEXICO, D. F.
NUEVA ORLEANS, LA., EUA.,
17 SEPTIEMBRE DE 1963.
Firma del interesado
ENTRADA SET 26 1963
SALIDA
Sello fechador

COMMISSION EXHIBIT No. 2478

Figure 61. Oswald's visa to enter Mexico with number 24085.

There is more proof that the CIA was involved in Oswald's trip to Mexico. The man who was in front of him in the queue, and who received visa 24084,[808] was CIA agent William Gaudet. The Warren Commission was not aware of this, because the FBI claimed that they had not been able to find out who had received visa no. 24084. This information was released by mistake in 1975,[809] and the HSCA did interview Gaudet. He also regularly visited Camp Street 544, and was one of the witnesses who had seen Oswald and Banister together.[810] Gaudet admitted before the parliamentary commission that he did know Oswald – though not personally – but that it was purely by coincidence that he had been in front of Oswald in the queue when he applied for his visa for Mexico. Gaudet's CIA file just happened to be destroyed, of course, at the time the facts were being investigated.[811] We are slowly beginning to understand why Richard Sprague, the main counsel of the HSCA, said that, if he could do it all over again, 'he would begin his investigation of the Kennedy assassination by probing Oswald's ties to the Central Intelligence Agency.'

To complete the circle, Ruth Paine once again took care of Marina when Oswald left. From then on, Oswald's wife lived in Irving, where she prepared for the arrival of her second baby. Lee and Marina would never live under the same roof again. Oswald left on September 25.

Chapter 15 – Mexico

Oswald traveled to Mexico City by coach. After Kennedy's assassination, two adventurous, 23-year-old Australian women[812] recognized him as having been one of their fellow travelers. Lee reached his destination on Friday morning, September 27. According to the Warren Commission, he hardly left the Hotel Commercio during the next six days, and ate all his meals in complete solitude. This is credible. Oswald was not on vacation, and, besides that, he was broke.[813] He obviously had another reason for the trip. Immediately after he had checked into the hotel at 11 a.m., he proceeded to the Cuban consulate[814] to apply for a visa for a two-week stay in Cuba, after which he would travel on to Moscow. Oswald was hoping to board the plane to Havana on September 30, three days after his application. Silvia Duran, the assistant of the Cuban consul, told Oswald to return with passport photos. One hour later, he arrived at the Cuban consulate for the second time, with the photographs. Duran filled in his visa application form and explained the further procedure to him. She clarified that the transit permit for Cuba depended on a prior entry visa for the Soviet Union. Oswald seemed perplexed, and stressed that he was a friend of the Cuban revolution, that he was the 'director' of the Fair Play for Cuba organization and a member of the Communist Party. Surely obtaining a visa wouldn't be a problem for him? Duran insisted that the visa depended entirely on the Russians. All Oswald could do was to make his way to the Russian embassy, where he was told by diplomat Oleg Nechiperenko that only the Russian embassy in Washington could handle visa applications, and that this would take about four months. Oswald realized that he should not expect cooperation from the Russians, and that the Cuban people were also not prepared to open the border for him out of gratitude and hospitality. This was just too much for the exhausted Oswald, and he became angry. The Soviet diplomat showed him the door. As soon as he had recovered from the shock, Oswald returned to the Cuban consulate. He lied to Silvia Duran, saying that the Russian embassy had no problem at all with his entry visa, and that she could therefore surely now provide him with the Cuban visa without any problems. Duran, of course, asked him for proof of the unlikely favorable decision by the Russian embassy. As Oswald could not give her that, she phoned the Russian embassy. She asked for the person with whom the American had spoken there, and whether it was correct that he would be given a Russian visa. The clerk at the Russian Embassy promised to check this. Twenty minutes later, he returned the call: a quick Russian visa for the short-tempered American was out of the question. Oswald became so angry once again that the Cuban Consul Euzebio Azcue himself came out to see what was going on. They continued the noisy altercation in Azcue's office. [815] When Azcue had had enough, he insisted that Oswald leave the consulate immediately. Oswald left, slamming doors.[816] To summarize, Oswald visited the Cuban consulate three times and the Russian embassy once on Friday, and was conspicuously shown the door at both locations.

BIG BROTHER IS WATCHING

The Mexican regime was very anticommunist. Mexico City had therefore become a major base for the anti-Castro operations of their neighbor, the USA, and the Cold War was in full swing. Eavesdropping and spying on the embassies of political opponents was a relatively harmless pastime. The attempts to infiltrate each other's intelligence departments by an unfathomable net of spies, double agents, covert operations, blackmail and true and faked information leaks were a little less innocent. At yet another level, assassination squads were in operation, and intervened in the interest of the state when they saw fit. This whole make-believe world was beyond any form of democratic control. Despite the huge budgets and the immense political consequences of the information gathered, the CIA in 1963 still emanated an aura of cloak and dagger that primarily attracted adventurers and mavericks. The personality and preferences of Allan Dulles defined the DNA of the entire organization. Dulles was the head of the CIA during the explosive expansion of the organization, and was fully protected, as his own brother, who was Secretary of State under Eisenhower, was autonomously calling the shots in the foreign affairs of the United States. But, for both the CIA and the KGB, the fun of pestering each other prevailed over the actual collection of useful information. Everyone was aware that there were bugs everywhere, and that a number of their own officials were inevitably operating as double agents. Nobody therefore let important or sensitive information slip in a local embassy. If this happened anyway by mistake, the counterparty immediately mistrusted what they had heard: it just had to be false information that had been consciously leaked.[817] It was therefore advisable to never believe what you heard or saw. Even concrete and useful information remained unusable, because using it could unmask its source, who would then no longer be able to pick up new, equally unusable, information.

Oswald had been in and out of the Cuban consulate and the Russian embassy. The CIA continuously spied on these two buildings, of course, and, from secret locations, took pictures of everyone entering and leaving them. For the CIA, this photograph observation was an important state secret, and the agency vehemently denied the existence of the cameras. The Cubans therefore themselves provided the American HSCA investigator Lopez with a photograph of the CIA photographers in action.[818] There is not a shadow of a doubt that the CIA clearly had the resources in place to record Oswald's presence on diplomatic premises on film.

The Cuban consulate was also covered in wiretaps. The CIA tapped Silvia Duran's phone, and had discovered that she had had an extra-marital affair with her former boss. In the case of embassy personnel, this is invaluable information. Intelligence agencies are always eager to find weak spots in order to recruit a spy, and the CIA knew quite a lot about Silvia Duran. At the time of Oswald's visits, the tapes of the recorded conversations were first processed by the translator, Boris Torasoff, and were then typed up and passed on to Anne Goodpasture, a highly skilled and intelligent officer[819] with an excellent memory for details. She assessed what should happen with the information. If the content of a phone conversation was relevant, the message took a different bureaucratic path within the agency, often in multiple copies if the message was about different people or situations. Eventually, all this paperwork ended up somewhere in a top secret file that was forever labeled as a state secret.

The CIA listened into Silvia Duran's conversation about Oswald with the Soviet Embassy. That was relevant enough to attract attention, because an unnamed American wanted to go to Cuba, which was against the law. The transcript of the conversation ended up on the desk of Bob Shaw, an associate of David Phillips, and also with Win Scott, the big boss of the CIA base in Mexico.

It ultimately took more than four days before the name Oswald was mentioned. Oswald phoned the Russian embassy himself at 10.30 a.m. on Tuesday, October 1. He, or at least a person claiming to be him, asked if there was any news from Washington about his visa. There are good reasons to doubt that it was really Oswald who called. According to the interpreter, this man, unlike Oswald, spoke 'terrible, hardly recognizable Russian.' The Embassy clerk had the man call back at 10.45 a.m. This time, he mentioned his name: 'This is Lee Oswald speaking. I was at your place last Saturday and spoke to a consul, and they said that they'll send a telegram to Washington, so I wanted to find out if you have anything new. But I don't remember the name of that consul.' The clerk, who was also a KGB agent, asked whether this could have been Kostikov, a consul with an exceptionally dark skin for a Russian. 'Yes', replied the American, and added once more that his name was Oswald. According to this conversation, Oswald had also visited the Russian embassy on Saturday. The spies now for the first time also had a name: Lee Oswald. But this didn't ring a bell. The name Kostikov, on the other hand, set off all the alarm bells.[820] Afterwards, the CIA reported to the Warren Commission that 'Kostikov is believed to work for [...] the Department responsible for executive action, including sabotage and assassination.'[821] The phone call raises a lot of questions. We already mentioned the 'terrible, hardly recognizable Russian.' There is another problem: the man on the phone said he had visited the embassy on Saturday, but that was impossible, because the embassy was not open to the public then.[822] And the confusion gets worse: after the assassination of Kennedy, the CIA sent photographs to the FBI on November 22, showing their 'Oswald' leaving the Russian embassy. The man was photographed no less than twelve times, wearing different clothing and at different times,[823] but he was *not* Oswald. There was no investigation into who the man was, and what he was doing at the embassy.[824] It was also not a question of a simple mix-up that was rectified later. Not a single photograph emerged at any point of the real Oswald, who had been going in and out of the embassy at roughly the same time.

Figure 63. The man who entered the Soviet embassy is certainly not Oswald.

Once the existence of the camera surveillance was confirmed, David Phillips needed, an explanation for why there was no photo of Oswald. The CIA asserted that the camera aimed at the entrance to the Russian embassy did not work during the weekend. However, this was not true according to HSCA investigator Lopez, reporting after his visit on site: 'We definitely saw photos from the period Phillips said the cameras were not working.' The same problem occurred at the Cuban consulate. We know that Oswald or 'Oswald' had entered the building at least four, and maybe five, times. The Americans had installed an automatic camera there, which clicked every time somebody came through the door. Why was there no photo of Oswald? The camera happened to be out of order according to the CIA and/or the entrance to the building had been changed and the camera still had to be adjusted to the new situation. The CIA lied once again, because we know that pictures of Oswald had existed. Win Scott, the big boss of the CIA base in Mexico, confirmed that in 1970.[825] He had seen the photos himself. In 1970, Scott was, of course, well aware of what the real Oswald looked like. We can therefore assume that the photos he referred to were those of the real Oswald. Perhaps the photos were overlooked? No. Edwin Lopez flipped through the three thick folders with hundreds of contact prints from around the last week of September to mid October.[826] They didn't include a single photo of Oswald. There is only one possible explanation for this: someone at a high level had deliberately removed those photographs.

Then, of course, in the absence of the pictures, there are the tape recordings of the tapped phones. A copy had been made of the disturbing conversation in which Kostikov was named. But Murphy's law affected the case once again. According to the CIA, the original tapes were reused for other recordings. This means that the other phone conversations of Silvia Duran and Oswald with the Russian embassy had long been deleted on November 22, and only existed on paper. But what about the one recording mentioning Kostikov, the tape that had been copied? According to the CIA, this copy had also been destroyed before November 22. That is once more a lie, for the following reasons:

— After the assassination of Kennedy, John Whitten (CIA) and Gordon Shanklin (FBI) reported independently of each other that they had heard the tape recording.

— In 1964, Anne Goodpasture confirmed that the voice on the tape had been compared with Oswald's voice.[827]

— Hoover himself not only reported that the tapes were listened to after the assassination, but also that the person on the tape was not Lee Harvey Oswald. He wrote to the head of the Secret Service on November 23: 'Special Agents of this bureau who have conversed with Oswald in Dallas, Texas, have [...] listened to a recording of his voice.[828] These Special Agents are of the opinion that the above-referred-to individual was not Lee Harvey Oswald.'

— Hoover also informed President Johnson on November 23. When Johnson asked Hoover whether he had found out anything more about Oswald's visit to the Soviet embassy in Mexico in September, he replied: 'No, that's one angle that's very confusing for this reason. We have up here the tape and the photograph of the man who was at the Soviet Embassy, using Oswald's name. That picture and the tape do not correspond to this man's voice and his appearance. In other words, it appears that there is a second person who was at the Soviet Embassy down there.'[829]

— Warren Commission staff member William Coleman confirmed the following in writing to investigators Joseph Heyer and Jennifer Gersop on December 18, 1991: 'We read the transcripts of what was actually said and we heard the words being spoken.'[830]

— Warren Commission counsel Slawson did not give a clear answer to the question of whether he had heard the recording. But in 1992, he agreed to answer some questions from a schoolgirl, Amanda Rowell, within the context of an innocent-looking school project. The girl was actually the daughter of Gary Rowell, however, the publisher of the JFK investigation magazine *The Investigator.* Charmed, the unsuspecting Slawson wrote to Amanda: 'Yes I listened to the tape of Lee Harvey Oswald's telephone conversations with the Soviet Embassy in Mexico City.'[831]

— Even the summary report that was prepared by the CIA itself on December 13 states: 'As soon as our Mexico City Station realized that Lee Oswald was the prime suspect [...] actual tapes were also reviewed.'[832] (Notice the plural 'tapes.')

— With 21 years of professional experience in intelligence work, Dr. John Newman understands like no other the meaning of hermetically sealed documents, and the stamps, corrections and initials on them. In his lectures, he demonstrates beyond reasonable doubt that the tapes were listened to and compared with Oswald's voice after the assassination.[833]

It is therefore certain that at least the tape recording of the conversation of October 1 still existed on November 22. But there were presumably even more tape recordings. A senior CIA officer 'who played [the lawyers] the tapes,' [834]confirmed their existence after November 22 in an interview with *Vanity Fair*. Anthony Summers probably refers to the same source when he mentioned 'three qualified witnesses who flatly contradicted the Agency's story.'[835] Two of those witnesses were – we suppose – the attorneys Coleman and Slawson. These two witnesses off the record also gave Summers the name of the third witness, a CIA agent. Summers tracked this agent down and received confirmation that 'the tapes existed as late as the spring of 1964.'

It is obvious why this evidence disappeared, and why it was lied about. The voice on the tape was not that of Lee Harvey Oswald. Torasoff, the interpreter who had listened to the tape in order to translate it, confirmed this. He recalled that the man on the phone spoke hardly recognizable Russian, while Oswald, by then, spoke the language reasonably well. Someone had passed himself off as Oswald on the phone. There could be a fairly innocent explanation for this. Author David Kaiser wonders whether the CIA perhaps had an undercover agent call the Russian embassy using Oswald's name, just to find out whether the real Oswald would obtain a visa. In any case, the terrible Russian demonstrates that this was a matter of pure improvisation. The problem with this hypothesis is that the name 'Oswald' had never been mentioned in the previous calls, so how could the CIA know under whose name they had to make this call?

All this does not rule out, however, that the 'real' Oswald visited the embassy and the consulate. A number of members of the Cuban consulate staff met in person the man who presented himself as Oswald. Could they confirm that the man in Mexico was the same person as the suspect in Dallas?

The Cuban consul Azcue would certainly remember Oswald well after the fierce altercation he had with him. Consul Azcue was no longer in office at the time of Kennedy's assassination, and had already left Mexico City. Only two or three weeks after the attack, he saw a close-up of Oswald in the news report in a movie theater. He immediately realized that the Oswald in Dallas was not the man with whom he had argued at the end of October in Mexico.

According to Azcue, the man didn't even look like Oswald.[836] The man who had visited the consulate was about 35, of medium size and had dark blond hair. The young face of the real Oswald was 'in radical contrast to the deeply lined face' of the man who came to apply for the visa.[837] The former consul maintained that 'this gentleman was not, is not, the person or individual who went to the consulate.'

Bugliosi minimized the problem. He said that Consul Azcue was 'virtually the sole basis for the allegation of imposture.' Just like the Commission, he dismissed Azcue's statement. Because there was, in fact, another reliable witness for Oswald's presence in Mexico: Silvia Duran. The consul's assistant had seen Oswald several times, and she confirmed his identity.[838] She claimed that the man in Mexico was the same man as in Dallas. Upon closer investigation, however, this statement appeared to be highly unreliable. In her original statement of November 27, Duran had described the man in question as 'blond, short, dressed inelegantly and whose face turned red when angry.'[839] This description did not fit Oswald at all. We also know why Duran changed her statement so drastically afterwards. She was roughly[840] arrested after the assassination of Kennedy. David Phillips, using the pseudonym Lawrence F. Barker,[841] spread the false rumor that Silvia Duran had been spotted in two cars with Texas license plates.[842] Soon after, a second rumor emerged about Duran and Oswald having had a sexual relationship during his short stay in Mexico. These rumors made Duran appear to be a major suspect. But the Americans could not arrest her. She was a Mexican citizen on Mexican soil. Win Scott, who did not know that the rumors were false and spread through his own department, called Luis Echevarria, a secretary of the Mexican Minister of Home Affairs. Echevarria was a reliable CIA asset and 'had shown the ability to get things done.' The CIA was counting on him to ensure the arrest of Silvia Duran. Win Scott then phoned the minister himself and demanded his full cooperation.[843] The CIA urged him to 'interrogate Duran vigorously and exhaustively.'[844] The woman was arrested without a warrant. 'Call the police, call the police,' she cried desperately as she was taken away and made to get into a van. The man who held her down snarled at her: 'Scandalous old woman, shut up. Because where we are going we will see what's going to happen to you.'[845] She already suffered a few blows during the arrest. The Cuban ambassador later saw and reported to the Cuban President that his assistant had dark marks on her arms.[846]

Years later, Duran stated that she had been beaten until she admitted that she had had an affair with Oswald. Through the Mexican authorities, the CIA forced Duran to make a statement implying the involvement of Cuba in the assassination of Kennedy. The Mexicans only released her after eight hours of rough interrogation and intimidation. The document that proves that the Mexican authorities had indeed arrested Duran at the request of the CIA was released in 1993.[847] The CIA station in Mexico had acted completely autonomously in this move, because, at the same time, the headquarters in Langley already tried to suppress any rumor hinting at a conspiracy, and at Cuban involvement on behalf of Johnson. When Win Scott proudly reported to headquarters that he had had a possible accomplice arrested – no less than a diplomatic officer of the Cuban consulate – headquarters got a dreadful shock. John Whitten, who was responsible in Langley for covert operations in Mexico, immediately blew the whistle on Scott. He told them that they could not arrest Silvia Duran. Although it was already too late for that, Scott saw no reason to panic, because the Mexican security service, when necessary, could be very discreet. Dick Helms, the deputy director of the CIA, also got a shock because of the possible consequences of the arrest. The slightest hint of any involvement of the Cubans in the assassination of Kennedy could trigger a war. To make sure that the station in Mexico had clearly understood what was at stake, a written confirmation from Langley followed: 'Arrest of Silvia Duran is extremely serious matter [...] request you ensure that her arrest is kept absolutely secret, that no information from her is published or leaked, that all such info is cabled to us...'[848] But Helms in Langley and Scott in Mexico were not aware that there were elements operating within the CIA who wanted to provoke an invasion of Cuba, instead of trying to prevent it.

Phillips continued to pour oil on the fire, and played his last joker, the young Nicaraguan Gilberto Alvarado. This man claimed to have witnessed Oswald being given $6,500 by someone at the Russian consulate: $1,500 for expenses and $5,000 as advance payment for the assassination of Kennedy. Phillips launched an alarming story for the umpteenth time.[849] His main ally in Mexico was Thomas Mann, the US ambassador in Mexico. On November 26, he sent a message to the Ministry of Foreign Affairs to the effect that someone in the Russian embassy had given Oswald money as an advance for the assassination. The FBI and the White House also received this message.

Only much later did it become clear that Alvarado was a CIA agent.[850] In the crisis atmosphere of 1963, however, the story of Ambassador Mann was believed, and this led to the renewed arrest of Silvia Duran. Mann wrote in his memorandum: 'Her only chance for survival is to come clean with the whole story and cooperate fully. I think she'll crack when confronted with the details. The Mexicans should be asked to go all out to break her.'[851] The Mexican security police followed the suggestion of the ambassador, and held Sylvia Duran for more than two days.[852] The headquarters in Langley, worried by the adverse evolution of the situation, sent another urgent telegram to the CIA post in Mexico. 'We want to ensure that Silvia Duran gets no impression that Americans are behind her rearrest. In other words we want Mexican authorities to take responsibility for the whole affair.'

In the meantime, the wind had definitively changed in Washington. There would be no invasion of Cuba. Johnson took charge of the Warren Commission, and, together with Hoover, decided which way they would finally go. Deputy Attorney General Katzenbach wrote in a memorandum: 'The public must be satisfied that Oswald was the assassin; that he did not had confederates who are still at large; and that the evidence was such that he would have been convicted at trial.'[853] Hoover dispatched one of his best agents, Larry Keenan, to Mexico in order to convince Ambassador Mann: an invasion of Cuba was out of the question, and that decision was final.

The fact that President Johnson did not want to hear of Alvarado's story did not prevent him from using it for his own purposes. On the basis of this story, he persuaded Warren that 40 million American lives were at stake. 'You were a soldier in World War I, but that was nothing comparable to what you can do for your country in this hour of trouble,' Johnson said to the Chief Justice. Warren declared himself ready to serve his country, and the crafty Johnson successfully used the story that was intended to provoke an invasion to actually prevent it.

But this means that Silvia Duran's role in it now had to be completely rewritten. And so her final statement would fully support the official version of the story: the man who had visited the consulate in Mexico was the same person as the prisoner in Dallas. Anthony Summers tracked Duran down in Mexico, in 1979. She stated – very much on her guard – that the memory of Oswald had faded, and that it had never crossed her mind at the time 'that the Dallas Oswald and the Embassy Oswald might be different people.' But she also told Summers that the man she had seen in Mexico had been very short in stature – 'about my size'[854] – and quite a bit older than Oswald. Silvia was only 1.61 meters in size, so she surely must have noticed this in a man. The real Oswald was 1.77 meters tall. A word is enough to the wise to understand exactly what Duran meant.

But as far as the Warren Commission was concerned, the problem was solved. Duran's final statement had put the genie firmly back in the bottle. At its own initiative, the Warren Commission increased Duran's credibility by claiming that other witnesses confirmed her statement, namely 'confidential sources of extremely high reliability available to the United States in Mexico.' The identity of these sources had to be kept secret to ensure that they could still be useful to the USA in the future. This meant that the Commission in fact referred to CIA sources in Mexico. But how could the CIA station there have had such a high degree of reliability with respect to Oswald's visit to the city? HSCA investigator Fonzi was given the following reply by a 'former high-ranking CIA-officer': 'the "clandestine mentality" that is drilled into the CIA operatives until it is instinctual would permit most of them to commit perjury because in their view, their secrecy oath supersedes any other.' The same person also said the following to Fonzi: 'You represent the United States Congress, but what the hell is that to the CIA?'[855] Allen Dulles, Commission member and former CIA Director, answered this question. During a secret session of the Commission on January 27, 1964, Commission Member Boggs asked whether a CIA member who recruited an agent would know whether that man was an agent. Dulles replied: 'Yes, but he wouldn't tell.' 'Wouldn't tell it under oath?' Warren then asked. Dulles said: 'I wouldn't think he would tell it under oath, no.' 'Why not?' asked the Chief Justice. Dulles clarified: 'He ought not tell it under oath.' Commission member McCloy then asked: 'Wouldn't he tell it to his own chief?' 'He might or he might not. If he was a bad one then he wouldn't,' was Dulles's reply. It seems that CIA agents can be expected to lie, even under oath, and the 'bad ones' could even autonomously decide what they communicated to their superiors. David Atlee Phillips seems to fit perfectly into this picture. Edwin Lopez, who investigated the situation in Mexico for the HSCA, heard from a deputy head at the base in Mexico 'that Phillips was really a bizarre character. He was a loner and reported only to the Station Chief Win Scott. But Scott just let him do whatever he wanted. He was really autonomous. He said he thought that Phillips was running his own operations that no one else knows about. He did know that whenever Phillips was working on an operation he was careful not to leave his fingerprints anywhere. That's the word he used: "fingerprints."'[856] Jefferson Morley, an authority in the field of the Mexico chapter, phrased it as follows: 'In a less ethically flexible world than the one Phillips inhabited, one would say that the CIA man told a series of bald-faced lies.' For the Warren Commission, these were the highly reliable sources[857] that were relied upon to confirm Duran's final statement.

The eyewitnesses therefore also did not dispel the doubts about Oswald's identity in Mexico, quite the contrary. Yet there is one solid piece of evidence that the real Oswald did apply for a visa at the Cuban consulate. Silvia Duran asked Oswald to return with four passport photos. She stapled one of those photos to the application form. This was most certainly a photo of the real Lee Harvey Oswald, the man who was arrested in Dallas.[858] Oswald did not have these photo's made in the vicinity of the consulate,[859] and the Warren Commission assumed that Oswald had them with him.[860] According to Bugliosi, a negative that was later found in his possessions[861] confirms this.

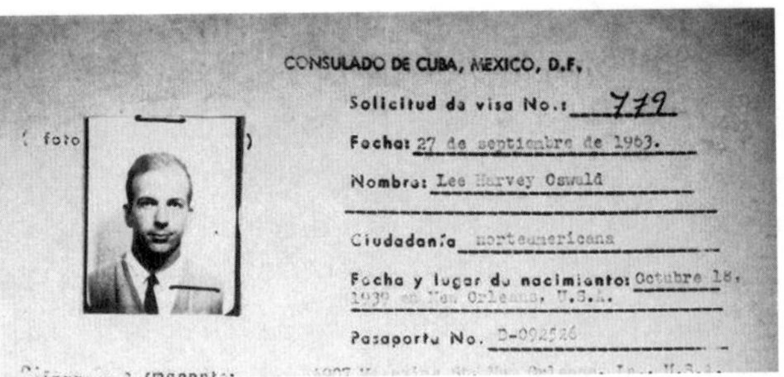
CONSULADO DE CUBA, MEXICO, D.F.

(foto)

Solicitud de visa No.: 779

Fecha: 27 de septiembre de 1963.

Nombre: Lee Harvey Oswald

Ciudadanía norteamericana

Fecha y lugar de nacimiento: Octubre 18, 1939 en New Orleans, U.S.A.

Pasaporte No. D-092526

Figure 64. Oswald's application for a visa for Cuba.

Before we assume that the photograph on the application was replaced later by a photograph of the real Oswald, it is important to know that the Warren Commission stated that the handwriting on the application was indeed Oswald's, and that 'nothing on any of the documents raises suspicion that they might not be authentic.'[862]

A KEEN INTEREST

The events that took place between Oswald's stay in Mexico and the assassination of Kennedy are also illuminating. The CIA station in Mexico City only informed headquarters in Langley ten days after Oswald's first visit to the Cuban consulate. On October 8, a telegram with the following content was received in Langley[863]: 'On October 1, an individual, who identified himself as Lee Oswald, had been overheard telling the Soviet Embassy that three days earlier, on September 28, he had been at the Soviet Embassy, when he spoke with a Consul whom he believed to be Valeriy Vladimirovich Kostikov.'[864] This telegram was clearly intended to link the Russian embassy, through the professional assassin Kostikov, to Oswald and, by extension, to the assassination of Kennedy, seven weeks prior to the assault. The content of the telegram was very misleading. The phone call it refers to was not conducted by Oswald, but by someone who claimed to be him. Moreover, it was not the man who claimed to be Oswald who mentioned the name Kostikov, but the Russian clerk on the other end of the line.[865] Another, more important, shortcoming is that the message did not mention Oswald's four visits to the Cuban consulate, but only that to the Soviet embassy. It also didn't mention that the wiretapped conversation was about a visa for Cuba. The word 'Cuba' was apparently still taboo on October 8.

The reply from headquarters came on October 10 and was no less misleading. The draft of this text went through several hands at the highest level. The reply was especially significant in the way in which it also withheld essential information. It mentioned that Oswald had defected to the Soviet Union and had returned with a Russian wife and a child. This was true, but the message also said that the latest information the CIA had about Oswald dated back to May 1962, when Oswald arrived back in the US.[866] This was a lie, because the CIA was well aware of the following information after May 1962:

- The report of FBI agent Hosty concerning Oswald's move to New Orleans;
- The FBI reported, among other things, that Oswald had extreme leftist sympathies and that he had a subscription to the *Socialist Workermagazine;*
- An FBI report about the incident in which Oswald got into a fight while distributing FPCC pamphlets;

— Most likely information from de Mohrenschildts about Oswald's situation in Dallas and the possibility that he was involved in the attempt on Walker's life;
— More than likely information from the Paines regarding the current situation of the Oswalds;
— Information from Banister about Oswald's activities in New Orleans, including the establishment of a pro-Castro organization, an arrest during a pro-Castro demonstration, an attempt to infiltrate the DRE, a radio interview and participation in a debate in which Oswald openly outed himself as a Marxist, CIA agent Gaudet, who applied for a tourist visa at the same time as Oswald, etc.

Why did the CIA claim that their latest information on Oswald dated back to May 1962, when this was not the case? On the basis of the routing slips of the documents, researcher Jefferson Morley found that Jane Roman was closely involved in drafting the telegram of October 10. When he questioned her, she admitted in the end: 'Yeah, I mean I'm signing off on something that I know isn't true.'[867] Roman also admitted that the gaps in the information meant that Oswald was involved in a covert operation in some way. The CIA had a strict rule for communication regarding its covert operations: not to disclose more than was absolutely necessary. According to Roman, this explained the gap in the communication regarding Oswald, which was 'held very closely on the need-to-know basis.' Phillips explained later that Oswald was still a purely routine matter in September, no more than a blip on the radar, but all the documents contradict this. It is clear that the information withheld about the connection between Oswald and Cuba had an operational meaning. Morley expressed this as follows: 'CIA agents with a "keen interest" in Oswald did not want to share what they knew [...] because they did not want to commit details of a deniable operation to the record.'[868] Oswald was clearly part of a clandestine CIA operation in connection with Cuba.

THE HSCA INVESTIGATION

In 1975, the Senate set up a subcommittee to investigate the activities of the intelligence services in more detail. This Church Commission – as usual named after its chairman – quickly came upon a significant number of literal and metaphorical skeletons in the CIA closets. It also looked into the assassination of Kennedy again, for the first time since Garrison. Church left 'his' commission, however, in order to join the fight for the nomination as the Democratic presidential candidate in 1976, a fight he lost to Jimmy Carter. Senator Schweiker inherited the chairmanship of the commission in 1975, and, as a result, became one of the best informed politicians about the strictly top-secret facts surrounding the assassination of President Kennedy. Schweiker had his personal staff put together a parallel file containing 'a fat stack of informal memos.'[869] Most of these memos concerned information that investigator Gaeton Fonzi had uncovered on behalf of the Church Commission. Unfortunately, the time, money and political will of the Church Commission were already consumed before it was able to force a breakthrough in the investigation. The HSCA, which was to pick up from where the Church Commission had left off, was only formed in 1976. The Chief Counsel of the HCSA, Richard Sprague, recruited the 33-year-old Robert R. Tanenbaum as Deputy Chief Counsel for the Kennedy investigation. Tanenbaum was an intelligent and courageous District Attorney in New York. He was only willing to come and join the HSCA if he would be allowed to apply the same bold methods he used in New York to deal with homicide cases. That was not a problem for Sprague, quite the contrary. Senator Schweiker had passed his personal Kennedy file on to Sprague, and he was therefore at the top of the list of people Tanenbaum interviewed. Schweiker gave his opinion straight away: 'The CIA was involved in the murder of the President.'[870] The 33-year-old Tanenbaum, who until then had believed the Warren gospel, did not know what he was hearing. But he got stuck into the file and came to the conclusion that they indeed had to take the CIA idea sufficiently serious. 'The more we looked into it, the most productive area of investigation was clearly the CIA – namely those operatives who had worked with the anti-Castro Cubans,' he said later in an interview.[871] He particularly wanted to challenge David Atlee Phillips, meanwhile promoted to head of covert operations for the entire western hemisphere. Phillips despised the parliamentary control over the activities of the CIA. Author David Talbot describes his attitude as follows: 'Phillips had mastered the aloof, country-club attitude of the agency's WASP-elite[872]. Like his boss, Dick Helms, he acted as if he were doing committee members a favor by granting them his time.' But Tanenbaum was well prepared, and he refused to be bullied by the arrogant chain smoker.[873] 'These guys act like they're totally above the law,' he said irritated. Phillips insisted that the tapes of the wiretapped phone calls had already been destroyed weeks before the assassination and lied about his regular meetings with Antonio Veciana. He also lied about the meeting with Oswald in Dallas in early September, which Veciana had witnessed.[874] This meeting was not insignificant, however, because Oswald emerged in Mexico three weeks later. When it came to Mexico, Phillips's memory and the bare facts blatantly opposed each other. Tanenbaum, for example, asked Phillips where the photos of the man who entered and left both the Cuban and Russian embassies in Mexico were. He replied unperturbed that they had been destroyed before November 22. When Tanenbaum confronted Phillips with the FBI report that spelled out in black and white that the FBI had seen the photographs *after* the assassination, he observed with amazement the extent to which Phillips defied parliamentary supervision: 'He read the memo. And then he just folds it up and leaves the room.'[875] Tanenbaum then tried to persuade the Commission members to use their authority, but the politicians shied away from a confrontation. Their survival instinct was better developed than that of Sprague and Tanenbaum. It was not long before the *New York Times* published a number of articles that incriminated Chief Counsel Sprague, and questioned his methods. Sprague didn't take the smear campaign very seriously initially, but an invisible hand kept sawing the legs from under his seat. The Commission's chairman, Congressman Gonzalez, soon introduced economy measures with respect to its expenses. He had the expenses of the investigators blocked, and eventually even their salaries. Gonzalez went as far as to recommend to the Attorney General to no longer forward the FBI files on the assassination to the parliamentary commission of which he himself was the Chairman. 'I am the Chairman. You are my employee. Do not forget that,' he wrote incensed to the bewildered Sprague. The moment he started to make life difficult for the CIA,[876] politicians and the media waged open warfare against Sprague. To date, Sprague is convinced that this was no coincidence. The climate deteriorated to the point that Gonzalez called his Chief Counsel a 'rattlesnake' in public. The situation became untenable, and Gonzalez dismissed Sprague on the spot. He was given just a few hours time to clear his HSCA desk. Tanenbaum preferred the honorable way out, and resigned from his job. He declared afterwards: 'I didn't want to participate in an historical fraud.'

Sprague was replaced as Chief Counsel by the low-key Professor Robert Blakey. Some of Blakey's most brilliant law students followed in his wake, and gave the investigation team new zest.[877] One of them was Danny Hardway. Arrogant as he was, Phillips failed to recognize in time that the casual Dan Hardway – with his long hair, jeans and bright red shirt – was a dangerous opponent. Hardway knew where and how Phillips had lied in his previous statements, and forced him firmly into a corner. As a fellow HSCA investigator, Gaeton Fonzi was present when Hardway informally questioned Phillips. The initially imperturbable CIA man became increasingly disheveled. According to Fonzi, he lit up a cigarette even though he already had two going[878] and, in the end, Phillips had to use all his talent as amateur actor to do the same to Hardway as he had done with Tanenbaum. He angrily got up and declaimed that he had had enough: 'I'm just sick and tired of having to live with this nonsense.'[879] Once more, he succeeded in getting away with it without further consequences. And so it came to pass that also the HSCA never found out what exactly had happened in Mexico in 1963, and what role the CIA and Phillips had played in it.

What is more, the CIA was even rewarded for all its deceit, lies and secrecy when the HSCA decided to completely exonerate the agency of any involvement: 'The committee found no evidence of any relationship between Oswald and the CIA. Moreover, the Agency's investigative efforts prior to the assassination regarding Oswald's presence in Mexico City served to confirm the absence of any relationship with him.' Although everyone was well aware that Phillips had lied and had committed perjury, the HSCA's quest for truth stopped abruptly when the Commission bumped into the closed door marked with the name 'CIA.'

OBSCURE RIDDLES

The events in Mexico are among the most obscure of all the riddles that surround the assassination of John Kennedy. The HSCA investigation was the last chance to figure out what had been going on. Chief Counsel Robert Blakey hadn't had the guts to prosecute Phillips for perjury, contempt and obstruction of justice, and even less on the grounds of conspiracy. Blakey's overriding aim was to maintain a workable relationship with the CIA, and he was convinced that he had succeeded in this. The members of his investigation team knew better. At some point, the CIA appointed George Joannides as new liaison with the aim of improving cooperation with the HSCA. Joannides was unable to locate the files on DRE anywhere in the CIA archives. He could also not ascertain who had been the CIA control officer for DRE at the time. The HSCA mandate terminated before Joannides had been able to find the answer. Thanks to investigation journalist Jefferson Morley of the *Washington Post*, we now know that this CIA control agent for DRE was George Joannides himself. To appoint this man as a liaison to help the parliamentary commissioners was in itself pure insolence by the CIA. Joannides had previously been employed at the Psychological Warfare department of the CIA station in Miami. He had, incidentally, also worked closely together with Phillips. It only dawned on Professor Blakey[880] that the HSCA had been deceived when Morley[881] disclosed the bare facts about Joannides to him.

Fighting a conflict with fake mustaches, microphones and men in raincoats seems a very humane form of warfare at first glance. But a secret organization that considers itself above the law is toxic to democracy. It puts the society it is supposed to protect at great risk. This is what President Truman, the founder of the CIA, warned about in the *Washington Post* of December 22, 1963. He said this exactly one month after the assassination of President Kennedy, to ensure that it would be clear to everyone what he was alluding to: 'For some time I have been disturbed by the way CIA has been diverted from its original assignment. It has become an operational and at times a policy-making arm of the Government. This has led to trouble and may have compounded our difficulties in several explosive areas. I never had any thought that when I set up the CIA that it would be injected into peacetime cloak and dagger operations. [...] There is something about the way the CIA has been functioning that is casting a shadow over our historic position and I feel that we need to correct it.'[882] Truman touched upon the core of the problem that surfaces everywhere in the Kennedy case. The CIA arrogantly believed that it could impose its own political choice on an elected president. The agency used deceit, lies and deception in the exercise of its covert operation. Mostly, these operations fell within its official mission. But the organization also used the same methods to run its own agenda in the sidelines. The agency knew that it could do this with impunity, and was convinced that nobody would ever be able to figure out what it was really doing.

In the normal world, we try to understand events logically. According to Descartes, this is only possible if there is no malevolent god who is keen on playing tricks on people and keeping them ignorant. Cartesian thinking also forms the essential basis of our legal system. In the Kennedy case, however, our logical deduction gets stuck all the time. The CIA created an environment that responded to Descartes's worst nightmare, a world in which an evil genius played tricks on the others. It created and destroyed evidence at will, pushed false witnesses forward and intimidated solid ones. In such circumstances, an inquiry no longer leads to the real perpetrator, the absence of evidence is no longer an indication of innocence, and a reply to a question, even under oath, becomes worthless.

It's clear that a crime cannot be solved in such a context, nor can the truth be uncovered. But, excluding all other possible perpetrators, the methods used in the Kennedy case are typical of the CIA. The next question, of course, is why was it so important for the CIA that no one would ever uncover the truth about the Kennedy assassination?

Chapter 16 – The Odio incident

On October 2,[883] Oswald took the #332 bus from Mexico to Dallas. After Silvia Duran, he would also meet Silvia Odio in this week. It is even possible that he met her before Silvia Duran, because it's not sure if the incident with Odio took place just before or after Oswald's trip to Mexico. I am largely using the account of Gaeton Fonzi here, because he met all those involved. He has thoroughly analyzed the incident for years, and will always remain the best source for this aspect of the case.

Silvia Odio was the pretty daughter of a very rich Cuban, Amador Odio. Before the Cuban revolution broke out, her father was the owner of one of the largest transport companies. *Time Magazine* described him as the 'transport tycoon of Latin America.'[884] But he was also an idealist, and initially supported the rebels. However, when he found that Castro had betrayed the revolution by becoming a communist, he became a fervent opponent of the new regime. Castro put Amador Odio and his wife behind bars for eight years. Silvia was then 24. She had studied law for a while, but she was now married and had four children. After the arrest of her parents, her husband left his family in the lurch. Amador Odio's children fled to the United States. Silvia had a hard time as a single mother without money and sometimes fainted due to stress. She sought help from a psychiatrist. She was also active to some extent in the anti-Castro movement. She supported the *Junta Revolutionara* (JURE), a group that was founded by Manolo Ray, an old friend of her father. When she found work she was able to look for a larger house. She would move in early October. Her 17-year-old sister Annie moved in with her temporarily to look after the children while Silvia prepared the move.

On September 24 or 25 – or on October 3 – three men called on her in the evening, and she had a brief conversation with them. The men, two of whom were darker types – one Cuban, while the other looked more Mexican – and one white man, seemed very tired and were unshaven, as if they had had a long journey behind them. The Cuban introduced himself with his 'war name,' Leopoldo. The Mexican man was probably called Angel, but Silvia was not quite sure about this anymore in hindsight. The American was introduced as Leon Oswald. Leopoldo did the talking, and claimed that their unexpected visit was about fundraising for JURE. He had to provide a well-written

English letter that they could then send to local businessmen, asking them for financial support for the organization. Although the men seemed to know some details about her father that only his confidants could be aware of,[885] Silvia was very suspicious, and promised nothing. About twenty minutes later, the men left in a red car. Annie also saw the men and heard the conversation.

The following day, or at the most two days later, Leopoldo called Silvia to inform her that the *gringo* was a former Marine, a marksman and was a little *loco*. Leon had apparently even told him that Cubans had no guts, because they should have assassinated Kennedy after the Bay of Pigs incident. According to Leopoldo, you could expect anything of Leon, and he was capable of anything.[886]

On November 22, just like half the world population, Silvia heard with bewilderment that the president had been assassinated. She immediately recalled the strange visitors and the phone call, and remembered Leopoldo's story about the gringo and his willingness to shoot Kennedy. This caused Silvia to have an anxiety attack; she lost consciousness and was hospitalized. Annie was not with Silvia when she heard about the assassination of the president. She saw a photo of Oswald on the television, and was convinced that she knew the man. She had met him sometime somewhere, but couldn't remember where. When Annie heard that Silvia was in the hospital, she rushed over. Silvia was crying hysterically. Annie told her that, from somewhere, she recognized the guy who the TV said had killed the president. Silvia asked her whether she remembered the three men who had come to her house. Annie then also realized that the American in the group was Oswald.

A STRAW

There is little doubt that the Odio sisters were telling the truth. They gave their statements separately, and these were consistent. Silvia had already written to her father about the incident with the three men before Kennedy's assassination. She had also talked about it with the psychiatrist, Dr. Einspruch. The sisters were also not looking for media attention, on the contrary. In the hospital room, they even agreed that they would not mention a word about the strange visit in September. But their sister Sarita also knew about the incident, and she told Lucille Connell, a friend of the family. Connell happened to know an FBI agent, and the next thing that happened was an FBI agent appearing at Silvia's door. But, according to the instructions, any clues that pointed towards a conspiracy were not to be thoroughly investigated. After the first statements by the sisters on December 12, 1963, there was silence regarding the investigation of the incident.

When the Warren Commission was finalizing its report, they realized that there was an unacceptable gap in the case. Chief Counselor J. Lee Rankin urged Hoover to investigate the Odio case further to see whether the incident could be refuted or confirmed. The Commission assumed that it would be yet another fabricated story. After November 22, dozens of people claimed to have seen Oswald in places or at times where he could never have been. Due to the concurrence with Oswald's trip to Mexico, the incident with Silvia Odio also seemed to be one of these claims. But the story of Silvia and Annie turned out to be much more reliable than the Commission had assumed. There was no refutation, and a confirmation was undesirable. If the story of the sisters was true, then Oswald had two accomplices, at least one of whom was aware of his assassination plan. This presented the Commission with a major problem. In a memo, Commissioner Liebeler described the dilemma as follows: 'There are problems. Odio may well be right. The Commission will look bad if it turns out that she is. There is no need to look foolish by grasping at straws to avoid admitting that there is a problem.' Actually, the Commission should only have been interested in the truth and shouldn't have referred to a possible confirmation of Oswald's visit to the sisters as a 'problem,' but Liebeler at least gave them the right advice: it was better to acknowledge that there was a problem than to ignore the issue. The Commission itself still opted for the straw. It found a maverick, one Loran Eugene Hall, who was willing to declare that he was the American visitor and that two friends, Lawrence Howard and William J. Seymour, had accompanied him that day. The fact that Hall was a member of the *International Anti-Communist Brigade*, an anti-Castro organization that was notorious for spreading false information, created no problem for the Commission. It could now conclude that Lee Harvey Oswald 'was not at Mrs. Odio's apartment in September of 1963.'[887] But, like a sand castle, Hall's story quickly fell apart: his two friends did not at all resemble the men who had met the Odio sisters, and the men also denied that they were in Dallas then. Hall soon admitted that he had fabricated the whole story, and he later even denied that he had ever made the statement. In the HSCA report, his story is reduced to a 'certified fabrication.'[888] The HSCA also asked Hall about his relationship with the CIA. He replied evasively: 'I had probably been as closely affiliated with them without being affiliated to them as you could possibly be...'[889] The HSCA also found that the FBI actually knew that the story was not true at the time they presented it to the Warren Commission.[890] As Liebeler had feared, the reputation of the Warren Commission took a firm dent. But Liebeler's own reputation also took a hit.

A QUICK CURTSY TO HONESTY

When Gaeton Fonzi again tracked down Silvia and Annie Odio for the Church Commission, the two women were living a normal, peaceful life. They had never been in the spotlight, had turned down every interview – even if they were offered a lot of money for it – and had not cashed-in on their role in history by publishing a book. Silvia did not know what to tell Fonzi, because it had become clear to her in the meantime that no one wanted to hear the truth and she refused to say anything other than what she had already stated. After fifteen years, she was still severely disillusioned with the government. The most shocking for her was her encounter with Liebeler, who had begun the hearing by saying how lucky he was that he could question the most beautiful witness. He afterwards invited her to a restaurant under the guise of having a number of additional questions. After the meal, he had bluntly asked her to accompany him to his hotel room. The young woman was deeply shocked. When the Warren Report later also branded her a liar, her confidence in the government disappeared completely. She was therefore very reticent with regard to Fonzi. 'Why are they bringing it all up again?' she asked defensively. But when she felt that Fonzi was of a different caliber than Liebeler, she promised her cooperation in his research.

After his deployment for the Church Commission, Fonzi also became an investigator for the HSCA. He afterwards felt personally responsible for the undeniable fact that the HSCA had also used Silvia Odio 'just as the Warren Commission did, "handling" her testimony, much more subtly but just as deceptively, making certain that her story was not prominently presented to the American people.'[891] When Fonzi told Silvia that the HSCA would not hear her, she was very angry: 'Now I really know that they don't want to know. They don't really want to know because they don't have any answers for the American public. They should never have started this charade in the first place.'[892]

Yet it was not quite all for nothing, because the parliamentary committee at least believed Odio and her sister. But the HSCA only dared to communicate even that reluctantly: 'The Commission was *inclined* to believe Silvia Odio.'

But what was Oswald doing there, and who were the men who accompanied him? According to the Commission, it was possible that he was associating with anti-Castro activists for some other reason unrelated to the assassination of the president. This sounds unconvincing. Fonzi came to the final conclusion: 'The Committee did not speculate on that "other unrelated reason." That door was marked "CIA," and it had already concluded that the Agency had nothing to do with Oswald." The HSCA therefore firmly kept the lid on this.

Although the purpose of the visit, the identity of the men and the exact timing of the visit remained unsolved mysteries, there can be no doubt about the importance of the incident. The incident with the Odio sisters was decisive for Fonzi in his analysis of the assassination case. He wrote: 'I have no hesitation in declaring the Kennedy assassination a conspiracy based strictly on Silvia Odio's consistently credible testimony and, more important, the fact that our investigation proved it true.'[893]

I can fully support that view. There are, in fact, only two possibilities:

— Oswald did not visit Silvia Odio himself. Someone strongly resembling him masqueraded as him two months before the attack. Another conspirator phoned Silvia shortly afterwards in order to already explicitly link the unsuspecting 'Leon' to the future attack.
— Oswald himself visited Silvia. He then offered his help to this woman who was unknown to him for a cause that he was completely opposed to, and which did not concern him at all. To do this, he made a detour of hundreds of kilometers to Dallas on his transit from New Orleans to Mexico, or, it was his very first concern on his return from a two-day bus trip. Furthermore, he was with two accomplices, at least one of whom was aware of his plan to murder the president.

In both versions, someone had already linked Oswald to the Kennedy assassination in early September. That is incompatible with the official assumption that Oswald was an opportunity killer who only realized just before November 22 that Kennedy would drive past, and with the assumption that he thereby acted alone.

Depending on whether we believe version one or two, there were three or two people who later went up in smoke. Just at the moment that the story was threatening to fall apart, the false witness Loran Hall appeared to rock the Commission back to sleep. The man later turned out to have links with the Mafia,[894] anti-Castro fanatics and the CIA.

The aim of the Odio incident was apparently to lay false and confusing clues which, after the attack on Kennedy, could become more significant or could be denied, whichever was better. This is a recurring pattern. Oswald introduced himself to Silvia Duran as a supporter of Castro, and to Silvia Odio as an opponent. Oswald supposedly shot at the conservative Walker and the progressive Kennedy because of the same political motives. Oswald set up the branch office of the pro-Castro organization FPCC in a building that was as good as the headquarters of the anti-Castro activity in New Orleans.

Oswald took a test drive at a car dealership, but didn't have a driver's license. Everything indicates that he shot at Walker, but there are as many witness statements that rule him out as the perpetrator. Within a period of 24 hours from 11 a.m. on September 25, Oswald, who could only move about with slow public transport, appeared in New Orleans, where he cashed a check, in Austin, where he complained very prominently about his dishonorable discharge from the army, in Dallas at Silvia Odio's house, and, finally, in Houston, where he got on the bus to Mexico. Oswald went to a shooting range to prepare himself for a murder, but there he mainly made efforts to be noticed and to have his weapon seen by as many witnesses as possible. Oswald appeared at the Red Bird Airfield in the company of a man and a woman on November 20. The man and the woman tried to persuade Wayne January, the owner of the American Aviation Company, to rent them a plane for the afternoon of November 22. Afterwards, the accomplices no longer fit into the final story, and the whole incident disappeared from the records. After the assassination of JFK, CIA-friendly channels drove the press pack firmly in the direction of Cuba's involvement in the assassination. These accusations disappeared as soon as the chance of an invasion of Cuba was definitively lost. All these conflicting clues can only have served one purpose: to create an inextricable tangle, a tangle that allowed the truth to be labeled as nonsense, and to sell deception as truth.

There is only one logical explanation for the endless series of contradictory findings. Oswald apparently joined the 'hell's kitchen' of the CIA in 1963. Under the delusion that he had succeeded in becoming a CIA spy, he did what he was told to do: he set up an FPCC branch, had a fight with Bringuier so that he would be arrested, went to Dallas to meet 'Bishop', traveled back and forth to Mexico, applied for an adjustment of his dishonorable discharge in Houston, visited Silvia Odio in Dallas as a JURE sympathizer in the company of two strangers, and, finally, was present in the School Book Depository when Kennedy drove by there. The scenario of leading three lives was just child's play compared to this. According to the rules of the CIA, he received only the minimum necessary information about the overall picture of the actions in which he participated. He therefore did not know that he had ended up in a select group of potential scapegoats for the assassination of Kennedy.

Chapter 17 – Hurt

The last file on Oswald deals with an event that took place twelve hours before his death. It seems like a detail, but is an intriguing piece of the big puzzle. The story again displays all the typical characteristics of the Kennedy case. From jail, Oswald allegedly tried to call a certain John Hurt on Saturday evening. If this is true, it has significant consequences for the entire file. We mainly have to thank historian Grover Proctor for the deciphering of this Rosetta stone, particularly through his essay *The Raleigh Call and the Fingerprints of Intelligence.*

On Saturday, November 23, at around 10.30 p.m., Oswald was permitted to contact the outside world by phone. He had previously been trying in vain to reach lawyer Abt through Ruth Paine. He was allowed to make a second attempt more than thirty hours after his arrest. By chance, two ladies were operating the switchboard at the police office at that time. Alveeta Treon was scheduled for the night shift, and she had arrived a little early to take over from her colleague, Louise Swinney. Louise had big news: Lee Harvey Oswald, now famous all over the world, would be requesting a phone connection in a few moments. Two men in suits were to tap into this conversation, but Louise was not sure whether they were from the Secret Service, the homicide squad or some other body. While awaiting Oswald's call, Alveeta briefly contacted her daughter, who suggested that she should make sure to keep a souvenir of the memorable event. The two men, who were never identified later, set themselves up in an adjacent room to tap into the calls. Then Oswald's request came through. He again wanted to call the famous left-wing lawyer John Abt in New York, and, once more, this was unsuccessful. This is where the official story ends.

The fact that listening into Oswald's phone conversations is a blatant violation of the rights of the accused is the least of the problems here. Twelve hours later, Oswald was dead, and, from then onwards, only the historical truth is important. Whether or not Oswald was in touch with anyone the night before should certainly be considered to be an essential element in the case. The Warren Commission was not interested in this, however, probably because it did not want to run the risk of discovering that Oswald had perhaps sought to contact an accomplice the night before he died. As the men who had listened into the calls on behalf of an official body remained anonymous, and the switchboard operators of the Dallas Police were never questioned, the Commission could truthfully argue that the file only contained proof of Oswald's futile attempt to reach New York lawyer John Abt.

But, in reality, Oswald did try to also reach a certain John Hurt in Raleigh, North Carolina, that night. The proof of this is a slip of paper in the possession of switchboard operator Alveeta Treon. It was an LD *slip*, a piece of paper that switchboard operators used for logging long distance calls. It enabled the police to justify the cost of the calls afterwards, and to possibly recover them from the caller. According to the strip of paper in the possession of Alveeta Treon, Oswald had given two phone numbers for contacting Hurt. The abbreviations *da* and *ca* on the document stand for *did not answer* and *canceled* respectively. The name at the bottom of the strip is Louise Swinney.

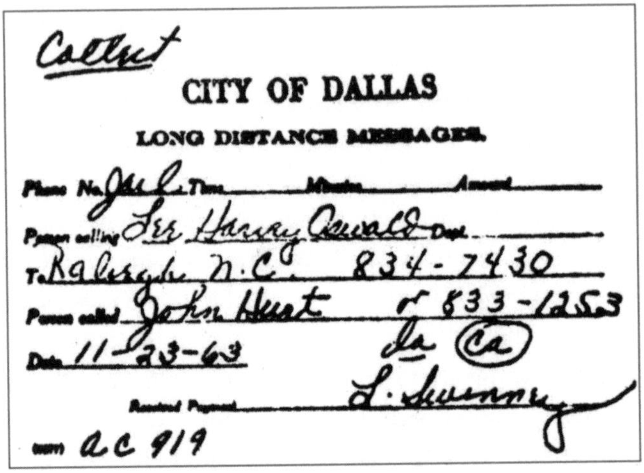

Collect
CITY OF DALLAS
LONG DISTANCE MESSAGES
Phone No. Jail Time Minutes Amount
Person calling Lee Harvey Oswald
To Raleigh N.C. 834-7430
Person called John Hurt or 833-1253
Date 11-23-63 da ca
Received Payment L. Swinney
ac 919

Figure 65. The long distance call slip.

Alveeta Treon did not seek any publicity and simply kept the slip of paper as a souvenir in a drawer. In 1965 she moved to Missouri. Three years later, while chatting to an acquaintance, a Mr. Smith, she briefly mentioned the small role she had played in the drama of November 22, 1963. He related the story to the local sheriff Mickey Owen. The sheriff considered it interesting enough for further investigation, and informed the FBI. This is how Alveeta Treon suddenly received a visit from the FBI in 1968. She informed them that Oswald had tried to call a certain John Hurt while in jail. The FBI agents assumed that this was just another wild story for which there was no evidence. But Alveeta Treon countered this and produced the slip of paper. The agents took it along for further investigation. The FBI was not really worried, and Alveeta even got her keepsake back after a while. The agents had their own idea about what must have happened: Oswald had only asked to make a call to lawyer Abt. Louise had noted this number down, and had thrown it into the wastepaper basket later. When hunting for a souvenir, Alveeta retrieved a scrap of paper from the trash, but not the one with Abt's number on it. As a result, she supposed that Oswald had tried to call someone called John Hurt, a man who had nothing whatsoever to do with the Kennedy case. Then, still working on the same assumption, she had prepared a fake slip and signed it with the name of her colleague to make it all look real. The agents drafted a statement along these lines, and distributed this within the FBI, but never submitted the document to Alveeta for her signature.

But who was this John Hurt, and how had his telephone number ended up in Louise's wastepaper basket? In 1970, this question led investigator Paul Hoch to add another hypothesis for the scenario. Furious about the assassination of Kennedy, and in a state of drunkenness, John Hurt had phoned the police in Dallas and demanded to speak to Oswald on the phone. He was obviously not put through, but he left a number where Oswald could reach him. The scrap of paper in the bin was therefore an incoming call from some drunk guy, not an outgoing call from the prisoner. Sounds all very logical, right?

Another eight years later, the HSCA investigation looked into this strange issue once more. For the first time, Alveeta Treon was now confronted with the statement she was supposed to have given the FBI ten years earlier. She immediately pointed out that she had never seen that statement, and that she had certainly not made it. The fact that her signature is missing from the document is a strong indication that she was right. The story she told the HSCA was quite different from the version the FBI had invented on her behalf. Yes, she had been at the switchboard with Louise Swinney when Oswald had asked to make a call. Both ladies had picked up the call at the same time, but Louise had spoken first and had asked which number Oswald wanted to contact. Alveeta let her colleague handle the call and, as her line was open too, she heard everything that was said. She noted down the name and the numbers of the other call Oswald wanted to make. This request was indeed for a John Hurt, and Oswald even gave her two phone numbers. The preparation of the slip for the call was a simple bookkeeping routine. But as no connection had been established, there were no costs, and the slip was no longer necessary. Alveeta decided to keep it as a souvenir. As it had been Louise who had tried to make the call, Alveeta had rightly written the name Swinney underneath. It all came down to working together: Louise spoke with Oswald and tried to make the connection to the numbers he had given, and Alveeta wrote down the administrative details for her colleague.

HSCA investigator Harold Rose decided to seek out Louise Swinney in order to hear her version of the story. When he informed her of the reason for his visit, the woman became very nervous and suspicious. In the first interview, she admitted that Oswald had tried to make two calls that evening, 'one to Lawyer Apt (*sic*) in New York and she doesn't remember where the other call was to.' She could not put either call through for Oswald. Her implicit message seemed to be that the men in suits had knowingly interrupted the call. In a second interview, Louise made drastic changes to her version of the facts: she denied that Oswald had tried to make a second call, and said she had never heard the name John Hurt.

In order to find out what we can believe of all this, we should answer three questions:

1. Who was John Hurt?
2. Was it an incoming or an outgoing call?
3. Did Oswald try to contact Hurt?

WHO WAS JOHN HURT?

The two phone numbers on the slip of paper belonged to two different individuals called John Hurt, who both lived in Raleigh, North Carolina. One of the Johns was living on New Bern Avenue, the other one on Old Wake Forest Road. The man from New Bern Avenue was apparently the person Oswald was trying to get hold of. John David Hurt was a former US Army Counterintelligence agent. In the fifties, Hurt had worked from a military base in Japan. The state where he lived was also the state where the training camp for potential defectors to the Soviet Union was based. All in all, Hurt was just a paper pusher who classified the files – and this only until 1955 – and was certainly not a master spy. In 1963, he was unemployed, disabled, and struggling with a serious alcohol problem. He was in bad shape: his advanced arthritis had caused so much pain and discomfort in his hands that all his fingers had had to be amputated. That didn't stop him from smoking and drinking excessively. He also suffered from an unpleasant skin disorder, psoriasis, and had serious psychological problems. According to his first statement, he had not phoned Oswald on November 23, and had also not received a call from him. He only knew Oswald from the TV, and had no idea why the man who was suspected of assassinating the president had wanted to contact him a day later. The HSCA could also not think of any reason why Oswald would use his last chance to make a phone call to try to call an unstable and disabled former administrative member of the military counterintelligence. The issue therefore ended up on the stack of unsolved riddles.

In 1980, Anthony Summers's book *Conspiracy* was published, and historian Doctor Proctor was commissioned by a newspaper to write a review on it. Summers's book included the story about the phone call to Hurt. Proctor became intrigued, as he himself came from Raleigh, and started his own investigation. He first contacted the author, Summers, who told him that he was actually sorry that he had not deleted this particular section because there was insufficient evidence that something had been going on, and because the story contained too many inconsistencies. But Summers called Dr. Proctor again a week later. By chance, Summers had, a few days before, spoken with Robert Blakey, the former Chief Counsel of the HSCA. He had repeated his concern that he should have probably left the entire section about the call to Hurt out of the book, because it was presumably not true anyway. Much to his surprise, Blakey didn't agree with him at all. He assured him that the story about the phone call to Hurt was 'real,' 'substantiated,' 'very troublesome' and 'deeply disturbing.'

An internal HSCA report on the matter consisted of 28 pages, and concluded that the information 'provided by Mrs. Treon, her daughter, and Louise Swinney all indicate that Oswald did in fact attempt to place a call from the Dallas City Hall Jail on the night of November 23, 1963.'

John Hurt passed away in 1981. His widow told author Henry Hurt – not a relative – that her husband had admitted the truth before he died: 'Terribly upset on the day of the assassination, he got extremely drunk – a habitual problem with him – and telephoned the Dallas jail and asked to speak to Oswald. When this was refused, he left his name and number.' This story is suspiciously reminiscent of the hypothesis that Paul Hoch had forwarded as a possible explanation in 1970. Bugliosi copied it indiscriminately, and referred to 'a slip of paper [that] for several years stirred the hearts of conspiracy theorists everywhere.'

With this sketchy information on John Hurt, we'll move on to the second question.

WAS IT AN INCOMING OR AN OUTGOING CALL?

John Hurt did not call the Dallas jail in a drunken stupor. Hoch had guessed wrong, and the widow had lied. This can be easily proven: where did the second number come from? Had Hurt in his delirium also passed on the phone number of a namesake in Raleigh? The simple fact that there were two numbers of two men who were both called John Hurt on the slip of paper demonstrates that someone wanted to call Hurt, and had found two of them in the Raleigh phone directory. The caller gave the switchboard the two numbers because he didn't know which of them was the right person. This means that an attempt was made from the jail to reach a certain John Hurt in Raleigh, and not the other way around. Former Chief Counsel Blakey also came to the same conclusion. In an interview with Proctor, he clearly said: 'The call apparently is real and it goes out. It does not come in. That's the sum and substance of it. It was an outgoing call, and therefore I consider it very troublesome material. The direction in which it went was deeply disturbing.'

DID OSWALD TRY TO CONTACT HURT?

Did the outgoing call come from Oswald, and not from someone else inside the building? A link to the story of the canceled attack in Chicago could help us further here. We recall that Agent Martineau of the Secret Service in Chicago did all he could to erase all traces of what had happened there before Kennedy was to visit the city – a visit that was canceled at the very last minute. This was not to the liking of Sherman Skolnick, an alert citizen who was confined to his wheelchair. He loudly denounced all the irregularities he believed were going on in Chicago. The rumors about a planned attempt on Kennedy's life had also not escaped him. In 1970, he started a FOIA procedure for the disclosure of the documents related to those events. But, in 1970, Skolnick obviously knew nothing about the mysterious phone call Oswald had tried to make. In his FOIA procedure, however, he casually mentioned that Agent Martineau had inquired about a certain John Heard after the assassination of Kennedy. In addition, the unfortunate colored Secret Service Agent Bolden – the man who ended up in jail and in psychiatric care after his attempt to inform the Warren Commission about the assassination attempt in Chicago – had also stated before the HSCA, on January 19, 1978, that Agent Kelly of the Secret Service had mentioned the name John Heard or Hurt in Chicago around November 26. At that moment, the Secret Service was not yet aware of the call slip that Alveeta Treon had kept, because that slip of paper would only emerge ten years later. The uncertainty about the spelling of the name also implies that the information was auditory. The Secret Service therefore had *heard* the name John Hurt. The fact that the agents linked this information to Oswald can only mean that they had heard the name when they were tapping into Oswald's telephone conversations in jail.

There is a second element that demonstrates that it was Oswald who tried to get hold of Hurt. The lie once again points towards the truth. The official story acknowledged the version with the drunken Hurt, provided by his widow. This implicitly confirms that Hurt is the man we are looking for. Hurt's widow turned the direction of the call around, but, in this way, she confirms that there was an attempted contact between her deceased husband and Oswald.

WHY DID OSWALD TRY TO CONTACT JOHN HURT?

His search for the reason why Oswald had wanted to contact the former staff member of the military intelligence department eventually led Dr. Proctor to Victor Marchetti, a former Executive Assistant of the CIA, who had turned his back on the agency. Marchetti wrote the book *The CIA and the Cult of Intelligence*, which caused a stir because of the drastic censorship the CIA applied to it. Marchetti was one of the few who broke the wall of silence surrounding the clandestine CIA operations. He knew the CIA from the inside, and only had one explanation for the story relating to the call to Hurt: Oswald tried to contact Hurt as a *cutout*. In its urge for compartmentalization, the CIA avoided direct contacts between the various parts of its operations as much as possible. The *case officer*, the agent who coordinated the case, could contact the agent who carried out a mission, but the contact in the opposite direction always took place through an unknown third party. David Atlee Phillips could, so to speak, contact Oswald directly, but Oswald could only get in touch with Phillips via a cutout, a kind of middleman. He thereby didn't mention his identity, nor the reason why he wanted the contact. The cutout didn't need to know anything about the whole business; he only had to report to the case agent that his agent was asking him to urgently get in touch with him. In an interview with Proctor, Marchetti explained the situation in which Oswald presumably found himself as follows:

> Proctor: I would contact you by telephone, right?
>
> Marchetti: Yes. But [...] I contact you, you don't contact me. But I give you a [unintelligible] number. So you call him.
>
> [...]
>
> Proctor: But you would use, for that middle man, people who were not necessarily active agents or agency people, right?
>
> Marchetti: That's right. Most likely they would be cut-outs. You would have to call indirectly.
>
> Proctor: Could Oswald have had a name ...
>
> Marchetti: He was probably calling his cut-out. He was calling somebody who could put him in touch with his case officer. He couldn't go beyond that person. There's no way he could. He just had to depend on this person to say: 'Okay, I'll deliver the message.'

John Hurt may have been a wreck in 1978, but that doesn't mean he could not have acted as a cutout in 1963. The CIA often used lack of credibility as a cover. Because of his condition, it seems at first sight highly unlikely that the CIA would use someone like John Hurt, but precisely this situation provided the CIA with the necessary 'deniability'. A second indication that he was probably Oswald's cutout is the fact that the two men in suits cut off the call to Hurt. A third element is Veciana's credible testimony about a meeting between Phillips and Oswald. If Phillips was Oswald's case officer, it makes sense that there was also a cutout to enable Oswald to contact Phillips in an emergency.

In any case, Oswald tried to reach John Hurt from jail, and there is no innocent explanation for this. Oswald didn't know Hurt, and he had no reason whatsoever to make his very last phone call to him. By itself, the story is by no means decisive, but it is completely in line with all the other findings, namely the indications that, on November 23, Oswald believed himself to be part of a CIA operation that had gotten out of hand, and he was still hoping against hope that the agency would rush to his aid in Dallas.

Chapter 18 – A wilderness of mirrors

Our starting point was as follows: Oswald was not the sniper, but he was certainly involved in Kennedy's assassination. In the run-up to November 22, he and the conspirators must have been in touch with each other. We assumed that an investigation of Oswald's surroundings could possibly put us on the trail of the perpetrators. While following Oswald's footsteps, we repeatedly come across the CIA. Without trying to be exhaustive, we can enumerate the following list of the links between Oswald and the CIA:

1. Both George de Mohrenschildt and the Paine couple had connections with the CIA. It would at least appear that they acted as Oswald's watchdogs.
2. Under the supervision of Phillips, the CIA had already urged a student, Court Wood, to establish a branch of the Fair Play For Cuba Committee. The CIA had always wanted to infiltrate and discredit the FPCC. Upon his arrival in New Orleans, Oswald had also suddenly established a local FPCC branch, which had its office in the building where Guy Banister was in charge of the covert CIA operations against Castro.
3. Oswald described his clash with Carlos Bringuier in a letter, before it actually took place. Bringuier was a member of the DRE, an organization that was closely related to, and funded, by the CIA. Following the fight with Bringuier, Oswald's communist sympathies became conspicuous and publicly known.
4. In the aftermath of the skirmish with Bringuier, Oswald was given notable media attention, particularly thanks to CIA cronies William Stuckey and Edward Butler.
5. Antonio Veciana had no reason to lie when he stated that he was absolutely sure that he had witnessed a meeting between CIA agent Phillips and Oswald in Dallas.
6. Oswald succeeded in paying off his debts in a relatively short time, although he actually didn't have the means to do so. CIA accountant James B. Wilcott distributed the funds for the agents in Japan. Payments took place on the basis of a code name. When asked by the

HSCA whether such a code name existed for Oswald, Wilcott replied that he thought so.[895]

7. When Oswald applied for a visa for Mexico, the man in front of him in the queue was CIA agent William Gaudet.
8. The strangest things happened during Oswald's stay in Mexico City. Someone apparently passed himself off as Oswald, and, despite the heavy CIA surveillance of the Russian and Cuban embassies, Oswald could not be seen in any of the photographs, even though he entered and left several times. The evidence of what really happened disappeared. The only trail the CIA left was a fake trail leading to a false witness, who claimed he saw Oswald receive money in the Russian embassy as an advance on a contract killing.
9. Immediately before or immediately after his trip to Mexico, Oswald and two men visited Silvia Odio. In this way, he created a trail that was diametrically opposed to the trail he had left behind in Mexico. The Odio operation therefore served as a mirror, an anti-story to create confusion, which was typical of the methods of the CIA.
10. Shortly before the assassination, several people passed themselves off as Oswald. These people always left traces which, where necessary, could either be used or denied. This, again, reflects the modus operandi and the logistic power of the CIA.
11. We have already demonstrated that Oswald could not possibly have been the gunman in Dealey Plaza. The evidence, however, all pointed towards him. Only the CIA can come into consideration for staging something as complex as this.
12. Oswald tried to call John Hurt, who was unknown to him, from jail. The only logical explanation for this is that Hurt was his cutout, and that Oswald tried to give a prearranged sign to his CIA contact through a middleman.
13. When Oswald was arrested, the fifth column sprang into action. Sources in favor of the CIA buzzed with information about Oswald's links to Russia and Cuba. Publicist Clare Booth Luce, wife of the owner of the *Time*, *Life* and *Fortune* magazines, kept her typewriter at the ready. George Bush Senior, Frank Sturgis, John Martino, Hal Hendrix and many others were the 'powerbrokers' on duty. CIA moles unobtrusively leaked to the press the well-prepared information about Oswald

that they wanted to publicize. Any traces of this disinformation were subsequently thoroughly erased.[896]

14. Shortly after the assassination of the president, six letters sent from Havana were intercepted that all attempted to indicate Cuba's involvement in the assassination.[897] The letters seemed to originate from different authors, but were all written on the same typewriter. They were addressed to the *Voice of America* radio station, the *Daily of New York* newspaper, Robert Kennedy, the leader of the *Sentinels of Liberty* organization and two of them to Oswald. The combination of the dates, i.e. the dates of their posting, stamping in the post office and arrival is impossible.[898] According to Fabian Escalante, the former head of the Cuban Counterintelligence, there were clear indications that the original language of the texts was not Spanish. According to Cuban intelligence, the text had been translated from English into Spanish. The six letters had been sent from Havana, or had been secretly added to the Cuban mail in Mexico City, where the Cuban airmail made a stopover. According to Hoover, the letters were not important,[899] but Escalante came to a different conclusion: 'This clearly shows that the letters were fabricated before the assassination occurred and by somebody who was aware of the development of the plot, who could ensure that they arrived at the opportune moment and who had a clandestine base in Cuba from which to undertake action. Considering the history of the last 40 years, we suppose only the CIA had such capabilities in Cuba.'[900]
15. When the Warren Commission started to believe the Odio tale, Loran Hall emerged from nowhere as a witness to debunk the story again. He later admitted that his statement had been fabricated, and, before the HSCA, described his relationship to the CIA as 'as closely affiliated with them without being affiliated with them.'
16. The CIA lied and withheld information from the Warren Commission. The agency infiltrated, bugged and sabotaged Jim Garrison's investigation. David Atlee Phillips arrogantly lied in his statements to the HSCA. The agency constantly deceived HSCA investigators such as Gaeton Fonzi.
17. During the Watergate scandal, President Richard Nixon ordered his Chief of Staff Bob Haldeman to put heavy pressure on the unhelpful

CIA Director Richard Helms: 'The President asked me to tell you this entire [Watergate] affair may be connected to the Bay of Pigs, and if it opens up, the Bay of Pigs may be blown.' *Bay of Pigs* was code language for the Kennedy assassination. CIA Director Helms, panic-stricken, responded to the message: 'The Bay of Pigs had nothing to do with this. I have no concern about the Bay of Pigs!' But, on second thought, he wisely decided to help Nixon.[901] Nixon and Helms apparently both knew how damaging a revelation about 'the whole Bay of Pigs' could be for the CIA.

18. Several CIA agents have confirmed the involvement of the Agency in the assassination of Kennedy.[902] David Sanchez Morales is just one typical example. Morales was part of the CIA *Black Operations department*. Among other operations, he was closely involved in the coup against Jacobo Arbenz in Guatemala in 1954, after Arbenz had had the audacity to nationalize the United Fruit Company. Morales later became known as the 'CIA's top assassin in Latin America,'[903] and was under Phillips' supervision. Fonzi called Morales 'the kind of action-oriented guy Phillips needed.'[904] Morales was an extreme patriot for whom Kennedy was a despicable coward. In 1973, Morales's hatred still hadn't cooled off. In the presence of three witnesses (his friend Ruben Carbajal, his lawyer Robert Walton and the latter's wife), while blind drunk, he cursed Kennedy in the most extreme terms for several minutes. He ended his furious diatribe with: 'Well, we took care of that son of a bitch, didn't we?'[905]
19. David Phillips's brother Jim did not speak another word with him from the moment he suspected that David was involved in the assassination of Kennedy. After six years of silence, David, terminally ill at the time, decided to phone his brother. Jim asked him: 'Were you in Dallas on that day?' When David confirmed this, Jim put the phone down.[906]
20. Even now, the CIA is doing everything to withhold as many documents related to the assassination of President Kennedy as possible, because they present a danger to the state. Why is the CIA so afraid of an investigation into the truth?

Regardless of whether one believes each of the above-mentioned items one hundred percent, we can conclude, based on all our findings, that certain elements within the CIA manipulated Lee Harvey Oswald intensively in the period that preceded the assassination of JFK. The attempts to assassinate Castro had united the Cuba department of the CIA, the Mafia and the most aggressive Cuban exiles in a diabolical plot. All the conspirators hated Kennedy, and knew that if they could point the finger at the right scapegoat, this would create the best chance for an American invasion of the island. The CIA was therefore not on its own, but the role they played was decisive. Corrupt elements within the Dallas police force, the Mafia and the militant anti-Castro movement each carried out their part of the mission. Perhaps they even provided the sniper(s). But they did not manipulate Oswald. The Soviet Union and Castro never even came close to Oswald. All the clues that pointed towards the USSR and Cuba were demonstrably false, and were laid by the CIA. Johnson and Hoover were certainly complicit in the cover-up operation, but they were in no way the masterminds behind the assassination. We also know that Oswald did not shoot. Based on all these elements, the final conclusion of our investigation is that, on the executive level, anti-Castro elements within the CIA organized Kennedy's execution. But they could never have gotten away with it without very high protection. So the question becomes: Who gave these CIA rogues permission to act? The answer to that question lies within the answer of another one: qui bono? Who profited from the murder? In other words, what was the motive behind the murder?

PART II

THE MOTIVE

For centuries man lived in the belief
that truth was slim and elusive and that once
he found it the troubles of mankind would be over.
And here we are in the closing decades of the 20th century,
choking on truth ... the mind is silent as the world spins
on its age-old demonic career.

Ernest Becker

Chapter 19 – Rumba heaven

Cuba is omnipresent in the Kennedy case. To answer the question of why Kennedy was assassinated, we must first look there.

On the paradise island group of Cuba, very few legal objections mattered under the regime of the corrupt operetta general Fulgencio Batista. Havana was the ideal destination for those who loved gambling, drugs, young women, booze and rumba. Everyday was a party in the Tropicana, the Lido and other popular nightclubs. In the brothels of Zanja Street you could fill your boots for 2 pesos,[907] the equivalent of 1 dollar. Havana was the kingdom of tolerance and lawlessness:[908] everything was possible and everything could be done. If there was a problem, the government was always ready to oblige for an appropriate fee. But while the tourist attractions wallowed in opulence and waste, most of the eleven million inhabitants lived in absolute poverty. The impoverished peasants were condemned to slave labor on the sugar plantations. More and more beggars, orphans, sick people and outcasts were seen on the streets. Fidel Castro, a law student from a good family, complained about the abuses, but was driven into the mountains of the Sierra Maestra with his improvised rebel mini-army. The regime did not regard them as a real threat. Nevertheless, the rebels had to keep themselves out of the hands of the regime, because if they were caught, torture or execution without due process awaited them.

The Mafia was the breeding ground of this complete lawlessness, and was plucking the benefits at the same time. The *Mob* had already made a fortune in Cuba in the twenties, when the country offered a dream smuggling route for illegal liquor during Prohibition in the US. That became the basis of an impressive criminal empire. After the end of Prohibition in 1933, the Mafia had its eye on heroin and cocaine, and Cuba was an obvious stopover between the production areas in South America and the end users in the United States. Thanks to the corrupt regime and the many small private airfields and jetties, Cuba was the ideal hub for drug trafficking. And the decadent atmosphere in Havana was cozy too. Following their old habits, the Mob hermetically sealed the territory off for outsiders – the monopoly position was too valuable to let adventurers participate. At the same time, there was fierce, often cutthroat competition between themselves. Cuba was a field of action reserved for the heavyweights, and, at the start, Charles "Lucky" Luciano was the most prominent Mafioso and the uncrowned *Capo dei Capi*, or Boss of the Bosses.

LUCKY LUCIANO

In 1907, the ten-year-old Charles was still called Salvatore Luciano. The cash-strapped Luciano family left Sicily, and went to try their luck in New York. Luciano was a tough guy. He worked his way up in a violent and ruthless way from a street thief and racketeer to the undisputed head of the New York Mafia gangs. At the age of 21, Luciano was working as a pimp. When he caught one of his girls servicing a 14-year-old boy for free, it came to blows, and the half-naked Benjamin Siegel fearlessly pulled his knife. A 16-year-old passerby, Maier Suchowljansky, heard the girl call for help and did not hesitate. He had a wrench in his bag, and gave Luciano a good whack with it. At that moment the police intervened, and arrested the unlikely threesome. But no one said a word at the station, and the police couldn't do anything except let them go again.[909] It was the beginning of a long friendship. Lucky Luciano had already made a name for himself. But the other two would also go far. Like most immigrants, Maier Suchowljansky changed his name to Meyer Lansky, and, despite his Jewish origins, became the financial brain of the Mafia. Benjamin 'Bugsy' Siegel built the Flamingo, the first casino-hotel in the unsightly village of Las Vegas, in 1931.

Before that, the three street crooks kept themselves busy in the Lower East Side of New York of the 1920s by picking pockets, smuggling, extorting shopkeepers, fencing stolen goods, burglary and running small gambling operations. Siegel, an inveterate playboy, sometimes sorted things out in a heavy-handed way for the capos, but had no sense of money. Lansky was the ice-cold accountant, and Luciano the undisputed leader. He seized every opportunity to move up the hierarchy. A gang war broke out in 1930 when Salvatore Maranzano challenged the supremacy of Giuseppe 'Joe' Masseria. After the murder of Masseria, Luciano took over his role as leader of one of the five Mafia families, and he established an armed peace between the clans. A committee now settled differences and territorial agreements. Golden years followed until 1933, when Prohibition was repealed. But even then, prostitution, drugs and gambling ensured a huge income. The Mafia also had its eye on the well-filled war coffers of the trade unions.

Figure 66. Charlie 'Lucky' Luciano, the head of the Mafia.

In 1936, Luciano's 25th arrest had fatal consequences for him. A number of prostitutes summoned up the courage to testify against him, and Luciano was sentenced to a prison term of 30 to 50 years. He was allowed to keep his private chef in jail, and could even manifest himself as a benefactor by donating the building materials for a church within the jail walls. But maintaining his power outside jail seemed a hopeless task. The Second World War changed 'Lucky' Luciano's luck, however. In 1940, he offered the US intelligence his secret contacts in Sicily, and also claimed to have vital information regarding a military landing operation in Europe via Sicily. From jail, Luciano could also guarantee that there would be no strikes by the dock workers during the war. His services had a price, however: his early release from jail. After the war, following ten years of imprisonment, he did, in fact, obtain an early release, but he was definitively expelled from the United States. Cuba looked like a good alternative. He took up residence in Suite 924 at the Hotel Nacional in Havana. Even now, the hotel offers a beautiful view of the Gulf of Mexico. Lucky would always remember the memorable day of his arrival in Havana: 'When I looked down over the Caribbean from my window, I realized somethin' else; the water was just as pretty as the Bay of Naples, but I was only 90 miles from the United States. That meant I was practically back in America.'[910]

Luciano felt the time was right to reaffirm his authority over the organization through some new agreements. If Luciano couldn't go to America, America could come to him. Under the guise of a tribute to the young crooner Frank Sinatra, more than five hundred gangsters gathered in Havana in December 1946. All the heads of the Mafia clans and their *consiglieri*, or counselors, were present for a congress under the chairmanship of Luciano. Only Al Capone was missing, due to advanced syphilis, but even he did not fail to send Lucky Luciano his best wishes. The special guests were pampered around the clock. In between, the men discussed their business. The capos concluded deals to the satisfaction of all regarding alcohol, casinos, cheese, olive oil, strip clubs, scams, horse racing, money laundering, trade union pension funds, political influence, transportation routes and distribution of territory. If they had any practical questions, they drummed the Cuban president out of his bed at any time they liked. One thorny issue was the question of what should be done with Bugsy Siegel in Las Vegas. The construction costs of his Flamingo had risen to six times the original budget. But Lansky and Luciano defended their childhood friend, and Siegel and his hotel, which would finally open on Christmas Day in 1946, were given another chance.

But things were not all hunky dory between the three friends. Lansky had built up his own power base in Luciano's absence. He had a good time in Havana, and preferred to call the shots himself. Lansky was also in favor of more discretion – Lucky was in the spotlight too much, and was too flashy parading with his gorgeous girlfriend Beverly Paterno. Lansky also believed much more than Luciano in a gradual transition from illegal to legal business. He got his way: on February 23, barely two months after the successful Mafia summit, the Cuban police deported Luciano from the country as an undesirable alien. On March 29, 1947, he was on a Turkish freighter traveling to Palermo. Lansky now had Cuba all to himself again. Every political and business agreement of any importance had to have his approval,[911] but, as far as the outside world was concerned, the ruthless businessman kept himself carefully in the background at all times. He never made notes of meetings or appointments, and drank milk rather than rum. His empire included nine casinos and six hotels. The network was gradually expanded to include banks, insurance companies and even an airline.

Bugsy Siegel, on the other hand, remained the unguided projectile that he had always been. He made the unpardonable mistake of holding back some of the casino profits for his own use. On June 20, 1947, the Mob finished him off with a bullet in his eye.

Another driving force in the Cuban Mafia empire was Amadeo Barletta, originally from Calabria in Italy. He became the exclusive importer of American cars: General Motors, Cadillac, Chevrolet, Oldsmobile. The cars that he sold in 1950 are still driving around Cuba today. Barletta was also involved in the pharmaceutical industry, construction projects and the newspapers and television. The Banco Atlantico was indispensable for his empire. In its report of August 7, 1951, the National Bank of Cuba reported a staggering pyramidal structure of the business interests of Banco Atlantico. The bank had no auditor to check the accounts, and did not even keep records of the incoming and outgoing payments, even when they amounted to millions of dollars in cash. It was clear that criminals were using the Banco Atlantico and other traditional banks such as Citibank and the Chase National Bank in order to launder massive amounts of money via fake companies.

Santos Trafficante, the godfather in Florida, also had a finger in the pie on the island in his backyard, of course. He was in charge of the construction and operation of casinos and other gambling houses.

Big industry followed in the wake of the Mafia. Among others, the Rockefellers settled down there with their Standard Oil Company, the largest oil company in the world.

CARLOS PRIO

In 1948, Carlos Prio became the new president of Cuba. During his reign, the culture of greed really bordered on madness. The fraudulent practices ran into millions of pesos according to Enrique Cerules, a Cuban who examined the original sources in the *Archivio Nacional de Cuba*. Cirules wrote that: 'Prio accentuated the corruption to the point of delirium.' The Autentico party acted 'as a force at the service of the financial Mafia-intelligence services groups of the United States.'[912]

Unbridled greed can only proliferate within a matrix of relentless shortsightedness. Cuba in 1950 was a poignant example of this. What prevented Prio and his entourage from using a part of the enormous windfall profits for the benefit of the local people? Why did they also have to run the country itself into the ground? The answer is clear: short-sightedness. Instead of perpetuating the criminal profits by investing a minimum in domestic tranquility, their greed was too great. With American help, the Cuban political caste shamelessly picked its population bare, and emptied the state coffers. As long as the Americans were allowed to do as they wanted, they weren't bothered about it.

President Prio clearly didn't properly understand this last nuance. He took it into his head to antagonize Rockefeller. Prio snatched the nickel mining rights in eastern Cuba from under the nose of the Americans, and granted the mining operation to the Dutch company Billiton. When he then also refused to limit the production of sugar cane, a demand from the Americans to raise the price of sugar on the world market, their patience ran out. The Americans didn't want to hear that their demand was unreasonable due to the monoculture on Cuba. Sugar was the only significant export product. The island had to import virtually everything, and the export of sugar was vital for the balance of payments. But the Americans' will was law, and Prio was becoming a millstone for them. If they could no longer deal with Prio, then they'd deal without him.

The Cuban people were also at the end of their patience. The moral outrage over the kleptocracy in Havana increased by the day. The politician Eduardo Chibas of the Orthodox Party openly complained about the corruption, including through radio broadcasts, and gradually won the support of the man in the street. Everything seemed to indicate that he would be the new president, but the CIA considered it their duty to prevent anyone with leftist ideas gaining political power in a neighboring country of the US. The political chess pieces were arranged so that the new strong man would either be the progressive Chibas by means of elections, or the reactionary General Batista by means of a coup. The liquidation of one would inevitably lead to the victory of the other. Chibas's opponents knew what to do, and skillfully lured the progressive presidential candidate into a trap. After a smear campaign of the worst kind, Chibas had to resign as an MP and lost his immunity. The exhausted Chibas committed suicide on August 16, 1951.

But the elimination of the political opposition and the economic shortsightedness also ensured that a popular uprising and a revolution came a step closer. A political or economic middle class no longer existed in Cuba, and there remained only a small, corrupt elite ruling over a large, impoverished mass. The poverty was harrowing and hopeless, even inhumanly cruel. In order to survive, young boys in Havana would even sell their sister for a few pesos.[913] And yet the revelers at the top had no intention of stopping.

The rebels received the benefit of the moral high ground. Anyone with an ounce of a sense of justice, everyone with their heart in the right place was opposed to the regime, and against the American bloodsuckers who followed in its footsteps. In this way, the rebels managed to represent the national honor. Anyone who really loved Cuba ultimately had no choice left but to support the armed resistance. In the meantime, the country deteriorated into chaos, and the greedy political class lost all its credit, not only with the Cuban people, but, and perhaps above all, with the Americans.

FULGENCIO BATISTA

The shocking corruption now gave the Americans a pretext for a military coup. There was an urgent need for a strong man who would sort things out in the interest of the Cuban people. The military seized power on March 10, 1952, and General Batista declared himself to be the head of state. There were only a few deaths. The Prios were allowed to go into exile unhindered, and the fortunes that had been amassed during the years of corruption disappeared without a trace. For the rest, it was immediately back to *business as usual*.

Things had become rather hot for the Mafia in the United States during the fifties. In 1950, Senator Estes Kefauver finally opened the discussion about the growing threat to society of organized crime. As chairman of a Senate Committee investigating organized crime, Kefauver bluntly wrote:[914]

> A nationwide crime syndicate does exist in the United States of America, despite the protestations of a strangely assorted company of criminals, self-serving politicians, plain blind fools, and others who may be honestly misguided.
>
> Behind the local mobs that make up the national crime syndicate is a shadowy, international criminal organization known as the Maffian so fantastic that most U.S. citizens find it hard to believe it really exists.
>
> [...] Infiltration of legitimate business by known hoodlums has progressed to an alarming extent in the United States. The committee uncovered several hundred instances where known hoodlums, many of them employing the "muscle" methods of their trade, had infiltrated more than 70 types of legitimate businesses.

After the revelations of the Kefauver Committee, the Mafia thought it was high time to legalize their amassed fortunes. The Cuban banks, which were hardly subject to any kind of checks, were ideal for laundering criminal money. Cuba seemed like a good destination for a quieter life, and, with a friendly dictator in power, the way also lay open for further US industrial exploitation of the island. The Rockefeller Group quickly gained control of the coveted nickel mines, and the sugar industry acquiesced to the American restrictions.[915] The sugar production per capita fell from 1.56 tons in 1925 to 0.89 tons in 1953. That was a dramatic situation for a country in which the majority of the population had to survive on the basis of this monoculture. In the 1950s, the major landowners only used a little more than half the surface area of their sugar plantations. The rest were left fallow on American command. Because the selling price increased as a result of the artificial scarcity, their profits remained intact, but the Cuban plantation workers suffered. Companies under the influence of the consulting firm Sullivan & Cromwell were prominent in Cuba. The brothers Allen and John Foster Dulles were leading partners of this business company. Even Richard Nixon had financial interests on the island through his lawyer friend Bebe Rebozo.[916]

A diabolical coalition of crime, politics and business kept the island in a stranglehold. US investment in Cuba from 1934 to 1956 delivered between 650 and 700 million dollars profit annually. An average of only 150 million dollars was re-invested. The country was literally drained dry.

However bad it may have been under Prio, the floodgates were really opened with the arrival of Batista in 1952. In a fever of insanity, the rulers mercilessly ruined the country. Poverty-stricken Cuba had to cough up nearly a billion pesos for various prestige projects that only benefited the Mafia and US multinationals. There were roads and services to places like Varadero and Pinar del Rio, where the Mafia wanted to set up hotels for wealthy tourists. The cost was 100 million dollars. A marina, a golf course and the millionaire hotel Monte Carlo de la Habana amounted to 20 million. Cuba invested 76 million in the mining industry and 94 million in the petrochemical industry. The profit from the investments went exclusively to America, after the necessary commission for the Batista clan, of course. Another 61 million was invested in tourist centers, 20 million in air transport, 36 million in railways and 96 million in waterways, all exclusively for the needs of foreigners. And the list is even longer. This expenditure had nothing to do with the real needs of the Cubans. In order to finance all this, Batista emptied all the popular banks, mortgage, savings and pension funds, and replaced the money with government bonds. On top of this, he also added another 300 million dollars to the national debt.

As we have already mentioned, General Batista had no worries about the motley crew in the mountains who called themselves the rebel army. That nasty little job would be sorted out by the Americans in due time. On the occasion of his visit on July 15, 1955, CIA Director Allen Dulles assured the dictator that he could count on America in the 'common struggle against the enemies of freedom': 'Allow me to say again, Mr. President, what a great honor and pleasure it has been to meet and talk with you, and I trust that we will be in a position to assist you and your country in our mutual effort against the enemies of liberty.'[917]

FIDEL CASTRO

This American support could not prevent three hundred guerrilleros inflicting a humiliating defeat on the government army in July 1958. It's hard to fight someone who would rather die than give up the fight for justice. The Americans reaped what they had sown all those years. The rebel army defeated Batista's troops again in November. The CIA slowly realized that the cause was lost, and President Eisenhower warned of impending doom.[918] Fidel Castro and Che Guevara advanced inexorably in the direction of the capital.

Eisenhower was not too worried at first. He sent his envoy William D. Pawley, a good friend of Batista and owner of the bus company that could operate public transport in Havana after the scandalous destruction of the Cuban tram system. On December 9, Pawley tried for three hours to convince Batista, who the Americans wanted to leave the country. He would be allowed to keep the 300 million dollars in his foreign accounts. The White House based the scenario for Cuba after Batista purely on the preservation of US interests. The Americans were prepared to support any new ruler as long as he was not called Fidel Castro. By removing Batista, they would force Castro to show his colors: if he was only fighting to oust Batista, he could then lay down his arms; if he continued to fight, then he was only after personal power. But Batista refused to leave. Ambassador E.T. Smith was also unable to persuade the dictator to step down. The choice of Smith as a negotiator was significant: the ambassador was also a stockbroker and a major shareholder in the Moa Bay Mining Company, which owned the nickel mines in Cuba. Discussions were currently taking place that would lead to a tax exemption for Cuban nickel exports, which would cost the Cuban state 40 million dollars a year and would produce the same amount of extra profit for the Americans. Smith was therefore strongly motivated to convince Batista to accept a non-violent change of power. This shows once again how much the interests were inextricably entwined at all levels. The Dulles brothers were also not uninvolved either. Secretary of State Foster Dulles shamelessly declared that the US government was neutral. At the same time, his brother Allen was heading the covert operations that did everything possible to help an emergency government and a military junta to take power. Such a government would immediately have asked for American support in restoring domestic peace, and everything could then remain as it was, with a new puppet leader as head of state.

But Batista's unwillingness to comply with the wishes of the Americans cost too much time, and the population of Havana welcomed the triumphant rebels to Havana on New Year's night in 1959. The American government was now stuck with a communist neighbor, and the Mafia had starved their hen that laid the golden eggs. Cuban collaborators, still numbed by the shock, fled to Florida and Louisiana as homeless refugees. The CIA had messed up once again. Everybody was furious, and wanted revenge and the restoration of the lost glory and the old paradise. No one even considered taking the responsibility for the debacle themselves, and, apart from Castro, there was not yet a scapegoat to shift all the blame onto. But the invasion in the Bay of Pigs would soon change that.

Chapter 20 – JFK, all the way

GIANCANA

John F. Kennedy won the presidential election with the tightest majority ever.[919] For those in the know, his victory in Illinois stood out in particular.[920] A stunning 89 percent of the voters showed up in the city of Chicago, at least according to the official results. This unlikely high turnout gave Kennedy a lead of 456,312 votes. This allowed him to just about survive his losses in the rural areas of Illinois. In the end, Kennedy won Illinois with a tiny margin of 8,858 votes from a total of 4,746,000. To a large extent, Kennedy had to thank Sam Giancana, the undisputed godfather of the Chicago Mafia, for his election. Through trial and error, Giancana had made it from a reckless street urchin to gangster king of Chicago. Three hundred gangsters unconditionally obeyed him. Kennedy's father, a shrewd swindler of all colors, knew Giancana personally. But, three years earlier, no one would have dared to predict that Giancana and the Kennedys would become allies in the 1960s.

In 1957, the Senate set up a subcommittee to investigate the activities of the trade unions. Senator McClellan led this *Select Committee on Improper Activities in Labor and Management*. The all-powerful *International Brotherhood of Teamsters*, a trade union for truck drivers led by the unparalleled Jim Hoffa, was targeted in particular. The investigation of the Committee increasingly pointed at Mafia bosses. The virtually anonymous parliamentary Committee suddenly came into the spotlight after a tragicomic incident. In the village of Apalachin, near New York, a police sergeant suddenly noticed a rather large collection of long, black Cadillacs and Lincolns with license plates from far outside New York near the villa of bootlegger Joseph Barbara. This aroused his curiosity. On his own initiative, the police sergeant decided to seal off the only access road to the secluded villa with some of his deputies, and to then move in on the select group. The result was hilarious: panic broke out among the Mafiosi, and no less than seventy villains in tailored silk suits made a dash for it into the swampy forests. The police were able to arrest sixty of the fugitives, including several heavyweights such as Vito Genovese, the don of New York, and James Civello, Jack Ruby's idol from Dallas. Giancana was also present at the meeting, but he was one of the few who managed to escape.

The meeting made the headlines in the national news. One of the major consequences was that FBI boss J. Edgar Hoover could no longer deny the existence of a national organized crime syndicate. From then on, the Bureau in Chicago continually tapped into the calls of the Mafia organization Outfit. The microphones were illegal, but provided the FBI with an invaluable amount of concrete information on the movements of the Mafia.

Another result was that the TV broadcast the debates of the McClellan Committee live. This is how the general public was introduced for the first time to the young, handsome Senator John Kennedy from Massachusetts, and his driven younger brother Robert, who, as protégé of Senator McCarthy, had made it to Chief Counsel of the parliamentary Committee. In that position, Robert Kennedy determined the direction the investigation would take, which witnesses were called, and how the hearing would proceed. Bobby Kennedy was a passionate fanatic in everything he undertook, but he lacked the legal experience to lead the interrogations. He attacked the arrogant Mafia bosses with relentless aggressiveness. As a result, the debates degenerated into vulgar slanging matches. The top lawyers of the Mafiosi were able to keep Bobby away from concrete results without really trying too hard. According to the Fifth Amendment, every citizen, including a Mafioso, had the constitutional right to remain silent if he might incriminate himself by answering.

On June 8, 1959, the Committee also questioned Sam Giancana, who ostentatiously drew the Fifth Amendment ticket and read out its text after every question with a sardonic grin. This irritated Robert Kennedy so much that he asked Giancana: 'Are you going to tell us anything or just giggle? I thought only little girls giggled?' The whole spectacle gave the Mafia some very bad publicity, but, legally, the Mafiosi held their own. The McClellan Committee experienced first hand what 'omertà' means: all Mafiosi kept silent. The Committee was dissolved after one year, and John and Bobby Kennedy were able to fully devote themselves to the preparations for the presidential campaign.

Giancana was not pleased with the political theatrics of the Kennedys, but larger issues temporarily demanded his full attention. In Cuba, Fidel Castro had come to power on New Year's day. After the initial confidence that a few kickbacks would make Castro a part of the deal, the mood changed. The new regime confiscated all US property on the island, and therefore also Giancana's investments. Meanwhile, the incident in Apalachin and the McClellan Committee had also woken up the FBI. Giancana was shadowed wherever he went, his phone was tapped and his life was generally made miserable. The Mafia was gradually considered to be a major threat to a civilized society and a normally functioning state. Organized crime was all set for a battle to the death, and such a battle could not be won against a determined government. But two unexpected incidents, which would merge into each other in a peculiar manner, made things look up for Giancana.

The first incident was a bizarre request from the CIA. Through their middleman Robert Maheu, the intelligence service contacted Johnny Roselli, one of Giancana's henchmen who managed his interests in Las Vegas. The Covert Operations department of the CIA was in the middle of Operation Mongoose, a secret plan to assassinate Castro. Maheu sounded Roselli out on whether the Mafia would be willing to do away with Castro for the round sum of 150,000 dollars. Roselli put Maheu in touch with Giancana and Santos Trafficante, the Mafia boss in Florida.[921] The idea of a power shift in Havana was not unwelcome to them, but, despite several grotesque attempts, the Mafia did not succeed in eliminating Fidel Castro. They had experience with brutal assassinations, but a well-prepared, sophisticated hit was out of their league. For Giancana, however, it wasn't bad news that the CIA had asked him for his help. That fact alone opened up some interesting perspectives.

The second incident took place in 1960, and, at first glance, seemed positive. Giancana was visited by an old acquaintance: Joe Kennedy urgently needed votes in Chicago, in order to get his son into the White House. That was more up Giancana's alley. If Kennedy won the electoral votes from Illinois, and thereby the presidency, the political backing of the Mafia would be assured for the next four or even eight years. So the young senator received his support.

BAY OF PIGS

The election season in the United States was also a windfall for Castro. He now had some time to stabilize his regime,[922] and to push through the first major measures, such as the redistribution of farmland. The Americans had no choice but to initially accept this situation. Very reluctantly, the military remained in the sidelines. An election year was certainly not the right time to start a war, but the plans were ready to be put on the desk of the new president. Whether that would be Nixon or Kennedy made little difference to the military chiefs. No president would or could afford to adopt a submissive attitude towards this arrogant Castro. It was precisely this rigid ideological approach of the Americans that drove Cuba into the arms of the Soviet Union.

Castro was well aware that America would not easily give up its influence on the island. He therefore expected attempts to destabilize his regime, politically or economically. America wouldn't miss a single opportunity to first create chaos in Cuba, in order to afterwards appear on the scene like a knight in shining armor, restore order and install a head of state who was more to the liking of the CIA. Castro had no choice but to turn to a strong Russian ally in order to consolidate his power. In the logic of the Cold War, a confrontation was inevitable. The plan that the army command and the CIA put on the table was for an invasion by Cuban exiles in the Bay of Pigs, followed by a spontaneous overthrow of the Castro regime by the liberated Cubans. The risky operation would be a first test for the brand new President Kennedy. The CIA and the military made him believe that 1,200 rebels would be enough to force an army of 200,000 to capitulate on an island with a length of more than 1,000 kilometers. They presented the chances of success of the invasion in a way that was much too promising. From a memorandum dated November 15, 1960, it later appeared that the CIA was perfectly aware that the paramilitary operation of the Cuban exiles had no chance of success without direct American support.[923] The intelligence service assumed that, once he had authorized the invasion, Kennedy would have no other option but to up the ante. They were certain he had no other choice but to provide the exiles with American military support. This is how the CIA advisors also sold the plan to the Cuban exiles. They imagined that Kennedy had no room for maneuvering, because the option of 'losing face' was a choice that a young, inexperienced president would never make so early in his first term of office. But they seriously misjudged Kennedy. JFK was a unique politician. Jack *always* got what *he* wanted. When he found that his army commanders and intelligence agencies had been messing with him, he took this as a violation of his authority and an insult to his intelligence. But he was indeed facing an extremely difficult choice. He could either let himself be bullied by the hawks in Washington and lose an important *internal* showdown, or suffer serious public loss of face and concede international embarrassment and an *external* defeat. As an officer during World War II, however, Kennedy had already proven that he didn't shy away from taking his responsibility in difficult times. He had a sincere interest in the opinions of others, even if they differed from his own, but only if they were open about it and could substantiate their point of view with the necessary arguments. If successful, he shared the merit, but if the final choice turned out to be wrong, he took the consequences himself. This philosophy was totally foreign to the entourage he had inherited from Eisenhower. They did just about everything that Kennedy despised. He had an aversion to war, especially if you fought an opponent with unequal weapons, as was the case with Castro. When Vice President Johnson once tried to persuade him to come deer shooting at his ranch, Kennedy said to a friend: 'That will never be sport until they give the deer a gun.'[924] Kennedy also had an aversion to advisers who gave him inaccurate or incomplete information, especially if they were trying to manipulate him. He hated stupidity and, as president, he did not want to accept any situation in which he did not have the final say. Confronted with a dilemma that was likely to define his place in history, his need for autonomy prevailed in the inner struggle he must have had. At that point in time, Castro was not the opponent he wanted to confront tit-for-tat. He was now in a power struggle with the army leadership and the CIA, and his first instinct was to win this battle. He therefore firmly refused to provide American air support for the Cuban exiles, and they were mercilessly crushed. The generals and the CIA responded with disbelief and outrage when they realized that Kennedy refused to play their game. Annoyed, Admiral Arleigh Burke and CIA man Richard Bissell stormed into the Oval Office in an attempt to bring Kennedy to reason. Five times Burke received 'no' for an answer with regard to military intervention.[925] When he persisted, Kennedy clearly stated his point: 'Burke, I don't want the United States to be involved.' The Admiral couldn't believe his ears: 'Hell Mr. President, but we *are* involved.' Ten years later, Burke still believed that Kennedy didn't get it right at the time: 'Mr. Kennedy was a very bad president ... He permitted himself to jeopardize the nation.'[926] Allen Dulles also believed that Kennedy had shown a lack of leadership. That evening, he sank exhausted onto Nixon's couch, asked for a whiskey and spoke of the 'worst day of my life.' From that day on, the Cuban exiles in Little Havana in Miami also hated Kennedy.

Kennedy was also seething, of course. 'I've got to do something about these CIA bastards,' he said later. He also didn't have a good word to say about his heavily decorated Joint Chiefs of Staff. 'Those sons-of-bitches with all the fruit salad just sat there nodding, saying it would work.' He was genuinely indignant about the basis for the decision the CIA and the military tried to impose on him. He was still angry weeks later, when he told his friend Paul 'Red' Fay, Secretary of the Navy, what it really was all about: 'Nobody is going to force me to do anything I think is not in the best interest of the country. We're not going to plunge into an irresponsible action just because a fanatical fringe in this country puts the so-called national pride above national reason.'[927] The president was the only one among the parties involved who was brave enough to shoulder the public blame for the disastrous operation. Kennedy could quietly congratulate himself on winning this first arm wrestling match with the military leaders and the CIA, but he was, of course, well aware that this would inevitably cause some issues. He took it in stride, because that was the reality of a politician's life.

The attraction of Kennedy's boundless self-confidence had a downside: he also tended towards recklessness. The ultimate proof of this would eventually cost him his life – when he drove through a dangerous city in an open car. But his decision to go against his advisors in the Bay of Pigs conflict was also a reckless political gamble. He might have won one pawn, but he considerably compromised his position on the big chessboard of global power at the same time. His military leadership felt hurt in their professional pride. The Cuban community felt betrayed. The CIA, who never wore their beaver up, were planning revenge. Public opinion was wondering whether it would perhaps have been better to have the more experienced and forceful Nixon at the helm of the national ship. What was more, Cuba was only one battle, the real ideological enemy was in the Kremlin. Kennedy was aware that he had got himself into a considerable mess. The elections were still a long way off, but the president had to score points in order to put enough weight into the political debate.

He tackled the problems one by one. Topping the list was the CIA. CIA Chief Allen Dulles was sacked, and Kennedy swore a solemn oath: he would break the power of the CIA.

He never trusted the military commanders again, which had far-reaching consequences during the missile crisis two years later. The solution of the

Cuba issue became a personal matter for him and his brother Bobby. The Kennedys had been raised in a very competitive environment. The word 'losing' was not in the family dictionary, and they would not tolerate that being changed by a man with a beard in Havana. In the greatest secrecy, the Kennedys decided to eliminate Castro at the first opportunity. For the president, this was important enough to put his brother at the head of a working group that coordinated the secret war against Cuba. Operation Mongoose was the collective name for the secret operations aimed at destabilizing the Castro regime. *Executive Action*, or the assassination of the head of state, topped the list of missions. The covert operation existed already before the Bay of Pigs fiasco, but with the president's brother at its helm, the Cuba issue rose in the priority list of the administration, and the urgency of the actions changed. As in everything he undertook, Robert Kennedy was very serious about it. He kept everyone on their toes until he saw results. On October 4, 1962, two weeks before the missile crisis, he strongly urged for the umpteenth time that pressure on Cuba should be increased. The memorandum of the meeting of the *Special Group (Augmented)*, which dealt with the issue, stated the following: 'The Attorney General opened the meeting by saying that higher authority is concerned about progress on the MONGOOSE program and feels that more priority should be given to trying to mount sabotage operations.'[928] The following phrase demonstrates that the assassination of Castro was openly one of the options: 'General Landsdale said that another attempt will be made against the major target which has been the object of three unsuccessful missions, and that approximately six new ones are in the planning stage.' During his hearing before the Church Commission in 1975, Roswell Gilpatric,[929] who was present at this meeting, minimized the significance of these words. The Senate Commission asked what exactly Robert Kennedy had meant by 'direct action.' Gilpatric answered: 'I don't recall anything other than this drum beating, reiteration of doing something which really would shake the Castro regime. He just wanted more effective steps than he consider the pin pricks that some people were trying to get in here and there.'[930] But nobody who was aware of the situation believed that the aim of Operation Mongoose was limited to pin pricks. Gilpatric did confirm, however, that Robert Kennedy had the absolute leadership of the Special Group (Augmented).

The fact that the Americans did not like the Castro regime was apparently sufficient reason to plan the assassination of the head of state of a neighboring country at the highest level. The Kennedys were no choirboys, but they probably did not know that the CIA had been foolish enough to outsource the assassination plans to the Mafia. One would have to be very cynical indeed to assume that Bobby, who prosecuted organized crime as the Attorney General, would approve outsourcing an assassination contract to them as the head of the Special Group. In any case, the Kennedy administration set to work on the Castro issue in a none-too-gentle manner.

THE OIL INDUSTRY

The implementation of a fairer tax system was an item in Kennedy's program that he wanted to work on during his first term of office. He also had an idea of where he could obtain the funding for the tax cuts for the middle class. In the 1960s, the oil industry was the largest legally-operating industry in the US, with a turnover of 50 billion dollars, bigger than the steel, automotive and chemical industries put together. It was also an extremely profitable industry. In Kennedy's opinion, the oil billionaires contributed unreasonably little to the community in proportion to their monster profits. On October 16, 1962, he pushed a bill through Congress that would cost the oil industry a loss of 15 to 30 percent on their foreign investment returns. And that was just the start. He went a lot further on January 17, 1963. Kennedy announced that he aimed to finance a general tax cut by abolishing preferential regimes such as the *Oil Depletion Allowance*. This tax loophole saved the oil industry about 280 million dollars in taxes annually.[931] This was a very risky plan. The bulk of the American oil was extracted in Texas. Anyone who wanted to be – or remain – president, was better off staying on friendly terms with the oil barons. In 1960, like Nixon, Kennedy proclaimed himself a supporter of the favorable tax regime the oil industry enjoyed. On October 13, 1960, he explicitly reconfirmed this to the campaign manager in Texas, Gerald C. Mann: 'I have consistently, throughout this campaign, made clear my recognition of the value and importance of the oil-depletion allowance.'[932] But a fairer distribution of the burden simply means that some people have to pay more. The tax exemption for oil extraction only made a small group of billionaires even richer, and no longer served the targets for which it had been introduced early in the 20th century. The abolition therefore seemed an ideal way to help finance a tax benefit that all Americans would be able to enjoy. But revoking a tax benefit from the oil industry was not an easy matter. Merely the mention of such an intention was enough to enrage Clint Muchinson, Sir Richardson, Haroldson Hunt, D.H. 'Dry Hole' Byrd (the owner of the book depository) and their friends. They were powerful enemies. The oil barons even had a senator in their ranks: Robert Kerr, the owner of the Kerr-McGee Oil Company, and a close friend of Prescott Bush, the father and grandfather of two of Kennedy's successors. The oil barons were certainly a part of the 'invisible government' that held control over the economic power, and was in no way willing to be pushed aside by the political power. People like Haroldson Hunt were not to be mocked. Hunt had already stated in 1961 that, with Kennedy, they had arrived at a point where there 'seems to be no way left to get those traitors out of our government except by shooting them out.'[933] The fact that the Texan Vice President Johnson, a friend of Hunt, was Kennedy's legal successor, obviously made this idea even more attractive. As far as Hunt was concerned, this was no more than a way of venting his frustration. He and his companions would and could never proceed to such a bold action, but the mood was so poisoned that they would not have opposed someone with more concrete plans in that direction.

Chapter 21 – Bobby Kennedy

Although the Bay of Pigs caused John Kennedy more than enough headaches already, his brother, as a member of his government, generously added to them.[934] The idea to give Bobby a top department came from their father, Joe Kennedy. He was still calling the shots in the family, and insisted that his 34-year-old third son would be put at the head of the 30,000 officials of the Department of Justice. But this was highly ambitious, as Bobby had no legal experience apart from his role as counsel to a Senate Committee. The crafty FBI Director Hoover saw a golden opportunity in Bobby's inexperience. In his mind, he could already see Bobby inevitably creating a power vacuum, and he would be there to rope in the powers that were left unmanaged. Hoover saw his way clear, and he gave Bobby the fatherly advice to put his doubts aside and to firmly seize the opportunity to become Attorney General. Hoover had already been Director of the FBI before Bobby was born. On paper, the Attorney General might be his boss, but the old fox believed that, with Bobby in charge, this would only remain 'on paper.' Apart from Kennedy senior and Hoover, however, few others were enthusiastic about the plan to catapult Bobby into the position of Attorney General.

Jack was not really in favor of the idea, and he could do without all this commotion at the start of his term of office. The brothers were undoubtedly a unique team, but, in addition to the striking similarities, there were also major differences, especially with regard to their temperament. Compared to the relaxed style of the talkative Jack, Bobby was a hyper-nervous, taciturn fanatic. When he got his teeth into something, he pursued it with an aggressive, relentless zeal. Jack preferred to downplay issues, and his vision of life was lighter. These differences in character constituted a potential risk: Bobby's uncompromising directness was not always the best strategy in the political arena. Moreover, a minister served 'at the pleasure of the President,' who could dispose of any member of the government at any time. When a blunder occurs, the minister in charge usually takes the blame, while the president remains unaffected as far as possible. But how would you sack your own brother without fallout? Without the interference of his father, Jack would never have given his brother such a high government post. Half seriously, he himself said the following about making the official announcement: 'Well, I think I'll open the front door of the house some morning about

2 a.m., look up and down the street, and, if there's no one there, I'll whisper: "It's Bobby!'" But the decisions of Mr. Kennedy senior were unassailable within the clan, and not even a president-elect could change this. Jack, who always had to have the final say, set a condition, however: Bobby had to at least comb his hair before facing the press.

Bobby himself also knew that humor was the best method to keep one step ahead of the critics. When he spoke to his department, he summarized his curriculum as follows: 'I started in the department in 1950 as a young man, worked hard, studied, applied myself... and then my brother was elected President of the United States.'[935] But the critics of his appointment had a point. The responsibility that Bobby Kennedy took on in his brother's government was mind-blowing. In addition to being Attorney General, he also became the principal adviser to the president. It was not in Jack's nature to bring job sharing into the presidency, but Bobby became his main sounding board, because he was the only person the president could be certain was loyal in all respects. Joe Kennedy also intended the principled Bobby to be something of a moral keeper for his more frivolous brother, so that, if necessary, he could discreetly remove the debris of Jack's amorous capers. Bobby did, in fact, act as a kind of super chief of staff around the clock, and that was already more than a full day's work on its own. Through the Special Group, he also controlled the top secret aspects of foreign policy. He constantly had an eye on Havana after the Bay of Pigs. In between, he had to manage the entire American judicial system in his position of Attorney General, and keep Hoover in line. He was very keen about doing all this, and was an indispensable aid to the president. Bobby might not have been an outstanding and experienced lawyer, but he had proven himself to be an efficient and tough manager during the campaign for the presidency. He worked incredibly hard, and was a control freak. His efforts gained him the respect and trust of his best personnel. If they did exactly what he asked them to do, this trust was mutual. His younger staff members in particular also appreciated his casual style: he rarely wore a tie, decorated his office with drawings from his children, and sometimes even brought his Labrador, Brumus, along to the office. This all helped to foster the team spirit, and, under his administration, the dusty Department of Justice soon turned into a productive think tank of political and legal activism. But so much diligence also stirred up ill feelings among those who felt victimized by it. It didn't take long for the predictable problems to surface.

For John Kennedy, politics was like a martial art. He accepted the challenge, but was also able to relax, and he refushed to be drawn into a conflict. Politics was a business affair, not something personal. For Bobby, this was different. He saw every confrontation as a personal duel and was very vindictive. 'Bob is the only man I've met in government who is willing to go all the way all the time,'[936] said a staff member of his department, admiringly. Expressed in a less positive manner, he could also be called a ruthless despot. Due to his personal relationship with the president, Bobby had almost unlimited power over his department. Even a trivial task from the personal confidant of the president was the equivalent of a direct presidential order. Bobby was so certain of presidential backing that, within his own area of responsibility, he started making autonomous decisions without asking the prior consent of the president. The first thing he did in his zeal as Attorney General was to tackle the Mafia. He had not forgotten the confrontation with union leader Hoffa and Mafia boss Giancana in the Senate Committee. He described the Mafia issue as a fight to the death: 'Either we are going to be successful or they are going to have the country,' he told his staff. He was thereby not far from the truth. The amount of money spent on gambling in the United States in the sixties was hallucinatory: in excess of 50 billion dollars a year, more than the entire defense budget. Kennedy saw a trend in the growing ambitions of the Mafia: they first took over their competitors, then the legal economy, and finally the government. The corrupting power of the crime syndicate was indeed life threatening for democracy. 'The racketeer is at his most dangerous not with a machine gun in his hand but with public officials in his pocket,'[937] Bobby often repeated when he held an address. For Kennedy, Hoffa was no less a gang member than the real gangsters, a hypocritical poser who cultivated his image of defender of the common man, and loudly complained about the shameful persecution he had to suffer. In Hoffa's eyes, Bobby was 'a spoiled rich kid' who was only out to crush the union of the underprivileged. Kennedy was right in this case. In reality, Hoffa was anything but socially motivated. He lived like a pasha, with intense contempt for anyone who dared to put any obstacle in his path. The marriage of his huge trade union, the International Brotherhood of Teamsters, with organized crime speaks volumes about his true intentions. Looking at it a little closer, this marriage was really not so strange. On request, the Mafia was able to efficiently enhance the effect of strikes and other union actions, but the number of Mafiosi was very limited. Conversely, the union could mobilize crowds of people and huge resources, but did not have the unscrupulous, professional implementers. The criminal imagination of the Mafia was also a couple of decades ahead of the ingenuity of the trade unions. The Mafia could coach the Teamsters in the most lucrative use of their organization with many members, plenty of money and a lot of power. Both groups were always looking for more power and more money, and were therefore dangerous to the state. Bobby was absolutely right, but he made it into a personal vendetta against the Mafiosi he already knew by name following his experience as chief counsel of the Senate Committee. Giancana and Trafficante were in the line of fire, but it was above all trade union boss Hoffa and Carlos Marcello, the godfather of New Orleans, who came into the cross hairs. Bobby's despotic trait was clearly seen when he had Marcello unceremoniously put on a plane to Guatemala in April 1961 after he had used a fake Guatemalan passport. The Justice Department was well aware that the passport was a forgery, but nevertheless dropped Marcello in the middle of the Central American jungle in his civilian suit. He was getting what he deserved for using a Guatemalan passport, ruled Kennedy. Marcello rescued himself from this predicament with great difficulty, and returned illegally to the United States, probably with the help of pilot David Ferrie. Once he was back on American soil, Marcello was like a man possessed in his efforts to avoid another expulsion. He forged documents, intimidated witnesses, bribed the jury, appealed and went to the Supreme Court. But whenever Marcello had a lucky escape, Bobby became even more determined. Ronald Goldfarb, one of Kennedy's special prosecutors, wrote: 'Marcello demonstrated both the elusiveness and power of our quarry.' He added, however, that it needed 'Kennedy's commitment to fight back as hard as it took to put them out of business.'[938] Bobby was not the kind of man to confine himself to pruning the branches of the criminal tree, he also put the ax to the roots. Every day, he would ask his staff how far the prosecution of the Mafiosi had progressed. He also urged the legal department to 'creative pursuit.' The Mafiosi constantly covered themselves against all possible facts for which they could expect full prosecution. The department therefore came up with the craziest offenses. For example, after an unsuccessful search, one Mafioso was prosecuted for having more frozen pigeons in his pantry than the statutory maximum number of slaughtered animals allowed outside the hunting season. Hoffa was prosecuted for mail fraud. For Bobby, the end justified the means. He had Giancana shadowed around the clock, even to the extent that the shadowers ostentatiously moved along with Giancana on the golf course, one hole behind him. The Mafia boss won a case of blatant stalking in court because of this, however, and even received an indemnity of 500 dollars.[939] But this didn't stop Bobby's staff. They kept punching, and, in the end, one of the gangsters cracked. Joe Valachi was intensively interrogated for eight months, and thereby remembered all the names and dates of crimes in which he had been involved as a gang member. He also provided colorful details about the habits and rules of the organization. Words like 'omertà,' 'capo' and 'consigliere' made their appearance in the legal reports. The admirable courage and perseverance of Robert F. Kennedy was gradually paying off. The graph of the Department of Justice showing the prosecution of Mafiosi spoke volumes:

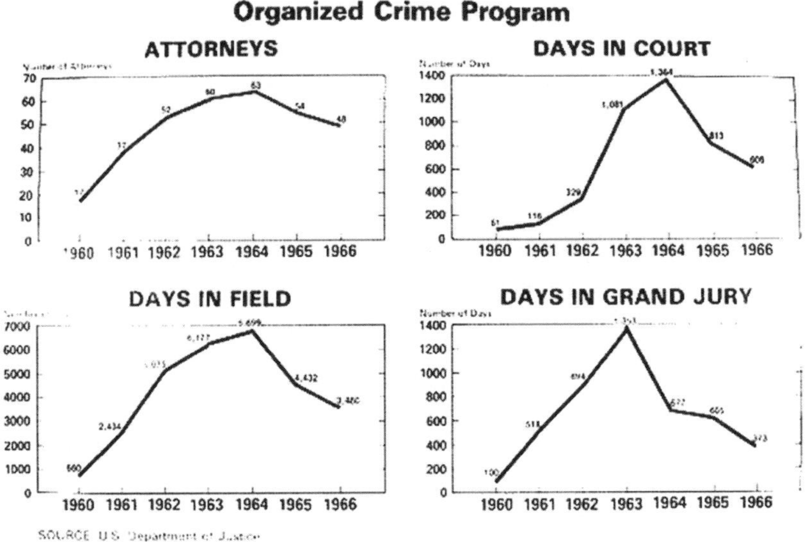

The trade union could also no longer evade the law. In the end, Bobby's special team prosecuted 201 Teamsters, 161 of whom were convicted. The graph clearly shows that Bobby Kennedy's offensive was life-threatening to organized crime, and that the assassination of his brother made a huge difference to any later progress in this battle. Bobby believed in the power of constantly increasing pressure. The opponent should not be given a chance to recover. Not until Bobby's power was broken after November 22 could organized crime slowly recover from the reign of terror that had lasted three years. Bobby had forced the Mob onto the defensive, and was left with at least four powerful and sworn enemies: Hoffa, Giancana, Trafficante and Marcello.

But he also had a deep resentment for Hoover and Vice President Johnson, which he often showed openly. At the same time, he also angered Desmond Fitzgerald of the CIA. In the secret fight against Castro, Bobby constantly put pressure on the intelligence agents or suddenly whistled them back brusquely. This caused plenty of irritation among the agents, who didn't understand why the Attorney General was actively interfering with their covert international operations. They considered this to be an expression of immature, exaggerated activism, but, as Bobby was the direct sounding board of the commander in chief, any protest was restricted to the gnashing of teeth behind closed doors. In addition, Bobby made even more enemies by having former General Walker referred to a psychiatric clinic. The incident with Walker was also an early sign of the Kennedys' cautious support of the civil rights movement. Bobby had come to the moral conviction that Martin Luther King had a point. From his position in the Department of Justice, he seemed to be prepared to actively participate in the call for equal rights for the black population. And this was also a thorn in the side of many opponents. Bobby Kennedy really did move mountains, but he left a trail of formidable enemies in his wake, who were whispering: 'This cannot go on any longer with the Kennedys. Something has to be done.'

Chapter 22 – From Dulles to Dallas

DULLES

Before the Second World War, the United States had no real intelligence service. The pioneers learned their trade from the British during the war, and, above all, improvised. The British Empire collapsed after the war, and the USA became the undisputed leader of the free world. Because the following war was a cold war, spies became the new front-line soldiers. The CIA mainly developed into the agency it would be in 1963 during the reign of its flamboyant director Allen Dulles. He had turned the bulk of the American intelligence service into a band of smug adventurers in his own image and likeness. Dulles is a remarkable historical phenomenon. For decades, he was involved in almost every major international event. Rather by chance, he met Lenin in 1917[940] and Hitler in 1933.[941] As a legal adviser to the League of Nations, he spoke with Mussolini and the leaders of Britain and France.[942] In 1943, Prince von Hohenlohe asked him about the possibility of ending the Second World War if a Gestapo coup were to bring Himmler to power.[943] He was also well informed about the planned assassination attempt on Hitler. Dulles snatched Fritz Kolbe from under the noses of the British MI6, which was the undisputed leader among Western intelligence services at the time. Kolbe passed on 1,200 top-secret Nazi documents, including the plans for the V2 and the reports of Hitler's summits. Almost single-handedly, Dulles brought about the Nazi capitulation in Northern Italy. Through his intervention, Tito became president of Yugoslavia and not a certain Mihailovic, of whom the world then heard nothing more.[944] His brother, Foster Dulles, also sat at the table in all major post-war conferences that redistributed world power. He managed to include a treaty with Japan, and was closely involved in keeping China out of the UN. Allen was also on board when Dewey failed to become president in 1948, and it was the Dulles brothers who ultimately decided that Eisenhower should stand as a candidate for the presidency in 1952: Foster personally flew to Paris to persuade the former general.[945] Under Eisenhower, Allen Dulles received the coveted post of Director of the CIA, while Foster became Secretary of State. He was a straightforward and gifted diplomat, but whether Allen was the man to single-handedly determine a large part of US foreign policy is another matter. According to Kim Philby, the most famous double agent in the CIA, Dulles created an 'unprofessional delight in cloak and dagger for its own sake.'[946] Philby thought that Dulles was quite a nice person. 'He was nice to have around: good comfortable, predictable, pipe-sucking, whiskey sipping company.' But he very much doubted whether Dulles, 'basically a line-of-least resistance man,' had ever made an intellectual effort that wasn't for his own sake. Walter Bedel Smith, Allen's predecessor as CIA Director, was on the same wavelength. He found Dulles downright unsuitable as his successor: 'Allen was far too romantic about the practical business of espionage, too interested in the excitements of covert operations and too little concerned with the hard painstaking slogging research and analysis which was now the essence of the modern intelligence machine.'

Figure 67. Allen Dulles, CIA Director from 1953 to 1961.

Dulles had a low opinion of Kennedy. He did not care about the course the new president wanted to sail, and felt no need to move with the times. Instead, he stated without hesitation that he had no desire to carry out the careful, progressive politics of Kennedy. For him, the right-wing political line that his brother Foster had mapped out as Secretary of State under Eisenhower was still good enough to be continued under Kennedy, with or without the latter's consent. Like a jealous husband, Dulles guarded his own privileges and those of his brainchild, the CIA. This overt insubordination had to result in a confrontation with the president sooner or later. Unlike Eisenhower, Kennedy assumed that he decided what the CIA was doing, and not vice versa. Even though Kennedy knew how dangerous this confrontation was, this did not prevent him from taking it on. Quite the opposite: he loved a good fight, and considered it to be his duty to effectively carry out the supreme command. Kennedy assumed that he could not lose this confrontation, like the many others he had had. But did he realize just how perilous the CIA could be for somebody who was trying to break its power?

THE WATCHDOG OF CAPITALISM

The CIA had grown extremely fast, and had thereby never encountered any budgetary or other obstacles in its path. The secret and uncontrolled budgets for the organization were hallucinatory. In 1954, the CIA was allowed to spend 500 million dollars on whatever it wanted. Without any additional funds, the agency financed the construction of the U2, the first plane that could carry out espionage flights in the stratosphere. The revolutionary airplane was already in use a year later. The CIA also dug a 550-meter-long tunnel under the Berlin Wall in order to install the required bugging devices under a telephone exchange in East Berlin. The tunnel was actually equipped with a cooling system in order to avoid it becoming obvious above ground when there was snow. These projects fitted perfectly into the goal for which Truman had called the intelligence service into life: intelligence gathering.

But the still relatively new organization had to grow up during the period of the Cold War, and there was no time for illusions and naivety in a world where the perfidious KGB was operating. The core activity of the CIA therefore quickly turned to clandestine ideological warfare, thereby creating the association between the agency and US imperialism. In the atmosphere of the Cold War, it was unthinkable that the United States would support a progressive, democratic government, let alone help it into the saddle. Progressive, popular and social sounded far too left-wing and socialist for the CIA, so they fought it with all possible means and, preferably, smothered it in the bud. The CIA thereby became more and more the aggressive watchdog of capitalism, the ally of various dictators or military juntas, but never the friend of the local population. This reality was at odds with the image of the generous and benevolent Americans that had arisen after World War II. The CIA did not provide development assistance. For the agency, politics was not a *res politeia* or people's cause, but a very nasty form of favoritism. In Egypt, Nasser received 12 million dollars from the CIA, with which he promptly built the Cairo Tower – also known as the CIA monument by those in the know. In Jordan, the Queen Mother also received 12 million dollars to lead her son King Hussein onto the right path. Things were completely out of control in Saudi Arabia: the CIA boosted the bank accounts of King Saud by almost 40 million dollars. The monarch mainly used the kickbacks to satisfy his 'enormous appetite for virgins and small boys'[947] and had his 'talent scouts' search the whole of the Middle East for these. King Saud used the rest of the millions for bribes, a proven method for keeping the peace. In the meantime, working together with the US American oil barons, the Shah of Iran was placed back on his peacock throne.

In the shadow of his charming director Allen Dulles, the head of the counterespionage department, James Jesus Angleton, had the freedom to develop his own specific ideas about the main task of an intelligence service. Angleton was a terrifying figure, an antisocial icy fiend who could only show tenderness for his collection of rare orchids. Dulles had no moral objections to the sometimes extreme practices of the CIA. Howard Roman, a CIA officer, said the following about Dulles: 'He was never against the unclean side of intelligence, so long as he could convince himself, as he usually could, that it was being done for a cause.'[948] The paranoid delusional world of a small clique was the dark glasses through which the CIA looked at the world. Under President Eisenhower and Director Dulles, the CIA arbitrarily determined a large part of the foreign policy of the United States. The intelligence service became a worldwide network, a secret network that had as good as unlimited financial resources and total impunity. It could tell lies, cheat, falsify and murder. It could withhold any proof of its misdeeds from the elected representatives as a state secret, and did not even have to account for the spending of its gigantic budget. By the time anyone well and truly realized what was going on, it was already too late to be able to do something about it. They could barely control the monster that Truman had created with the best of intentions, and which had been able to escape the attention of Eisenhower during the eight years of unbridled growth under Dulles. Only during the Bay of Pigs incident did Kennedy realize that the CIA was actively making political decisions, and thereby deemed themselves to be above the president. It was also very clear that the CIA was totally untrustworthy as an intelligence service. But Kennedy would be defeated in his attempt to put things right.

LEGACY OF ASHES

The scope and budget of the CIA had long since assumed excessive proportions in 1960. The activities, which had begun with wiretaps, infiltration, secret codes and mutual deception with double agents, expanded rapidly to include the destabilization of democratically elected regimes and the heavy-handed protection of American business interests. They culminated in cold-blooded murder and right-wing coups. The targets were Guatemala, the Dominican Republic, the Congo, Venezuela, Iran, Vietnam, Indonesia and, of course, Cuba. The CIA had beginner's luck in overthrowing regimes, but the organization was actually already largely dysfunctional by the second half of the 1950s. It failed completely when it had to provide reliable information, which was the original reason for its existence. This also often frequently happened consciously and deliberately. The CIA agents colored their reports ideologically in order to steer the political decisions in the desired direction. The more important the issue, the more chance there was that the CIA would 'adjust' the information provided to the political decision makers.

Two famous examples illustrate how dramatic the situation really was. The CIA systematically overestimated the nuclear power of the Soviet Union, and Dulles constantly reported that a dramatic 'missile gap' was arising. From 1957, the CIA reported to President Eisenhower that the Russians had more ICBMS, intercontinental missiles equipped with nuclear warheads, than the Americans. In 1960, the CIA estimated the number of ICBMS that the Soviets would have in 1961 at 500. That led to a frenzied American investment in nuclear weapons, no doubt to the delight of their manufacturers. But it later turned out that the Russians possessed exactly four ICBMS.[949] That is no innocent mistake. How many investments in schools, health and social services would the community have been able to afford without all that spending on this totally useless nuclear armament budget? But the CIA was never at any moment held accountable for the economic damage it caused with its outrageous misinformation. And the damage was not limited to the economic cost of excess nuclear warheads. At a certain moment, this situation brought the world to the brink of destruction when voices were raised in military circles to make use of the nuclear superiority, created by the misinformation, for a surprise nuclear attack on the Russians. Here also, the CIA was never called to account.

The second example dates from 1960. President Eisenhower wanted to end his tenure successfully (*reed*: on a high note). Later, at the inauguration of Kennedy, he would warn the world about the danger to liberty through what he described as the "military-industrial" complex. In that same line of reasoning he wanted in his last year in the White House, to cautiously explore the possibility of a mutual arms limitation with Khrushchev in Paris. Eisenhower explicitly told Dulles that, in view of the discussions, he felt it was too risky to have U2 flights taking place. He believed in an intelligence service that was made up of 'only spies, not gadgets.' His vision was that they needed to know what the Russians were thinking, and who was making the decisions, in order to have an idea of Russian intentions.[950] A photograph of an internal memorandum was worth more than any aerial view of an army camp, and therefore he preferred that the CIA stopped carrying out U2 flights. An incident could have far-reaching implications on the chance of mutual arms limitation. Dulles listened politely, but had his own opinion. The inevitable happened on May 1, 1960: the Russians shot down a U2 aircraft that was carrying out a mission without the consent of the president. Again without consulting the president, the CIA lied that this was a 'weather aircraft' that had gone missing over Turkey, instead of a spy plane being downed over Central Russia. But the pilot of the U2 was captured alive by the Russians. On top of the other diplomatic problems that the incident created, the Americans now also appeared as liars in the eyes of the world community. Eisenhower could not even blame the CIA for the blunders, because that would have proved publicly that he did not have enough authority to prohibit the agency from carrying out U2 flights. The tired president was so disgusted by the whole situation that he even considered resigning. The international summit to which he had been looking forward for so long began in Paris thirteen days later. The initial discussions with the Russians at Camp David had been promising, but Khrushchev opened the summit in Paris with a demand for a public apology from the Americans over the U2 espionage issue. Eisenhower refused to apologize openly, and the Russians left with slamming doors. That meant the end of the summit and the start of a new, costly cycle in the arms race. It is even possible that the CIA deliberately provoked the U2 incident in order to sabotage the summit, but that is speculation. In any case, the CIA had had its own way again, with far-reaching negative consequences.

These embarrassing blunders did not lead to more restraint or discretion. There was work to do in Cuba, where they had misjudged the chance of Castro bringing the revolution to a successful conclusion. In the short-term, the elimination of Castro was right up the CIA's street. In the official memorandum, someone replaced the word 'eliminate' with 'remove from Cuba.' This sounded somewhat less criminal. According to the CIA, the counter-revolution would start on its own once Castro was out of the way. The agency drew up the first plans together with Vice President Nixon. Eisenhower himself was hardly interested: he was looking impatiently towards the end of his illustrious career, and spent most of the day doing nothing. In this relaxed atmosphere, the CIA was able to quietly do its own thing in terms of the foreign policy of the United States. The heads of the intelligence services arbitrarily made decisions on state affairs, about which the president should preferably hear as little as possible. But the CIA underestimated the problems in the Cuba case once again, and they also overestimated the manipulability of the world. The Cold War atmosphere was grim, and made the case more complex. The Americans wanted to be able to fall back on 'plausible deniability' at any time. No evidence of US interference in Cuba must therefore ever be turned up. This led to scenarios that were sometimes more nonsensical than a comic spy movie. The most ridiculous idea was perhaps the plot to smear Castro's boots with a product that would make his beard fall out. That would certainly inevitably trigger a successful popular uprising. Another plan was to add LSD to Castro's drinking water. This would then result in even more verbal garbage than usual during his hour-long speeches on Revolution Square, and the people would again spontaneously overthrow the regime. The CIA even considered promising the deeply religious Cubans the second coming of Christ on earth if they would first chase away the Antichrist Castro.[951] Marita Lorenz, a German beauty, was to share Fidel's bed, and make use of the opportunity to put poison pills in his champagne. She carefully hid the pills in a jar of night creme, but they dissolved in it.[952]

Because they were so unsuccessful with all their homemade murder plans, the CIA finally brought in the Mafia. This demonstrates yet again the lack of civic responsibility within the agency. In 1960, the CIA had even set up a fully-fledged department for the 'assassination of foreign political leaders': ZR/RIFLE. William 'Bill' Harvey, who had also thought up the Berlin tunnel, headed it. Kennedy was taken aback a year later when he first shook hands with Bill Harvey. The so-called American version of James Bond turned out to be an obese alcoholic and an unscrupulous, uncouth cynic. Harvey came up with the misbegotten idea of sending Robert Maheu as a mediator to Johnny Roselli, a Mafioso of the first water. This showed a total disregard for morality, a lack of respect for the rule of law, but, above all, a lack of realism. The gangsters had no experience at all in political assassinations. For them, murder was a brutal matter of honor and revenge. If a war broke out between the families, it could be dangerous on the street for a while, but the victims were usually within their own virile community. Above all, a murder proved that the murderer was not to be trifled with, or that indiscretion was usually paid for with death. This was something completely different from carrying out a political assassination without leaving any evidence of American involvement. In fact, the godfathers were not really happy with the CIA's Castro project, but they didn't dare to flatly refuse. They didn't accept the offered 150,000 dollars for the hit contract, and let the matter muddle on for a while. In the meantime, the CIA kept itself busy with the preparations for the Bay of Pigs operation, but as this would not be possible before the election, they postponed it in anticipation of Nixon's succession of Eisenhower. But Nixon did not win the White House, which was, in fact, also partly due to a blunder by the CIA. Dulles indiscreetly explained something about the planned operation in Cuba to the presidential candidate Kennedy. Kennedy then used this against Nixon during the crucial television debate. He accused the Vice President of having done nothing to overthrow Castro. Nixon was obviously not allowed to mention the existence of the secret operation on television. The exchange between the candidates left the impression that the Eisenhower administration was indeed soft on Castro, and that hugely benefited Kennedy in the public opinion.

Only at the very end of his tenure did it occur to President Eisenhower how dysfunctional the CIA had become under his control. After the incident with the U2, a study group investigated the agency, and its report was placed on the desk of the outgoing president on December 15, 1960. It was devastating. Eight years long, Dulles had amused himself by doing what he preferred to do: launching exciting, clandestine operations. But he had completely failed to develop and manage a professional intelligence service that was adapted to the changed needs. Three weeks later, there was another confirmation of this in a report from the *President's Board of Consultants on Foreign Intelligence Activities*, a presidential advisory council for espionage activities abroad. The report warned that: 'the CIA's concentration on political, psychological and related covert action activities have tended to distract substantially from the execution of its primary intelligence-gathering mission.'[953] Dulles laughed off the findings of the report, but Eisenhower was not in the mood to listen to him anymore: 'The structure of our intelligence organization is faulty. It makes no sense, it has to be reorganized, and we should have done it long ago.' The old president understood that he had never been able to keep the CIA under control. 'I have suffered an eight-year defeat on this,' he stated bitterly, and added that he had left his successor 'a legacy of ashes.'[954] The supreme commander who had brought Hitler to his knees proved powerless when faced with a roguish, pedantic clown with a pipe and bow tie. Eisenhower could not correct his mistake, and Kennedy would pay the highest price for it.

COUNTERPRODUCTIVE OPPOSITION

The utter failure of the Bay of Pigs operation confronted Kennedy with the incompetence and unreliability of the CIA for the first time. All the defects of the CIA were clearly present in the debacle. Dulles had lied about the feasibility of the invasion: 'Mr. President, I stood right here at Ike's desk and told him I was certain that our Guatemalan operation would succeed, and Mr. President, the prospects for this plan are even better for this plan than they were for that one.'[955] Kennedy soon experienced how little the word of his CIA director was worth. The CIA proved yet again that it understood very little about intelligence, and that its handling of its top-secret operations was as leaky as a sieve. After the catastrophe, Kennedy vowed he would break the CIA into a thousand pieces and scatter them to the wind. But he did not have the luxury of putting this into practice. The popular Eisenhower had sedately allowed things to follow their course, but after the failed Bay of Pigs operation, Kennedy's political start-capital was significantly affected. He urgently needed to score political points in the Cuban issue. That was not possible through an open war, and therefore, however angry he was, the president had to continue to work with the CIA and their covert operations. Allen Dulles, Deputy Director Charles Cabell and Deputy Director for Plans Richard Bissell had already been sacked in the meantime. John McCone, a Kennedy confidant without any experience in intelligence work, became the new director, and Richard Helms moved up the hierarchy and became Deputy Director. So there still was a CIA man who could ensure continuity, and keep the lid on some smelly jars firmly closed for the new director. McCone knew what Kennedy expected of him: to take control of the whole thing and carry out a major clean-up. The most problematic division, the Clandestine Operations, was hit the hardest. McCone sacked hundreds of officials, starting with the 'accident-prone,' the 'wife-beaters' and the 'alcohol-addicted.'[956] In accordance with Kennedy's wishes, he succeeded in substantially reducing the Clandestine Operations department, but caused the morale of the remaining troops to drop to freezing point. The anti-Kennedy sentiments grew, and Kennedy had some new enemies on his back.

Because Kennedy had no confidence at all in the department of Clandestine Operations, but also needed to quickly take revenge on Castro, the president now entrusted the secret war against Cuba to the only man he dared trust blindly: his brother. Operation Mongoose received unlimited means. The budgets are still a state secret, but insiders estimate that the annual budget in the critical period was between 50 and 150 million dollars.[957] 'We were hysterical about Castro,' wrote Secretary of Defense McNamara about the mood after the Bay of Pigs operation.[958] The Kennedys never left a humiliation unanswered. Castro had to be dealt with tit for tat. Robert Kennedy demanded that 'no time, money, effort or manpower be spared' to overthrow the Castro regime. The failure in the Bay of Pigs stimulated the Kennedys' competitive nature to the limit. They couldn't resist the temptation to intervene in the daily operations of the CIA. Perhaps they had no choice, but it remains a classic example of bad governance. The errors were numerous, and mutually reinforced the negative consequences. Removing an iconic director and replacing him by a friend without political experience was still acceptable. But to then install your brother as the head of a secret cell for whom arson, sabotage, assassination and kidnapping stood on the agenda was playing with fire. Unlike the fierce fight against organized crime in his own ministry, Bobby was not surrounded by loyal and motivated employees in Operation Mongoose. On the contrary, the CIA agents never accepted his authority. Sam Halpern, executive assistant of the CIA *Cuba Desk*, and an expert in the field of intelligence, had serious misgivings about Bobby's dynamic approach: 'We thought it was stupid, silly, ineffective, and wasteful. But we were under orders, and we did it.'[959] The fact that no team spirit emerged was primarily Bobby's fault. He made it quite clear that he did not trust the CIA. Without consultation, he constantly took initiatives that were contrary to the house rules. He also had his private favorites in the community of Cuban exiles. These direct contacts were unprofessional, according to the CIA, and were in any case unwise for a serving Attorney General. But Castro was a personal matter for Bobby, and that made him quite unmanageable. Thomas Parott, executive secretary of the Special Group Augmented, summed it up as follows: 'Bob Kennedy was very difficult to deal with. He was arrogant. He knew it all, he knew the answer to everything. He sat there, tie down, chewing gum, his feet on the desk. His threats were transparent. It was, "If you don't do it, I'll tell my big brother on you."'[960] In another typical encounter, a frustrated Bobby Kennedy fired a series of questions at Bill Harvey, which he concluded with: 'And I've got ten minutes to hear the answer.' Harvey exceeded the limit of ten minutes with his response, whereby Kennedy got up without a word and left the meeting. It was typical of the poisoned atmosphere that Harvey imperturbably continued talking to the Attorney General's empty chair.[961] General Charles Johnson listened to another one of Bobby's minute-long harangues against Harvey. 'I was surprised at the vehemence of this thing,' recalls the general. 'It couldn't have been a tirade for just a failure to make Mongoose succeed, I don't think. It seemed to be something beyond that – a failure beyond that.'[962] Subordinates who were not familiar with the contradictions in Bobby's personality didn't know where they were. Was he the moral, principled knight from the Department of Justice who attacked every injustice with a flaming sword, or a ruthless, pragmatic politician who saw no problem with assassinations or bombings? Was he the skilled manager who brought Kennedy's campaign to a successful conclusion, or an arrogant amateur?

Bobby may well have stuck to his guns, but that did not mean he was actually in charge of the clandestine operations. It was unthinkable that the Attorney General should organize murder squads. The new director, McCone, was also not in charge of them, because he didn't know anything about the assassination attempts on Castro, although he bore the ultimate responsibility for these operations.[963] The old boys' network quickly sensed the power vacuum and filled it themselves, as the Kennedys would soon find out. An anonymous CIA source who worked with Harvey and Rosselli on the murder plots of ZR/RIFLE told author Gus Russo that Harvey deliberately sabotaged the plots against Castro. According to this source, Harvey said that the Kennedys 'thought of it as a game.' But, for Bill Harvey, this was no private contest between Kennedy and Castro. 'Bill knew that this was no game. It was serious business. I know that Bill personally stopped the plots in their tracks,' said the anonymous source.[964] A little later, Harvey was 'relieved of his command,' and exiled to the CIA station in Rome. This again raised bad blood among the CIA loyalists. The CIA operatives who wanted to keep things more or less on track in the area of the Cuba case were constantly bombarded with interference and blame. They had a glowing dislike of Bobby Kennedy. Everyone who had been on the side of the CIA in the past shared their dislike of the Kennedys. Even Deputy Director Desmond Fitzgerald of the CIA, who was actually a personal friend of Jack, thought Bobby was a 'young rookie' and an 'amateur' when it came to intelligence matters.[965]

This misguided approach made Kennedy's problem with the CIA even worse than it already was. That was very dangerous, because there was no more room for error. In the meantime, John Kennedy also realized that there had better be no second, similar incident after the Bay of Pigs. Red Fay quoted the president's words about the possibility of a coup in the United States: 'If there was another Bay of Pigs, then the country's reaction would be: "Is he too young and inexperienced?" The military would almost find it their patriotic duty to stand ready to maintain the integrity of the nation and God alone knows which segment of the democracy they would defend if they had to topple the elected system ... Then, if there were a third Bay of Pigs, it could happen that...' But, self-confident as ever, Kennedy added with a smile: 'But that's not going to happen on my watch.'[966] The president was a born optimist, but his rosy assessment shows that he did not realize how counterproductive his attempts to restrict the CIA would turn out in the field.

CIA ROGUES

When it came to the resources to carry out a sinister plan, the CIA was in a unique position. It had people available everywhere in the world and for every task. The CIA recruited both local terrorists and amorous secretaries for its actions. Every station also had a selection of conscientious and competent bureaucrats. Only a very small proportion of all the teams could come into consideration for the really delicate operations, and an even smaller portion were used for subversive operations on domestic soil. The conspiracists refer to that select group as CIA *rogues*. That is very vague and general, but a more specific description of the phenomenon is impossible because of the total clandestine nature of the operation. We can therefore only attempt to sketch a prototype of the CIA villain who could qualify for the conspiracy. The CIA rogue was politically right-wing, and felt himself superior to his environment in the host country but just as much with regard to the sour prunes in Washington. He was cynical and inscrutable, and could easily switch from one to the other role by taking on a new identity, a different appearance, or another job. He could make cold-blooded decisions when necessary. His silent reticence was eternal. Although he perhaps wore a civilian suit and sat behind a desk, he never felt himself to be a bureaucrat, but a man of action. In his own view, he was no less a soldier than the best trained military man. The CIA rogue carried out immoral deeds with a clean conscience because someone simply had to do the dirty work. In his own eyes, whatever he may have done in the field, he was not a criminal or a traitor, at most a nonconformist. This individuality was often a problem. The staff of the Clandestine Operations department was not recruited on the basis of a political exam or a blank criminal record. They were guys like E. Howard Hunt,[967] whose arrogant rashness brought Nixon to ruin in the Watergate scandal a few years later. Many of these incorrigible individualists climbed the ranks of the CIA because, early in the origins of the agency, they had been friends with the men who had afterwards made it to the top of the organization. They had rigid and pessimistic ideas about how the world was, and would continue to be. In their view, the dangerous work they did provided others with the luxury to sweet talk about morality. They took the risks, and knew they would be all alone if anything went wrong. They were the true idealists, who protected their country against dangerous internal and external enemies. These men did not need the revolution of the golden 1960s. Through their own strength, they had become much freer than the long-haired liberation movement could ever make them. The CIA rogue regarded racial integration, beat music, flower power, sexual liberation and counterculture only as a form of degeneration and moral decadence. The Kennedys were naturally a part of that decadence, if they were not actually the cause. For the CIA rogues, the Kennedys were spoiled kids who cheerfully woke up in their silk pajamas at eleven o'clock in the morning with the pleasant prospect of spending the rest of the day pestering the servants who did all the work. It was not the front-line soldiers of the CIA who had betrayed the country, but the Kennedys. It was this conviction that meant these rogues could be used to take part in the very exceptional mission in the autumn of 1963. They were professionals who were willing to perform certain duties in the interest of the country, based on strongly segregated information. The only condition to execute any given order was blind faith in the direct line of command. If that trust was there, they never asked about the reason for an assignment. They had only contempt for Bobby Kennedy, but blindly trusted men like David Atlee Phillips.

When it came to the use of these rogues, Phillips was at the source. The cauldron of the Cuba operations teemed with anti-Kennedy villains. Phillips could select and control, take the initiative and whistle back to his heart's content. He knew exactly how he could divide up shameful and harmful plans in small, digestible pieces. He could complete an action without any outsider realizing the final end purpose of the parts, and without leaving behind any traces of the true operation. We mention Phillips because we met him in the wake of Oswald. But he is not the only one who qualifies as the architect for the operation. There are other candidates such as David Morales, who collaborated closely with Phillips. In 1954, Morales helped to remove Jacobo Arbenz in Guatemala because he wanted to implement a land reform that was not to the liking of the United Fruit Company. Allen Dulles was a shareholder in UFC and his brother had been their lawyer for some time.[968] In 1961, Morales was promoted to Head of Clandestine Operations at the Miami station. His mission was to train Cuban exiles, fill their hands full of money and to support infiltration and sabotage actions in Cuba. Morales knew what he was talking about when he described his colleagues at the CIA: 'They are the most ruthless motherfuckers there is and if they want to get somebody, they will. They will do their own people up.'[969] Morales was also assigned to the ZR/RIFLE operation and was thus directly involved in the ongoing, disruptive interventions of Bobby Kennedy.

Whoever the CIA experts were who knew the scenarios, one thing was sure: freedom from prosecution. The improper approach of the Kennedys actually had one big advantage: any investigation into the background of the events in 1962 and 1963 would be sabotaged from above. With every blunder of Bobby Kennedy in regard to the prevailing rules of intelligence work, the impunity of the future conspirators increased. The errors of Bobby could only stay under the mat if all other events were also covered up. The creators of the plan were experts in the manipulation of information. They understood that it was sufficient to link their action to the Cuba file in one way or another in order to be sure that the matter would never be investigated down to the bones. The Kennedys had hatched crazy assassination plots with the Mafia ... the potential harm to the prestige of the presidency were enormous. The conspirators knew that it sufficed to sidetrack from their plot to the Cuba fiasco to ensure that even the Kennedys themselves would agree that it was better to keep the whole affair under wraps until the end of times. Documents would disappear and, if necessary, an epidemic of heart attacks and suicides would break out among the witnesses, but the case would never become public. Whoever was the president, he would be guaranteed to sit on the lid of the cover-up with his full weight. And, if it was really necessary, the CIA would quickly undertake 'executive action,' solely in the interest of the nation, of course.

Chapter 23 – The missile crisis

Kennedy tackled the problems that arose from the Bay of Pigs failure one by one. The CIA ended up in the sin bin, and the pressure on Castro was substantially increased. The Cuban exiles were intensively sponsored, and the prisoners who had been bought free after the Bay of Pigs operation heard Kennedy promise that he would hand over the flag of the Bay of Pigs brigade to their commander again in a free Cuba.

The third and biggest problem, which would bring the world to the brink of destruction, was the Kremlin. Moscow had followed Kennedy's first international steps with Argus eyes. It was to be expected that they would confuse Kennedy's military restraint in the Bay of Pigs incident with a lack of decisiveness and courage. Because the Russians only showed respect for political and military brutality, they considered the time ripe for a game of geopolitical bluff. This was completely in line with the personality of Soviet leader Khrushchev. Nixon, himself a poker enthusiast, was convinced that Khrushchev would have been an excellent poker player. First, he is out to win. Second, he plans in advance, like any good poker player, so he can win the big amounts. And above all: 'he loves to bluff.'[970] If the decadent Western democracy was foolish enough to put a weakling in the White House, the Russians felt they owed it to themselves to exploit the opportunity as much as possible. At that level, Kennedy's top military commanders had correctly judged the reaction of Russia. Like an animal tamer who steps into a lion cage, you cannot allow yourself any hesitation, because a predator never lets an opportunity pass. The apparent sign of uncertainty that Kennedy had shown was perilous in a strategy of mutual deterrence. Historian Thomas G. Patterson therefore places a large part of the responsibility for the missile crisis on Kennedy himself.[971]

The president reaped what he had sown in mid-October 1962, when he was shown photos of a Russian launch pad complete with nuclear missiles only one hundred miles from the coast of Florida. The generals had warned Kennedy previously, and assumed that Kennedy had now learned his lesson about how you had to keep Russian imperialism under control. The strategic error made at the Bay of Pigs must not be repeated, argued the army top brass. The crisis with the missiles in Cuba was an ultimate test, and offered a final chance to prove to the Russians that they should not be under any illusions. Even Kennedy would now realize that he had to give the army commanders the order to properly carry out their duty. A serious crisis is always an opportunity to push through an agenda, and the hardliners saw the incident as a perfect opportunity to attack Cuba. The generals considered that Kennedy had deprived himself of all freedom of movement because of his half-hearted response in 1961. He had only one option: to grant the wishes of the high command and to strike hard. An air of optimistic tension and restrained euphoria prevailed in the Pentagon. The US forces had a temporary but undeniable superiority. Military force was inevitably restrained in peacetime, like a dog on a chain. But the Russians had been foolish enough to provoke the Americans, and had given them a perfect opportunity. They had challenged the US, and the army would finally have a free hand to teach them a lesson.

But to their great amazement, the generals were mistaken in their president, who refused to start a war of aggression. He wrongfully bypassed all the official channels, and sent his cocky, inexperienced little brother to negotiate with the Russian dyed-in-the-wool professional diplomats. After thirteen sleepless nights, the crisis was supposedly averted by diplomatic means. But the golden opportunity to attack was in jeopardy, and the generals feared that the Russians would once again strengthen their condescending opinion about the indecisiveness of Kennedy. It would only inspire the enemy to initiate new efforts to see how far they could go with the pacifist in the White House. To make matters worse, and in order to achieve that dubious outcome, Kennedy had promised that the US would never invade Cuba. There was even a deal involving the American nuclear warheads in Turkey. In the eyes of many in the military, this was treason. But the frivolous playboy knew very well how to sell his ignominious defeat and desertion as the ultimate victory. Incited by the leftist press, the voters swallowed it like hot cake. The man in the street was relieved that no nuclear war had broken out thanks to the 'statesmanship' of Kennedy. The president didn't add, of course, that it had all gotten out of hand due to his own cowardice at the Bay of Pigs. Instead, he misrepresented the valiant efforts of the army to defend the country's interests and honor, and presented it as if the dangerous lunatics were not in the Kremlin, but in his own Pentagon. Castro had allowed the Russians to point a loaded pistol at the head of the USA. But according to the Kennedys, it was not Castro who brought the world to the brink of war; the culprit was the US military command. General Curtis LeMay almost swallowed his inseparable cigar stub in indignation.

The extreme challenge brought out the best in Kennedy. He was very well-read, with a preference for history[972] and the biographies of great predecessors, and had traveled extensively. JFK had a sincere and broad interest in what concerned ordinary people, sometimes down to the voyeuristic level. TV journalist Lisa Howard used her natural charms to persuade Castro to give an exclusive interview. When Jack Kennedy spoke to her about that meeting, he wanted to know every detail. The fact that Fidel did not even remove his boots when making love fascinated the president. 'Jack liked details like that,'[973] wrote Gore Vidal. But his interest went beyond the salacious. Unlike his military command, he intuitively felt the changing times, and had a talent for geopolitics. The range of the weapon determines the size of the arena, argued Kennedy. In 1963, the arena had grown to an intercontinental scale. It was not only a matter of Cuba. If the Americans invaded Havana, the Russians would occupy Berlin, and a global conflict was inevitable. The excessive cost of participation in the nuclear arms race also limited the number of participants. The very nature of nuclear weaponry led to two spheres of influence that divided the world, and therefore everything hung together. Regarding Cuba as an isolated conflict was rubbish according to Kennedy. The inability of the generals to understand this connection during the Cuban missile crisis was a dangerous form of tunnel vision. Like a crazed Dr. Strangelove, LeMay openly advocated a nuclear war of aggression. He was not the only one who believed in the possibility of a winnable nuclear war. In 1961, General Lemnitzer, as Chairman of the Joint Chiefs of Staff, has informed Kennedy that 'a surprise attack in late 1963 preceded by a period of heightened tensions' was the best scenario for a nuclear attack on Russia'[974] A committee of military men, the *Net Evaluation Subcommittee*,[975] even regularly calculated the losses that would occur on both sides in the case of a nuclear confrontation. Dulles had also pointed out to Kennedy that 1963 would be the best time for a nuclear attack. According to him, the USA would have the most favorable 'window of superiority' at that time. And now, according to LeMay, this period of increased tension, and an optimal window of superiority, had arrived. The Americans briefly had a large superiority in the number of intercontinental missiles. The USA didn't need more missiles – you could only bomb Russia flat once. But each additional Soviet bomb would make that gap smaller, until the USSR could also guarantee the total destruction of the enemy. It would then be too late to win the nuclear confrontation.

There were also more acceptable arguments for proceeding with military action. Men in uniform are not generally in favor of war, and even less of the use of nuclear weapons. That is exactly why they considered the immediate destruction of the missiles on Cuban territory mandatory and urgent. Taking action against this intolerable aggression was a hard decision, but was nevertheless necessary in their eyes. Kennedy, however, took a wider view. It was not the nuclear weapons in Cuba that were his main concern, it was the existence of nuclear weaponry itself that had become the issue. This nuclear madness would eventually and inevitably lead to self-destruction. Kennedy understood that one misunderstanding could be enough to have a crazed madman press the launch button in one of the two camps. A mere technical error could destroy the whole world in 1963. Kennedy gradually saw the Soviet Union more as an ideological enemy, and no longer as a military one. The Soviets did not want to invade or destroy the territory of the USA. They only wanted to stabilize the existing power balance, and Kennedy was willing to start a conversation about the terms of such a mutual containment. The solution to the missile crisis lay in this new context. If the intention was to maintain the balance, both parties could just as well take a step back, the president believed. Taking away the threat of the invasion of Cuba therefore offered the solution to the Cuban puzzle. Kennedy was always carefully to ensure that he saved Khrushchev a loss of face wherever possible. The removal of obsolete US missiles in Turkey was just a sham maneuver to give Khrushchev a victory for domestic use. This mindset also helped to defuse conflicts. While the army leadership believed that greater permissiveness increased the problem, Kennedy understood that threat reduction offered an equivalent outcome from the standpoint of the balance of power. The Politburo in Russia also understood this, and a global catastrophe was thereby averted. We have only Kennedy's cool-headed approach to thank for the very existence of our contemporary environment. In the years following the missile crisis, it became clear that the information from the CIA and military intelligence was again totally wrong. The Soviets had 40,000 soldiers stationed in Cuba, a multiple of the US estimates in 1962. But, in addition, strategic nuclear weapons were already operational in Cuba at the time of the missile crisis in 1962. Here also, the Americans were not fully informed. An invasion would have thereby turned into an unmitigated disaster, and would have brought about a direct confrontation with Russian troops. If the army command had had its way, the unfortunate survivors of the nuclear conflict would have found themselves in a nuclear wasteland.

But such practical considerations were wasted on the army command. At the highpoint of the missile crisis, LeMay formulated it in his barbaric style as follows: 'The Russian Bear has always been eager to stick his paw in Latin American waters. Now [that] we've got him in a trap, let's take his legs off right up to his testicles. On second thought, let's take off his testicles too …'[976] In his book *Eyeball to Eyeball*, Dino Brugioni described LeMay's attitude as 'petulant and childish' and that he 'was characterized by one observer as always interjecting himself into situations "like a rogue elephant barging out of the forest."' Defense Secretary McNamara testified that LeMay was 'extraordinary belligerent and even brutal,' even towards his subordinates – how would he then have behaved in front of his enemies?[977] LeMay also did not shrink from reprimanding Kennedy about the Cuba crisis during a meeting in the Oval Office: 'And you … have made some pretty strong statements … that we would take action against offensive weapons. I think that a blockade and political talk would be considered by a lot of our friends and neutrals as being a pretty weak response to this. And I'm sure a lot of our own citizens would feel that way, too. In other words you're in a pretty bad fix at the present time.' The general casually insulted the president once more by suggesting that he would be prepared to risk a nuclear war just to avoid a political loss of face. Kennedy did not believe what he was hearing at first, but when LeMay once again repeated that he was really in trouble, the president kept a cool head and replied: 'You're in there with me.'[978] He left the meeting a few moments later in order to adhere strictly to his agenda, so that the outside world, and especially the Russians, would not realize that there was a serious crisis in the air. The generals did not know that Kennedy recorded all his conversations in his office.[979] These recordings revealed that LeMay was not alone. After Kennedy had left, General Shoup said to LeMay: 'You pulled the rug right out from under him Goddamn.' LeMay chuckled, and Shoup continued: 'I just agree with that answer. General, I just agree with you a hundred per cent.'[980] But history proved Kennedy to be right. There were indeed operational nuclear warheads in Cuba, and many more Russian soldiers than the CIA suspected. The generals could not even ensure Kennedy that they could eliminate all the known nuclear warheads with a lightning air strike. In 1991, officers of the Red Army who were stationed in Cuba in 1962 unanimously confirmed that the atomic bombs would have been launched in the event of an American attack.[981] Historians agree that the invasion of Cuba that the army leadership proposed as an alternative to the blockade would have led to a devastating escalation worldwide. It also became clear later that the American victory scenario would have plunged half the planet into a nuclear winter.

After two years in the White House, Kennedy had been through quite a lot. When asked by a journalist what he had learned, he replied: 'In the first place, the problems are more difficult than I had imagined and secondly there is a limitation on the ability of the United States to solve these problems.'[982] Kennedy was a more realistic, determined and experienced president as he began the second half of his term. He had acquired the taste for it, and was determined to vigorously lead America and the world in accordance with his convictions.

THE AFTERMATH OF THE MISSILE CRISIS

LeMay was an extreme exponent of the prevailing mentality, but the less verbally aggressive star-generals also shared his opinion. In their eyes, it was the mission of the USA to save the world from a red dictatorship. Communism openly aspired to world domination, and any sign of weakness would encourage the Russians to go one step further. After World War II, the Americans had seen how their Russian ally had degenerated into an imperialist dictatorship in no time at all. Sweet talkers like Kennedy were dangerous in their naivety. The diplomatic solution to the missile crisis that Kennedy was finally able to achieve thereby did not in the least convince the military leadership that he was right. Yet Kennedy proved once again that he had the right attitude as Commander in Chief. After the crisis, he called the generals together to congratulate them. Kennedy shared the success that he actually did not have to thank them for in any way at all, and said 'Gentlemen, we've won.' But he also warned them that it would not be wise to rub the Russians' nose in the defeat again: 'I don't want you to ever say it, but you know we've won and I know we've won.' But Admiral Anderson disagreed with this: 'We've been had!' LeMay naturally did not want to be upstaged, and banged his fist on the table: 'Won? Hell! We lost! We should go in and wipe them out today!' LeMay actually called the missile crisis 'the greatest defeat in our history' and once again urged them to carry out an invasion on the very same day.[983] McNamara testified that Kennedy was so shocked by the attitude of LeMay that he even stuttered in his reply. Defense analyst Daniel Ellsberg was stunned at the anger within the military after the missile crisis: 'There was virtually a coup atmosphere in Pentagon circles. Not that I had the fear there was about to be a coup – I just thought it was a mood of hatred and rage. The atmosphere was poisonous, poisonous.'[984]

Ted Dealey, the publisher of the *Dallas Morning News* newspaper, and the man whose father had Dealey Plaza named after him, has also dared to let off steam against the president in 1961 during a lunch at the White House: 'You and your administration are weak sisters ... We can annihilate Russia and should make that clear to the Soviet Government.' He added that America needed 'a man on a horseback' to lead the country, and that 'many people in Texas and the Southwest think that you are riding Caroline's tricycle.'[985] It is inconceivable that someone should say something like that to a president in the White House, but clearly shows how bad the atmosphere already was before the missile crisis erupted, and how some of the real people with power did not recognize Kennedy as president, and considered themselves miles above him. Things did not get better afterwards. The army leadership remained convinced that the president had not got it right. Admiral Anderson of the navy, who had also taken part in the crisis meeting in the Oval Office, still gave a stunning example of hardheadedness, and did not conceal his disappointment in 1981 in an interview for the US *Naval Institute*. 'It could have been rather bloody, but I would say with a relatively low degree of casualties on the part of American forces. I think the Cuban people would have immediately rallied to our support and I think we could have installed a good government in Cuba.'[986] Kennedy knew what this admiral thought about it at the time. After the missile crisis, he was wisely kicked upstairs as the ambassador to Portugal. What Anderson understood as a 'good government' for Cuba was shown by his later views on the Portuguese dictator Salazar, with whom he became good friends: 'an extremely polite, decent quiet man.'

Unlike his generals, Kennedy had indeed learned something. 'The military are mad,' he said bluntly to his assistant, historian Schlesinger[987] from Harvard. For him, a war for Cuba was no longer negotiable. The population apparently supported him, because the missile crisis caused his popularity to soar. But there was a small minority who would never forgive him. Those who wanted to turn back the clock to the time of Batista foamed at the mouth from rage. Thousands of exiles dreamed of the good old days in Havana, a triumphant return and installing a suitable strong leader on the island. Kennedy's policy of cowardice and lies made them furious. Those Americans with a rabid anti-communist ideology were also ready to drink Kennedy's blood. And then, of course, there was the Mafia, which wanted to see the roulette wheels turning again in their hotels that had been confiscated by Castro, the army commanders who imagined themselves to be superior, and the arms manufacturers who saw their ambitious business plans threatened.

Kennedy had made a U-turn in his solution of the missile crisis. The CIA had to be restrained even more rigidly from now on. Its infiltration and secret war, its assassination plans and the whole Operation Mongoose suddenly had to be placed on the back burner. The CIA, once almighty on the terrain, all of a sudden could not fulfill the promises and commitments it had made to its shadowy partners in clandestine operations. The CIA adventurers had been peddling suitcases full of dollars and wild dreams of a triumphant entry into Havana for many years. They had taken on an air of importance and the power of decision, but they were now ignominiously rebuffed. Everyone who was involved in the Cuba operations was angry, not the least because the Kennedys had largely started Operation Mongoose themselves, and now – once again – had deserted in the heat of battle. The missile crisis thereby caused much grinding of teeth. It was the second incident in a series of three that could lead to a coup.

The Mafiosi were perhaps the least annoyed by the Cuba issue. Cuban profits had been so high that even in case of loss of the assets, they had already recouped all their Cuban investments several times over. The Mafia had also survived the end of Prohibition. Las Vegas was the new gambling Eldorado, and the big illegal money was now being earned in drug dealing. The former street rascals were now elderly millionaires. Cuba would have been nice, but organized crime has to constantly reinvent itself. That process was in full swing. It was no longer Cuba that caused the Mafia bosses to lose sleep, but Bobby Kennedy, and the personal humiliations he made them swallow. It was above all the latter fact that made them hate Kennedy. Father Joe had personally assured them that the anti-Mafia rhetoric from Bobby was only pretense for the public, and that things actually wouldn't be too bad with Jack in the

White House. Frank Sinatra passed on the same message. The Mafia grumbled, but took a safe rather than sorry attitude, and gambled on both Nixon and Kennedy. Cuba was thereby never mentioned. The agreement was that the prosecution of the Mafia would be limited, as usual, and would not really hurt them. The Mafia had supported Kennedy's campaign financially, and had provided crucial votes in Chicago. Perhaps even more important was that the Mafia had not hampered Kennedy, which they certainly could have done. In their eyes, JFK had made a contract, and had now broken it unilaterally. This was something the Mafia simply couldn't allow.

In Cuba, Castro had no real reason to want Kennedy dead. The Great Leader knew he was very lucky to still be alive and in power. The incidents surrounding the Bay of Pigs and the Russian missiles had caused Kennedy to officially renounce any invasion of Cuba. That was also good news. The bad news was that the Russians had unilaterally decided to withdraw the nuclear weapons. This was against the wishes of Castro, and had even taken place without consulting him. If he still was only a vassal and not a full comrade, Cuba might just as well decide on a more independent course. Castro now only half trusted the Russians, and, at the same time, he seemed ready to also partly trust Kennedy – you can never trust Americans all the way. In addition, nobody knew whether Kennedy could curb the military and imperialist elements in his environment. The Kennedy era was perhaps only a breather. In South America, a political puppet who thwarted the plans of his own army would not survive long. But the Americans never knew whether they wanted to use their imperial power for good or evil, and Kennedy seemed to be leaning towards the right side. Maybe he was not such a bad guy, and it could be possible to live side by side as peaceful neighbors. It was a toss-up, but everything still went well for Castro for now.

If one of the two heads of state had to worry about his political survival, then it was Kennedy. His first term was half over. By downplaying the dangers of the Cold War, he showed the reactionary populists in his own country his vulnerable side, where they could kill him politically. But he got a kick out of doing the very thing that everyone said he had to put out of his head. He was addicted to risk and to the implementation of his plans.

Chapter 24 – The road to Dallas

A POLITICAL TESTAMENT

The missile crisis was the turning point in Kennedy's presidency. Kennedy realized that he alone had taken the decisive action. He had found a moral conviction, a fight that he could fully identify with, and against formidable opponents. As a true Kennedy, this gave him a taste for more. He was also chastened, and had matured as a result of the confrontations, but was certainly also strengthened in his belief that his fellow Americans would support him in his approach. That was not obvious. The domestic Cold War rhetoric was still a political factor that was not to be underestimated. The Kennedys knew this better than anyone, because the brothers had both used this tactic to advance their political rise. Taking a sufficiently tough attitude against the Communists in order to keep the national security issue out of the hands of the Republicans, while giving detente a chance at the same time, was no simple balancing act. A delicate pas de deux was therefore required on the political stage. Did Kennedy have enough political talent to convey his complex and paradoxical message to the general public? That was not evident.

The domino theory was still a dogma in American political and military circles in 1963. This soon became clear after Kennedy's assassination. Johnson could picture it quite clearly: 'I knew that if the aggression succeeded in Vietnam, then the aggressors would simply keep on going until all of Southeast Asia fell into their hands ... at least down to Singapore and almost certainly Djakarta ... and soon we'd be fighting in Berlin or elsewhere. And so would begin World War III.'[988] When Kennedy cautiously tested the limits of the domino theory, he was still a pioneer in unknown territory. But he was sure of what he was doing, because the Cuba crisis had opened his eyes. In his opinion, it was possible to talk to the Russians. Soviet Foreign Minister Kosygin had sent out tentative diplomatic signs for a possible rapprochement. As the risk of nuclear war still remained, JFK felt that the USA should not take this opportunity for rapprochement lightly. He calmly prepared the visionary speech he was to hold on June 10, 1963, at the *Commencement*, the promotion and graduation ceremony of the American University in Washington. Kennedy spoke about the Russians as fellow human beings, fellow inhabitants of a small planet. This language was unheard of in the Cold War. It was far more politically comfortable to demonize the enemy, and to exalt the American superiority and way of life. Kennedy did the opposite. He asked the Americans to look at their own shortcomings and to recognize the good qualities of the opponent: 'Every graduate of this school, every thoughtful citizen who despairs of war and wishes to bring peace, should begin by looking inward – by examining his own attitude toward the possibilities of peace, toward the Soviet Union, toward the course of the Cold War and toward the freedom and peace here at home.' The inspiring end of his speech has lost none of its power, more than half a century later: 'We all inhabit this small planet. We all breathe the same air. We all cherish our children's future. And we are all mortal.' Kennedy meant what he said. He had finally found his authentic political voice, and knew that he had a unique opportunity to have a positive effect on the history of the world. His Secretary of Defense Bob McNamara said in 2007: 'The American University speech laid out exactly what Kennedy's intentions were. If he had lived, the world would have been different. I feel quite confident of that. Whether we would have had détente sooner, I'm not sure. But it would have been a less dangerous world.'[989] The *Commencement Speech* of June 10, 1963, was the indisputable highlight of Kennedy's presidency. His public call for world peace became his main political legacy, but it was probably also one of the reasons for the death sentence that was pronounced on him shortly afterwards.

A HELL OF A HORSE TRADER

At the end of his speech, Kennedy announced that he had unilaterally suspended all nuclear tests in the atmosphere, provided other nations followed his example. The result of that unexpected offer was spectacular: one month later, Kennedy was able to put his signature on a limited nuclear test ban treaty with the Russians that curbed nuclear testing in the atmosphere, under water and in space. But the Senate still had to ratify the treaty before it would become valid. A fierce counter-campaign therefore started at the Pentagon, with the financial backing of the arms producers, who made clever use of fervent, flag-waving patriots to influence public opinion. The military commanders even ventured to the brink of mutiny. When Kennedy asked if it was possible to identify Russian nuclear underground tests with certainty, the army command did not want the president to know the answer to that question, and kept the seismologist who could have provided the answer hidden from him.[990] The CIA also put up a good show. They dispatched their nuclear experts to the senators to convince them that the Russians could not be trusted. Dean Rusk, Kennedy's Secretary of State, urged the president to seek the advice of the most powerful senators, but Kennedy had another plan. On July 26, he addressed the nation live on television: 'I speak tonight to you in a spirit of hope. Eighteen years ago the advent of nuclear weapons changed the course of the world as well as the war. Since that time, all mankind has been struggling to escape from the darkening prospect of mass destruction on earth. [...] Each increase of tension has produced an increase of arms; each increase of arms has produced an increase of tension.' Kennedy stressed that the treaty did not solve all the problems, and that there was no guarantee that the agreements would be respected, but that it was a first step in the right direction. The only alternative was a further increase in the risk that the unthinkable might happen: an accidental nuclear war. At the end of this address, he placed his masterstroke on the political chessboard: 'This limited test ban, in our most careful judgment, is safer by far for the United States than an unlimited nuclear arms race. For all these reasons, I am hopeful that this nation will promptly approve the limited test ban treaty.'[991]

The president had considerably increased the stakes. After this emotional appeal, the congressmen who were intent on bringing the nuclear test ban down would have to come up with some very good arguments. If the treaty was not ratified, however, Kennedy's loss of face would be nothing less than dramatic after this very personal speech. The president had openly admitted that he would do anything to have the treaty approved – a signal that was also not lost on the Russians. He mobilized activists from the peace movement, scientists, religious leaders, civil society groups, movie stars, and anybody he could involve in order to win the favor of public opinion. The military leadership resisted with all available means. At a meeting in the White House on August 7, Kennedy told some members of the citizens' committees that the generals did not want to have any restrictions whatsoever on their nuclear toys. Some generals 'believed the only solution for any crisis situation was to start dropping the big bombs.' If he then asked them how bombing would solve the problem, the military heads were suddenly 'far less confident or articulate.'[992] The disagreement between the president and the military leadership was an open secret. But by openly referring to it in front of members of the citizens' committees, Kennedy committed a dangerous form of insubordination. A commander in chief cannot dissociate himself from his generals with impunity. The struggle with the military lobby about what was no more than an initial and small step on a very long road towards arms reduction was difficult, but Kennedy threw his entire political weight into the balance. He stated openly that he would be 'happy' to sacrifice his re-election for this treaty. When a president is actually prepared to give up everything for a single political purpose, he has a very good chance of getting what he wants. But, beforehand, Kennedy still had another extra trump card up his sleeve. Former President Eisenhower was scornful about the treaty, and asked in public whether the word 'victory' had now been deleted from Kennedy's New Frontier politics[993]. Eisenhower was indebted to Kennedy, however. One of his former loyal members of staff was on the verge of federal prosecution, and Bobby dealt with the file strictly. Eisenhower contacted Kennedy. It would mean a lot to him if the prosecution could disappear. Of course, Ike assured, it was a round-trip ticket. If Kennedy needed his predecessor in some delicate matter, he would be willing to return the service. This was equivalent to promising Kennedy a blank check if he would do the favor. Bobby didn't want to hear about it, but Jack was a pragmatist, and suspected that Eisenhower had a code of honor that would oblige him to respect his promises. The court file of his staff member therefore ended up in the shredder. And now, in the heat of the battle over the nuclear test ban treaty, Kennedy decided to cash in his blank check. He asked Eisenhower for a big favor: a public statement to the effect that his criticism of the treaty had been misquoted, and that he was actually a supporter of the treaty. Senator Everett Dirksen, the Republican Minority Leader, was asked to convey the message to Eisenhower. 'Mr. President, you're a hell of a horse trader,' said the senator when he heard what Kennedy was asking of his elderly predecessor. But Eisenhower fulfilled his promise, and his word on military matters was the gold standard in public opinion. Kennedy won the battle on September 24, 1963. When he signed the treaty, the president took an extra pen, added a flourish to his signature and then put the pen into his breast pocket. 'This one is mine!' he smiled.

In all the political turmoil surrounding the limited test ban treaty, John Kennedy also had a personal loss to deal with. According to his close friends, this loss had a considerable influence on the final political choices of the president. His wife Jackie, gave birth to a boy of barely 4 pounds 10 ounces (2.1 kg) on August 7, 1963, five weeks premature. Kennedy immediately suspended his activities and flew to the hospital. It didn't look good for the baby. He was given the name Patrick, and was christened as soon as possible. Shortly after his birth, the baby was sped to a specialized children's hospital in Boston. JFK, who had looked death in the eye more than once himself, stayed with his courageous fighting little boy. The baby was put in a steel hyperbaric chamber in the hope that he would live through the first difficult days. But, at 2 o'clock in the morning of August 9, when the doctors realized that the baby was not going to make it, they allowed the president to be near his little son. Patrick Kennedy died two hours later, his tiny fingers in the hand of his great father.

VIETNAM

Kennedy did not remain idle after the signing of the Limited Test Ban Treaty. Fewer than three weeks later, on October 11, he signed NSAM263, the *National Security Memorandum* ordering the withdrawal of the first thousand soldiers from Vietnam. Kennedy considered it to be the first responsibility of any president 'to keep the nation out of war if at all possible.' But in the case of Vietnam, his conviction was even stronger. He had always known that he didn't want to fight a war in the Vietnamese jungle. French President Charles de Gaulle had warned him against it. Indochina was a bottomless military quagmire.[994] As a young congressman, Kennedy had been in Indochina in 1951, together with his brother. 'We were there! ... We saw what happened to the French.'[995] was how Bobby gave an explanation for the fact that his brother was vehemently against sending ground troops to Vietnam. In 1954, Senator John Kennedy also warned President Eisenhower: 'No amount of American military assistance in Indochina can conquer an enemy which is everywhere and at the same time nowhere...'[996] Once he was in the White House himself, Kennedy immediately made it clear that he considered a ground war in Southeast Asia to be nonsense. In the spring of 1961, the military asked for 3,600 combat troops to support President Diem in Vietnam. Kennedy gave them five hundred advisers.[997] After a visit on site, Vice President Johnson advised sending more troops, and General Taylor also urged him to do so. But Kennedy was more inclined to listen to the counsel of General McArthur, who had once led troops into battle in Korea. He was on the same wavelength as Kennedy: 'Anyone who advocated putting American ground troops in Asia should have his head examined.' In November 1961, in front of the president, George Ball predicted that there would be 300,000 Americans stationed in Vietnam within five years. Kennedy found the idea preposterous: 'George, you're just crazier than hell. That just isn't going to happen.'[998] Kennedy never believed that America had anything to gain in Vietnam at a military level. The concrete decisions in the fall of 1963 were a logical consequence of this. The time was right to reduce the American military presence in Vietnam, while the issue was still manageable in all respects. 'It was a minor blip on the administration's screen. Vietnam was not central to the foreign policy of the Kennedy Presidency. Berlin was, Cuba, and the Soviet Union – but not Vietnam. Vietnam was a low-level insurrection at that point,' said Ted Sorensen, Kennedy's speech writer, about this in March 2006. Kennedy therefore had some room for maneuvering. But the proponents of an escalation did not give in. The participants of no less than three fact-finding inspection missions returned from Southeast Asia in 1963 with the recommendation to send in more troops. According to Sorensen, the president did not yield: 'JFK listened to the hawkish advisors, but he never did what they wanted.'[999] Once again, he was on his own in his decision not to dispatch troops. General Taylor recalled that no one was opposed to sending in more troops 'except one man, and that was the President.'[1000] The president imposed his own way, going against all others. In this context, he liked to tell an anecdote about Abraham Lincoln and his cabinet: 'He says: "All in favor say "Aye" and the whole cabinet voted Aye, and then "all opposed no" and Lincoln voted No, and he said 'the vote is 'no."'[1001] But going against everybody turned out to be a double-edged sword. Because the opposition was unanimously against the decision of the president, they could easily sabotage or ignore his instructions afterwards. Three times, Kennedy urged his ambassador to South Vietnam, Henry Cabot Lodge, to start talks with President Diem again. Lodge ignored these orders, fully aware that, by shunning Diem, he was signaling to the Vietnamese military command that a coup might not be unwelcome for the Americans. The biggest problem was not the Pentagon, however, but the CIA, who controlled the situation on the spot. William Colby, the head of the CIA station in Saigon, stated: '[by early 1962] the station had contacts and influence throughout Vietnam, from the front to the rear doors of the Palace, to the rural communities, among the civilian opponents of the regime and the commanders of all military units.'[1002] That was even more true eighteen months later. The CIA left it in no doubt that they alone were in charge. One of its front organizations was the *Agency for International Development*, which controlled the money flow for development aid. The CIA turned off this money supply of their own accord,[1003] well aware that the discontent among the population would increase if the humanitarian aid dried up. Moreover, it was a signal to the military that the Americans were abandoning Diem. This unilateral initiative of the CIA thwarted Kennedy's attempt to keep the dialogue with the regime open. The hawks deliberately set out to cause an escalation of the problems in Vietnam, and it was the CIA, not Kennedy, who controlled the situation locally.

In the meantime, Kennedy was working on the idea of a complete withdrawal of American troops from Vietnam by 1965. Kennedy assumed that he would be able to conclude an agreement with Russia about a reunified Vietnam. The other international cards were also somewhat more favorable than they appeared to be at first sight. The Chinese had more than enough headaches already with their Cultural Revolution and the border disputes with India. A neutral Vietnam was perhaps not a bad idea for them either. Moreover, the North Vietnamese would certainly prefer a guaranteed independence rather than Chinese intervention, from which they had been trying to get away for a thousand years. Besides, were the Vietnamese not nationalists in the first place like everyone else, and only then communists? What was so valuable about having a pro-Western government in South Vietnam that American taxpayers and soldiers had to defend it? Moreover, the South Vietnamese civilians, for whom the Americans were actually fighting, were helping the enemy as much as they could. They apparently disliked Americans even more than communists. Finally, there was the question of how the Americans could hope to win far away from home against a guerrilla army, something in which a conventional army had never succeeded. A war was anticipated to be long, expensive and dirty, and, even though many Americans disapproved of the withdrawal of forces at the time, they always turned against a war sooner or later once it had started. In 1963, an expensive war still meant that taxes had to be raised and/or domestic programs had to be cut. The United States could provide economic aid to a reunified Vietnam for a fraction of the cost of a ground war. That would increase the reputation and prestige of the US, and provide other communist satellite states with food for thought, and encourage them to open talks. Kennedy preferred all that instead of a war. His decision about the withdrawal of American troops from Vietnam was therefore final, but he was waiting for the right moment to translate it into political and military decisions.

On September 2, a relaxed Kennedy gave an exclusive interview to Walter Cronkite. He first gave the South Vietnamese government a shot across the bows: 'In the final analysis, it is their war. They are the ones who have to win or lose it. We can help them, we can give them equipment, we can send our men out there as advisers, but they have to win it, the people of Vietnam, against the communists.'[1004] Kennedy put the Vietnamese in charge of their victory, but did not yet openly talk of withdrawal. On the contrary, he said the following in an interview for NBC on September 9: 'I think we should stay. We should use our influence in as effective way as we can, but we should not withdraw.'[1005] The reason for this was that, immediately after this interview, Kennedy had a meeting with Senator Henry 'Scoop' Jackson, a pronounced hawk. At that moment, Kennedy was still frantically searching for a majority for the ratification of the Limited Test Ban Treaty. He therefore didn't want to upset Scoop. Ken O'Donnell, a member of staff and friend of the president, also wondered how they could limit the political damage that the withdrawal could cause. Pragmatic as ever, the president replied: 'Easy. Put a government in that will ask us to leave.'[1006] But it was not as easy as that, and Kennedy was well aware of it. 'It haunts me day and night,'[1007] he said to his neighbor in Hyannis Port on October 20, 1963.

Kennedy, once again, asserted his will. The decision to recall one thousand American troops from Vietnam before the end of 1963 was made at the cabinet meeting of October 2. The military advisors strongly opposed the decision, and even more the fact that it would be made public, but Kennedy was adamant. The decision was not only a risk from a military perspective: the situation was also very delicate politically. Speaking to columnist Bartlett, the president summed up the dilemma between wisdom and electoral reality as follows: 'Those people hate us. They are going to throw our tails out of there at almost any point. But I can't give up a piece of territory like that to the communists and then get the American people to reelect me.' The Kennedy administration therefore presented the withdrawal as a proposal from Secretary of Defense McNamara. On October 5, Kennedy approved this 'recommendation' of McNamara, and it was communicated to Ambassador Lodge in Saigon[1008] by State Department Telegram No. 534. The document stressed that the US should focus its efforts on the social, economic and political strengthening of the regime. The improvement of the living conditions of the Vietnamese would strengthen the regime and turn the population away from their inclination to convert to communism. The instructions for the ambassador referred, for example, to fertilizers for the farmers in the Mekong Delta and boats for the fishermen – that would undoubtedly have made more friends for the Americans than Johnson's later choice of pouring tons of poisonous Agent Orange over the country. The cabinet decision of October 2 regarding the initial withdrawal was recorded as official policy line NSAM 263 *(National Security Action Memorandum)*.

Maybe this decision on Vietnam was the third and decisive factor, because Kennedy was assassinated before he could effectively implement the planned withdrawal, which was very limited. But significant from a symbolic point of view.

CUBELA OR ATTWOOD

Vietnam was a relatively simple decision, at least for Kennedy. From the start of his presidency, he didn't believe in the benefit and the feasibility of a war in Southeast Asia. The fact that there were more than 16,000 American troops in Vietnam was for strategic reasons. From the perspective of the Cold War, the US had no choice: South Vietnam should not fall into communist hands. But except from the viewpoint of the domino theory, South Vietnam was a territory without strategic or economic value. Kennedy no longer believed in the domino theory, and became an advocate of a kind of reverse domino theory. That had worked for the missile crisis, so why not also in Vietnam? As soon as the elections were over, a diplomatic offensive to give the status of independence to a reunited Vietnam would have a reasonable chance, according to the Kennedy doctrine. If the Russians and the Chinese also backed off, an American military presence in Vietnam would no longer be required. For Kennedy, it was only a matter of timing.

Cuba, on the other hand, was a much trickier issue. The island was only 90 miles off the American coast, a hundred times closer than Vietnam. In this context, it made sense that the island should fall under the American sphere of influence. Unlike Vietnam, it was also a problem that could not wait until after the elections. Patiently tolerating the communist presence in Cuba was not unlike sitting on a political bombshell. The Cuban exiles were mostly living in Florida. If Kennedy couldn't gain a victory in Florida and Texas, he would certainly not be reelected. Postponing an intervention in Cuba increased the electoral risk, while a quick, successful action would assure Kennedy an extended stay in the White House in one fell swoop. But on the other hand, an American intervention in Cuba would block the rapprochement with Russia, and jeopardize the great mission Kennedy had meanwhile set himself as a goal. Consequently, Kennedy could do nothing else in 1963 but blow hot and cold about Cuba. There was no invasion of the island to solve the missile crisis, but the clandestine war continued. This contradiction was a problem. That is evident, for example, from the discussion Kennedy had with Director McCone and Desmond Fitzgerald of the CIA on November 12. Both men defended the sabotage operations on behalf of the CIA. The position of Dean Rusk, the Secretary of State, was that all these 'hit and run operations were complicating relations with the Soviets and causing too much trouble internationally.'[1009] Ambiguity makes everyone angry. Castro and Khrushchev reproached Kennedy because the CIA was providing the anti-Castro rebells with logistic and financial support. But the CIA and the rebels were even angrier with Kennedy because they sensed that his support was no longer sincere. They could see what was coming, and were afraid that Kennedy would betray them a third time. There were rumors that he was trying to come to an agreement with Castro behind their backs.

Kennedy actually only had one chance to escape from this deadlock: a quick, internal coup in Cuba. The Cubans had to overthrow Castro themselves, without too much bloodshed. A pro-American regime could then come to power after the coup. Kennedy kept this option open. The Americans were negotiating in secret with Rolando Cubela, a high-ranking military leader with direct access to Castro. Cubela had earned his spurs during the revolution, and could allegedly count on widespread support from the Cuban population. He seemed willing to assassinate Castro, and was also in his immediate vicinity often enough to implement such a plan. He would afterwards confirm his takeover of power with the support of the United States. The CIA correspondent's report of the last meeting with Cubela (with code name AMLASH) in Brazil on October 31 confirmed Cubela's willingness to overthrow Castro, but was otherwise not exactly positive about the man: 'AMLASH cocky totally spoiled brat who will always be control problem but feel his feelings against regime sincere and he basically honest.'[1010] Whether he was honest was still to be seen, because, according to Fabian Escalante, the then head of the Cuban counterespionage, Cubela's political loyalty very much depended on his state of mind: 'Cubela was a voluble, unstable and ambitious person, with a misguided view of friendship that blinded him to the defects of those around him and influenced his ideas.' Escalante also confirmed the negative image the CIA informant had about Cubela: 'He drank too much and regularly frequented nightclubs and cabarets, places in which he was involved in various public disturbances.'[1011] Still, the Cubela scenario was too tempting to start questioning it. Desmond Fitzgerald met Cubela in Paris on October 29. He confirmed that he spoke on behalf of Robert Kennedy, and that the United States was prepared 'to give full support to [Cubela] and his group if they are successful in a real coup against the [Castro] regime.'[1012]

The chances of success with Cubela, however, were completely in the hands of the man himself. The Americans could do little else than await the big day, and its result. Kennedy therefore also unilaterally kept the path of peaceful coexistence open. UN diplomat William Attwood received signals that Castro was willing to talk to the Americans, and Kennedy was willing to open that door a crack. Attwood first had to resign from the diplomatic service in order to meet Castro as a citizen. Kennedy remained very cautious, but he could not resist the temptation. Attwood also informed the president that Jean Daniel, a journalist for the French left-wing weekly *L'Observateur*, was about to meet with Castro. Kennedy had a stunned Daniel called into the White House, and asked the journalist to convey a startling message: Castro's entire revolution was a logical reaction of the Cubans to economic colonization. The Americans had been guilty of the unnecessary humiliation and extreme exploitation of the island. Even Batista's errors were, in fact, American errors, according to Kennedy: 'Batista was the incarnation of a number of sins on the part of the United States. Now we shall have to pay for those sins.' This confession alone must have horrified the CIA, who must have been informed about the meeting. Kennedy asked Daniel to convey the following concrete proposal to the Cuban leader: 'If Castro stopped trying to export communism to other nations and became the Tito of the Caribbean, then, like Tito, he could receive U.S. recognition and aid.'[1013]

The meeting between Castro and Daniel was scheduled for Friday, November 22, 1963.

Kennedy therefore did have concrete plans in November 1963 for a revolutionary second term. He also mentioned this in his speech at the Amherst College on October 26: 'I look forward to an America which commands respect throughout the world not only for its strength but for its civilization as well.'[1014] Insiders knew that Kennedy meant what he said. His enemies didn't believe their ears, however, when they heard him proclaim his intention of conducting international politics on the basis of civilized behavior. In their eyes, a nation that unilaterally adopted moral obligations and constraints that did not apply to the same extent in other countries was simply committing diplomatic suicide.

The list of Kennedy opponents had become impressive: Johnson, Hoover, the Cuban exiles, rabid conservatives, the anticommunists, the Mob, the CIA, the military leadership, the oil industry, the racists in the South, the arms industry ... they were all irritated by the arrogant naivety of the president. They considered the Kennedys to be hypocritical crypto-communists who had themselves become wealthy through stolen money, and were now looking down on others. They loathed the self-willed character traits of the brothers, their disdain for the consultants who tried to make them see reason, the pleasure they took from antagonizing everyone ... But these were only superficial issues. Worse was that, at a much deeper level, the Kennedys also behaved as if they had the right to experiment with the American concerns of state, and the associated economic interests. Mr. Kennedy privately felt he had to top up his feeling of moral superiority, and put this need above that of the nation. He tried to gain the good graces of America's enemies, openly expressed national self-reproach and was selling out American interests, just because this happened to make him feel better as a person. Through the complicity of the press, the American people did not realize just how incompetent and dangerous Kennedy was: a traitor, an unworthy commander in chief, an unreliable bigmouth. He arrogantly behaved as if he had been elected president of the world, and, in the exercise of this mandate, American interests were but a side issue, secondary to the general interests of the entire world. He confused his role with that of the Secretary General of the UN. He concluded treaties that deliberately limited the effectiveness of his own armed forces. He was willing to ignominiously capitulate to the communists in Vietnam and Cuba. A president who was intent on conducting an internationalist and pacifistic policy was committing treason. He harbored the dangerous illusion that conflicts were only due to avoidable mistakes that America had made in the past. Kennedy's opponents, however, were certain that the world was not a huge sunny estate in Hyannis Port, and that mutual respect and civilization wouldn't lead to peace and order. Their world was a dark and dangerous snake pit. The CIA only believed its own dismal logic in this respect. What you didn't defend tooth and nail would be violated and trampled upon. Stop being a hunter, and you become the prey. America's enemies lowered everywhere, patiently awaiting the first sign of weakness … And now the American president was even waiting on them hand and foot.

But all those factors did not add up to a conclusive reason to eliminate JFK. In the eyes of his enemies, Kennedy was a threat to the system, the system to which they owed their position of power and wealth. That was the true motive for the assassination. We can say that the anti-Castro elements within the CIA masterminded the assassination. But the CIA is not an independently thinking being, and can therefore not nurture a motive for a crime. More than anyone, the CIA had the staff, the knowhow and the resources for an intervention at its disposal. By virtue of the secrecy surrounding its mission, the external and internal control of its operations was lax. That systemic fault was the weakest point, where an undercurrent of primitive motives from an occult elite came explosively to the surface. The hard truth is that an elected president is only a temporary, ceremonial member of an exclusive club of leaders. He keeps some useful illusions going, and, in return, can claim his place in the spotlight for a while, and leave behind some personal touches. But he should not exceed his role, and he must never interfere with the system itself.

The system was never endangered again after November 22, 1963. But the plans Kennedy had in the back of his mind would indeed have been a threat. Kennedy wanted to change America and the world, coincidentally at a time that was extremely favorable for change. Major changes can only happen at a moment of grace, and that is exactly what became clear in Dallas. Kennedy's hopes for a more open, freer, more civilized world were also reflected in the eyes of the smiling and waving people. The Golden Sixties had truly begun, and the feeling of widespread social change was in the air. Deeply conservative Dallas was enthusiastically greeting a progressive president. Kennedy had gradually gained the trust of the American people, and was now about to finally capture their hearts. Kennedy was an incorrigible optimist, but he was also a realist, and, like no other, could sense the minutest change in the electoral winds.

While he was driving along Main Street in his dark-blue open limousine, the cheering must have sounded like music to his ears. If the Republicans were to nominate the belligerent Goldwater, he could turn the elections into a referendum on war or peace. The response of the American public to the peaceful resolution of the missile crisis had been encouraging. The adoption of the Limited Test Ban Treaty by the Senate with the required two-thirds majority was close to a political miracle. He had done it yet again. The elections should not become a pessimistic referendum about defeatism with regard to Cuba and the Cold War, but an optimistic debate about the beginning of a new era of openness, peace, civilization, freedom and prosperity for all. The first thousand soldiers were ready to return from Vietnam. In Havana, a French journalist was conveying Kennedy's cordial greetings to Castro. The next step would be a visit of the presidential couple to their friend Nikita Khrushchev in the Kremlin.[1015] When the jovial Khrushchev greeted the Kennedys with open arms on the balcony in Red Square, the Russian people would also cheer, and the Cold War would then be over.

While the limousine drove onto Dealey Plaza and approached a red brick building, John Kennedy lifted his hand to smooth an unruly lock of auburn hair. He waved to the enthusiastic spectators, his *fellow Americans*, and gave them his irresistible boyish smile. One second later a shot sounded, the first of a carefully prepared assault.

Flip de Mey
Mechelen, Belgium, September 2015

EPILOGUE

Lyndon Johnson, Richard Nixon and George H. Bush were in Dallas on November 22. Gerald Ford became a member of the Commission that would determine the official truth about the assassination. Bush, a CIA informer on the day of the assassination, was later appointed to be director of the intelligence agency. These four men, who knew more about the events that took place in Dallas on November 22 than anyone else, later became presidents themselves. At no time at all did they constitute a threat to the system.

Bobby Kennedy was on the wrong side. He only made it to presidential candidate, and was assassinated on June 6, 1968. The killer was a 'lone nut.'

NOTES

1. The fifth floor for Europeans, who do not count the ground floor as the first floor.
2. (HSCA, Appendix Vol. III, 1978) p. 595
3. Dallas Police, FBI, Warren Commission, Ramsey Clark Panel, Rockefeller Commission, Church Committee, House Select Committee on Assassinations (HSCA) and the Assassinations Records Review Board (ARRB).
4. (Brown W., Treachery in Dallas, 1995) p. 269
5. The jury in *On Trial* found Oswald guilty.
6. (Brown W., *The People v. Lee Harvey Oswald*, 1992). In this book, the judge, in the interest of the truth, orders a verdict of "innocent" after the case had to be stopped for procedural reasons.
7. The Probe Interview: Bob Tanenbaum Probe July-August 1996, p. 24 (http://www.ctka.net/pr796-bti.html)
8. The HSCA was a *select committee*, a specially appointed commission with no *standing committee*, and no permanent commission. Insiders knew that the mandate would not be extended, and that no additional appropriations would be provided. Anyone who wanted to sabotage the committee simply had to win time by occasionally leaking misinformation that provided the investigators with extra work and caused delays. An illuminating account of this method can be seen in the video of the lecture by Dan Hardway and Edwin Lopez on September 26, 2014, at the AARC conference. The video is available on: http://aarclibrary.org/aarc-conference-2014-the-hsca-and-the-cia-the-view-from-the-trenches-and-the-view-from-the-top/
9. http://jfkfacts.org/assassination/news/key-jfk-files-ignored-in-obama-declassification-drive/
10. Posner, 1993, 2003, p. 418
11. Morley, Jefferson, The Holy Grail of the JFK Story: David Phillip checked up on Oswald in Mexico, and Brich O'Neal, head of the CIA's Special Investigation Group, compiled the information in Washington. Morley wrote the following about this in 2011: 'With Lesar's help I discovered that the National Archives retains 605 pages of CIA records about David Phillips in the JFK Assassination Records Collection in College Park, Md. The Archives also has 222 pages about Birch D. O'Neal, Angleton's aide, who regularly received reports on Oswald between 1959 and 1963. The Agency says it will not release the Phillips and O'Neil material until at least 2017.' (http://www.salon.com/2011/11/22/the_holy_grail_of_the_jfk_story/). Morley also took legal action against the CIA over 10 years for the release of the documents referring to George Joannides. In September 2014, the CIA finally admitted in its defense that Joannides was a CIA agent, and that the DRE, an anti-Castro student group, was coordinated and financed on behalf of the CIA. There are at least five known interactions between the DRE and Oswald. The DRE was also quick to spread information about Oswald being a pro-Castro activist after the assassination.

12. Hurt, 1985, p. 22
13. Goldfarb, 1995, p. 281
14. Cassie Parnau, http://kilgallenfiles.wordpress.com/what-happened-to-dorothy/
15. Hurt, 1985, p. 22
16. One of the first critics of the report, Silvia Meagher, noted that the very fact that many thick books were required to defend the story of the Warren Commission, which is in itself 888 pages long, says a great deal. Other fervent prominent supporters include Gerald Posner (Case Closed), Gerald Ford (Portrait of the Assassin), two books by Commission attorney David Belin (Final Disclosure – November 22, 1963 You are the jury), Jim Moore (A conspiracy of one) and Arlen Specter, who devotes a part of his memoirs to the Commission's defense. The major newspapers and television networks CBS, NBC and ABC have also repeatedly defended the official line in their documentaries.
17. Bugliosi was also a District Attorney in Los Angeles. He obtained a conviction of the accused in 105 of his 106 cases. His most high-profile case as prosecutor was the murder of Sharon Tate, the wife of the film guru Roman Polanski. Bugliosi wrote a highly critical book about the controversial decision of the Supreme Court to award George W. Bush the presidency after a highly contentious electoral battle in Florida. Although he was himself a republican, he also wrote a book in which he stated his opposition to the witch hunt against Clinton. The humiliation of the President could only take place at the expense of national prestige and the governability of the country, concluded the author. He was also the prosecutor who, in 2008, dared to publish his criticism of the Iraq invasion under the title "The Prosecution of George W. Bush for Murder."
18. Bugliosi, 2007, p. 987
19. https://www.youtube.com/watch?v=20gvMWkU1jo Interview V. Bugliosi, October 16, 2013.
20. Warren Commission, Hearings and Exhibits, Vol. II, 1964, p. 162
21. Warren Commission, Hearings and Exhibits, Vol. VI, 1964, p. 157
22. Warren Commission, Hearings and Exhibits, Vol. II, 1964, p. 162
23. Warren Commission, Hearings and Exhibits, Vol. XIV, 1964, p. 470
24. Warren Commission, Hearings and Exhibits, Vol. II, 1964, p. 162
25. de Mey, 2013, pp. 280-306
26. FBI 62-109060 JFK HQ File, Section 5, p. 119
27. Warren Commission, Hearings and Exhibits, Vol VII, 1964, p. 58
28. Warren Commission, Hearings and Exhibits, Vol VII, 1964, p. 228
29. It is often claimed, even in *Cold Case Kennedy*, that the Kennedy investigator Lattimer had an identical Carcano 91/38 for research purposes in the 1970s, also with serial number C2766. But Lattimer apparently stated in an interview in 2004 that this was a mistake, which was only realized after the book was already in print. Henry Bloomgarden (*The Gun: A Biography of the Gun that Killed John F. Kennedy*, 1975), is the authority in connection with the Carcano and he assumes that there were several Carcanos with the number 2766, but not preceded by a 'C'. It is also a happy coincidence that the Carcano had a serial number. The weapons were checked upon arrival in the United States, and the serial number was often omitted when replacing parts.
30. HSCA Appendix Vol. VI, p. 66
31. *On Trial*, part 9: Cecil Kirk. https://www.youtube.com/watch?v=t5nEqR26cL4
32. Warren Commission, *Hearings and Exhibits*, Vol. VII, 1964, p. 229.
33. Warren Commission, *Hearings and Exhibits*, Vol. VII, 1964, p. 177.

34. The search of Oswald's rented room apparently also took place without a search warrant (Warren Commission, *Hearings and Exhibits*, Vol. VII, 1964, p. 117), but Agent Fay Turner claims that there was a search warrant (Warren Commission, *Hearings and Exhibits*, Vol. VII, 1964, p. 222).
35. HSCA, Final Report, 1978, p. 55 HSCA, Appendix Vol. VI, p. 89
36. HSCA, Appendix Vol. VI, p. 88, marginal number 320
37. Original photo from the estate of Cecil Kirk, property of Flip de Mey.
38. HSCA Appendix Vol VI, p. 88 marginal number 230
39. Twyman, *Bloody Treason. The Assassination of John F. Kennedy*, 2010, p.101
40. For example, Regh Templin, a weapon expert from the Wisconsin State Crime Lab, claimed in an interview that 'there is not now and never was a test to administer on a firearm to give an approximate time period as to when a firearm has been fired. He stated that analyzing swabs taken from a firearm can detect gun powder, but nothing more can be drawn from such analysis.' Source: http://mcadams.posc.mu.edu/factoid1.htm
41. Warren Commission, Hearings and Exhibits, Vol. III, p. 395
42. Meagher, 1967, reprinted, p. 101. Meaghers source is said to be a letter sent to the Analog of John P. Conlon. But according to John McAdams, the context in the letter from Conlon is a comparison between the Carcano and a machine gun. Source: http://mcadams.posc.mu.edu/factoid9.htm
43. The problem with the clip is one of many that we have discussed here. When Inspector Day carries the weapon out, the clip is apparently in. That suffices to demonstrate that a clip was present in the TSBD. Unfortunately, the clip is not included in the inventory of the evidence and it is not even in the photo of the weapon or the photo of the other evidence that was taken on November 22.
44. Meagher, 1967, reprinted, p. 117
45. Warren Commission Report, 1964, p. 555
46. Meagher, 1967, reprinted, p. 118
47. Lattimer, *Kennedy and Lincoln. Medical and Ballistic Comparisons of their Assassinations*, 1980, p.298
48. Warren Commission, *Hearings and Exhibits*, Vol. IV, 1964, p. 23
49. https://www.youtube.com/watch?v=3WOgdyTvWjU
50. HSCA, Appendix Vol. VI, p. 616
51. It would have been agents Hendrix, Staley and Miller, but the committee did not hear these important witnesses.
52. Warren Commission, Hearings and Exhibits, Vol. III, p. 404
53. Warren Commission, Hearings and Exhibits, Vol. III, p. 443
54. Warren Commission, Hearings and Exhibits, Vol. III, p. 405
55. Warren Commission, Hearings and Exhibits, Vol. III, p. 407
56. Warren Commission, Hearings and Exhibits, Vol. III, p. 443
57. Warren Commission, Hearings and Exhibits, Vol. III, p. 444
58. Warren Commission, Hearings and Exhibits, Vol. III, p. 799
59. 1 mil is approximately 1/1000 of a radial. 17.7 mil is a deviation of 1 degree.
60. Warren Commission, Hearings and Exhibits, Vol. III, p. 445
61. Warren Commission, Hearings and Exhibits, Vol. III, p. 448
62. Warren Commission, Hearings and Exhibits, Vol. III, p. 50

63. Lattimer, *Kennedy and Lincoln. Medical and Ballistic Comparisons of their Assassinations*, 1980, p. 301
64. Warren Commission Report, 1964, p. 195
65. Warren Commission, Hearings and Exhibits Vol. x, p. 361
66. Warren Commission, Hearings and Exhibits, Vol. xi, 1964, p. 312
67. Epstein E. J., *Legend. The Secret World of Lee Harvey Oswald*, 1978, 2011, Kindle version, loc.1100
68. Warren Commission, Hearings and Exhibits, Vol. xvi, 1964, p. 639
69. Warren Commission, Hearings and Exhibits, Vol. xix, 1964, p. 18
70. Warren Commission Report, 1964, p. 192
71. Brown W., *Treachery in Dallas*, 1995, p. 26 quotation by Leo Sauvage, Oswald Affair p. 58
72. Lattimer, *Kennedy and Lincoln. Medical and Ballistic Comparisons of their Assassinations*, 1980, p. 304
73. Lattimer, *Kennedy and Lincoln. Medical and Ballistic Comparisons of their Assassinations*, 1980, p. 293
74. Lattimer, *Kennedy and Lincoln. Medical and Ballistic Comparisons of their Assassinations*, 1980, p. 294
75. DiEugenio, 1992, p. 106
76. Warren Commission, Hearings and Exhibits, Vol. xxI, 1964, p. 141
77. Warren Commission, Hearings and Exhibits, Vol xxii, 1964, p. 763
78. Warren Commission, Hearings and Exhibits, Vol xxii, 1964, p. 778
79. Warren Commission, Hearings and Exhibits, Vol. xxvi, 1964, p. 63
80. Warren Commission, Hearings and Exhibits, Vol. xxvi, 1964, p. 64
81. Brown W., *Treachery in Dallas*, 1995, p. 293
82. Warren Commission Report, 1964, p. 553
83. Warren Commission, Hearings and Exhibits, Vol vii, 1964, p. 226
84. FBI 62-109060 JFK HQ File, Section 176, p. 90
85. Warren Commission, Hearings and Exhibits, Vol. xxii, 1964, p. 765 and 776
86. Warren Commission, Hearings and Exhibits, Vol. ii, 1964, p. 466
87. Warren Commission, Hearings and Exhibits, Vol. ii, 1964, p. 466
88. Warren Commission, Hearings and Exhibits, Vol. xxii, 1964, p. 763
89. Warren Commission, Hearings and Exhibits, Vol. xxii, 1964, p. 778
90. Warren Commission, Hearings and Exhibits, Vol. i, 1964, p. 14
91. Warren Commission, Hearings and Exhibits, Vol. xxii, 1964, p. 785
92. HSCA, Final Report, 1978, p. 55
93. Warren Commission, Hearings and Exhibits, Vol. xxii, 1964, p. 196
94. Warren Commission, Hearings and Exhibits, Vol. xxvi, 1964, p. 65-68
95. Commission Document 206, Gemberling Report, p. 31. According to the Gemberling report, there are also some confused statements that have nothing to do with Oswald.
96. There is even a problem with the *dry runs*, the practice exercises needed to become acquainted with the awkward loading mechanism of the Carcano. The loading of the bullet leaves a scratch on the shell. The shells that were found showed no traces of repeated loading during practice sessions.
97. Price first saw Oswald on Saturday, September 28. He is sure of this date because September 28 was the opening day of the shooting range. This is impossible, because the real Oswald was supposed to be in Mexico City on that day. Price saw Oswald again on the last Sunday before Thanksgiving. That makes sense, because there was a shooting

contest with a turkey as the first prize. The problem is that Thanksgiving fell on December 1 that year, and Sunday, November 24, is the day of Oswald's death.

98. Warren Commission, Hearings and Exhibits, Vol. XXIII, p. 390
99. Warren Commission, Hearings and Exhibits, Vol. XI, 1964, p. 154
100. Warren Commission, Hearings and Exhibits, Vol. XXIII, p. 392
101. Warren Commission, Hearings and Exhibits, Vol. III, p. 372
102. Warren Commission, Hearings and Exhibits, Vol. VII, 1964, p.225 – 226
103. Warren Commission Report, 1964, p. 320
104. Warren Commission, Hearings and Exhibits, Vol. X., p. 385 and further.
105. Warren Commission, Hearings and Exhibits Vol. X., p. 390
106. Warren Commission, Hearings and Exhibits, Vol. XXIV, 1964, p. 303
107. Commission Document 87 – Secret Service report of 08 Jan 1964 re: Oswald p. 678
108. http://www.jfk-online.com/oswaldrifle.html
109. Warren Commission Report, 1964, p. 319
110. Lattimer, *Kennedy and Lincoln. Medical and Ballistic Comparisons of their Assassinations*, 1980, p. 304
111. de Mey, 2013, p.179
112. Warren Commission, Hearings and Exhibits, Vol. III, p. 395 Frazier: 'The length of the barrel is 34.8 inches (88.39 centimeters).'
113. http://jfkassassination.net/russ/testimony/frazierb4.htm Affidavit of Buell Wesley Frazier.
114. Warren Commission, Hearings and Exhibits, Vol. VII, 1964, p. 230
115. Russo, 1998, loc. 6522 Interview Gus Russo with Buell Frazier 16/02/1987
116. Warren Commission, Hearings and Exhibits, Vol. II, 1964, p. 249
117. Warren Commission, Hearings and Exhibits, Vol. II, 1964, p. 250
118. Warren Commission, Hearings and Exhibits, Vol. XXII, 1964, p. 751
119. Warren Commission, Hearings and Exhibits, Vol. II, 1964, p. 248
120. Warren Commission, Hearings and Exhibits vol. XXI, 1964, p. 4, Paine Ruth Exhibit nos. 275 and 276
121. Warren Commission, Hearings and Exhibits, Vol. XXI, 1964, p. 3, Paine Ruth Exhibit nos. 272 and 273
122. Warren Commission, Hearings and Exhibits, Vol. IV, 1964, p. 267. Day himself was hedging his bets: 'I wrote that at the time the sack was found before it left our possession.' The first part of the statement refers to the time it was found, shortly before 2 p.m. The second part refers to the time of transfer to the FBI, which was at 11:45 p.m.
123. Warren Commission, Hearings and Exhibits, Vol III, 1964, p. 286 286
124. Warren Commission, Hearings and Exhibits, Vol VI, 1964, p. 268
125. Warren Commission, Hearings and Exhibits, Vol VII, 1964, p. 65
126. Warren Commission, Hearings and Exhibits, Vol VII, 1964, p. 162
127. Warren Commission, Hearings and Exhibits, Vol. IV, 1964, p. 220
128. C.D. 5 Gemberling Report p. 129
129. Warren Commission, Hearings and Exhibits, Vol. III, 1964, p. 231
130. Warren Commission, Hearings and Exhibits, Vol VII, 1964, p. 104
131. Warren Commission, Hearings and Exhibits, Vol VII, 1964, p. 98
132. Warren Commission, Hearings and Exhibits, Vol VII, 1964, p. 138
133. Warren Commission, Hearings and Exhibits, Vol VII, 1964, p. 144
134. Warren Commission Report, 1964, p. 79

135. The Commission may actually be closer to the truth than they themselves suspect. Photos were obviously taken immediately on Friday afternoon, but I believe they were subsequently replaced with other photos. The reason for this was that one of the shells was missing. Chief Inspector Fritz had apparently nonchalantly put a shell in his pocket while helping the press. This took place very early in the process. As a result, the whole chain of evidence only existed for two shells, instead of three. This was later corrected with lies and falsifications. There is enough evidence of this. In *Cold Case Kennedy* (p. 197), I mentioned that I presumed that only two shells were visible on the original photos, and that these photos therefore had to be replaced. The paper bag was not available during the reconstruction, so that it does not appear on the final photos.
136. Warren Commission, Hearings and Exhibits, Vol. IV, 1964, p. 267
137. Warren Commission, Hearings and Exhibits, Vol VII, 1964, p. 289
138. Warren Commission, Hearings and Exhibits, Vol. XVI, 1964, p. 613
139. See also Tony Fratini – http://www.jfkassassinationforum.com/index.php?topic=11622.948. Investigators like Pat Speer dispute whether this is the same bag.
140. Warren Commission, Hearings and Exhibits Vol. X, 1964, p. 579
141. FBI file 105-82555, sec. 39 p. 7
142. Warren Commission, Hearings and Exhibits, Vol. IV, 1964, p. 90-94
143. Warren Commission, Hearings and Exhibits, Vol. VI, 1964, p. 357
144. Warren Commission, Hearings and Exhibits, Vol. IV, 1964, p. 97 and Warren Commission, Hearings and Exhibits, Vol. XXIV, 1964, p. 263
145. de Mey, 2013. For the photo, see *Cold Case Kennedy*, p. 178
146. Warren Commission, Hearings and Exhibits, Vol. IV, 1964, p. 267
147. Warren Commission, Hearings and Exhibits, Vol. VII, 1964, p. 144
148. FBI 62-109060 JFK HQ File, Section 5, p. 156. FBI memo Jevons to Conrad, 23/11/63.
149. Warren Commission, Hearings and Exhibits, Vol. IV, 1964, p. 6 and FBI 62-109060 JFK HQ File, Section 5, p. 157
150. Warren Commission Report, 1964, p. 236
151. Warren Commission, Hearings and Exhibits, Vol. XXIV, 1964, p. 766, CE2146
152. Warren Commission, Hearings and Exhibits, Vol. IV, 1964, p. 21
153. Warren Commission, Hearings and Exhibits, Vol. XXIV, 1964, p. 263, CE 2003 p. 134
154. Warren Commission, Hearings and Exhibits, Vol. XXIV, 1964, p. 263, CE 2003, and Warren Commission, Hearings and Exhibits, Vol. IV, 1964, p. 88
155. Warren Commission, Hearings and Exhibits, Vol. II, 1964, p. 252
156. The Mannlicher Carcano – A practical experiment in its Reassembly, Weisberg Archive. R-disk/Rifle Accuracy Item 07
157. Griggs, 2005, p. 165
158. Warren Commission, Hearings and Exhibits, Vol. XXII, 1964, p. 480
159. Griggs, 2005, Photo Section Two
160. Griggs, 2005, p. 169
161. Warren Commission, Hearings and Exhibits, Vol. III, p. 397
162. HSCA Appendix Vol VI, p. 79, Fig. III-4d Photo from the estate of Cecil Kirk, property of Flip de Mey
163. http://jfk.hood.edu/Collection/Weisberg Subject Index Files/P Disk/Paraffin
164. Warren Commission, Hearings and Exhibits, Vol. XXIV, 1964, p. 764
165. Warren Commission, Hearings and Exhibits Vol. XV, 1964, p. 750
166. Warren Commission, Hearings and Exhibits, Vol III, 1964, p. 286

167. Warren Commission, Hearings and Exhibits, Vol. III, 1964, p. 494
168. Warren Commission, Hearings and Exhibits, Vol. VII, 1964, p. 591
169. Warren Commission, Hearings and Exhibits Vol. XXV, 1964, p. 800
170. Warren Commission, Hearings and Exhibits Vol. XV, 1964, p. 746
171. Chambers, 2010, p. 171
172. Chambers (2010, p. 172) refers to: Paraffin test records, 75-226 file, Weisberg Archives. Despite an intensive search in the Weisberg Archives, I have been unable to find the document to which he was referring. Chambers said the following: 'Concomitant with these tests, the FBI had also conducted a control study where seven different men fired the Mannlicher Carcano rifle and subsequently had paraffin casts taken of their cheeks. Therefore this controlled experimental analysis demonstrated that Oswald had not fired a rifle on November 22, 1963.'
173. FBI Lab Report, March 6, 1964, 105-82555-2384 Oswald HQ File, Section 94 p. 171
174. 1 gram dissolved in a liter of water is 1000 ppm.
175. FBI 62-109060 JFK HQ File, Section 5, p. 139
176. FBI Lab Report, March 6, 1964, 105-82555-2384 Oswald HQ File, Section 94
177. Ongeldige bron opgegeven. P. 491
178. Weisberg Archive, General Atomic Report GA-6152 to the U.S. Atomic Energy Commission pages 7 and 9-11
179. Guinn wrote: 'the levels of Sb (Antimony) on the casts were still well above normal levels, even after the casts were treated by the chemical test. It appears, therefore, that performing the diphenylamine test on the paraffin casts removes the Ba fairly completely but does not remove significant amounts of Sb.'
180. In that context, Lieutenant Day carelessly destroyed important evidence. To my knowledge, this is the first time that this has been indicated. While looking for a fingerprint under the butt, he dismantled the weapon before it had been tested with regard to the accuracy with which it had been adjusted before the assassination. Because of its disassembly, we'll never be able to figure this out. All we know now is that the weapon was poorly adjusted after Day had re-assembled it again. If the weapon was accurate *before* Day so rashly pulled it apart, this would be a very strong indication that it was not brought into the building as twelve pieces and five screws.
181. Warren Commission, Hearings and Exhibits, Vol. IV, 1964, p. 31. Only four boxes were examined for fingerprints. These are the large box the shooter is presumed to have sat on, and the three smaller boxes that would have been used as support for the weapon. On box A, the 'top box' of the three smaller boxes, one fingerprint and one handprint were located with the help of the aggressive agent silver nitrate. This is why, in the evidence (HXVII, p. 292 CE 641), this box has the specific discoloration, just like the paper bag. On the larger box, 'Box D', the Dallas Police were able to make a palmprint visible with carbon powder. The piece of cardboard with this palmprint was only handed over to the FBI on November 27, however, five days after the assassination (HIV p. 37). Despite the treatment with silver nitrate, Oswald's prints were not detected on boxes B and C (HIV p. 42). FBI expert Latona was cautious, and would only confirm that the one palmprint that was still visible with carbon was less than three days old. The fact that the other prints were only visible with silver nitrate would indicate that they were older than this particular palmprint.
182. Curry, quoted in the *Dallas Morning News*, November 6, 1969, article by Tom Johnson, and in his book JFK *Assassination File*.

183. Warren Commission, Hearings and Exhibits, Vol. VII, 1964, p. 46
184. Warren Commission, Hearings and Exhibits, Vol. III, 1964, p. 288
185. Warren Commission Report, 1964, p. 68
186. Warren Commission, Hearings and Exhibits, Vol. III, p. 202
187. Warren Commission, Hearings and Exhibits, Vol. III, p. 203
188. Frontline PBS Special *Who was Lee Harvey Oswald?* Interview of Harold Norman, 13 June 1993. Russo, 1998, loc. 6778
189. Posner, 1993, 2003, p. 227
190. Warren Commission, Hearings and Exhibits, Vol. III, p. 169. At the same time, Williams' statement refutes the testimony of Arnold Rowland, a witness who was in Dealey Plaza and who claimed to have seen two people on the sixth floor, one of whom was armed, at 12.15 p.m. (Warren Commission, Hearings and Exhibits, Vol. II, 1964, p. 169). Rowland claimed that he saw someone with a weapon at the window of the sniper's nest at 12.15 p.m. For 15 seconds, he saw a heavy, tall man (100 kg, later downsized in his statement to 70/75 kg), standing about one meter away from the window. The man was holding a rifle, of the type used for deer hunting. He had black hair, 'appeared to be in his early thirties,' was not going bald, had a tanned complexion and was wearing a white or light blue shirt. Rowland saw an older, black man leaning out of the window on the opposite side of the sixth floor.
191. Commission Documents 5, FBI Gemberling Report p. 329. Rowland was first questioned by Officer Fay Turner (Warren Commission, Hearings and Exhibits, Vol. VII, 1964, p. 220). He noted that Rowland mentioned 'two floors from the top.' It is not clear whether he was referring to the fifth or the sixth floor with this.
192. Commission Document 87 – Secret Service report of 08 Jan 1964 re: Oswald p. 292
193. Warren Commission, Hearings and Exhibits, Vol. VI, 1964, p. 354
194. Warren Commission, Hearings and Exhibits, Vol. VI, 1964, p. 350
195. Posner, 1993, 2003, p. 224
196. Warren Commission, Hearings and Exhibits, Vol. V, 1964, p. 35-36
197. Warren Commission, Hearings and Exhibits, Vol. VII, 1964, p. 390
198. Warren Commission, Hearings and Exhibits, Vol. VI, 1964, p. 383 and Warren Commission, Hearings and Exhibits, Vol. XIX, 1964, p. 499
199. CD 735 p. 295
200. Warren Commission, Hearings and Exhibits, Vol. XXIII, CE 1974, p. 873
201. Bugliosi, 2007, p. 828-829
202. Warren Commission hearings and Exhibits, Vol. III, p. 161
203. de Mey, 2013, see page 340, fig. 92 for the comparative photographs
204. Warren Commission, Hearings and Exhibits, Vol. XIV, 1964, p. 470
205. Warren Commission Report, 1964, p. 62
206. In the Zapruder film, Brennan is visible until frame Z208, less than one second before the second shot from the sniper's nest, when the magic bullet hit Kennedy in the back. At that moment, Brennan was still looking at the limousine. He can therefore only be referring to the third shot when he said he saw the gunman aiming and then firing.
207. Commission Document 87 – Secret Service report of 08 Jan 1964 re: Oswald p. 272
208. Warren Commission, Hearings and Exhibits, Vol. III, p. 161
209. http://www.maryferrell.org/wiki/index.php/Essay_-_Rewriting_History_-_Bugliosi_Parses_the_Testimony
210. Warren Commission, Hearings and Exhibits, Vol. XXIV, 1964, p. 522

211. Warren Commission, Hearings and Exhibits, Vol. II, 1964, p. 171
212. Warren Commission, Hearings and Exhibits, Vol. VI, 1964, p. 194 and Fay Turner who questioned him (Warren Commission, Hearings and Exhibits, Vol. VII, 1964, p. 223)
213. Warren Commission, Hearings and Exhibits, Vol. VI, 1964, p. 203
214. Warren Commission Report, 1964, p. 68
215. Warren Commission, Hearings and Exhibits, Vol. III, p.145
216. Warren Commission, Hearings and Exhibits, Vol. XVI, 1964, p. 5
217. Warren Commission, Hearings and Exhibits, Vol. III, p. 161
218. Warren Commission, Hearings and Exhibits, Vol. III, p. 257. Roy Truly recalled seeing Oswald in a T-shirt when they met on the second floor, shortly after the shots. But Truly ran on to the upper floors almost immediately, and did not meet Oswald directly, as Baker did. Commission Document 87 – Secret Service report of 08 Jan 1964 re: Oswald p. 778
219. Warren Commission, Hearings and Exhibits, Vol. II, 1964, p. 255
220. Warren Commission, Hearings and Exhibits, Vol. II, 1964, p. 250
221. Warren Commission, Hearings and Exhibits, Vol. III, 1964, p. 61
222. e.g. Warren Commission, Hearings and Exhibits vol. XXI, 1964, p. 467, Shaneyfelt Exhibit 24.
223. Warren Commission Report, 1964, p. 622
224. Warren Commission Report, 1964, p. 144
225. Warren Commission, Hearings and Exhibits, Vol. III, p. 160
226. CD 329 FBI Gemberling Report of 22 Jan 1964 re: Oswald/Russia/Cuba, p. 8
227. CD 1549 p. 2
228. Warren Commission, Hearings and Exhibits, Vol. XI, 1964, p. 217
229. Warren Commission, Hearings and Exhibits, Vol. III, 1964, p. 154
230. Roffman, 1976, p. 102. CBS News Extra: 'November 22 and the Warren Report', broadcast over the CBS Television Network, September 27, 1964, p. 20 of the transcript prepared by CBS News.
231. Roffman, 1976, p. 104, Life October 2, 1964, p. 42, 47
232. Hurt, 1985, p. 89
233. Warren Commission, Hearings and Exhibits, Vol. XXII, 1964, p. 676
234. Warren Commission, Hearings and Exhibits, Vol. XXII, 1964, p. 632
235. Warren Commission Report, 1964, p. 153
236. Warren Commission, Hearings and Exhibits, Vol. VII, 1964, p. 389. This also invalidates the statement of Eddie Piper that he saw no one go down the stairs before Truly and Baker started to go up them, because Piper entered the central hall together with the officer and the superintendent.
237. Source: http://thegirlonthestairs.wordpress.com/2014/01/07/the-sixth-floor-escape/.
238. Besides the standard statement of where she was at the moment of the shooting. Warren Commission, Hearings and Exhibits, Vol. XXII, 1964, p. 648
239. http://www.whokilledjfk.net/another_witness.htm
240. For a copy of the Stroud letter, see de Mey, 2013, fig. 102, p. 354
241. The girls made a mistake about the place and the time of their meeting with two other employees shortly after the assassination, but that does not excuse the blatant manipulation by the Commission.
242. http://educationforum.ipbhost.com/index.php?showtopic=17359, reply 15

243. In addition to Dorothy Garner, Elsie Dorman, Betty Foster Mary Hollies, Ruth Smith and Sandra Styles were also situated on the fourth floor at the time of the assassination. They were not questioned, except for the standard statement that was taken from all TSBD employees. The Commission only heard Vicki Adams, and a meaningless FBI statement exists from Yola D. Hopson. On the first floor, Roy Edwards was standing near the glass access door, Mrs. Carol Hughes sat near a window on the second floor, and Mrs. Edna Case and Mrs. Sandra Sue Elerson were on the fourth floor. There are also no known official statements from them.
244. CD 706 p. 7: Mr. O. V. Campbell, Mrs. L. C. (Bonnie) Richey, Mrs. Barney (Betty) Dragoo, Mrs. Don (Virgie) Baker née Rackley, and Miss Judy Johnson, 915 Sunnyside, Dallas
245. CD 5, Gemberling Report p. 41
246. Warren Commission, Hearings and Exhibits, Vol. XXII, 1964, p. 632
247. CD 706
248. Warren Commission, Hearings and Exhibits, Vol. XXII, 1964, p. 645
249. Warren Commission, Hearings and Exhibits, Vol. XXII, 1964, p. 656
250. Warren Commission, Hearings and Exhibits, Vol. XXII, 1964, p. 671
251. Summers, Not in your lifetime, 1998, p. 81
252. Summers, Not in your lifetime, 1998, p. 60
253. Warren Commission Report, 1964, p. 600
254. Warren Commission, Hearings and Exhibits, Vol. XXII, 1964, p. 672. She also made a statement on 24 November, but in this statement she did not explicitly mention where she was before she left the book depository. Warren Commission, Hearings and Exhibits, Vol. XXII, 1964, p. 844
255. Warren Commission, Hearings and Exhibits, Vol. VI, 1964, p. 383
256. CD 5, Gemberling report p. 329
257. Thomas, Don, *Rewriting History. Bugliosi Parses the Testimony.* http://www.maryferrell.org/wiki/index.php/Essay_-_Rewriting_History_-_Bugliosi_Parses_the_Testimony
258. Warren Commission, Hearings and Exhibits, Vol. VII, 1964, p. 390
259. Warren Commission, Hearings and Exhibits, Vol. IV, 1964, p. 203
260. Warren Commission, Hearings and Exhibits, Vol. VII, 1964, p. 314: 'myself, T. J. Kelley of the US Secret Service, David B. Grant of the US Secret Service, Robert I. Nash, Commander of the US Police and detective Billy L. Senkel and Fay M. Turner of the Homicide and Robbery Bureau of the Dallas Police Department. This interrogation was primarily conducted by Chief Inspector Fritz.' Apart from Bookhout and Fritz, none of the others present were questioned on the content of the intensive interrogation of Oswald. Fay Turner even contested that he had been present at the interrogation. Warren Commission, Hearings and Exhibits, Vol. VII, 1964, p. 223
261. Warren Commission Report, 1964, p. 200
262. Warren Commission, Hearings and Exhibits, Vol. IV, 1964, p. 213
263. Warren Commission Report, 1964, p. 622
264. Commission Document 329 – FBI Gemberling Report of 22 Jan 1964 re: Oswald/Russia/Cuba
265. Warren Commission, Hearings and Exhibits, Vol. III, p. 201
266. Italics in the original text.
267. Bugliosi, 2007, p. 830
268. Warren Commission, Hearings and Exhibits, Vol. III, p. 189
269. Warren Commission, Hearings and Exhibits, Vol. XXII, 1964, p. 632

270. Myers, *With Malice. Lee Harvey Oswald and the murder of Officer J.D. Tippit*, 1998, p. 279
271. Craig Ciccone's map of Dealey Plaza with the position of 338 spectators.
272. Bugliosi, 2007, p. 837
273. Posner, 1993, 2003, p. 264
274. Warren Commission, Hearings and Exhibits, Vol. XVII, 1964, CE 497 p. 212
275. Warren Commission, Hearings and Exhibits, Vol. XXII, 1964, p. 585
276. Jerry Dealey, The Dealey Plaza Echo, March 2008, *The Ups and Downs of the* TSBD. (http://www.dealey.org/updown.pdf)
277. Warren Commission, Hearings and Exhibits, Vol. VI, 1964, p. 367
278. Warren Commission, Hearings and Exhibits, Vol. II, 1964, p. 162 195
279. http://jfkassassination.net/russ/testimony/carrshaw.htm
280. Douglas J. W., 2008, p.276
281. Douglas J. W., 2008, p. 452
282. Warren Commission, Hearings and Exhibits, Vol. III, p. XIX, 1964, p. 524
283. September 18th 1964, letter from J. Edgar Hoover to J. Lee Rankin
284. Escalante, 2006, p.164
285. Matthews, *Jack Kennedy. Elusive Hero*, 2012
286. On the occasion of the 50th anniversary of the assassination, John Kerry, as Secretary of State, publicly said to NBC reporter Tom Brokaw: 'To this day, I seriously doubt that Lee Harvey Oswald acted alone.' This shows the extent to which the conspiracy theory is gradually becoming discussible among the highest echelons of power.
287. Mosley, 1978, p. 170
288. Douglas J., 2008, p. 169
289. Warren Commission, Hearings and Exhibits, Vol. II, 1964, p. 386
290. Jones Steve, *New Evidence Regarding Ruth and Michael Paine*. Source: http://jfklancer.com/pdf/Paine.pdf
291. Joseph McBride made this public in *The Nation*.
292. Fonzi, 1993, p. 358
293. Shane, 2013, interview with Joan Mellen.
294. Posner, 1993, 2003, p. 85
295. http://educationforum.ipbhost.com/index.php?showtopic=17690, Spartacus, Lee Forley Blog *Lost in translation*.
296. Warren Commission, Hearings and Exhibits, Vol. III, 1964, p. 3
297. Douglas J., 2008, p. 169
298. CD 206, Gemberling Report p. 66
299. Lee Farley, http://educationforum.ipbhost.com/index.php?showtopic=19806. On December 19, 2012, without giving his source, Farley stated in his blog *Lost in Translation* on the Spartacus Education Forum that 'Southwestern States Telephone Company had this telephone call listed as taking place on November 22nd and if it did take place at 1:00 PM on 11/22/63 then not only were the pair of them discussing Oswald being the assassin 45 minutes before he was arrested but it also means that their phone was being listened to prior to it officially being tapped and would also explain the bizarre comments from the pair.'
300. Warren Commission, Hearings and Exhibits, Vol. II, 1964, p. 48
301. Warren Commission, Hearings and Exhibits, Vol. II, 1964, p. 433
302. Posner, 1993, 2003, p. 77
303. Warren Commission Report, 1964, p. 703

304. Warren Commission, Hearings and Exhibits, Vol. II, 1964, p. 438
305. Mohrenschildt, 2014, p. 22 and 132: 'He spoke fluent Russian, but with a foreign accent, and made mistakes, grammatical mistakes, but had remarkable fluency in Russian.'
306. Summers, *Not in your lifetime*, 1998, p. 94 and 99
307. Warren Commission, Hearings and Exhibits, Vol. II, 1964, p. 450
308. Mohrenschildt, 2014, p. 30
309. Warren Commission, Hearings and Exhibits, Vol. II, 1964, p. 470
310. Warren Commission, Hearings and Exhibits, Vol. II, 1964, p. 472
311. Warren Commission, Hearings and Exhibits, Vol. II, 1964, p. 468
312. Warren Commission, Hearings and Exhibits, Vol. II, 1964, p. 492
313. Warren Commission, Hearings and Exhibits, Vol. II, 1964, p. 492
314. Warren Commission, Hearings and Exhibits, Vol. II, 1964, p. 495
315. Warren Commission, Hearings and Exhibits, Vol. II, 1964, p. 493
316. Warren Commission, Hearings and Exhibits, Vol. II, 1964, p. 509
317. Warren Commission, Hearings and Exhibits, Vol. I, 1964, p. 477
318. Kaiser, 2008, p. 263
319. Warren Commission, Hearings and Exhibits, Vol. XXII, 1964, p. 759
320. Douglas J. W., 2008, p. 173
321. Warren Commission, Hearings and Exhibits, Vol. II, 1964, p. 446
322. Ruth Paine Interview 1963, https://www.youtube.com/watch?x-yt-cl=84503534&v=xT-b2ZKIhDRQ&x-yt-ts=1421914688.
323. Warren Commission, Hearings and Exhibits, Vol. III, 1964, p. 34
324. Warren Commission, Hearings and Exhibits, Vol. II, 1964, p. 247
325. Warren Commission, Hearings and Exhibits, Vol. III, 1964, p. 213
326. Warren Commission, Hearings and Exhibits, Vol. XI, 1964, p. 391
327. Warren Commission, Hearings and Exhibits, Vol. IX, 1964, p. 390
328. Warren Commission, Hearings and Exhibits, Vol. VII, 1964, p. 228
329. Warren Commission, Hearings and Exhibits, Vol. VII, 1964, p. 230
330. Warren Commission, Hearings and Exhibits, Vol. XXII, 1964, p. 614, CE 1362
331. Posner, 1993, 2003, p. 99
332. Horne D., *Inside the Assassination Records Review Board Vol. V*, 2009, p. 1394
333. Warren Commission, Hearings and Exhibits, Vol. XXI, 1964, p. 563
334. Edwin Black, *The Plot to Kill Kennedy in Chicago*. The Chicago Independent, November 1975, http://www.thechicagoplot.com/The%20Chicago%20Plot.pdf
335. Douglas J. W., 2008, p. 203
336. Waldron, *Ultimate Sacrifice*, 2005, p. 247, reference to the CIA document dd. 27.01.64 F85-0272/1, declassified 8/16/83; CIA F820272/1, 82-1625 (4)
337. Waldron, *Ultimate Sacrifice*, 2005, p. 248
338. Waldron, *Ultimate Sacrifice*, 2005, p. 280
339. Edwin Black, *The Plot to Kill Kennedy in Chicago.*
340. HSCA Record 180-10070-10273, January 19, 1978, pp. 2-6
341. HSCA, Final Report, 1978, p. 231
342. The Ministry of Finance contacted Moyland. At the time, the Secret Service fell under the jurisdiction of this Ministry.
343. Douglas J. W., 2008, p. 207
344. Epstein E. J., *Legend. The Secret World of Lee Harvey Oswald*, 1978, 2011, Kindle version loc. 1152

345. Douglas J. W., 2008, p. 203
346. In his capacity as Deputy Counsel for the HSCA, Tanenbaum allegedly saw a film among the evidence in which CIA agent David Atlee Phillips, David Ferrie and Oswald can all be seen. He described this in his fiction book *Corruption of Blood* and confirmed the story in the Probe interview. *The Probe Interview: Bob Tanenbaum*, Probe July-August 1996, http://www.ctka.net/pr796-bti.html.
347. Douglas J. W., 2008, p. 204. Pilot David Ferrie, who played a prominent role in the events in New Orleans shortly after the assassination, also participated in these camps near Lake Pontchartrain.
348. https://www.maryferrell.org/wiki/index.php/Transcript_of_Milteer-Somersett_Tape
349. Waldron, *Legacy of Secrecy. The Long Shadow of the JFK Assassination*, 2009, p.78
350. Waldron, *Legacy of Secrecy. The Long Shadow of the JFK Assassination*, 2009, p. 197. Waldron had obtained independent confirmations, among others from Police Chief Mullins in Tampa, who only acknowledged the situation in an interview in 1996 – when he was 82 years old. According to the ARRB, the documents from the Secret Service about the threat in Tampa were destroyed, in breach of the JFK act.
351. Waldron, *Ultimate Sacrifice*, 2005, p. 707
352. Waldron, *Ultimate Sacrifice*, 2005, p. 707
353. Waldron, *Legacy of Secrecy*. Waldron, *The Hidden History of the JFK Assassination*, 2009, p. 293.
354. According to author Dick Russell, Richard Case Nagell had himself deliberately arrested in September 1963 by committing an armed robbery. By landing in jail, he prevented his further involvement in the plot. For a good deflation of Nagell's story, refer to Dave Reitzes' *Truth or Dare. The lives and lies of Richard Case Nagell.* http://mcadams.posc.mu.edu/nagell3.htm
355. Oswald 201 File (201-289248)/Oswald 201 File, Vol. 1 / p. 1 to 6.
NARA Record Number: 104-10021-10030
356. Hancock, 2006, p. 294 and CIA report 306-701 : https://www.maryferrell.org/mffweb/archive/viewer/showDoc.do?docId=1992&relPageId=3
357. Oswald 201 file, Vol. 1. According to Waldron, the informant of CIA man David Morales was a Cuban exile (code-named 'Amot'). Waldron, *The Hidden History of the JFK Assassination*, 2013, p. 293.
358. Myers, *With Malice. Lee Harvey Oswald and the Murder of Officer J.D. Tippit*, 1998, p. 87
359. Warren Commission, Hearings and Exhibits, Vol. XXIII, p. 833 and p. 858 CE1974
360. Warren Commission, Hearings and Exhibits, Vol. XXIV, 1964, p. 202
361. Warren Commission, Hearings and Exhibits, Vol. III, p. 307
362. Warren Commission, Hearings and Exhibits, Vol. III, p. 315
363. The Portal to Texas History (http://texashistory.unt.edu/ark:/67531/metapth49426/)
364. Warren Commission, Hearings and Exhibits, Vol. XIX, 1964, p. 522
365. Warren Commission, Hearings and Exhibits, Vol. XXIV, 1964, p. 18
366. Warren Commission, Hearings and Exhibits, Vol. VI, 1964, p. 431, and Warren Commission, Hearings and Exhibits, Vol. II, 1964, p. 293
367. Warren Commission, Hearings and Exhibits, Vol. XXIV, 1964, p. 18
368. Warren Commission, Hearings and Exhibits, Vol. VI, 1964, p. 429
369. Warren Commission, Hearings and Exhibits, Vol. VI, 1964, p. 434
370. Warren Commission, Hearings and Exhibits, Vol. VI, 1964
371. Warren Commission, Hearings and Exhibits, Vol. XXIV, 1964, p. 18

372. Warren Commission, Hearings and Exhibits, Vol. VI, 1964, p. 440
373. https://www.youtube.com/watch?v=15fRNaFQczc
374. Myers, *With Malice. Lee Harvey Oswald and the Murder of Officer J.D. Tippit*, 1998, p. 352
375. Measurement on Google Maps. Neely Street is located at the very end of the 700 block. But the 600 block is only 100 meters long, and the 700 block itself only 55 meters.
376. Warren Commission, Hearings and Exhibits, Vol. XXIV, 1964, p. 18, CD 1987. The FBI covered the 4.2 km route three times: with a maximum speed of 35 km/h (7 minutes), 30 km/h (8.5 minutes) and 25 km/h (7 minutes, but with fewer stop lights). Together, that is 22.5 minutes for 12.6 km, converted to 33.6 km/h.
377. de Mey, 2013, see *Cold Case Kennedy*, p. 152-159
378. Warren Commission, Hearings and Exhibits, Vol. VII, 1964, p. 273
379. Warren Commission, Hearings and Exhibits, Vol. VII, 1964, p. 69
380. Warren Commission, Hearings and Exhibits, Vol. XXIV, 1964, p. 415 CE2011
381. Myers, *With Malice. Lee Harvey Oswald and the Murder of Officer J.D. Tippit*, 1998, p. 278
382. Warren Commission Report, 1964, p. 559
383. At least the following persons saw/heard Oswald walking, shooting and/or running away in 10th Street: Jimmy Burt (1) stood talking with his friend Bill (William) Smith (2); Burt saw Oswald pass by in a westerly direction. Waitress Helen Markham (3) was on her way to the bus that would take her to work. Taxi driver William Scoggins (4) was behind the police car on 10th Street, and Jack Tatum (5) and Domingo Benavides (6) were also driving in 10th Street as Oswald was crossing the street and went to the police car. Scoggins (7) saw Tippit step out of his patrol car, and the shots occurred shortly afterwards. From his front yard, Frank Wright (8) saw a man running away from the scene of the crime; his wife (9) called the police. Masons Francis Kinneth (10) and Elbert Austin (11) were working on a neighboring site. The 16-year-old Barbara Davis (12), her father-in-law Louis Davis (13) and her sister-in-law Virginia Davis (14) walked to their front yard and saw how the murderer removed the shell from his weapon. Frank Cimino (15) also came running out. Aquilla Clemmons (16) saw two men running away in different directions. T.F. Bowley (17) arrived at the scene of the crime just after the murder. Car salesman Ted Callaway (18) saw the killer run past in Patton Street. Garage owner Warren Reynolds (19) and his black worker Sam Guinyard (20), Harold Russell (21), B.M. 'Pat' Patterson (22) and L.J. Lewis (23) all saw the killer run past in the direction of Jefferson Boulevard. Robert Brock (24), a mechanic in the Texaco tank station and his wife Mary (25) saw the killer passing by their car parking. Shoe salesman Johnny Brewer (26) saw Oswald sneak into the cinema.
384. Warren Commission Report, 1964, p. 6
385. Commission Document 291 – AG Texas Radio Log Channel II p. 7
386. Warren Commission, Hearings and Exhibits, Vol. VI, 1964, p. 321
387. Warren Commission, Hearings and Exhibits, Vol. XIX, 1964, p. 470
388. Warren Commission Report, 1964, p. 144. The 68 kilogram according to the autopsy report seems more realistic than the 61 kilogram in the arrest form in New Orleans.
389. https://www.youtube.com/watch?v=3yO-ko-gDDo
390. Myers, *With Malice. Lee Harvey Oswald and the Murder of Officer J.D. Tippit*, 1998.
391. Dale Myers, *Solving the Tippit Murder's Wallet Mystery: How the Truth Got Twisted into the Big Lie*. Source: http://jfkfiles.blogspot.be/2014/03/solving-tippit-murders-wallet-mystery.html
392. Hosty, 1996, p. 62

393. Myers, *With Malice. Lee Harvey Oswald and the Murder of Officer J.D. Tippit*, 1998, p. 298-299
394. The Fourth Decade, Volume 5, Issue 6, p. 23
395. Myers, *With Malice. Lee Harvey Oswald and the Murder of Officer J.D. Tippit*, 1998, p. 290
396. Commission Document 735 – FBI Gemberling Report, p. 265 (http://www.maryferrell.org/showDoc.html?docId=11133&search=%22Julia_Postal%22#relPageId=274&tab=page)
397. Warren Commission, Hearings and Exhibits, Vol. VII, 1964, p. 12
398. Jones Harris interview with Kenneth Croy, 11/02/02
399. Simpich, source: http://www.maryferrell.org/pages/State_Secret_Conclusion.html
400. Warren Commission, Hearings and Exhibits, Vol. XXIV, 1964, p. 421
401. Warren Commission, Hearings and Exhibits, Vol. XXIV, 1964, p. 793
402. Warren Commission, Hearings and Exhibits, Vol. II, 1964, p. 463
403. Warren Commission, Hearings and Exhibits, Vol. XXVI, 1964, p. 485 e.v.
404. Warren Commission, Hearings and Exhibits, Vol. XXVI, 1964, p. 486
405. Warren Commission, Hearings and Exhibits, Vol. XXVI, 1964, p. 494
406. Wikipedia mentioned the source: Appleton, Roy (November 2, 2013). "For slain officer J.D. Tippit's family, 'normal' life gone in a flash". dallasnews.com. Retrieved August 15, 2014.
407. Warren Commission, Hearings and Exhibits, Vol. XXIV, 1964, p. 1
408. Commission document 1002 FBI Letter from Director of 02 Jun 1964 with Attachments re: J.D. Tippit.
409. Warren Commission, Hearings and Exhibits, Vol. XXIV, 1964, p. 389
410. Warren Commission, Hearings and Exhibits, Vol. XXIV, 1964, p. 1
411. Warren Commission, Hearings and Exhibits, Vol. XXIV, 1964, p. 488
412. Livingstone H. E., 2004, p. 327
413. Livingstone H. E., 2004, p. 325
414. Dixie Dea, 11 January 2005, on John Simkin's Blog The Education Forum (http://educationforum.ipbhost.com/index.php?showtopic=2862)
415. De Voice of America is the official mouthpiece of the Americans. Pulitzer prizewinner and Watergate journalist Carl Bernstein investigated the relationship between the press and the CIA during the Cold War. The CIA was naturally keen on journalists, especially foreign ones. On the one hand, it allowed them to steer the media in the appropriate direction, but journalists were also perfect undercover agents abroad. Carl Bernstein, *The Cia and the Media*, Rolling Stone, October 20, 1977, (http://www.carlbernstein.com/magazine_cia_and_media.php)
416. https://larryhancock.wordpress.com/2014/10/10/loose-ends-in-dallas-and-the-house-on-harlandale/ Hancock stated: 'Avila's activities also included his services as an interpreter for Cuban exiles in Dallas, apparently also including visitors. Amelia Diaz, who had emigrated from Cuba in 1959, worked for Avila, was an active DRE supporter and reportedly moved to the house in Harlandale during the short period that it was used by the members of DRE and Alpha 66 [...] Jose Salazar had rented the house in Harlandale, was vice-president of the Alpha 66 division in Dallas and was a friend of Oswaldo Aurelio Pino – Pino was notably one of those questioned by the FBI as to whether they knew, and possibly visited Sylvia Odio.'

417. Warren Commission, Hearings and Exhibits XXV, 1964, p. 370. Pino said that he was only at a barbecue at which Sylvia Odio gave a short speech, but did not know her more closely.
418. https://larryhancock.wordpress.com/2014/10/10/loose-ends-in-dallas-and-the-house-on-harlandale/
419. Hancock, 2006, p. 174
420. Commission Document 385 – FBI Gemberling Report of 11 Feb 1964 re: Oswald, p. 86
421. Commission Document 897 – FBI Gemberling Report of 04 Ap. 1964 re: Oswald – Russia/Cuba p. 420
422. Warren Commission, Hearings and Exhibits, Vol. XI, 1964, p. 435
423. Conspiracy literature, but also Dale Myers o.c. p. 325, stated that the incident took place in February 1964. In January 2010, Jean Davison examined the case, and the correct year appeared to be 1965. (Source: http://jfkassassination.net/deaths.htm, Jim Marr's List Really So Mysterious)
424. Reference to Larry Ragle, *Crime Scene*, New York, Avon Books, 1995, p. 156 in Michael T. Griffith's article "Why Would Tippit have Stopped Oswald?", 1997, source: http://www.mtgriffith.com/web_documents/whytippit.htm
425. Warren Commission, Hearings and Exhibits, Vol. VI, 1964, p. 450
426. Warren Commission, Hearings and Exhibits, Vol. VI, 1964, p. 444
427. Warren Commission, Hearings and Exhibits, Vol. XXIV, 1964, p. 165
428. Commission Document 735 – FBI Gemberling Report p. 265, questioning of Julia Postal
429. Simpich, source: Anthony and Robbyn Summers, "The Ghosts of November", Vanity Fair, December 1994.
430. Myers, *With Malice. Lee Harvey Oswald and the Murder of Officer J.D. Tippit, 1998, p. 279*
431. Brown W., *Treachery in Dallas*, 1995, p. 249. Walt Brown explains that he learned from a number of sources that 'J.D. Tippit had a reputation for rousting anybody and everybody, and usually for the hell of it; some of them remember Tippit as "the neighborhood ***hole."'
432. Warren Commission Report, 1964, p. 6
433. Simpich, Chapter 6
434. Commission Document 290 – AG Texas Radio Log Channel I and Commission Document 291 – AG Texas Radio Log Channel II
435. Warren Commission, Hearings and Exhibits, Vol. XVII, 1964, p. 397
436. The five credible witnesses are: photographer Al Volkland and his wife Lou, both of whom knew Tippit [...] three employees of the Gloco Station, Tom Mullins, Emmett Hollingshead and J.B. 'Shorty' Lewis, who all knew Tippit, confirmed Volklands' story. http://mcadams.posc.mu.edu/car10.htm
437. Bill Drenas, 1997,1998, "Car #10. Where are you?" Source: http://jfklancer.com/pdf/Paine.pdf
438. Warren Commission, Hearings and Exhibits, Vol. II, 1964, p. 258
439. Dallas Police Department Radio Transcripts (Critics copy by Arch Kimbrough), p.16
440. Bill Drenas, 1997,1998, "Car #10. Where are you?"
441. Dallas Police Department Radio Transcripts (critics' copy by Arch Kimbrough), p. 25-34
442. Bill Drenas, 1997,1998, "Car #10. Where are you?", statement from Lowrey via Professor Bill Pulte Given to Bill Drenas.

443. Warren Commission, Hearings and Exhibits, Vol. III, p. 459; Warren Commission Report, 1964, p. 559
444. Warren Commission Report, Appendix 10: Expert Testimony p. 559
445. HSCA, Final Report, 1978, p. 59
446. Bugliosi, 2007, p. 1080
447. Psychological test report on Jack Ruby by Roy Schafer. Dallas Municipal archives JFK Collection, Box 4, folder 1, document 34 (http://jfk.ci.dallas.tx.us/11/1216-001.gif)
448. Bugliosi, 2007, p. 1080
449. Warren Commission, Hearings and Exhibits, Vol. XXI, 1964, p. 42
450. HSCA Report Appendix Vol. IX, p. 242
451. Bugliosi, 2007, p. 1096
452. Kaiser, 2008, p. 335
453. Kaiser, 2008, p. 333
454. Kaiser, 2008, p. 334. As a witness for the Senate Rackets Committee, Bright denied his own statement to the newspaper.
455. Kantor, 1978, p. 8 Ed Reid and Ovid Demaris, authors of *The Green Field Jungle*. Privately taped interview regarding conditions leading to Jack Ruby's arrival in Dallas from Chicago in 1947.
456. Bugliosi, 2007, p. 1131
457. Posner, 1993, 2003, p. 399
458. HSCA Appendix Vol. IV, 1978, p. 570
459. Posner, 1993, 2003, p. 360
460. FBI Clements Report, p. 31
461. FBI, Clements Report, p. 43, statement by Chief Inspector Fritz dd. 27.11.1963
462. Bugliosi, 2007, p. 1072 On December 29, Inspector Revill and McCaghren covered these distances in 73 seconds to the building and 22 seconds from the entrance to the crime scene, respectively.
463. Bugliosi, 2007, p. 1073
464. FBI interrogation of Seth Kantor, December 3, 1964, DL89-43 (p. 37) / DL 44-1639
465. Warren Commission, Hearings and Exhibits, Vol. XXIV, 1964, p. 434, CE 2019. According to another source, the phone call started at 10.10 a.m. NARA, Records of the John F. Kennedy Assassination, Key Persons Files, Ruby. DL 44-1639 p. 10 CR 105 p. 327
466. Warren Commission Report, 1964, p. 224
467. Posner, 1993, 2003, p. 373
468. FBI, Clements report, p. 39, statement by Chief Inspector Fritz dd. 25.11.1963
469. Warren Commission, Hearings and Exhibits, Vol. XXV, 1964, p. 523 CE 2420
470. Warren Commission, Hearings and Exhibits, Vol. XX, 1964, p. 481
471. Warren Commission, Hearings and Exhibits, Vol. XIII, 1963, p. 224
472. Interview by Elmer Gertz and Earl Ruby, in Parkland Memorial Hospital, Dallas, Texas. Gertz, 1968, p. 485-92
473. Warren Commission, Hearings and Exhibits, Vol. XII, 1964, p. 401
474. Dallas Municipal Archives JFK Collection, Box 4, folder 1, document 19 (http://jfk.ci.dallas.tx.us/11/1175-001.gif)
475. FBI, Clements Report, p. 20, report of Joseph J. Hanley & William Johnson dd. 24.11.1963
476. Warren Commission, Hearings and Exhibits, Vol. XIX, 1964, p. 772

477. Kantor, 1978, p. 65. In CE2002, the Commission (Warren Commission, Hearings and Exhibits, Vol. XXIV, 1964, p.65. In CE2002, the Commission (Warren Commission, Hearings and Exhibits, Vol. XXIV, 1964, p. 48) mentioned only 27 press representatives. Maegher (Meagher, 1967, reprinted, p 402-403) adds another seventeen to this, which already brings the total to at least 44. Missing names include Philippe Labro *(France Soir)* and Lawrence Schiller, who were standing less than a meter away from Oswald, yet did not make it onto the official list of reporters.
478. FBI, Clements report, p. ?? Statement of Chief Inspector Talbert dated November 25, 1963, p. 41
479. Kantor, 1978, p. 65
480. Meagher reports fourteen reporters, nine of whom were not checked in any way whatsoever with respect to their name or with reference to the source of their statement. (Meagher, 1967, reprinted, p. 403)
481. Warren Commission, Hearings and Exhibits, Vol. XXIV, 1964, p. 440 CE2027. Statement of Detective Brantley.
482. FBI 44-24016 Ruby HQ File, Section 64 p. 21, Statement of Assistant Chief Batchelor dated 11.24.1963
483. Warren Commission, Hearings and Exhibits, Vol. XV, 1964, p. 162
484. FBI 44-24016 Ruby HQ File, Section 75 p. 126, statement of Marvin (Bert) Hall
485. Warren Commission, Hearings and Exhibits, Vol. XV, 1964, p. 160
486. Warren Commission, Hearings and Exhibits, Vol. XV, 1964, p. 161
487. Kantor, 1978, p. 67
488. Warren Commission, Hearings and Exhibits, Vol. XV, 1964, p. 161
489. Commission Document 85 – FBI Clements Report of Dec 11, 1963 re: Ruby, p. 166
490. FBI, Clements report, November 30, 1963, p. 7. This recording is meanwhile available on the Internet, and is basically the equivalent of the Zapruder film, which captured the images of Kennedy's assassination.
491. Warren Commission, Hearings and Exhibits, Vol. XXIV, 1964, p. 52: Fritz Kuller of KDRL 'stated the videotape was continuous.'
492. Warren Commission, Hearings and Exhibits, Vol. XXIV, 1964, p. 51: 'Funeral home logged call at 11:21 a.m. [...] Dispatcher notified Ambulance 605 at 11:22 a.m.'
493. FBI, Clements Report, statement by DPD Deputy Chief Stevenson dated November 25, 1963, p. 35 and 36
494. Warren Commission, Hearings and Exhibits, Vol. XII, 1964, p. 339
495. Warren Commission, Hearings and Exhibits, Vol. XII, 1964, p. 427
496. Warren Commission, Hearings and Exhibits, Vol. XII, 1964, p. 420
497. Warren Commission, Hearings and Exhibits, Vol. XII, 1964, p. 361
498. The walls were already there in 1963, as can be seen, for example, from this plan. HSCA Appendix Vol. IV, 1978, p. 574
499. Warren Commission, Hearings and Exhibits, Vol. XXIV, 1964, p. 440, CE2026: length of the entrance: 30 meters.
500. HSCA Appendix Vol. IV, 1978, p. 575, JFK document F-562, report dated December 15 of the investigation commission of the Dallas Police.
501. Warren Commission, Hearings and Exhibits, Vol. XII, 1964, p. 433
502. Summers, *Not in your lifetime*, 1998, p. 357 and Davis, 1989, p. 207
503. Commission Document 302 – FBI Clements Report of January 17, 1964, re: Jack Ruby/Oswald/Civil Rights p. 16

504. FBI, Clements Report, p. 16, DL 44-1639, interview of November 25, 1963
505. Warren Commission, Hearings and Exhibits, Vol. XXIV, 1964, p. 56
506. FBI 44-24016 Ruby HQ File, Section 20, p. 124-125
507. FBI Supplemental Investigation of the Killing of Oswald, January 13, 1964, p. 6 'Sergeant Putnam also saw four or five people standing on the sidewalk,' but ibid p. 7 'Lieutenant Pierce saw two or three other persons as he left the ramp.'
508. Warren Commission, Hearings and Exhibits, Vol. XXIV, 1964, p. 56
509. Warren Commission, Hearings and Exhibits, Vol. XXIV, 1964, p. 51
510. Warren Commission, Hearings and Exhibits, Vol. XII, 1964, p. 401
511. Kantor, 1978, p. 75
512. Warren Commission, Hearings and Exhibits, Vol. XIII, 1964, p. 70
513. Summers, *Not in your lifetime,* 1998 p. 358
514. FBI 44-24016 Ruby HQ File, Section 9, p. 114
515. Warren Commission, Hearings and Exhibits, Vol. XIII, 1964, p. 52
516. FBI 44-24016 Ruby HQ File, Section 20, p. 171-172
517. Warren Commission, Hearings and Exhibits, Vol. XII, 1964, p. 412
518. Warren Commission, Hearings and Exhibits, Vol. XIII, 1964, p. 53
519. At 3.15 p.m., during the questioning by Captain Fritz, Ruby allegedly replied to the question of how he had entered the building as follows: 'That's something that I will not answer' or 'I'm not going to explain that.' He is also said to have stated that he came into the building using the driveway on Main Street just as Pierce drove out. But, at one moment, he asked Fritz: 'Don't you think I'd make a good actor?' Kantor, 1978, p. 76
520. Warren Commission Report, 1964, p. 221
521. Warren Commission, Hearings and Exhibits, Vol. XII, 1964, p. 324
522. FBI 44-24016 Ruby HQ File, Section 20, p. 141
523. Warren Commission, Hearings and Exhibits, Vol. XXIV, 1964, p. 79
524. Kantor, 1978, p. 145
525. Warren Commission, Hearings and Exhibits, Vol. XIII, 1964, p. 135
526. Warren Commission, Hearings and Exhibits, Vol. XIII, 1964, p. 136
527. Warren Commission Report, 1964, p. 221
528. Warren Commission, Hearings and Exhibits, Vol. XXIV, 1964, p. 180 CE2002
529. HSCA Appendix Vol. IV, 1978, p. 603
530. Warren Commission, Hearings and Exhibits, Vol. XII, 1964, p. 369
531. Warren Commission, Hearings and Exhibits, Vol. XII, 1964, p. 233
532. Warren Commission, Hearings and Exhibits, Vol. XIX, 1964, CE5327 p. 427
533. Warren Commission, Hearings and Exhibits, Vol. XIV, 1964, p. 50: 99 ft from the center of the sidewalk down the Main Street ramp to a line running East from the southeast corner of the Jail Office.
534. FBI Clements Report, p. 16, DL 44-1639, hearing of Ruby on November 25, 1963
535. Warren Commission, Hearings and Exhibits, Vol. XXV, 1964, p. 896
536. FBI Supplemental Investigation of the Killing of Oswald January 13, 1964, p. 13
537. FBI Supplemental Investigation of the Killing of Oswald January 13, 1964, p. 12
538. Warren Commission Report, 1964, p. 221
539. Warren Commission, Hearings and Exhibits, Vol. XXIV, 1964, p. 465
540. HSCA Appendix Vol. IV, 1978, p. 588
541. Warren Commission, Hearings and Exhibits, Vol. XII, 1964, p. 346

542. Warren Commission, Hearings and Exhibits, Vol. XII, 1964, p. 346
543. http://jfk.ci.dallas.tx.us/box14.htm, City of Dallas Archives. JFK Collection – Box 14, Item 91 (3131-001)
544. Warren Commission, Hearings and Exhibits, Vol. XIII, 1964, p. 327: 'Did he seem to be walking fast, slow, medium?' Doyle: 'Just ordinary gait.'
545. Warren Commission, Hearings and Exhibits, Vol. XXIV, 1964, p. 50: 'a distance of 339'6" from Westernmost doorway at the Western Union Office to the center of the ramp leading into the basement.'
546. Kantor, 1978, p. 68
547. Warren Commission Report, 1964, p. 221
548. http://jfk-archives.blogspot.be/2010/06/how-did-jack-ruby-enter-basement.html David von Pein's JFK Archives blog spot e-mail to Dave Von Pein dd. 2/4/2008
549. Kantor, 1978, p. 69
550. Warren Commission, Hearings and Exhibits, Vol. XII, 1964, p. 383
551. Warren Commission, Hearings and Exhibits, Vol. XII, 1964, p. 423
552. Warren Commission, Hearings and Exhibits, Vol. XIII, 1964, p. 179
553. FBI report of 13/1/1964 DL 89-43 p. 2
554. Warren Commission, Hearings and Exhibits, Vol. XV, 1964, p. 250
555. Dallas Municipal archives JFK Collection, Box 4, folder 1, document 18 (http://jfk.ci.dallas.tx.us/11/1166-001.gif)
556. Warren Commission, Hearings and Exhibits, Vol. XIII, 1964, p. 213
557. Warren Commission, Hearings and Exhibits, Vol. XIII, 1964, p. 286
558. Dallas Municipal archives JFK Collection, Box 4, folder 1, document 18 (http://jfk.ci.dallas.tx.us/11/1171-001.gif)
559. Dallas Municipal Archives Box 4, folder 1, document 16 (http://jfk.ci.dallas.tx.us/11/1166-001.gif)
560. FBI Report File DL 89-43, p. 289 statement of Karen Bennett on 03.01.1964.
561. Warren Commission, Hearings and Exhibits, Vol. XV, 1964, p. 644
562. Warren Commission, Hearings and Exhibits, Vol. XIII, 1964, p. 209
563. Warren Commission, Hearings and Exhibits, Vol. XV, 1964, p. 428
564. Warren Commission, Hearings and Exhibits, Vol. XV, 1964, p. 656
565. Warren Commission, Hearings and Exhibits, Vol. XIII, 1964, p. 210
566. Warren Commission, Hearings and Exhibits, Vol. XIX, 1964, p. 306
567. Warren Commission, Hearings and Exhibits, Vol. XIII, 1964, p. 210
568. Warren Commission, Hearings and Exhibits, Vol. XIII, 1964, p. 204
569. FBI report DL 44-1639 p. 43, statement of Huey Reeves dated 09.06.1964 and time stamp on receipt of 5$.
570. Warren Commission, Hearings and Exhibits, Vol. XIII, 1964, p. 248
571. Warren Commission, Hearings and Exhibits, Vol. XV, 1964, p. 663
572. Warren Commission, Hearings and Exhibits, Vol. XXV, 1964, p. 303
573. Warren Commission, Hearings and Exhibits, Vol. XV, 1964, p. 477
574. Warren Commission, Hearings and Exhibits, Vol. XV, 1964, p. 476
575. Warren Commission, Hearings and Exhibits, Vol. XX, 1964, p. 13
576. Warren Commission, Hearings and Exhibits, Vol. XXV, 1964, p. 191
577. NARA Records of the John F. Kennedy Assassination Collection. Key Person Files L. Meyers FBI report DL 44 1639, CR 86 p. 534. Fifteen years later, Lawrence Meyers claimed before the HSCA that he had had dinner with Ruby in the Cabana restaurant

that night. He was reasonably sure of that: 'Unless I have completely blown my mind we had dinner Saturday night.' But he was wrong: Ruby never had time for a meal in the Cabana on Saturday.

578. Warren Commission, Hearings and Exhibits, Vol. XIV, 1964, p. 427
579. Warren Commission, Hearings and Exhibits, Vol. XIII, 1964, p. 213
580. Warren Commission, Hearings and Exhibits, Vol. XV, 1964, p. 653
581. Warren Commission, Hearings and Exhibits, Vol. XV, 1964, p. 428
582. Warren Commission, Hearings and Exhibits, Vol. XV, 1964, p. 422
583. Warren Commission, Hearings and Exhibits, Vol. XIII, 1964, p. 210
584. Warren Commission, Hearings and Exhibits, Vol. XV, 1964, p. 663
585. Warren Commission, Hearings and Exhibits, Vol. XIX, 1964, p. 306
586. Warren Commission, Hearings and Exhibits, Vol. XIII, 1964, p. 212
587. Warren Commission, Hearings and Exhibits, Vol. XIII, 1964, p. 310
588. Kantor, 1978, p. 59: 'Payday in the Carousel was normally on Sunday.'
589. Warren Commission, Hearings and Exhibits, Vol. XIII, 1964, p. 210
590. Warren Commission, Hearings and Exhibits, Vol. XV, 1964, p. 620
591. FBI 62-109060 JFK HQ File, Section 74, p. 288
592. Warren Commission, Hearings and Exhibits, Vol. XV, 1964, p. 660
593. Dallas Municipal archives JFK Collection, Box 4, folder 1, document 16 (http://jfk.ci.dallas.tx.us/11/1166-001.gif)
594. Researcher Gary Shaw announced the following on the Burlesoncrowley.com/news site on October 18, 2010: 'Beverly Massagee called and said Karen died last month. Michael Carlin called [Massagee] to say Karen was cremated and the ashes buried in Tennessee.' Source: Peter Fokes https://groups.google.com/forum/#!topic/alt.assassination.jfk/K8M1O2gZhVE). In 1963, Beverly Oliver was one of Ruby's dancers. She later outed herself as the *Babushka lady* who filmed the murder close up.
595. John Rutledge, a journalist at *The Dallas Morning News*, knew Ruby, and saw him step out of the elevator on the third floor. Officer Eberhardt and Victor Robertson, a radio and TV reporter for WFFA, also confirmed Ruby's presence. According to the Warren Commission, there were two other unnamed witnesses.
596. Warren Commission Report, 1964, p. 340
597. Commission Document 1 – FBI Summary Report p. 13
598. Warren Commission, Hearings and Exhibits, Vol. XV, 1964, p. 484
599. Warren Commission, Hearings and Exhibits, Vol. XV, 1964, p. 486 Bugliosi (p. 195) claimed that Ruby was mentioned by name, but radio reporter Duncan denied this.
600. Warren Commission, Hearings and Exhibits, Vol. XV, 1964, p. 487
601. There is some confusion about the hour at which Ruby left KLIF. Duncan claimed that Ruby was there before 2:00 a.m., heard the news and stayed at the radio station for a half hour.
602. Warren Commission, Hearings and Exhibits, Vol. XIV, 1964, p. 630 The garage was located at the corner of Jackson Street and Field Street. Field Street is the first side-street from the Carousel on Commerce Street, in the direction of Dealey Plaza.
603. Warren Commission, Hearings and Exhibits, Vol. XIV, 1964, p. 631
604. Nara Records of the John F. Kennedy Assassination. Key Persons Files Harry Olsen p. 6, report of the hearing of Kay Coleman (Kathy Kay) on 11/12/63.
605. Warren Commission, Hearings and Exhibits, Vol. XIV, 1964, p. 643
606. Warren Commission, Hearings and Exhibits, Vol. XIV, 1964, p. 646

607. Warren Commission, Hearings and Exhibits, Vol. V, 1964, p. 191
608. Warren Commission, Hearings and Exhibits, Vol. XIV, 1964, p. 631
609. Nara Records of the John F. Kennedy Assassination. Key Persons Files Harry Olsen p. 3, report of the hearing of Olsen on 12.12.1963. According to an unknown source, Ruby, Kay and Olsen also drank a few beers in the garage.
610. Nara Records of the John F. Kennedy Assassination. Key Persons Files Harry Olsen p. 108, report of the examination of Olsen on 12.12.1963. Letter from the FBI dated 01.09.1964. CD1463. How Bugliosi (2007, p. 197) managed to conclude that this was about Johnny 'Johnson' is unclear. In September 1964, the FBI were finally able to identify the parking attendant who had taken part in the conversation: it was a certain John P. Simpson. He confirmed the nocturnal meeting, but firmly denied that he had been present there.
611. Nara Records of the John F. Kennedy Assassination. Key Persons Files Harry Olsen p. 3, report of the examination of Olsen on 12.12.1963.
612. Nara Records of the John F. Kennedy Assassination. Key Persons Files George Senator p. 2, affidavit of Senator on 24.11.1963.
613. Warren Commission Report, 1964, p. 371, HSCA, Appendix Vol. IX, 1978, p. 985-988
614. Warren Commission, Hearings and Exhibits, Vol. XXV, 1964, p. 235
615. Warren Commission, Hearings and Exhibits, Vol. XV, 1964, p. 672
616. Warren Commission, Hearings and Exhibits, Vol. XIV, 1964, p. 153
617. Warren Commission, Hearings and Exhibits, Vol. XX, 1964, p. 55
618. Warren Commission, Hearings and Exhibits, Vol. XXV, 1964, p. 297
619. Warren Commission, Hearings and Exhibits, Vol. XXV, 1964, p. 251
620. NARA Records of the John F. Kennedy Assassination Collection. Key Person Files Ralph Paul FBI report DL 44 1639, CR 86 p. 413 FBI hearing of R. Paul 24.11.1963 NARA Records of the John F. Kennedy Assassination Collection. Key Person Files Ralph Paul FBI report DL 44 1639, CR 86 p. 424 FBI hearing of Mrs. Bert Bowman 24.11.1963. NARA Records of the John F. Kennedy Assassination Collection. Key Person Files Ralph Paul FBI report DL 44 1639, CR 86 p. 426 FBI hearing of John Jackson 24.11.1963
621. NARA Records of the John F. Kennedy Assassination Collection. Key Person Files Ralph Paul FBI report DL 44 1639, CR 86 p. 412 FBI hearing of R. Paul 24.11.1963
622. Warren Commission, Hearings and Exhibits, Vol. XIV, 1964, p. 153
623. Only eight months later, he remembered the second encounter again.
624. Nara Records of the John F. Kennedy Assassination. Key Persons Files Harry Olsen p. 62 The telephone records of Kathy Kay indicated that there had been a 6-minute call to Olsen's father in Henriette from her apartment on November 22, 1963. According to her statement, she had driven all the way to Wichita Falls, Henrietta, that Sunday together with Olsen, a drive of 240 kilometers. She said she had arranged a babysitter and left with Olsen at around 4.00 p.m. She deduced this from the fact that it was already getting dark when they arrived in Henrietta after driving three hours. How could Olsen have forgotten that drive? According to Kathy, the reason was actually a visit to his parents, who were to meet her for the first time, the woman whom Olsen would marry a month later. That doesn't seem to be something you'd just forget. On the same evening, according to Kathy, the pair made their way back to Dallas at 10.00 p.m.
625. Ruby had skated over Olsen's leg during an ice hockey game, with the fracture as a result. This is hardly a believable story. A less sporty story would sound much more

credible: As a fervent gay hater, Olsen allegedly used to hang out with his knuckle-dusters in a public toilet that was known as a meeting place for homosexuals. Shortly before Kennedy's assassination, he is said to have under-estimated an opponent, and suffered a broken knee as a consequence. Olsen himself gave no explanation for his injury. He was in any case in a plaster cast in mid-November.

626. Livingstone H., p.341. There are only two buildings in 8th Street that can qualify as an 'estate'. Number 425E was a villa where heavy gamblers plied their trade. Ruby gratefully collected his percentage of the heavy losses of the gamblers who he passed on to the tender mercies of the establishment. The correct address of the property where Olsen worked was never proven.
627. Warren Commission, Hearings and Exhibits, Vol. XVII, 1964, p. 401
628. Bugliosi, 2007, p. 1107
629. Posner, 1993, 2003, p. 361
630. NARA Records of the John F. Kennedy Assassination Collection. Key Person Files Ruby_jack_nov_63_dec_63_2-4_business_and_financial_interests. CR46 p. 191, statement by Irving Mazzei dated 29.11.1963.
631. Wall learned about the Kennedy assassination through the TV. He and his friend responded with great sadness: 'I stayed in the bedroom and watched the television to find out what was, you know, going on. We stayed there all that night and we departed for Galveston to get away from Dallas the next day, which was Saturday, at around 3 or 4 in the afternoon.' Wall didn't even leave the bedroom to eat. He had thereby informed no-one that he would leave Dallas, and certainly not that he was going to Galveston.
632. Warren Commission, Hearings and Exhibits, Vol. XIV, 1964, p. 604
633. Warren Commission, Hearings and Exhibits, Vol. XIV, 1964 p. 601 Wall was with former vacation neighbors, the McKenna's. Both families had stayed in touch with each other.
634. Warren Commission, Hearings and Exhibits, Vol. XV, 1964, p. 551
635. Warren Commission, Hearings and Exhibits, Vol. XV, 1964, p.343
636. Warren Commission, Hearings and Exhibits, Vol. XIV, 1964, p. 529
637. Warren Commission, Hearings and Exhibits, Vol. XIX, 1964, p. 537
638. NARA, Records of the John F. Kennedy Assassination. Key Person Files J. Ruby CR876
639. Warren Commission, Hearings and Exhibits, Vol. XXIV, 1964, p. 429
640. Warren Commission, Hearings and Exhibits, Vol. XIX, 1964, p. 770
641. Warren Commission, Hearings and Exhibits, Vol. IV, 1964, p. 233
642. Warren Commission, Hearings and Exhibits, Vol. XXV, 1964, p. 233
643. DL 44-1639 p. 10 CR 105 p. 327 According to the FBI report, the conversation lasted eleven minutes, from 10.10 to 10.21 a.m. But the official statement of Southwestern Bell Telephone Company probably gives the correct time.
644. Warren Commission, Hearings and Exhibits, Vol. XIII, 1964, p. 211
645. FBI report DL 44-1639 11/12/1963
646. Dallas Municipal Archives JFK Collection, Box 4, folder 1, document 14 (http://jfk.ci.dallas.tx.us/11/1175-001.gif)
647. Secret Service hearing of November 24 by Special Agent Warner, file no. CO-2 34030, CR81 p. 423
648. Warren Commission, Hearings and Exhibits, Vol. XIII, 1964, p. 213
649. Warren Commission, Hearings and Exhibits, Vol. XIII, 1964, p. 213

650. Warren Commission, Hearings and Exhibits, Vol. v, 1964, p. 206. Witness Pastor Rushing remembers seeing Ruby in the police building at 9.30 a.m. But we know that he had a brief telephone conversation with Karen Bennett at 10.19 a.m. Ruby had also phoned his cleaning lady Elnora Pitts between 8.00 and 9.00 a.m. She stated that Ruby had sounded very strange, but that she was certain that it was him on the line. The pastor was therefore mistaken.
651. Warren Commission, Hearings and Exhibits, Vol. xii, 1964, p. 237
652. Warren Commission, Hearings and Exhibits, Vol. xii, 1964, p. 81
653. Kantor, 1978, p.61
654. Warren Commission, Hearings and Exhibits, Vol. xii, 1964, p. 82
655. NARA, Records of the John F. Kennedy Assassination. Key Persons Files L.D. Blackie Harrison, p. 28, FBI report of 20.07.1964
656. NARA, Records of the John F. Kennedy Assassination. Key Persons Files L.D. Miller p. 23, hearing of L.D. Miller dated 24.03.1964.
657. Warren Commission, Hearings and Exhibits, Vol. xii, 1964, p. 306
658. Kantor, 1978, p. 147
659. Warren Commission, Hearings and Exhibits, Vol. xii, 1964, p. 243
660. Warren Commission Report, 1964, p. 224
661. Bugliosi, 2007, p. 882l
662. Warren Commission, Hearings and Exhibits, Vol. xiv, 1964, p. 632
663. Hurt, 1985, p. 252, Source: Senate Select Committee, *Investigation of the Assassination*, p. 51
664. Hurt, 1985, p. 252
665. Titovets, 2010, p. 160
666. Epstein E. J., Legend. *The Secret World of Lee Harvey Oswald*, 1978, 2011, p. 365
667. Epstein E. J., Legend. *The Secret World of Lee Harvey Oswald*, p. 73
668. Epstein E. J., Legend. *The Secret World of Lee Harvey Oswald*, 1978, 2011, p. 60
669. Warren Commission Report, 1964, p. 423
670. Warren Commission, Hearings and Exhibits, Vol. xxiv, 1964, p. 269
671. Posner, 1993, 2003, p. 85
672. Posner, 1993, 2003, p. 79 and 81
673. Posner, 1993, 2003, p. 95
674. Posner, 1993, 2003, p. 83
675. Posner, 1993, 2003, p. 109
676. Posner, 1993, 2003, p. 94
677. Epstein E. J., Legend. *The Secret World of Lee Harvey Oswald*, 1978, 2011, loc 5652
678. Posner, 1993, 2003, p. 75
679. Posner, 1993, 2003, p. 6
680. Siegel Exhibit 1 – http://mcadams.posc.mu.edu/siegel1.htm. Siegel confirmed her opinion of 1953 in the Frontline documentary https://www.youtube.com/watch?v=n-uayVALahU
681. Posner, 1993, 2003, p. 7
682. Warren Commission Report, 1964, p. 381
683. Warren Commission Report, 1964, p. 380
684. Warren Commission Report, 1964, p. 381
685. Warren Commission, Hearings and Exhibits Vol. xx, 1964, p. 308

686. Epstein E. J., Legend. *The Secret World of Lee Harvey Oswald*, 1978, 2011, Kindle version, loc. 1069
687. Warren Commission, Hearings and Exhibits Vol. XX, 1964, p. 308
688. Epstein E. J., Legend. *The Secret World of Lee Harvey Oswald*, 1978, 2011, Kindle version loc. 1136
689. Warren Commission, Hearings and Exhibits, Vol. VIII, p. 315
690. Epstein E. J., Legend. *The Secret World of Lee Harvey Oswald*, 1978, 2011, loc. 1185
691. Epstein E. J., Legend. *The Secret World of Lee Harvey Oswald*, 1978, 2011, loc. 1429
692. Warren Commission, Hearings and Exhibits Vol. XX, 1964, p. 308
693. Marchetti published a critical book on the CIA in 1973: *The CIA and the Cult of Intelligence*. The CIA censored 399 sections of the book, later reduced to 168. In protest, Marchetti published the book with blank spaces replacing the omitted sections. This ensured the necessary additional publicity for the book, which made it into a bestseller.
694. Interview of Marchetti with Dr. Grover B. Proctor, in *The Raleigh Call and the Fingerprints of Intelligence*, http:/www.groverproctor.us/jfk/jfk80.html
695. Hurt, 1985, p. 243 and HSCA Appendix Vol. IV, 1978, pp. 178-186
696. Titovets, 2010, p. 165
697. There are authors (Summers, *Conspiracy*, p. 191 and Penn Jones, *Forgive my Grief*, Vol. 4, p. 169) who claim that Marina knew Robert E. Webster in Leningrad. Webster was also a former Marine who defected to the Soviet Union two weeks before Oswald, and who also returned to the US a few years later. If Marina had also been sent to him to find out whether Webster was interested in a relationship, that would obviously be quite significant.
698. Savodnik, 2013
699. Titovets, 2010, p. 234
700. Warren Commission, Hearings and Exhibits Vol. IX, 1964, p. 310
701. http://www.jfkassassinationforum.com/index.php?topic=1328.0;wap2
702. Epstein E. J., Legend. *The Secret World of Lee Harvey Oswald*, 1978, 2011, loc. 5540. From January 28 to April 25, Oswald had an income of 693 dollars, which – after paying the rent, transportation and the purchase of the weapons – left him 408 dollars to survive for 88 days (ibid. loc. 5618). That is around at least 4.60 dollars a day. But this was also nothing less than poverty, and it demonstrates once again how remarkable the rapid repayment of his debts really was. It seems hardly possible that Oswald had no other (unknown) sources of income, for example as an informer. From April 26 to September 1, Oswald had an income of 804 dollars, of which he spent 297 dollars on rent and 55 dollars on expenses for his political activities. That leaves him with 397 dollars for 127 days, or about 3.10 dollars a day (ibid. loc. 5690).
703. http://legal-dictionary.thefreedictionary.com/Adversary+system
704. Warren Commission Report, 1964, p. 187
705. Warren Commission, Hearings and Exhibits, Vol. V, 1964, p. 516
706. Commission Document 81.1 – AG Texas p. 12
707. Warren Commission, Hearings and Exhibits, Vol. XXIII, p. 760, CE 1953, Warren Commission, Hearings and Exhibits, Vol. XXIV, 1964, p. 40
708. Warren Commission, Hearings and Exhibits, Vol. XI, 1964, p. 423, Patrol Squad 26, Sgt. Hansen. Warren Commission, Hearings and Exhibits, Vol. XXIV, 1964, p. 40 (5)
709. Warren Commission, Hearings and Exhibits, Vol. XI, 1964, p. 415
710. Warren Commission, Hearings and Exhibits, Vol. XXIV, 1964, p. 41

711. Warren Commission, Hearings and Exhibits, Vol. XI, 1964, p. 415
712. Warren Commission, Hearings and Exhibits, Vol. XXIII, p. 767
713. Warren Commission, Hearings and Exhibits, Vol. XXIV, 1964, p. 39 CE 2001, circled (3) and Warren Commission, Hearings and Exhibits, Vol. XXIV, 1964, p. 40 CE 2001, circled (5) en Commission Document 81.1 – AG Texas p. 12
714. Meagher, 1967, reprinted, p. 288
715. The date of the newspaper was November 29, but the paper was printed on Monday, November 25. FBI 105-82555 Oswald HQ File, Section 201, p. 36
716. Warren Commission Report, 1964, p. 662
717. Warren Commission, Hearings and Exhibits, Vol. XXIV, 1964, p. 766
718. Warren Commission, Hearings and Exhibits, Vol. III, p. 86-87.
719. Warren Commission, Hearings and Exhibits, Vol. XXII, 1964, p. 765 CE 1403 and Commission Document 205 – FBI Report of 23 Dec 1963 re: Oswald p. 710
720. Commission Document 205 – FBI Report of 23 Dec 1963 re: CD 5, Gemberling Report p. 712
721. Warren Commission, Hearings and Exhibits, Vol. XXIII, p. 393
722. Warren Commission, Hearings and Exhibits Vol. IX, 1964, p. 393
723. Warren Commission Report, 1964, p. 184
724. FBI 62-109060 JFK HQ File, Section 36: http://www.maryferrell.org/mffweb/archive/viewer/showDoc.do?absPageId=759909
725. Warren Commission, Hearings and Exhibits, Vol. XXIII, p. 393
726. Warren Commission, Hearings and Exhibits, Vol. XXIII, p. 393 CE 1785
727. Warren Commission, Hearings and Exhibits, Vol. I., 1964, p. 16
728. Warren Commission Report, 1964, p. 405
729. Warren Commission, Hearings and Exhibits, Vol. XXIV, 1964, p. 41
730. Warren Commission, Hearings and Exhibits, Vol. XXIII, p. 762
731. Warren Commission, Hearings and Exhibits, Vol. XXIII, p. 762
732. Warren Commission, Hearings and Exhibits, Vol. XVI, 1964, p. 439 105-82555 Section 186 p. 121
733. Warren Commission, Hearings and Exhibits, Vol. XXVI, 1964, p. 440
734. Warren Commission, Hearings and Exhibits, Vol. XI, 1964, p. 416 – 417
735. Warren Commission, Hearings and Exhibits, Vol. XI, 1964, p. 436
736. Warren Commission, Hearings and Exhibits, Vol. XXIV, 1964, p. 40 CE2001, circled (6),
737. Warren Commission, Hearings and Exhibits, Vol. XI, 1964, p. 418
738. Warren Commission, Hearings and Exhibits, Vol. XXIV, 1964, p. 40 CE2001, circled (6)
739. Warren Commission, Hearings and Exhibits, Vol. XXIII, p. 762
740. Warren Commission Report, 1964, p. 187
741. Bugliosi, 2007, p. 694
742. Bugliosi, 2007, p. 350
743. Epstein E. J., Legend. *The Secret World of Lee Harvey Oswald*, Kindle version loc. 493
744. Epstein E. J., Legend. *The Secret World of Lee Harvey Oswald*, loc. 5611
745. Marrs, 1993, paperback edition, p. 129
746. HSCA, Appendix Vol. II, 1978, p. 234
747. Warren Commission, Hearings and Exhibits Vol. IX, 1964, p. 249
748. Warren Commission, Hearings and Exhibits Vol. IX, 1964, p. 316
749. Warren Commission, Hearings and Exhibits, Vol. I, 1964, p. 18

750. There was a discussion about the way the date was written. Melanie Swift points out the existence of a postcard (Warren Commission, Hearings and Exhibits, Vol. XVI, 1964, p. 885, CE 321) on which Oswald also wrote the date May 10, 1962, as 10/V/1962.
751. Epstein E. J., Legend. *The Secret World of Lee Harvey Oswald*, 1978, 2011, loc. 5589
752. Epstein E. J., Legend. *The Secret World of Lee Harvey Oswald*, 1978, 2011, loc. 5594
753. Warren Commission, Hearings and Exhibits, Vol. XXIV, 1964, p. 39 CE 2001, circled (3)
754. Warren Commission, Hearings and Exhibits, Vol. III, p. 439
755. Warren Commission, Hearings and Exhibits, Vol. III, p. 503
756. Warren Commission Report, 1964, p. 186
757. FBI 62-109060 JFK HQ File 2845, http://www.giljesus.com/Walker/bullet.htm
758. HSCA Appendix VII, p. 380
759. For example, Colin Crow on the JFK Assassination Forum, http://www.jfkassassinationforum.com/index.php/topic,9679.0.html
760. Warren Commission, Hearings and Exhibits, Vol. III, p. 439
761. Mailgram from Edwin Walker September 12, 1978, courtesy of Gil Jesus. Source: http://www.giljesus.com/Walker/bullet.htm. FBI number illegible 62-117290?
762. Warren Commission, Hearings and Exhibits, Vol. XXIII, p. 757 and following CE1953 p. 18 discrepancies
763. Warren Commission, Hearings and Exhibits, Vol. XXIII, p. 759
764. Warren Commission, Hearings and Exhibits, Vol. IV, 1964, p. 273
765. Warren Commission, Hearings and Exhibits, Vol. III, p. 503
766. Warren Commission, Hearings and Exhibits, Vol. III, p. 503
767. Warren Commission, Hearings and Exhibits, Vol. III, p. 438
768. Warren Commission, Hearings and Exhibits, Vol. III, p. 503
769. Epstein E. J., Legend. *The Secret World of Lee Harvey Oswald*, 1978, 2011, loc 5573
770. Warren Commission, Hearings and Exhibits, Vol. VII, 1964, p. 439
771. HSCA, Appendix Vol. II, 1978, p. 234
772. HSCA Appendix Volumes VIII, 1978, p. 236
773. For example, the letter says: 'should there be anything in the papers.' This could point to facts that were perhaps not serious enough to be picked up by the newspapers. Oswald assured Marina that she could count on the compassion and the help of the Red Cross. Wouldn't that would seem rather unlikely if he was about to commit a serious crime?
774. Interview of Volkmar Schmidt by William E. Kelly, dated 01.01.2008, source: http://jfkcountercoup.blogspot.be/2008/01/volkmar-schmidt-interview.html
775. Epstein E. J., Legend. *The Secret World of Lee Harvey Oswald*, 1978, 2011, loc. 3301
776. Hakl, 2014, p. 72
777. Russ Holmes Work File, Memorandum for: Article by Gaeton Fonzi: 'Who killed JFK?' *Washingtonian*, November 3, 1980, p. 15
778. Warren Commission, Hearings and Exhibits Vol. IX, 1964, p. 236 and Commission Document 555 – FBI Wood Report of 14 Mar 1964 re: George de Mohrenschildt p. 79
779. Staff investigation March 1979, Johanna Smith, http://jfkassassination.net/russ/jfkinfo4/jfk12/defector.htm
780. Oswald 201 File, Vol. 10, Part 1, Sect 2 p. 17 source: http://www.maryferrell.org/mffweb/archive/viewer/showDoc.do?mode=searchResult&absPageId=997521
781. Warren Commission, Hearings and Exhibits, Vol. VIII, p. 135. There is some uncertainty about the day of Oswald's arrival in New Orleans, as he left Dallas on Wednes-

day, April 24, and only arrived in New Orleans on Monday, April 29, five days later. Lillian Murret, his aunt who looked after him in New Orleans, was sure that he arrived on a Monday. Why did Oswald's trip take four days longer than normal? Presumably his aunt made a mistake.

782. HSCA, Final Report, 1978, p. 170
783. Fleming, 2013, loc. 1297
784. Summers, *Not in your lifetime*, 1998, p. 233
785. Summers, *Not in your lifetime*, 1998, p. 226
786. HSCA, Appendix Vol. X, 1978, p. 132
787. Summers, *Not in your lifetime*, 1998, p. 231
788. Escalante, 2006, p. 103
789. North, 2011, p. 273
790. North, 2011, p. 275
791. Hancock, 2006, p. 165
792. Memorandum: Fair Play for Cuba Committee, Nara Record Number 104-10310-10152
793. Summers, *Not in your lifetime*, 1998, p. 228
794. HSCA, Final Report, 1978, p. 128: Ross Banister, Guy's brother, and Ivan Nitschke. Hinckle and Turner, *Deadly Secrets*, pp. 234-5: George Higginbothan, Adrian Alba, Allen and David Campbell, Ronnie Caire, David L. Lewis, William Gaudet... Summers, *Not in your lifetime*, 1998, p. 228: Delphine Roberts, Banister's secretary and mistress, and her daughter (also named Delphine) also confirmed Oswald's regular presence in the building where they worked. Roberts confirmed that the formation of an FPCC branch was Banister's idea. When Delphine Roberts saw them together, Oswald and Banister spoke together for a long time behind closed doors.
795. Jack Martin hated Ferrie, and, in order to accuse him, laid a connection between Ferrie and Oswald in two ways: their participation in the same aviator camp several years before, and the fact that Oswald allegedly had Ferrie's library card in his possession. But he did not make a connection with respect to the presence of both men in the building in Camp Street. Martin therefore never saw Oswald and Banister together, although he was present in Banister's office almost 90 percent of the time. Banister's widow Mary found a pack of FPCC pamphlets among his papers, but we have to take her at her word. Russell Willie and Joseph Cambre of the Louisiana State Police acquired what was left of Banister's files from the widow. One of the files was entitled '23-7 'Fair Play For Cuba'. But the HSCA could only conclude that this file had been destroyed under the Privacy Act in the meantime.
796. Memo: Garrison's charges against CIA, NARA Record Number: 104-10435-10025
797. Mellen, 2007, p. 401
798. Kaiser, 2008, p. 214
799. Warren Commission, Hearings and Exhibits Vol. XX, 1964, p. 524, V.T. Lee Exhibit #5
800. Epstein E. J., Legend. *The Secret World of Lee Harvey Oswald*, 1978, 2011, loc. 5679. For the photograph of the action, see Warren Commission, Hearings and Exhibits, Vol. XXI, 1964, p. 139.
801. Mellen, 2007, p. 56
802. Kaiser, 2008, p. 206
803. AARC Conference Bethesda, November 2014
804. Summers, *Not in your lifetime*, 1998, p. 250
805. Fonzi, 1993, p. 141

806. Fonzi, 1993, p. 142
807. Commission Document 1154 – State Meeker Letter of 23 Jun 1964 with Attachments re: Mexican Dept Foreign Affairs, p. 4
808. Commission Document 75 – FBI DeBrueys Report dated December 2, 1963, re: Oswald Russia p. 573
809. Douglas J., 2008, p. 179
810. HSCA, Final Report, 1978, p. 219
811. Nara Record Number: 104-10135-10019
812. Warren Commission, Hearings and Exhibits, Vol. XI, 1964, p. 215.
813. Warren Commission Report, 1964, p. 234
814. Morley, 2008, p. 181
815. Lopez Report p. 193
816. Warren Commission, Hearings and Exhibits, Vol. XXIV, 1964, p. 573
817. Newman, *Where Angels Tread Lightly. The Assassination of President Kennedy.* Volume 1, 2015, p. 310. Dulles phrased it as follows: 'Often the very fear of deception has blinded an opponent to the real value of the information which accidents or intelligence operations have placed in his hands.'
818. Fonzi, 1993, p. 295
819. Lopez Report p. 49 and 101
820. Lopez Report p. 143
821. Commission Document 347 – CIA Information of 31 Jan 1964 re: Oswald's Trip to Mexico p. 16
822. HSCA, Appendix Vol. III, 1978, p. 30
823. Summers, *Not in your lifetime*, 1998, p. 272
824. Epstein E. J., Legend. *The Secret World of Lee Harvey Oswald*, 1978, 2011, loc. 5795
825. Lopez Report p. 127, referring to page 273 of a manuscript that Scott prepared in 1970 about his thirteen years of service with the CIA.
826. Fonzi, 1993, p. 294
827. Morley, 2008, p. 186
828. Lopez Report p. 11, HSCA, Final Report, 1978, p. 250
829. Summers, *Not in your lifetime*, 1998, p. 2276; Telephone Conversation between the President and J. Edgar Hoover, 23 Nov 1963 http://www.maryferrell.org/mffweb/archive/viewer/showDoc.do?docId=807&relPageId=2,
830. Fonzi, 1993, p. 286
831. Fonzi, 1993, p. 287
832. Hosty, 1996, p. 303 The annex to Hosty's book contains a copy of the CIA Summary Report.
833. Newman, 2010,
834. Waldron, *Legacy of Secrecy. The Long Shadow of the JFK Assassination*, 2009, p. 214
835. Summers, *Not in your lifetime*, 1998, p. 277
836. Fonzi, 1993, p. 288
837. Summers, *Not in your lifetime*, 1998, p. 266
838. There were other witnesses as well, such as Oscar Contreras, who described a person who introduced himself as Oswald, as blond and short. It is not entirely certain that Contreras really met Oswald, unlike Azcue and Duran. We will therefore not consider Contreras in further detail here.

839. Lopez Report p. 186 and Russ Holmes Work File/ NARA Record Number: 104-10404-10103
840. Fonzi, 1993, p. 288
841. Phillips had several identities he could use. He even traveled with a Belgian passport at some point. Source: Fonzi, 1993, p. 130. In addition to Barker and Bishop, he operated in Cuba under the names Jack Stewart and Andrew F. Morton. Newman, *Where Angels Tread Lightly. The Assassination of President Kennedy.* Volume 1, 2015, p. 90.
842. Waldron, *Legacy of Secrecy. The Long Shadow of the JFK Assassination*, 2009, p. 216 Nara 104-10169-10458, http://www.maryferrell.org/mffweb/archive/viewer/showDoc.do?docId=37974&relPageId=2
843. Morley, 2008, p. 210
844. Nara 104-10419-11024, https://www.maryferrell.org/mffweb/archive/viewer/showDoc.do?mode=searchResult&absPageId=236051
845. Castro was Prime Minister, Dorticos was the President.
846. Waldron, *Legacy of Secrecy. The Long Shadow of the JFK Assassination*, 2009, p. 217
847. NARA 104-10015-10055, https://www.maryferrell.org/mffweb/archive/viewer/showDoc.do?docId=1603&relPageId=3
848. HSCA Segregated CIA Collection, Box 28/NARA Record Number: 104-10088-10108; Morley, 2008, p. 210
849. Morley, 2008, p. 220
850. Morley, 2008, p. 224
851. Morley, 2008, p. 221
852. CIA Record 104-10127-10207, 'Mexico City Chronology', pp. 8–9
853. HSCA, Appendix Vol. III, 1978, p. 652
854. Summers, *Not in your lifetime*, 1998
855. Fonzi, 1993, p. 302
856. Fonzi, 1993, p. 295
857. Warren Commission Executive Session of 27 Jan 1964, p. 153
858. Warren Commission Report, 1964, p. 304
859. Warren Commission, Hearings and Exhibits XXV, 1964, p. 589
860. Warren Commission Report, 1964, p. 734
861. Bugliosi, 2007, p. 756
862. Warren Commission Report, 1964, p. 304
863. The full text of the telegram read as follows: '1. 1 Oct 63, American Male who spoke broken Russian said his name Lee Oswald (phonetic), stated he at Sovemb on 28 Sept when spoke with Consul whom he believed be Valeriy Vladimirovich Kostikov. Subj asked Sov guard Ivan Obyedkov who answered, if there anything new re telegram to Washington. Obyedkov upon checking said nothing received yet, but request had been sent. 2. Have photos male appears be American entering Sovemb 1246 hours, leaving 1222 on 1 Oct. Apparent age 35, Athletic build, circa 6 feet, receding hairline balding top. Wore khakis and sport shirt.'
864. MEXI 6453 of October 8, 1963; Incoming 36017 of October 9, CIA Document #5-1A, text in Lopez Report, 136-37
865. Oswald, or 'Oswald,' merely implied that Kostikov was indeed the man he had spoken with. In a letter to the Russian embassy dated October 12, Oswald referred to his 'meetings with comrade Kostin.' It was standard procedure of the CIA to open all letters to the Russian embassy. Kostikov was the only person at the Russian embassy whose

name resembled 'Kostin' (Commission Document 347 – CIA Information of 31 Jan 1964 re: Oswald's Trip to Mexico p. 15). Nechiporenko and Obyedkov also later confirmed that the American visitor had indeed spoken with Kostikov. The CIA did not have this information on October 8, however.

866. Morley, 2008, p. 192
867. Morley, 2008, p. 196
868. Morley, 2008, p. 198
869. Fonzi, 1993, p. 176
870. Talbot, Brothers. *The Hidden History of the Kennedy Years*, 2007, p. 383
871. Talbot, Brothers. *The Hidden History of the Kennedy Years*, 2007, p. 383
872. WASP: White Anglo-Saxon Protestants, a group of influential, socially high-ranking white Americans with protestant English ancestors.
873. Talbot, Brothers. *The Hidden History of the Kennedy Years*, 2007, p. 384
874. Fonzi, 1993, p. 142
875. Talbot, Brothers. *The Hidden History of the Kennedy Years*, 2007, p. 385
876. Fonzi, 1993, p. 284
877. Fonzi, 1993, p. 291
878. Fonzi, 1993, p. 368
879. Fonzi, 1993, p. 297
880. Fonzi, 1993, p. 419
881. Kaiser, 2008, p 321
882. *Washington Post*, 22 December 1963, p. A11
883. Warren Commission Report, 1964, p. 301
884. Fonzi, 1993, p. 109
885. Summers, *Not in your lifetime*, 1998, p. 297
886. The phone call with Leopoldo took place one or two days after the visit, on a weekday, possibly a Friday. This means that the men must have visited Silvia on a Wednesday or a Thursday. But Oswald had apparently cashed an unemployment check for $33 in New Orleans on Wednesday, September 25 (Warren Commission, Hearings and Exhibits, Vol. XXIV, 1964, p. 717). If Oswald then traveled 750 kilometers to Dallas by bus, he could not have arrived in time at Silvia Odio's house that evening. In addition, he was also said to be in Austin that day to complain about his dishonorable discharge from the army. After he left Odio, he then had to manage the 360 kilometers back to Houston in order to catch the bus to Mexico the next morning. We can certainly rule out Thursday evening, September 26, because Oswald arrived in Mexico City on Friday morning, after spending the previous night on the bus. It therefore seems impossible that Oswald was in Dallas on the last Wednesday or Thursday of September. On Thursday evening, October 3, on the other hand, Oswald was already two full days into his return from Mexico. We also know that Oswald visited Marina and Ruth in Irving on October 4, and that he slept in the YMCA that night (Warren Commission, Hearings and Exhibits Vol. X, p. 281). It is therefore sure that Oswald returned to Dallas from Mexico, and not to New Orleans, from where he had left. If he was the man that Silvia Odio met, we must assume that the encounter took place after his Mexico trip, not before.
887. Warren Commission Report, 1964, p. 324
888. HSCA, Final Report, 1978, p. 138

889. HSCA Immunized testimony of Loran Hall, NARA Record Number: 180-10118-10115, p. 24

890. Hancock, 2006, p. 471

891. Fonzi, 1993, p. 116

892. Fonzi, 1993, p. 254

893. Fonzi, 1993, p. 408

894. http://spartacus-educational.com/JFKhallL.htm

895. The HSCA hearing of James B. Wilcott that was kept secret, March 22, 1978, p. 19, (http://www.maryferrell.org/showDoc.html?docId=260)

896. An example: The FBI made a list of eight long distance calls that Seth Kantor allegedly made on a particular day. The list was included in the annexes of the Warren Report (WC Vol. XXV p. 236-237, Comm. Exhibit 2301). In 1975, Kantor discovered (Kantor, 1978, p. 201) that one phone call was missing from the list. It was a call to journalist Hal Hendrix. As early as 6 p.m., Hendrix was able to disseminate information that linked Oswald to Cuba. Only later did it became apparent that Hendrix was a fixed contact person for all kinds of disinformation campaigns of the CIA. He also had good contacts with David Phillips in the context of the propaganda efforts of the CIA. It was precisely this contact that had disappeared from the list of Kantor's phone calls.

897. Only one of these letters was mentioned in the Warren Report (Warren Commission Report, 1964, p. 307, with a footnote referring to CE2950), and was included as evidence in the annexes (Warren Commission, Hearings and Exhibits, Vol. XXVI, 1964, p. 421). Four other letters together made up Commission Document 295, but were not included in the annexes (Commission Document 295 – FBI Four Letters from Cuba Indicating Oswald Assassination Kennedy). The Cuban counterespionage succeeded in intercepting the sixth and last letter (Escalante, 2006, p. 136).

898. The Cuban counterespionage thereby knew about a telephone conversation Agent Kelly is said to have had on December 5 at 12.40 o'clock regarding a letter Marina Oswald had received 'yesterday.' This letter was addressed to Oswald and was dated November 10, but had a postmark of November 23, the day after the assassination. According to him, a letter from Havana could never have reached the United States in twelve days, because all mail from Havana always made a stopover in Mexico City.

899. CD295 p. 2, letter dated 17.01.1964 from Hoover to Commissioner Rankin of the Warren Commission.

900. Escalante, 2006, p. 145

901. David Talbot, *The Mother of All Cover-Ups*

902. CIA agent Donald Norton stated that Oswald was with the CIA 'and if he did it then you better believe the whole CIA was involved.' Former CIA agent Joseph Newbrough said: 'Oswald was an agent for the CIA and acting under orders.' Howard Hunt and John Martino allegedly even admitted that he had been involved in the assassination of Kennedy. CIA informant John Garrett Underhill is also often quoted. On May 8, 1964, just before Jim Garrison was to question him, Underhill was found dead with a bullet in his head. The official cause of death was suicide. McAdams (McAdams, 2011, p. 108) however, says the following about Underhill: 'He was quite simply a mentally unstable fellow who thought there was a JFK conspiracy, just as many other (stable and unstable) Americans did. Thus, there is no reason to doubt his death certificate, which says he "shot himself in the head with an automatic pistol."'

903. http://spartacus-educational.com/JFKmorales.htm

904. Fonzi, 1993, p. 383
905. Fonzi, 1993, p. 390
906. http://jfkmurdersolved.com/phillips.htm, email from Shawn Phillips, son of Jim, on what he was told about it by his father.
907. Cirules, 2010, p. 1
908. Cirules, 2010, p. 8: 'Havana was a kingdom of tolerance: anything could be arranged with the greatest impunity.'
909. Holt, 2013, p. xxi
910. Gosch, 1974, p. 305
911. Cirules, 2010, p. 18
912. Cirules, 2010, p. 63
913. Giancana S.A., 2010, loc. 2660, p. 208
914. Kefauver, 1951, p. 12-16
915. Cirules, 2010, p. 106
916. Newman J. M., 2015, p. 62
917. Cirules, 2010, p. 107. Letter from Dulles to Batista dated July 15, 1955, Archivo Museo del Ministerio del Interior, Havana Cuba.
918. Eisenhower, *The White House Years: Waging Peace (1956-1961)*, 1965, p. 520
919. Out of 68,329,141 votes cast, Kennedy had barely 112,827 votes more than Nixon, a difference of 0.17 percent.
920. Kennedy finally won 34 electoral votes more than Nixon, and could therefore claim victory even without the 27 electoral votes from Illinois. But the electoral votes of Mississippi, Georgia and Alabama, representing a total of 26 votes, could go to either Kennedy or the alternative Democratic candidate, Harry Byrd. Without Illinois, these obstructionists therefore held the balance, and their vote for Kennedy would certainly have to be negotiated at a high political price. Illinois was therefore crucial.
921. Giancana and Trafficante's home turfs were Chicago and Tampa respectively, which were, by coincidence or not, the two places where an attack on Kennedy had also been planned in November 1963. To complete the circle, Dallas is situated in the territory of Carlos Marcello.
922. Weiner, 2007, p. 189
923. Talbot, Brothers. *The Hidden History of the Kennedy Years*, 2007, p. 47
924. Clarke, 2013, p. 138
925. Talbot, Brothers. *The Hidden History of the Kennedy Years*, 2007, p. 46
926. Talbot, Brothers. *The Hidden History of the Kennedy Years*, 2007, p. 50
927. Talbot, Brothers. *The Hidden History of the Kennedy Years*, 2007, p. 51
928. Minutes of Meeting of the Special Group (Augmented) on Operation MONGOOSE, October 4
929. Nara Record Number: 157-10002-10050
930. Church Committee, Testimony of Roswell Gilpatric, 8 Jul 1975, p. 107. http://www.maryferrell.org/mffweb/archive/viewer/showDoc.do?docId=1375&relPageId=107
931. Nelson, LBJ *The Mastermind of the* JFK *Assassination*, 2011
932. http://www.intellectualtakeout.org/library/primary-sources/john-f-kennedy-letter-gerald-c-mann-oil-depletion-allowance
933. Statement of Doctor Albert Burke about a meeting with Haroldson L. Hunt in his home in Dallas in the course of 1961.

934. Nowadays, it is forbidden by law for a president to offer a ministerial position to a close relative. (Goldfarb, 1995, p. 11)
935. Goldfarb, 1995, p. 26
936. Goldfarb, 1995, p. 43
937. Goldfarb, 1995, p. 41
938. Goldfarb, 1995, p. 148
939. Goldfarb, 1995, p. 138
940. Mosley, 1978, p. 47
941. Mosley, 1978, p. 88
942. Grose, Peter 1994, *Gentleman Spy: The Life of Allen Dulles*. Boston: Houghton Mifflin, p. 100
943. Mosley, 1978, p. 145
944. Mosley, 1978, p. 223
945. Mosley, 1978, p. 265
946. Mosley, 1978, p. 282
947. Mosley, 1978, p. 350
948. Mosley, 1978, p. 289
949. Weiner, 2007, p. 183
950. Weiner, 2007, p. 183
951. Russo, 1998, loc. 1485
952. Fonzi, 1993, p. 89
953. Weiner, 2007, p. 193
954. Weiner, 2007, p. 194
955. Weiner, 2007, p. 204
956. Weiner, 2007, p. 216
957. Russo, 1998, loc. 1225
958. Russo, 1998, loc. 1611 Congressional testimony of McNamara
959. Russo, 1998, loc. 1667
960. Russo, 1998, loc 1895, bron: Evan Thomas, *The Very Best Men*, p. 297
961. Russo, 1998, loc. 2027 Source: David C. Martin 'The CIA's loaded gun,' article in the *Washington Post* of September 10, 1976.
962. Russo, 1998, loc. 2053 source: General Charles E. Johnson III, Church Committee interview, July 28, 1975
963. Fonzi, 1993, p. 334
964. Russo, 1998, loc. 2071 Interview by Gus Russo on 12/3/1995
965. Russo, 1998, loc. 2092 source: Evan Thomas, The Very Best Men, p. 297
966. Fay, 1966, quoted in Douglas J. W., 2008, p. 13
967. Frank Sturgis, a self-confessed suspect in the assassination of Kennedy, was also a Watergate burglar, but there is no evidence that he was involved in the CIA operations. On his deathbed, E. Howard Hunt admitted to his son that he was involved in the Kennedy assassination. A letter in Oswald's handwriting and dated November 8 was addressed to a certain 'Mr. Hunt.' In the letter, Oswald asked for more information before he could take further steps. (de Mey, 2013, p.96)
968. Mosley, 1978, p. 347
969. Fonzi, 1993, p. 357
970. Newman, *Where Angels Tread Lightly: The assassination of President Kennedy*. Volume 1, 2015, p. 13. Nixon, 1979, p. 324

971. Patterson, 1989, p. 129
972. The classic book *The Guns of August* by Barbara W. Tuchman deals with how the run-up to the First World War influenced Kennedy's strategy in the missile crisis, and especially his fear of a 'war by imprudence,' which was wished by neither side, but became inevitable by mutual incorrect assessments.
973. Talbot, Brothers. *The Hidden History of the Kennedy Years*, 2007, p. 224
974. Clarke, 2013, p. 165
975. Clarke, 2013, p. 164
976. Mosley, 1990, p. 469
977. Horne D. P., 2014, loc. 1765
978. May Ernest R. and Zelikow, 1997, p. 182
979. Kurtz, 2006, p. 14. Immediately after the assassination, Robert Kennedy gave the order to completely dismantle the installation before Johnsonended up in the Oval Office.
980. May Ernest R. and Zelikow, 1997, p. 188
981. Horne D. P., 2014, p. 2036
982. *Killing Oswald* DVD Shane O'Sullivan
983. Beschloss, *The Crisis Years 1960-1963*, 1991, p. 544
984. Talbot, Brothers. *The Hidden History of the Kennedy Years*, 2007, p. 173
985. Russo, 1998, loc. 5255
986. Talbot, Brothers.*The hidden History of the Kennedy Years*, 2007, p. 168
987. Beschloss, *The Crisis Years 1960-1963*, 1991, p. 545
988. Kearns, 1976, p. 330
989. Talbot, Brothers. *The Hidden History of the Kennedy Years*, 2007, p. 206
990. Talbot, Brothers. *The Hidden History of the Kennedy Years*, 2007, p. 210
991. http://www.military.com/Content/MoreContent1/?file=cw_speech_4
992. Talbot, Brothers. *The Hidden History of the Kennedy Years*, 2007, p. 212
993. Kennedy called his politics *New Frontier*, as an indication that the United States were finally moving again after years of stagnation under Eisenhower.
994. MacLear, 1981, p. 59
995. Hershman, 2002, p. 271
996. Talbot, Brothers. *The Hidden History of the Kennedy Years*, 2007, p. 217
997. Clarke, 2013, p. 59
998. Douglas J. W., 2008, p. 375
999. Talbot, Brothers. *The Hidden History of the Kennedy Years*, 2007, p. 215
1000. Clarke, 2013, p. 61
1001. Clarke, 2013, p. 61
1002. Douglas J. W., 2008, p. 185
1003. Douglas J. W., 2008, p. 193
1004. Douglas J. W., 2008, p. 189
1005. Clarke, 2013, p. 158
1006. O'Donnell, p. 16
1007. Douglas J. W., 2008, p. 182
1008. http://www.fas.org/irp/offdocs/nsam-jfk/nsam-263.htm
1009. Kaiser, 2008, p. 300
1010. Kaiser, 2008, p. 301
1011. Escalante, 2006, p. 57
1012. Kaiser, 2008, p. 302

1013. Clarke, 2013, p. 252
1014. Clarke, 2013, p. 260
1015. Douglas J., 2008, p. 379

INDEX OF PEOPLE

Adams, Vicki: office worker who ran downstairs from the fourth floor with her friend Sandra Styles shortly after the assassination, and neither saw nor heard Oswald on the way. Also did not meet motorcycle officer Baker and Supervisor Truly.

Angleton, James Jesus: paranoid head of the Counterespionage department of the CIA.

Arnold, Carolyn: witness who saw Oswald on the first floor just before the assassination. She also stated that she had seen Oswald on the second floor in the cafeteria, but that is doubtful, because Oswald never mentioned that he saw her there. He would certainly have done so as he could thus have proven his innocence.

Baker, T.L.: motorcycle officer in the Dallas police force. Drove up to the book depository as soon as he heard the first shot and ran up the stairs to the roof with Supervisor Truly, looking for the gunman. On the second floor, they met an outwardly calm Oswald in the cafeteria, less than 90 seconds after the first shot.

Banister, Guy: ex-FBI agent and CIA informant who coordinated the anti-Castro operations in New Orleans from a building in Camp Street. Oswald handed out pro-Castro pamphlets on the street with Banister's address on them.

Booth Lucė, Clare: wife of the owner of the Time, Life and Fortune magazines. After the assassination, she sent messages around the world that added to the misinformation that was also simultaneously disseminated by other CIA henchmen.

Bowley, T.F.: witness of the murder of police officer Tippit. Made contact with police headquarters at 1.16 p.m. using the car radio of the police car. According to his own statement, he was at the crime scene at 1:10 p.m., and the murder had already occurred. According to our analysis, Tippit was murdered between 1.12 and 1.13 p.m.

Braden, Jim: gangster who was arrested because he was in the building across from the book depository at the time of the assassination without any reason for being there. Lied about his presence there, but was released for lack of a case. It later appeared that there was not a single file in the police records that mentioned his name, because he had recently changed it. Had met with Lamar Hunt, son of Haroldson Hunt, the richest man in the world and a Kennedy hater, the day before the murder. Was also twice in the same building as Ruby the day before the assassination.

Brennan, Charles: crown witness for the Warren Commission. Sat on a wall opposite the book depository and saw a gunman firing the fatal shot at Kennedy. But his testimony, which claimed that he saw Oswald shooting, is very questionable.

Bringuier, Carlos: agitator from the pro-Castro student group DRE, which received financial support from the CIA. Had a fight with Oswald in New Orleans, thereby ending up in jail and receiving media attention. It's remarkable that Oswald described the fight in great detail in a letter four days before it actually took place. Bringuier also had contact with Guy Banister.

Bugliosi, Vincente: most important believer author. Wrote an extremely detailed book of 1,600 pages and as many pages of endnotes.

Bush, George H.W.: CIA informant who, after the assassination of JFK, tried to put the blame on the pro-Castro sympathizers. Lied about this afterwards. Happened to be in Dallas on November 22, 1963. Friend of Georges de Mohrenschildt. Later became CIA Director, and then President of the United States in 1988. Father of President George W. Bush.

Index of persons: 19-year-old stripper in Ruby's nightclub. Along with her 'husband' Bruce Carlin, she supported the story of the urgent payment made to Karen by Ruby on Sunday, November 24, 1963. Remained in hiding after the events in Dallas.

Carlin, Bruce: lived together with Karen Bennett. Apparently worked 60 hours free-of-charge in the weekend of the assassination, after which the couple started the weekend without a dollar in their pockets. The statements made by Bruce and Karen are very doubtful on more than one point.

Castro, Fidel: Prime Minister of Cuba after the fall of Batista in 1959. Sought the active support of the Soviet Union in order to keep his regime afloat.

An attempted coup by rebels in a raid at the Bay of Pigs ended badly for the Americans. Started an international crisis that brought the world to the brink of nuclear war when the Russians installed nuclear missiles in Cuba.

Coleman, Kay (Kathy Kay): Carousel stripper who was closely involved in the story about Karen Carlin Bennett's urgent need for money, whereby Ruby 'accidentally' came close to Oswald on Sunday morning. Also sat in a car on Friday evening with Jack Ruby and her lover, Officer Olsen, in a discussion that lasted more than an hour. All the participants lied about this encounter. Kathy also met Jack Ruby on the night before Kennedy's assassination.

Coleman, Kirk: witness of the attack on General Walker. His testimony seems to exclude the possibility that Oswald was the culprit.

Cubela, Rolando: played an important role in the Cuban revolution. Castro rewarded him with an important function. With an eye on a coup in Cuba, he had secret contacts with the Americans at the highest level. Was even willing to murder Castro himself. The planned coup in Havana was aborted after the assassination of Kennedy.

Day, J.C.: lieutenant in the Dallas police force. Responsible for the crime scene of JFK's assassination. Found a hand print of Oswald on the Carcano when no witnesses were present. Only submitted the proof of this after the murder of Oswald. Several of his interventions, in both the case of the attempted murder of General Walker and that of the Kennedy assassination, are very questionable.

de Mohrenschildt, Georges: eccentric baron who asked the CIA for permission to become Oswald's friend. Apparently acted as his watchdog. Left the country in a hurry when he suspected that Oswald was involved in the attack on General Walker.

Diem, Ngo: Catholic president of South Vietnam. Fell from power after a coup backed by the CIA and was brutally killed on November 2, 1963. This assassination was the official reason for the cancellation of the visit of JFK to Chicago.

Dulles, Alan: member of the Warren Commission. Former Director of the CIA, who was removed from office by Kennedy after the Bay of Pigs operation. Turned the CIA into an organization full of intrigue that failed terribly in its duty to provide the president with information. Openly disagreed with the foreign policy of Kennedy, and much preferred the policy line that his brother, Foster Dulles, had followed as Secretary of State under President Eisenhower. Lied to the Warren Commission and concealed information. Frankly admitted that this was also to be expected of CIA agents who were questioned under oath.

Duran, Sylvia: clerk at the Cuban consulate in Mexico City. Was dealt with harshly after the Kennedy assassination until her statement contained the desired version of the facts.

Eisenhower, Dwight (Ike): predecessor of Kennedy as president. War hero who became president during a quiet period in international affairs, and who followed things less closely during his second term of office. Among other things, this led to the derailment of the CIA.

Ferrie, David: eccentric homosexual, but also an outstanding pilot. Drove from New Orleans to Texas for no apparent reason during a heavy rain storm just after the assassination of Kennedy. Turned back when he heard that Oswald had been murdered. Worked together with Guy Bannister at the address at which Oswald's pro-Castro organization was also registered. Associate of Mafia boss, Carlos Marcello. Posed together with Oswald for a photo of a training camp years before the assassination. Died in mysterious circumstances when Jim Garrison wanted to question him in connection with the assassination of Kennedy.

Fonzi, Gaeton: dedicated investigative journalist who also ended up in the investigation team of the HSCA through the Schweiker Commission. Won the trust of key figures such as Antonio Veciana and Sylvia Odio. Ultimately became very disappointed by the bureaucratic strangulation of the HSCA investigation, and the constant misleading tracks laid by the CIA. Later wrote 'The Last Investigation', a book that stands out in the ranks of Kennedy literature.

Ford, Gerald: Republican member of Congress. Became part of the Warren Commission thanks to President Johnson, and served as an FBI informant there. Succeeded Richard Nixon as President of the United States after the Watergate Scandal.

Frazier, Buell Wesley: best friend of Oswald in Dallas. Regularly gave Oswald a lift to and from Irving, the suburb where the Paines lived. Also did this on the day before and the morning of the assassination. Was certain that the paper bag that Oswald had with him was too short to contain a rifle.

Fritz, Will: captain of the homicide squad of the Dallas police. Did not lead the investigation as he should have, with the result that there were later huge gaps in the official evidence. For example, he allowed the interrogations to take place without making an audio record or taking notes.

Garner, Dorothy: head of the office on the fourth floor of the schoolbook depository. Made an important statement in 1964 indicating that Oswald did not descend the stairs in the 90 seconds after the assassination. Her very credible testimony disappeared without a trace, but has been confirmed in the meantime through indirect documents and her statement to author Ernest Barry.

Gaudet, William: CIA agent who, through pure coincidence, stood in front of Oswald in the queue when he applied for a tourist visa for Mexico.

Giancana, Sam: Godfather of the Outfit, the Mafia in Chicago. Said to have helped Kennedy to a fraudulent victory in Illinois during the presidential election. Lost his investments in hotels and casinos in Cuba after the seizure of power by Castro. Was hounded by Bobby Kennedy, and found this unacceptable following his support of John Kennedy. His accomplice, Roselli, became involved in the clandestine CIA assassination attempts on Castro. Plotted a first attack on JFK in Chicago at the start of November 1963. Was executed Mafia-style just as he was about to make a statement to the HSCA.

Givens, Charles: employee at the book depository. According to his first statement, he saw Oswald on the first floor shortly before 12.00 noon. Later changed his statement and became a key witness for the Warren Commission, because he claimed to have seen Oswald on the sixth floor at around 12.00 noon. In a report, the FBI stated that Givens was willing to change his statement in exchange for money.

Harvey, William (Bill) King: head of the CIA base in Berlin up to 1960. On his return to headquarters, he was put in charge of the ZR/Rifle organization, the department which was responsible for the liquidation of foreign political leaders. Came up with the misbegotten idea of involving the Mafia in the plan to assassinate Castro. To JFK's surprise, he was not an American version of James Bond, but rather an ill-mannered, cynical, corpulent alcoholic.

Hidell, Alek: pseudonym used by Oswald to purchase the rifle. He had forged identity papers in this name with him when he was arrested.

Hoover, J. Edgar: corrupt and all-powerful director of the FBI. Good friend of Vice-president Johnson. Had a very strained relationship with the Kennedys. After the assassination, he did everything he could to have the Warren Commission conclude that Oswald had assassinated the president and had acted alone.

Howard, Lisa: TV journalist who, as Castro's mistress, was involved in one of the countless CIA plans to assassinate the Cuban leader.

Hurt, John: CIA contact person or 'cutout' of Oswald in jail. Oswald called him on the evening of November 23 so that Hurt could ask Oswald's case officer to contact him.

Johnson, Lyndon Baines: Kennedy's Vice President. Was already involved in a number of scandals, but the investigations ended up under the carpet after he succeeded JFK as president. Established a political commission to investigate the assassination of his predecessor, and was actively involved in the sabotage of the investigation to find the real perpetrators.

Kantor, Seth: journalist who called a generally well-informed colleague on November 22. As Kantor had also met Jack Ruby on that day, the Warren Commission published the list of his telephone calls on that day. The conversation with his colleague was missing, however. It later turned out that his colleague was a notorious CIA mole.

Kennedy, Robert (Bobby): younger brother of the president. Became Attorney General and was an absolute confidant in the JFK government. Was heavily at odds with FBI director Hoover, and came down hard on organized crime. Was partly responsible for the clandestine Cuba policy of the government, and was at least aware of the plans to eliminate Fidel Castro.

Khrushchev Nikita: leader of the Communist Party in the USSR. A farmer's son, which sometimes made his style of government harsh and unpredictable. Defied Kennedy, whom he didn't think much of at the start of his term of office, but he gradually came to respect him and then trusted him enough to sign a nuclear test ban treaty. Seemed prepared to allow a thaw in the Cold War.

Kirk, Cecil: leading member of the HSCA panel of photographic experts. Had the original photos of the Carcano and the backyard photographs that the HSCA had recorded as evidence. The photos indicated that the rifle that was found in the book depository is the same rifle that was in Oswald's hands in the backyard photos. Flip de Mey was able to buy these photographs after the death of Cecil Kirk.

Kostikov, Valery: KGB agent who was part of the death squad of the Russian secret service. Worked in the Soviet embassy in Mexico. Oswald is said to have mentioned his name in a telephone conversation with the embassy, which could possibly be used later as evidence of Russian involvement in the assassination.

LeMay, Curtis: energetic general who argued openly for a nuclear war initiated by the USA. Hated Kennedy and everything he stood for. The feeling was mutual.

Lopez, Edwin: dedicated young HSCA investigator who wrote the report about the events in Mexico.

Lopez, Gilberto Pollicarpo: suspect involved in the planned attack in Tampa, Florida. His background was very similar to that of Lee Harvey Oswald.

Maheu, Robert: adventurer who provided various services to the CIA. Contacted the Mafia on behalf of the intelligence service to ask them to help with the assassination of Fidel Castro.

Marcello, Carlos: officially a humble tomato grower, but was actually the Godfather of the Mafia in New Orleans and Dallas, the two places where Oswald lived in the period before the assassination. Bobby Kennedy pursued him aggressively – and not always only with legal methods. Hated the Kennedys. His accomplices, such as David Ferrie and Jim Braden, appeared prominently in the murder case. Won his lawsuit against the Justice Department at the exact moment of the assassination of JFK. It turned out later that he had once again bribed the jury.

Markham, Helen: witness of the murder of police officer Tippit. Saw how a police car slowly followed Oswald as he went by. Testified that nothing seemed to be wrong during the conversation between Oswald and Tippit, until the shots were fired.

McNamara, Robert: CEO of the Ford Motor Company until JFK appointed him as Minister of Defense. Supported Kennedy's military restraint in Southeast Asia, but loyally carried out Johnson's brutal war strategy in Vietnam afterwards.

Milteer, Joseph: racist who boasted in a tapped phone call shortly before the assassination that Kennedy would be shot down from a high building, and that, as far as the general public were concerned, everything would be blamed on a scapegoat.

Morales, David: head of the Secret Operations department of the CIA base in Miami, ally of David Phillips. Gained experience in the elimination of heads of state in Guatemala and was also closely involved in the ZR/Rifle operation, the endless series of CIA plots to assassinate Castro. Was the prototype of the CIA villain.

Nixon, Richard: candidate running against Kennedy in the presidential elections of 1960. Was coincidentally in Dallas on November 22 to attend a congress of Pepsi-Cola, an important client of his law firm. Knew more about the involvement of the CIA in the assassination of Kennedy, as he was later, when President, able to blackmail CIA director Helms in connection with the assassination in Dallas.

Odio, Sylvia: Cuban refugee who Oswald was supposed to have visited at a particular point in time. Oswald was suddenly anti-Castro again. Someone told Odio that Oswald was capable of doing anything, and that he was a sharpshooter who was convinced that the anti-Castro Cubans should assassinate Kennedy.

Olsen, Harry: police officer in Dallas. Took sick leave on November 22 in order to work as a private guard on an estate, but could not remember where the estate was afterwards. It was only two blocks from the spot where Officer Tippit was murdered. On the same day, he also talked with Ruby for more than an hour in a car. All the participants lied about this encounter. Also had a brief meeting with Ruby on Saturday evening on the sidewalk in front of the Carousel.

Paine Ruth: Quaker and school teacher, married to Michael Paine. Provided shelter for Marina Oswald. Had connections with the CIA through her husband and her sister. Looked after Marina after Georges de Mohrenschildt had left the country. Also helped Oswald to obtain his job in the book depository. Was also involved in the evidence about Oswald's involvement in the attack on General Walker. In a tapped telephone call after the JFK assassination, her husband told her that Oswald was not responsible for the attack, and that they both knew who was.

Paul, Ralph: owner of a number of restaurants in Dallas. Conducted several phone calls with Ruby the day before the latter shot Oswald. Was also supposed to have been in contact – at least indirectly – with Officer Tippit.

Phillips, David Atlee: propaganda specialist and head of the Cuban Operations of the CIA in Mexico. Was closely involved in the manipulation of the evidence of Oswald's stay in Mexico, just after the Kennedy assassination. Antonio Veciana also saw him once in Dallas together with Oswald.

Prayer Man: nickname given to an unidentified person who stood at the back of the entrance hall of the book depository. The man's clothing does not rule out that he was Oswald. Oswald is the only person from the book depository whose location we do not know at the time of the attack.

Prusakova, Marina: Oswald's Russian wife. Probably brought into contact with him by the KGB. Was one of the most important witnesses against her husband. The FBI put her under constant pressure to provide the statements they desired. Withdrew the statements later.

Ruby, Jack: nightclub operator in Dallas, who shot Oswald in the basement of the police building on Sunday,November 24.

Roselli, Johny: gentleman-gangster who looked after the interests of Sam Giancana in Las Vegas. Was the intermediary for contacts between the CIA and the Mafia with regard to the plans to assassinate Castro.

Saez, Miguel Casas: suspect who was present at the time of the planned attacks on Kennedy in both Chicago and Tampa. Was also in Dallas on November 22. Apparently would have served as a reserve scapegoat if the planned scapegoat was not blamed for some reason.

Senator, Georges: shared an apartment with Ruby. Lied about Ruby's whereabouts on November 22 and 23.

Schmidt, Volkmar: oil geologist. Had a long conversation with Oswald at de Mohrenschildt's home. Claimed that Oswald was dangerous and anti-Kennedy, a statement that closely followed the wishes of the CIA. According to the official story, the conversation with Schmidt gave Oswald the idea to assassinate General Walker.

Schweiker, Richard: senator who led a senate commission in 1978 to investigate the operations of the intelligence services. Thoroughly studied the Kennedy dossier and was convinced of the involvement of the CIA in the actions of Oswald.

Stevenson, Adlai: Democrat, US Ambassador to the UN. Gave a lecture in Dallas shortly before the assassination of Kennedy. An agitated crowd jeered him and spat at him.

Tippit, J.D.: police officer in Dallas. Was already frantically searching for someone near Oswald's rented room a quarter of an hour after the JFK assassination. Saw Oswald walking along 10th Street. Had a short conversation with him through the open window of the police car. Got out of the car calmly and slowly, after which Oswald killed him with four gunshots.

Titovets, Ernst: best friend of Oswald in Minsk, Belarus. Witnessed how Oswald met Marina through the active intervention of the KGB. Later became professor of neurology, and author of 'Oswald's Russian Episode', a good book about Oswald's stay in Minsk.

Trafficante, Santos: Godfather of the Mafia in Florida. Was actively involved in the CIA plans to eliminate Castro. A second attempt to shoot Kennedy took place in Tampa, Florida in mid-November.

Vallee, Thomas Arthur: suspect involved in the planned attack in Chicago. His background is very similar to that of Lee Harvey Oswald.

Veciana, Antonio: dictatorial leader of the terrorist anti-Castro group Alpha 66. Witnessed a meeting between Oswald and CIA man, Phillips, in Dallas.

Walker, Edwin: ultra-right-wing ex-general. Oswald was supposed to have carried out an attempt to assassinate him. Walker himself was convinced that Oswald was not the gunman who made the attempt on his life. The general and the president had, in fact, a mutual dislike of each other, and held strongly opposing political views. It seems quite unlikely that Oswald wanted to kill both men on the basis of political convictions.

Wall, Breck: chairman of the Dallas department of the AGVA strippers' union, which was actually an extortion mechanism of the Mafia. The AGVA apparently had a stranglehold on Ruby shortly before the assassination. Ruby called Wall in Galveston the night before the murder of Oswald.

Westbrook W.R.: captain in the Dallas police force. At the scene of the murder of Tippit, he held a wallet in his hand that closely resembled Oswald's. Was prominently present later during Oswald's arrest in the Texas Theatre. Was also involved with the wallet that was supposedly found in Oswald's back pocket and that was added to the evidence. Nothing more was then heard of the first wallet found at the crime scene. A news film is the only evidence of its existence. The wallet contained the identity card of Hidell, which was very incriminating for Oswald. It is hard to imagine that Oswald would have had this with him when he planned an attack on Kennedy on November 22.

Williams, Bonnie Ray: black worker in the book depository. Ate his lunch near the sniper's nest on the sixth floor in the period from shortly after 12 noon up to at least 12.20 p.m. Saw or heard no one.

Zapruder Abram: tailor who filmed the assassination of Kennedy with his new amateur camera. Life Magazine bought the images, and were able to prevent their disclosure to the public for ten years.

BIBLIOGRAPHY

Adams, D. (2012). *From an Office Building with a High Powered Rifle*. Waterville, OR: Jody Miller, Kindle edition.

Alabama Harbinger (May 26, 1998). *Beverly Oliver ('The Babushka Lady') Interview by Gary James*. Opgehaald van Mobile Alabama Harbinger: http://www.theharbinger.org/xvi/980526/james.html

Baker, B. (1978). *Wheeling and Dealing, Confessions of a Capitol Hill Operator*. New York: W.W. Norton & Company.

Belin, D. W. (1988). *Final Disclosure*. New York: McMillan.

Belzer, R. (2013). *Hit List. An In-Depth Investigation into the Mysterious Deaths of Witnesses to the JFK Assassination*. New York: Skyhorse Publishing.

Benson, M. (1993). *Who's Who in the JFK Assassination*. New York: Citadel Press Book.

Beschloss, M. R. (1991). *The Crisis Years 1960-1963*. New York: Harper Collins.

Beschloss, M. R. (1997). *Taking Charge. The Johnson White House Tapes, 1963-1964*. New York: Simon & Schuster.

Bishop, J. (1968). *The Day Kennedy was Shot. An uncensored minute by minute account of November 1963*. New York: Funk & Wagnals.

Brashler, W. (1977). *The Don. The Life and Death of Sam Giancana*. New York: Harper & Row Publishers.

Briody, D. (2004). *The Halliburton Agenda. The Politics of Oil and Money*. Hoboken, New Jersey: John Wiley & Sons.

Brown, M. D. (1997). *Texas in the Morning: The Love Story of Madeleine Brown and President Lyndon Baines Johnson*. Conservatory Press.

Brown, W. (1992). *The People v. Lee Harvey Oswald*. New York: Carol & Graf Publishers.

Brown, W. (1995). *Treachery in Dallas*. New York: Carol & Graf Publishers.

Brown, W. (2013). *Master Chronology of JFK Assassination – Book I – Dynasty*. Vigiliano Books, Kindle edition.

Brugioni, D. (1990). *Eyeball to Eyeball*. New York: Random House.

Bugliosi, V. (2007). *Reclaiming History*. New York: W.W. Norton & Company.

Buyer, R. (2009). *Why the JFK Assassination Still Matters*. Tucson, Arizona: Wheatmark.

Califano, J. A. (1991). *The Triumph and Tragedy of Lyndon Johnson. The White House Years. A Personal Memoir by President's Johnsons Top Domestic Adviser.* New York: Simon & Schuster.

Caro, R. A. (1990). *The Years of Lyndon Johnson. Means of Ascent*. New York: Albert A. Knopf.

Cirules, E. (2010). *The Mafia in Havanna. A Caribbean Mob Story*. North Melbourne, Australia: Ocean Press.

Chafe, W. H. (2010). *The Unfinished Journey*. New York: Oxford University Press.

Chambers, P. G. (2010). *Head Shot. The Science Behind the JFK Assassination*. New York: Amherst.

Charles Massegee Evangelistic Service (sd). *The Life Story Of Beverly Massegee.* Opgehaald van Massegee.org: http://www.massegee.org/newsRelease2.html

Chatterjee, P. (2009). *Halliburton's Army. How a Well-Connected Texas Oil Company Revolutionized the Way America Makes War.* New York: Nation Books.

Christianson, S. (2006). *Bodies of Evidence, Forensic Science and Crime*. The Lyons Press.

Ciccone, C. (2012). *Master List of Witnesses to the Assassination of President John F. Kennedy*.

Clarke, T. (2013). *JFK's Last Hundred Days. The Transformation of a Man and the Emergence of a Great President*. New York: The Penguin Press.

Connally, N. (2003). *From Love Field. Our Final Hours with President John F. Kennedy*. New York: Ruggedland.

Dallek, R. (1991). *Lone Star Rising: Lyndon Johnson and his times 1908-1960*. New York: Oxford University Press.

David, J. (1968). *The Weight of the Evidence. The Warren Report and its Critics.* New York: Meredith Press.

Davis, J. H. (1989). *Mafia Kingfish. Carlos Marcello and the Assassination of John F. Kennedy*. McGraw-Hill Publising Co: New York.

De Bruyn, P. (1998). *8 seconden in Dallas. Kennedy's rendez-vous met de dood.* Icarus: Standaard Uitgeverij.

de Mey, F. (2013). *Cold Case Kennedy*. Tielt, Belgium: Uitgeverij Lannoo.

de Morenschildt, G. (2014). *Lee Harvey Oswald as I knew him.* Kansas: United Press of Kansas.

Dicscovery Communications DVD (2011). *Unsolved History JFK Conspiracy Myths.*

DiEugenio, J. (1992). *Destiny Betrayed.* Delaware: Skyhorse Publishing.

Douglas, J. W. (2008). *JFK and the Unspeakable. Why He Died and Why It Matters.* New York: Orbis Books.

Dugain, M. (2005). *La Malédiction d'Edgar.* Paris: Gallimar.

Eisenhower, D. D. (1961). *Military-Industrial Complex Speech, Public Papers of the Presidents,* 1960, p. 1035-1040. Washington.

Eisenhower, D. D. (1965). *The White House Years: Waging Peace (1956-1961).* New York: Doubleday.

Epstein, E. J. (1978, 2011). *Legend. The Secret World of Lee Harvey Oswald.* New York: EJE Pubication/Kindle edition.

Epstein, E. J. (1992). *The Assassination Chronicles: Inquest, Counterplot and Legend.* New York: Caroll & Graff.

Epstein, E. J. (2011). *The JFK Assassination Theories.* EJE Single, Kindle edition.

Escalante, F. (2006). *JFK, The Cuba Files.* New York: Ocean Press.

Evans, R., & Novak, R. (1966). *Lyndon B. Johnson: The Exercise of Power.*

Farell, J. P. (2011). *LBJ and the Conspiracy to Kill Kennedy.* Illinois: Adventures Unlimited Press.

Fetzer, J. H. (1998). *Assassination Science.* Catfeet Press.

Fleming, G. B. (2013). *S-172 Lee Harvey Oswald Links to Intelligence Agencies.* Kindle edition.

Fonzi, G. (1993). *The Last Investigation. What Insiders Know about the Assassination of JFK.* New York: Skyhorse.

Franklin, B. (1787). *Dangers of a Salaried Bureaucracy.* Philadelphia, Oration to Constitutional Convention 1787: The World Famous Orations, edited by: Bryan, William Jennings.

Fursenko, A. A. (1997). *One Hell of a Gamble. The Secret History of the Cuban Missile Crisis.* London: W.W. Norton & Co.

George, A. L. (2013). *The Assassination of John F. Kennedy. Political Trauma and American Memory.* New York: Routledge.

Gertz, E. (1968). *Moment of Madness: The People vs. Jack Ruby.* Chicago: Follett Publishing Co.

Giancana, A. H. (2005). *JFK and Sam.* Nashville, Tennessee: Cumberland House Publishing.

Giancana, S. A. (2010). *Double Cross: The Explosive Inside Story of the Mobster who Controlled America (electronic version).* New York: Skyhorse Publishing.

Gilbride, R. (2009). *Matrix for Assassination. The JFK Conspiracy.* Trafford, Kindle edition.

Gillon, S. M. (sd). *The Kennedy Assassination – 24 Hours After. Lyndon B. Johnson's Pivotal First Day as President.* New York: Basic Books.

Goldfarb, R. (1995). *Perfect Villains, Inperfect Heroes. Robert F. Kennedy's War Against Organized Crime.* Herndon, Virginia: First Capital Books.

Gosch, M. A. (1974). *The Last Testament of Lucky Luciano.* Boston: Little, Brown and Company.

Griggs, I. (2005). *No Case to Answer. Essays and Articles on the JFK Assassination (1993-2005).* Southlake, Texas: JFK Lancer Productions and Publications.

Hagedorn, J. M. (2009). *A Genealogy of Gangs in Chicago.* Minnesota: University of Minnesota Press.

Hakl, H. T. (2014). *Eranos: An Alternative Intellectual History of the Twentieth Century.* New York: Routledge.

Hancock, L. (2006). *Someone would have talked.* Southlake, Texas: JFK Lancer Productions and Publications.

Hersh, S. M. (1997). *The Dark Side of Camelot.* Canada: Little, Brown & Company.

Hershman, D. J. (2002). *Power Beyond Reason. The mental collaps of Lyndon Johnson.* New Jersey: Barricade.

Hill, C. (2012). *Mrs. Kennedy and Me.* New York: Gallery Books.

Holt, C. (2013). *Self Portrait of a Scoundrel. A Memoir of Spooks, Hoods and the Hidden Elite.* Waterville, OR.: Trineday.

Horne, D. (2009). *Inside the Assassination Records Review Board Vol. I.*

Horne, D. (2009). *Inside the Assassination Records Review Board Vol. II.*

Horne, D. (2009). *Inside the Assassination Records Review Board Vol. III.*

Horne, D. (2009). *Inside the Assassionation Records Review Board Vol. IV.*

Horne, D. P. (2014). *JFK's War with the National Security Establishment: Why Kennedy was Assassinated.* Fairfax, Virginia: The Future of Freedom Foundation.

Hosty, J. P. (1996). *Assignment: Oswald.* New York: Arcade Publishing.

HSCA Appendix Vol. VII. (1978). Washington.

HSCA Appendix Vol. VI. (1978). Washington.
HSCA Appendix Vol. IV. (1978). Washington.
HSCA Appendix Vol. VIII. (1978). Washington.
HSCA Appendix Vol. II. (1978). Washington.
HSCA Appendix Vol. III. (1978). Washington.
HSCA Appendix Vol. IX. (1978). Washington.
HSCA Appendix Vol. X. (1978). Washington.
HSCA Appendix Vol. I. (1978). Washington.
HSCA, Final Report. (1978). Washington.
Hubbard-Burrell, J. (1992). *What Really Happened? JFK Five Hundred and One Questions & Answers*. Spring Branch, Texas: Ponderosa Press.
Hughes, J. (July 2007). *george-mcgann-8613*. Downloaded from Bluff Magazine: http://www.bluff.com/magazine/george-mcgann-8613/
Hurt, H. (1985). *Reasonable Doubt*. New York: Holt, Rinehart & Winston.
Joesten, J. (1968). *The Dark Side of Lyndon Baines Johnson*. Icconoclassic Books.
Jones, P. J. (1966). *Forgive my Grief, Volume 1*. Dallas: The Midlothian Mirror Inc.
Kaiser, D. (2008). *The Road to Dallas*. Cambridge, Massachusetts: Belknap Press of Harvard University Press.
Kantor, S. (1978). *Who was Jack Ruby?* Everest House.
Kearns, D. (1976). *Lyndon Johnson and the American Dream*. New York: Harper and Row.
Kefauver, E. (1951). *Crime in America*. New York: Doubleday.
Kennedy-Bouvier, J. (2011). *Mijn Leven met John F. Kennedy. Historische Gesprekken met Arthur M. Schlesinger Jr.* Houten-Antwerpen: Spectrum.
Kessler, R. (1997). *Wat is de titel van het oorspronkelijke Engestalige boek?* New York: Warner Books Inc.
Knebel, F. (1962). *Seven Days in May*.
Kritzberg, C. (sd). *Secrets from the Sixth Floor Window*.
Kurtz, M. L. (2006). *The JFK Assassination Debates. Lone Man vs. Conspiracy*. Kansas University Press.
La Fontaine, R. A. (1997). *Oswald Talked. The New Evidence in the JFK Assassination*. Gretna Louisiana: Pelican Publishing.
Landesco, J. (1933). *The Journal of Criminal Law and Criminology, March-April – pag 964-998 – The Life History of a Member of the '42' Gang*. American Institute of Criminal Law and Criminology.

Lane, M. (2011). *My Indictment of the CIA in the Murder of JFK*. New York: Skyhorse Publishing.

Lattimer, J. K. (1980). *Kennedy and Lincoln. Medical and Ballistic Comparisons of their Assassinations*. New York: Harcourt Brace Jovanovich, Inc.

Leaming, B. (2006). *Jack Kennedy: The Making of a President*. London: ORION Publishing Group.

Les Dossier des Grands Mystères de l'Histoire. (2003). *Le Mythe JFK. Commission Warren Le Rapport Truqué.*

Levine, R. (1993, 2001). *The Secret of the Century*. Smashwords Editions, Kindle edition.

Livingstone, H. E. (2004). *The Radical Right and the Murder of John F. Kennedy*. Victoria BC, Canada: Trafford.

M., S. L. (2003). *The JFK Myths. The Evidence Speaks Loudly*. St Paul, MN: Paragon House.

M., S. W. (2008). *To Kill a President. An Ex-FBI Agent Rips Aside the Veil of Secrecy That Killed JFK*. Lexington.

MacLear, M. (1981). *The Tenthousand Day War: Vietnam 1945-1975*. New York: St. Martin's Press.

Maier, T. (2004). *The Kennedy's: America's Emerald Kings. A Five Generation History of the Ultimate Irish-catholic Family*. Basic Books.

Manchester, W. (1967). *De Dood van een President*. Utrecht/Antwerpen: A.W. Bruna & Zoon.

Marrs, J. (1993, paperback edition). *Crossfire. The Plot that Killed Kennedy*. Basic Books.

Martin, O. (2010). *JFK Analysis of a Shooting. The Ultimate Ballistics Exposed*. Indianapolis: Dogear.

Matthews, C. (2012). *Jack Kennedy. Elusive Hero*. New York: Simon & Schuster, Kindle edition.

May Ernest R. and Zelikow, P. D. (1997). *The Kennedy Tapes*. Cambridge, Massachussets: Belknap Press.

McAdams, J. (2011). *JFK Assassination Logic. How to Think About Claims of Conspiracy*. Dulles, Virginia: Potomac Books.

McClellan, B. (2003). *Blood, Money and Power*. New York: Hannover House.

Mcgrayne, S. B. (2011). *The Theory that Would not Die. How Bayes' rule cracked the enigma code, hunted down russian submarines & emerged triumphant from two centuries of controversy*. New Haven & London: Yale University Press.

McMaster, H. (1997). *Dereliction of Duty: Lyndon Johnson, Robert NcNamara, the Joint Chiefs of Staff, and the lies that led to Vietnam.* New York: HarperCollins.

McNamara, R. (1995). *In Retrospect: The Tragedy an Lessons of vietnam.* New York: New York Times Books.

Meagher, S. (1967, reprinted). *Accessories After the Fact. The Warren Commission, The Authorities & the Report.* Ipswich: Mary Ferrell Foundation Press.

Mellen, J. (2007). *A Farewell to Justice.* Dulles, Virginia: Potomac Books.

Menninger, B. (1992). *Mortal Error. The Shot that Killed Kennedy.* New York: St Martin's Press.

Miller, D. (2002). *The JFK Conspiracy.* New York: Writers Club Press.

Minnery, J. (1970). *Kill Without Joy!: The Complete How To Kill Book.*

Moore, J. (1991). *Conspiracy of One.* Forth Worth Texas: The Summit Group.

Morenschildt, G. D. (2014). *Lee Harvey Oswald as I Knew Him.* University Press of Kansas.

Morley, J. (2008). *Our Man in Mexico. Winston Scott and the Hidden History of the CIA.* Kansas City Press.

Mosley, L. (1978). *Dulles. A Biography of Eleanor, Allen and John Foster Dulles and Their Family Network.* New York: The Dial Press.

Munitaglio, B. A. (2013). *Dallas 1963.* New York: Hachette Book Group.

Myers, D. (1998). *With Malice. Lee Harvey Oswald and the Murder of Officer J.D. Tippit.* Milford, MI: Oak Cliff Press.

Myers, D. (2007). *Secrets of a Homicide. Epipolar Geometric Analysis of Amateur Films Related to Accoustics Evidence in the John F. Kennedy Assassination.*

Neale, T. H. (1978). *Analysis of Reports and Data Bearing on Circumstances of Death of Twenty-one Individuals Connected with the Assassination of President John F. Kennedy.* Washington: Library of Congress, Congressional Research Service.

Nelson, P. F. (2011). *LBJ The Mastermind of the tht JFK Assassination.* New York: Skyhorse Publishing.

Newman, J. (2010). *Lee Oswald and the Mexico City Tapes (Disk one: Transcripts & documents).* JFK Lancer Conference.

North, M. (2011). *Act of Treason.* New York: Skyhorse Publishing.

O'Donnell, K. E. (sd). *Johnny, We hardly knew you. Memories of John Fitzgerald Kennedy.* New York: Open Road.

O'Reilly, B. (2012). *Killing Kennedy.* New York: Henry Holt & Cy.

Patterson, T. G. (1989). *Kennedy's quest for Victory.* Oxford: University Press.

Phillips, D. T. (2009). *A Deeper, Darker Truth. Tom Wilson's Journey into the Assassination of John F. Kennedy.* Illinois: DTP Companion Books.

Posner, G. (1993, 2003). *Case Closed.* New York: Anchor Books.

Prouty, F. L. (2011). *JFK. The CIA, Vietnam, and the Plot to Assassinate John F. Kennedy.* New York: Skyhorse Publishing.

Rem, E. P. (1992). *JFK Assassination Rifle Shots Phenomenon Exploded.* Washington: T.B.I. Publishing Co.

Rinnovatore, J. V. (2012). *Aftermath of the JFK Assassination Parkland Hospital to the Bethesda Morgue.* New York: Arje Books, Kindle edition.

Roffman, H. (1976). *Presumed Guilty.* A.S. Barnes and Co.

Rusk, D. (1990). *As I Saw It.* New York: W.W. Norton & Co.

Russel, D. (2008). *On the Trail of the Assassins.* New York: Skyhorse Publishing.

Russo, G. (1998). *Live by the Sword: The Secret War against Castro and the Death of JFK.* Baltimore: Bancroft Press.

Salandria, V. (2004). *False Mystery. Essays on the Assassination of JFK.* Louisville, Colorado: Square Deal Press.

Savage, G. (1993). *JFK First Day Evidence.* Monroe, LA: The Shoppe Press.

Savodnik, P. (2013). *The Interloper. Lee Harvey Oswald Inside the Soviet Union.* Philadelphia: Basic Books.

Scheim, D. E. (1988). *The Mafia Killed President Kennedy.* London: WH Allen.

Schlesinger, A. M. (1978). *Robert Kennedy and His Times.* New York: Ballantine Books.

Scholtz, E. M. (1996). *History Will Not Absolve Us. Orwellian Control, Public Denial and the Murder of President Kennedy.* Brookline, Massachusetts: Kurtz, Ulmer & DeLUCIA.

Shane, O. (2013). *Killing Oswald.* E2 Films.

Shaw, G. (1976). *Cover Up.*

Shesol, J. (1997). *Mutual Contempt. Lyndon Johnson, Robert Kennedy, and the Feud that Defined a Decade.* New York: W.W. Norton & Co.

Silver, N. (2012). *The Signal and the Noise. The Art of Science and Prediciton.* New York: Penguin Books.

Simpich, B. (sd). *State Secret. Wiretapping in Mexico City, Double Agents, and the Framing of Lee Harvey Oswald.* Mary Ferrell Foundation.

Sloan, B. (1993-2012). *Breaking the Silence (Revised 2012) The Kennedy Conspiracy: 12 Startling Revelations About the JFK Assassination.* Taylor Publishing, Kindle edition.

Sloan, B. W. (1992). *JFK The Last Dissenting Witness.* Gretna: Pelican Publishing Co.
Smith, M. E. (1968). *Kennedy's 13 Great Mistakes in the White House.* New York: National Forum.
Stone, R. (2013). *The Man Who Killed Kennedy. The Case Against LBJ.* New York: Skyhorse Pubishing.
Stone, R. (2014). *Nixon's Secrets.* New York: Skyhorse Publishing.
Summers, A. (1993). *Official and Confidential. The Secret Life of J. Edgar Hoover (Ned. uitgave: Het J. Edgar Hoover Dossier).* New York: G.P. Putnam's Sons.
Summers, A. (1998). *Not in your lifetime.* New York: Marlowe & Co.
Summers, A. (sd). *Conspiracy.*
Talbot, D. (2007). *Brothers – The Hidden History of the Kennedy Years.* New York: Free Press.
Thompson, N. (2003). *Kings: The True Stroy of Chicago's Policy Kings and Numbers Racketeers.* Chicago: Bronzeville Press.
Titovets, E. (2010). *Oswald Russian Episode.* Minsk, Belarus: Mon Litera.
Trask, R. B. (1994). *Pictures of the Pain.* Danvers, Massachusetts: Yeoman Press.
Trask, R.B. (2005). *National Nightmare.* Danvers, Massachussets: Yeoman Press.
Twyman, N. (1997). *Bloody Treason.* Laurel Mystery Books, e-book.
Twyman, N. (2000). *Illusion and Denial in the John F. Kennedy Assassination.* Laurel Mystery Books, Kindleedition.
Twyman, N. (2010). *Bloody Treason. The Assassination of John F. Kennedy.* Laurel Mystery Books, Kindle edition.
Van Egmond, G. (sd). *Bodemloos bestaan.* Amsterdam: Ambo.
Vary Baker, J. (2010). *Me & Lee. How I came to know, love and lose Lee Harvey Oswald.* Walterville, OR: Trine Day.
Vermeulen, P. (2008). *Lee Harvey Oswald. Via Rotterdam naar Dallas. De moord op JFK.* Eindhoven: De Boekenmakers.
Waldron, L. (2005). *Ultimate Sacrifice.* Berkeley: Counterpoint.
Waldron, L. (2009). *Legacy of Secrecy. The Long Shadow of the JFK Assassination.* Berkeley: Counterpoint.
Waldron, L. (2013). *The Hidden History of the JFK Assassination.* Berkeley: Counterpoint.
Warren Commission, Hearings and Exhibits, Vol. XV. (1964). Washington.
Warren Commission, Hearings and Exhibits, Vol. XXI. (1964). Washington.

Warren Commission, Hearings and Exhibits, Vol. XXV. (1964). Washington.
Warren Commission, Hearings and Exhibits, Vol. II. (1964). Washington.
Warren Commission, Hearings and Exhibits, Vol. III. (1964). Washington.
Warren Commission, Hearings and Exhibits, Vol. VIII. (1964). Washington.
Warren Commission, Hearings and Exhibits, Vol. XIII. (1964). Washington.
Warren Commission, Hearings and Exhibits, Vol. X. (1964). Washington.
Warren Commission, Hearings and Exhibits, Vol. XVIII. (1964). Washington.
Warren Commission, Hearings and Exhibits, Vol. VI. (1964). Washington.
Warren Commission, Hearings and Exhibits, Vol. VII. (1964). Washington.
Warren Commission, Hearings and Exhibits, Vol. XXII. (1964). Washington.
Warren Commission, Hearings and Exhibits, Vol. XXIII. (1964). Washington.
Warren Commission, Hearings and Exhibits, Vol. I. (1964). Washington.
Warren Commission, Hearings and Exhibits, Vol. IV. (1964). Washington.
Warren Commission, Hearings and Exhibits, Vol. V. (1964). Washington
Warren Commission, Hearings and Exhibits, Vol. XI. (1964). Washington.
Warren Commission, Hearings and Exhibits, Vol. XII. (1964). Washington.
Warren Commission, Hearings and Exhibits, Vol. XIV. (1964). Washington.
Warren Commission, Hearings and Exhibits, Vol. XIX. (1964). Washington.
Warren Commission, Hearings and Exhibits, Vol. XVI. (1964). Washington.
Warren Commission, Hearings and Exhibits, Vol. XVII. (1964). Washington.
Warren Commission, Hearings and Exhibits, Vol. XXIV. (1964). Washington.
Warren Commission, Hearings and Exhibits, Vol. XXVI. (1964). Washington.
Warren Commission, Hearings and Exhibits, Vol. IX. (1964). Washington.
Warren Commission, Hearings and Exhibits, Vol. XX. (1964). Washington.
Warren Commission, Report. (1964). Washington.
Weiner, T. (2007). *Legacy of Ashes*. New York: Anchor Books.
Weisberg, H. (1965). *Whitewash. The Report on the Warren Report*. Ipswich, MA: Mary Ferrell Foundation.
Weisberg, H. (1969, 2007). *Post Mortem. JFK Assassination Cover-up Smashed*. Ipswich, MA: Mary Ferrell Foundation.
Wills, G. A. (1967, unabridged republication 1994). *Jack Ruby*. New York: Da Capo Press.
Woods, R. B. (2006). *LBJ Architect of American Ambition*. Cambridge, Massachusetts: Harvard University Press.
Zirbel, C. (2010). *The Final Chapter on the Assassination of John F. Kennedy*. E-book.

INDEX

Illustration credits

Illustrations 2, 3, 4, 5, 7, 12 (right) and 40 (left) are part of the Dallas Municipal Archives (http://texashistory.unt.edu/).
Illustrations 12 (left), 15 (top), 16, 22 (top), 23, 26, 27, 33, 39, 49, 59, 61, 62 and 64 are evidence that the Warren Commission added to its report in the Hearings and Exhibitions volumes.
Illustrations 1, 6, 8, 9, 10, 11, 31, 37, 40 (right), 41, 42, 52, 54 (a, b, c and d), 55, 63 are part of the Warren Commission Documents, and are in the public domain.
Illustrations 13, 57, 63 (left) and (right) are evidence that the House Select Committee on Assassinations added to its report in the Appendix Volumes.
Illustrations 66 and 67 are in the public domain.
Illustrations 14, 15, 17, 25 (bottom) are from the legacy of Cecil Kirk; the rights were acquired by the author.
Illustration 20 (left) is a still from *A CBS News Inquiry: The Warren Report*, 1967.
Illustration 22 is included courtesy of Ian Griggs.
Illustration 53 is owned by the author.
Illustrations 43 (left and right) and 46 are included courtesy of Google Streetview.
Illustrations 47 and 48 are stills from the KLIF-AM Dallas documentary *Kennedy Assassination* are in the public domain.

We would like to thank all archives, foundations and institutes that have provided pictures for this book.

www.lannoo.com

Design: Studio Lannoo
Inside: Karakters
Cover photography: © Dallas Police Department, Dallas Municipal Archives
Author photo: Annelies de Mey

ISBN 978 94 014 3296 2